The Law of Nations in Early American Foreign Policy

Theory and Practice of Public International Law

Series Editor

Vincent Chetail

VOLUME 1

The titles published in this series are listed at *brill.com/tppi*

The Law of Nations in Early American Foreign Policy

Theory and Practice from the Revolution to the Monroe Doctrine

By

Willem Theo Oosterveld

BRILL
NIJHOFF

LEIDEN | BOSTON

Library of Congress Cataloging-in-Publication Data

Oosterveld, Willem Theo, author.
The Law of Nations in early American foreign policy : theory and practice from the Revolution to the Monroe Doctrine / by Willem Theo Oosterveld.
pages cm. -- (Theory and practice of public international law ; 1)
Includes bibliographical references and index.
ISBN 978-90-04-30567-0 (hardback : alk. paper) -- ISBN 978-90-04-30568-7 (e-book) 1. International and municipal law--United States--History. 2. International law--United States--History. 3. United States--Foreign relations--History. I. Title.
KF4581.O57 2015
341.0973'09033--dc23
2015029110

This publication has been typeset in the multilingual "Brill" typeface. With over 5,100 characters covering Latin, IPA, Greek, and Cyrillic, this typeface is especially suitable for use in the humanities. For more information, please www.brill.com/brill-typeface.

ISSN 2405-6847
ISBN 978-90-04-30567-0 (hardback)
ISBN 978-90-04-30568-7 (e-book)

This book is printed on acid-free paper.

Printed by Printforce, the Netherlands

To Andy (1941–2012)

Les Nations étant libres, indépendantes, égales, & chacune devant juger en sa Conscience de ce qu'elle a à faire pour remplir des devoirs; l'effet de tout cela est d'opérer, au moins extérieurement & parmi les hommes, une parfaite égalité de droits entre les Nations, dans l'administration de leurs affaires & dans la poursuite de leurs prétensions, sans égard à la justice intrinsèque de leur Conduite, dont il n'appartient pas aux autres de jugér définitivement...

—EMER DE VATTEL, *DROIT DES GENS*, PRELIM., PARA 21

•••

[Nur durch eine Verbindung] wie die der amerikanischen Staaten, [der] auf einer Staatsverfassung gegründet und daher unauflöslich ist, [kann] die Idee eines zu errichtenden öffentlichen Rechts der Völker, ihre Streitigkeiten auf civile Art, gleichsam durch einen Proceß, nicht auf barbarische (nach Art der Wilden), nämlich durch Krieg, zu entscheiden, realisirt werden.

—IMMANUEL KANT, *METAPHYSIK DER SITTEN*, PART 1, PARA 61

•••

International law (...) contributes more to the happiness of the human race than all the statues which ever came from the hands of the sculptor, or all the paintings that were ever placed on canvass.

—JOHN MARSHALL TO HENRY WHEATON, MARCH 24, 1821

Contents

Acknowledgements

The present monograph is the result of a long academic journey, the outcome of which I could not possibly have fathomed when I first entered university back in 1996. This journey saw several academic way stations: from the narrow canals of Amsterdam and Leiden past the Place du Panthéon in Paris and the shadow of the Heidelberger Schloss to the benches of New York's Greenwich Village back to the shores of Lac Léman in Geneva, and including a stopover enjoying the tranquil campus yards in Cambridge, MA. But apart from an academic journey, it has also been an intellectual journey. Starting out as a political scientist and later adding a law degree, when the time came to contemplate graduate school, I finally took the chance to study what I always wanted to study: history. My fear was that studying the subject would ruin my appetite for it, but picking the right subject for a study that is now culminating in a book made sure that my fears were more than allayed.

Throughout this project, I have received much support from many corners. The first drafts of this project were written at the Graduate Institute in Geneva, where thanks are due first of all to Jussi Hanhimaki and Peter Haggenmacher, in addition to the very helpful staff of the Institute's library. At Harvard, where much of this book was researched, a special thanks is due to David Armitage, who also read early drafts of the first chapters. Thanks are also due to the staff of the Law School and Widener libraries.

Financial support for this project was provided by the Graduate Institute through a series of scholarships, McKinsey Switzerland as well as by the Feris Foundation in Virginia, which generously supported me through an Albert Gallatin International Affairs fellowship that permitted me to undertake research in the United States.

The inspiration that helped me to persevere with this project knows many sources. First of all, it follows from a longstanding fascination with everything relating to the 18th century. Second, it is the result of an equally longstanding fascination with international law and politics. The key question for me is always: Why do countries voluntarily abide by rules? This study provides at least part of an answer to that question. But thirdly, and most importantly, it is friends and family that have inspired me. Friends, because they provide ideas, companionship, and sometimes a place to sleep when you're visiting, and family, because they made it possible for me to pursue my goals and ambitions in the first place.

After many twist and turns on my intellectual journey, I finally settled on a subject most congenial to my interests and tastes. And so it was to a dear friend of mine, who sadly did not live to see this book published. It is to him that this book is dedicated.

W.Th.O., The Hague, September 2015

Chronology of Events

1747	Jean-Jacques Burlamaqui publishes *Principles of Natural and Politic Law*
1754	Albany Plan of Union
1756–63	Seven Years' War (French and Indian Wars in North America since 1754)
1758	Emer de Vattel publishes *The Law of Nations*
1763	Royal Proclamation on settlements in the American West
1765	William Blackstone's *Commentaries*
	March: Parliament passes the Stamp Act
1766	March: Stamp Act repealed
1767	June: Townshend Acts passed
1770	March 5: Boston Massacre
	April: Townshend Acts repealed
1773	December 16: Boston Tea Party
1774	March: Parliament passes Intolerable (or Coercive) Acts
	September–October: First Continental Congress meets in Philadelphia
	October 20: Articles of Association adopted
1775	April 18: Paul Revere's "Midnight Ride" from Boston to Lexington
	April 19: Battles of Lexington and Concord
	May 10: Second Continental Congress convenes in Philadelphia
	June 17: Battle of Bunker Hill
	July 3: Washington takes command of Continental Army
1776	January 9: Thomas Paine publishes *Common Sense*
	June 7: Resolution for independence introduced by Richard Henry Lee
	July 2: Independence declared
	July 4: Independence proclaimed
	September 17: Model Treaty (Plan of 1776) presented to Congress
	December 25: Washington crosses the Delaware
1777	January: Americans beat British at Princeton
	October 7: American victory at the Battle of Saratoga
	November 15: Articles of Confederation adopted
1778	February 6: Treaties of Amity and Commerce with France
1780	February: League of Armed Neutrality formed
1781	March 1: Articles of Confederation ratified by Congress
	October 17: British surrender at Yorktown
1782	April 19: Dutch recognition of the United States
1783	September 3: Peace of Paris signed by Britain and the United States
1786	September 11–14: Annapolis Convention
	September 26: Shay's Rebellion in Massachusetts

1787	July 13: Northwest Ordinance adopted
	September 17: Federal Constitution adopted in Philadelphia
	October: *Federalist Papers* written by Jay, Hamilton and Madison
1788	Constitution is ratified
1789	February 4: Washington elected president
	April 30: Washington inaugurated as president
	July 14: Beginning of the French Revolution
	August 26: Declaration of the Right of Man proclaimed in France
1790	April 17: Benjamin Franklin dies
	September: Nootka Sound crisis
1792	September 21: French Monarchy abolished
1793	January 21: Louis XVI of France executed
	February 1: France declares war on Great Britain
	April 22: Proclamation of Neutrality
	April–May: Citizen Genêt affair
	September 5: Reign of Terror begins in France
	November 6: Britain issues Orders-in-Council, targeting American shipping
1794	Spring: Reign of Terror ends in France
	November 19: Jay Treaty signed
1795	October 27: Treaty of Madrid (Pinckney treaty) between Spain and the United States
1796	February 26: Jay Treaty ratified
	September 17: Washington's Farewell Address
1797	March 4: John Adams becomes president
	XYZ affair, resulting in Quasi War with France
1798	July 6 and 14: Alien and Seditions Acts adopted
	July 7: United States renounces Treaties of Alliance with France
1799	December: Napoleon becomes first consul; Directory overthrown
	December 4: George Washington dies
1800	September 30: Convention with France (Treaty of Mortefontaine)
1801	March 4: Thomas Jefferson becomes president
1801–05	United States undertakes naval operations against Barbary states
1803	February 24: *Marbury v. Madison* case ruled by Supreme Court establishing judicial review principle
	April 30: Louisiana Purchase treaty
1804	January 1: Haiti declares independence from France
	May 14: Lewis and Clark expedition begins
	July 12: Alexander Hamilton dies
1805	October 21: Battle of Trafalgar
	December 2: Battle of Austerlitz

1807	March 25: Britain adopts Slave Trade Act
	June: *Chesapeake* affair
	July 7–9: Treaties of Tilsit between France and Russia
	Jefferson secures imposition of Embargo Act
1808	January 1: Slave trade abolished in the United States
	May 2: Peninsular War begins
	Further Embargo acts adopted
	Viceroy of New Spain declares independence from Spain
1809	January–March: Embargo Act against Britain in place
	James Madison becomes president
1810	May 1: Macon's Bill no. 2 enacted
	October 27: Madison unilaterally annexes West Florida
	Parts of New Spain declare independence
1812	June 18: American declaration of war with Britain
	June 24: France invades Russia
1813	November 6: Mexico declares independence from Spain
1814	August 24: city of Washington is burned by the British
	September: Congress of Vienna convenes
	December 24: Treaty of Ghent with Britain
1815	January 8: American victory at Battle of New Orleans
	June 18: Battle of Waterloo
1817	March 3: Neutrality bill passed
	March 4: James Monroe becomes president
	November 20: First Seminole War in Florida
1818	April 20: second Neutrality bill passed
	October 20: Convention with Britain
1819	Adams–Onís treaty gives Florida to the United States
1823	December 23: Monroe Doctrine proclaimed
1826	July 4: Thomas Jefferson and John Adams die

Introduction

Debates about international law and the United States over the past 15 years have usually led to the conclusion that the world's remaining superpower has no interest in abiding by international rules. Many who would only regard the years of the War on Terror (2001–present), believe that America has apparently abdicated from commonly accepted norms of public international law.[1] The most conspicuous examples in this respect usually include ignoring treaty obligations, the unsigning of the Rome Statute for the International Criminal Court and, in the context of the war on terror, putting prisoners beyond the reach of the law in Guantánamo Bay and, topping the list, invading a country based on uncorroborated claims without the sanction of international law.[2] But sins of commission are not only attributed to the Bush administration. Under President Obama, concerns about drone strikes and more recently, scandals surrounding spy agencies have only helped to further feed the idea that the United States lives by a law of its own.

However, when considering the entire period since the end of the Cold War, the picture becomes more nuanced. The first point is that the very order of international law that the United States is allegedly breaching has been of its own making—having been "present at the creation" of the postwar order centered around the United Nations and the Universal Declaration for Human Rights, the United States, more than any other nation, has helped to bring about the current world order, including the tenets of today's international

---

1 According to Janis, "The thoughtless repudiation of international law and morality in too much of the conduct of the 2001–2009 Bush administration (…) have hurt, rather than helped, American international interests." Mark Janis, *America and the Law of Nations 1776–1939* (Oxford: Oxford University Press, 2010), p. 71.

2 See e.g. Philippe Sands, *Lawless World: America and the Making and Breaking of Global Rules from* FDR*'s Atlantic Charter to George W. Bush's Illegal War* (London: Allen Lane, 2005) and *Torture Team: Deception, Cruelty and the Compromise of Law* (London, Allen Lane, 2008); Dominic McGoldrick, *From 9–11 to the Iraq War: International Law in an Age of Complexity.* (Portland, OR: Hart Publishing, 2004). More favorable accounts on the Bush years include Jack Goldsmith, *The Terror Presidency: Law and Judgement inside the Bush Administration.* (New York: W.W. Norton, 2007) and John Yoo, *The Powers of War and Peace: The Constitution and Foreign Affairs after 9/11* (London: University of Chicago Press, 2005). For a more dispassionate account of the legal issues involved in the struggle against international terrorism, see Helen Duffy, *The 'War on Terror' and the Framework of International Law.* (Cambridge: Cambridge University Press, 2005), and John F. Murphy, *The United States and the Rule of Law in International Affairs* (Cambridge, UK: Cambridge University Press, 2004).

 | DOI 10.1163/9789004305687_002

legal system. What is more, the United States has also at times helped to uphold international law, having intervened in Iraq in 1991, Bosnia in 1994–1995, and having contributed to the founding of international criminal tribunals for the former Yugoslavia and Rwanda in the 1990s. As a result, it is not so easy to draw a uniform conclusion about American attitudes towards international law.

Especially in Europe there is often a tendency to look at the United States as a country that possesses an incorrigible inclination to ride roughshod across sacred pieties of international law.[3] Ideas such as manifest destiny, the vision of a new world an ocean away from the old and, yes, American exceptionalism, all add to the notion that Americans must always have been ill-disposed and insincere in their commitment towards international law. This European—and increasingly global—belief is often attributed to cultural differences. On both sides of the Atlantic, there is arguably a lot of support to be found for this explanation. However, in a seminal essay in 2003, one prominent and iconoclastic historian of American foreign relations, Robert Kagan, argued that between Americans and Europeans, "differences in strategic culture do not spring naturally from the[ir] national characters."[4] As such, he contested the idea that Americans, in their foreign policy dealings, are inherently more apt to use force than Europeans, and to ignore international law. Instead, he argued that a country's behaviour is dependent on its relative power in the state system. Thus, "for the United States, [as a child of the Enlightenment] there is nothing timeless about the present heavy reliance on force as a tool of international relations, nor about the tilt toward unilateralism and away from a devotion of international law."[5] He adds that, like Europeans today, "American statesmen [in the 18th century] appealed to international law (…), claimed to abjure power and assailed as atavistic the power politics of the eighteenth – and 19th-century European empires." As a result, "[the Founding Fathers] could play by European rules when circumstances permitted (…) [but] were realistic enough to know that they were weak, [and therefore] denigrated power politics [claiming] an aversion to war and military power, all realms in which they were far inferior to the European great powers."[6]

What Kagan is contending here is essentially that hegemonic powers behave differently from small powers, and that they are naturally inclined towards

3 As one observer says: "that the U.S. is above international [is a] given (…) traditional Washington stance." Geoffrey Robertson, *Crimes Against Humanity: The Struggle for Global Justice* (New York: The New Press, 2006), p. 423.

4 Robert Kagan, *Of Paradise and Power* (New York: A.A. Knopf, 2003), pp. 7–8.

5 Kagan, *Of Paradise and Power*, p. 9.

6 Kagan, *Of Paradise and Power*, p. 9.

disobeying rules of international law.[7] Since traditionally, the early United States has been seen as a weak power, it would be expected according to this theory that international law as a foreign policy instrument was employed as a defensive means. Indeed, this is also how it is portrayed in much of the literature on American legal history.[8] However, when looking at the early republic, this picture requires to be nuanced further. For one, it has been argued that in the early United States, international law was not merely used as a 'shield' but also as a 'sword.'[9] Such a perspective opens up different ways for framing the issue. First, it could suggest that the United States in its early decades was perhaps not a weak as has been traditionally believed, and that it already began to assert itself as a powerful country—using international law as one of its instruments. Alternatively, it could point towards the existence of a particular predisposition towards international law independent from its relative position in the international system. These were some of the propositions that prompted this investigation into how the law of nations—as international law was called over 200 years ago—was used and appreciated in the early American republic.

Perhaps surprisingly, historians and lawyers have rarely addressed this issue before.[10] Most major historical surveys of the era show little interest in how

7 Historian David Hendrickson suggested however that Kagan meant to imply that the early American statesmen only subscribed to international law because they "anticipat[ed] the day of their strength when they could repudiate these once convenient views," an idea that would allegedly better fit neoconservative ideology which Kagan seeks to support. See "Of Power and Providence" *Policy Review* 135 (March 2006), p. 2.

8 Typical examples are e.g. Stewart Jay, "The Status of the Law of Nations in Early American Law" *Vanderbilt Law Review* 42 (1989), pp. 819–842; Jens Westengard, "American Influences upon International Law" *Journal of Comparative Legal & International Law* 18, New Ser., No. 1. (1918), pp. 2–14; and Felix Gilbert, *To The Farewell Address* (Princeton, NJ: Princeton University Press, 1961).

9 See Douglas Sylvester, "International Law as Sword or Shield? Early American Foreign Policy and the Law of Nations" *New York University Journal of International Law and Politics* 32, no. 1 (1999), pp. 1–87.

10 The only directly relevant studies to have appeared that address international law in the early American republic both in terms of doctrinal development and its practical application in foreign policy are David Hendrickson, *Peace Pact: The Lost World of the American Founding* (Lawrence, KS: University Press of Kansas, 2003); Peter and Nicholas Onuf, *Federal Union, Modern World: The Law of Nations in an Age of Revolutions 1776–1814*, (Madison, Wisc.: Madison House, 1993); and Eliga Gould *Among the Powers of the Earth: The American Revolution and the Making of a New World Empire*, (Cambridge, MA: Harvard University Press, 2013).

international legal questions were handled by the generation of the Founders.[11] But lawyers have also shown little interest in this period.[12] The studies that do exist generally deal only with some specific aspects or only cover a limited period of time.[13] As of yet, there is no general survey on how the law of nations was 'received' and became part of American law, and how it was then deployed as a means for foreign policy in the era of the early republic (1776–1823).

Providing just such an overview is one aim of this study. Another is to show that the role and significance of international law in the early United States went beyond being merely instrumental, or that is was just a reflection of the nation's relative weakness, but that it was an integral part of the political ideology that helped bring about American independence. Hence, this narrative will challenge views that conceive of the law of nations as a reflection of balance of power politics, and show that in fact, it was firmly embedded in the foundational ideas that were at the heart of the early republic itself.[14] As I hope to demonstrate, this perspective will help to explain American attitudes

11 See for instance Samuel F. Bemis, *A Diplomatic History of the United States* (New York: Henry Holt and Co., 1950); Bemis, *John Quincy Adams and the Foundations of American Foreign Policy.* (New York, A.A. Knopf, 1949); Dexter Perkins, *The Monroe Doctrine 1823–1826.* (Cambridge, MA: Harvard University Press, 1926); Alexandre Deconde, *Entangling Alliance: Politics and Diplomacy under George Washington.* (Durham, NC, Duke University Press, 1958). More recent studies on the early period include Jonathan Dull, *A Diplomatic History of the American Revolution* (New Haven: Yale University Press, 1987); Jerald Combs, *The History of American Foreign Policy: to 1920* (Armonk, NY: M.E. Sharpe, 2008) and Bradford Perkins, *The Creation of a Republican Empire* (Vol. 1 of the Cambridge History of American Foreign Relations, Cambridge and New York: Cambridge University Press, 1993); Michael Hogan and Thomas G. Paterson, *Explaining the History of American Foreign Relations* (2nd ed., New York, NY: Cambridge University Press, 2004).

12 Stephen Presser and Jamil Zainaldin (eds.), *Law and Jurisprudence in American History* (St.Paul, MN: Thomson/West, 2003), Kermit Hall and Peter Karsten (eds.), *The Magic Mirror: Law in American History* (New York: Oxford University Press, 2009) and Hendrik Hartog (ed.), *Law in the American Revolution and the Revolution in the Law* (New York/London: New York University Press, 1981).

13 Some good—and useful—examples include Daniel G. Lang, *Foreign Policy in the Early Republic: The Law of Nations and the Balance of Power* (Baton Rouge: Louisiana State University Press, 1985); Douglas Sylvester, "International Law as Sword or Shield? Early American Foreign Policy and the Law of Nations" *NYU Journal of International Law and Politics* 32, no. 1, 1999, pp. 1–87; Stewart Jay, "The Status of the Law of Nations in Early American Law" *Vanderbilt Law Review* 42 (1989), pp. 819–842.

14 Some authors hint at this notion, but not explicitly so. Even less do they pursue this idea in a systematic fashion. See e.g. Stewart Jay, "The Status of the Law of Nations in Early American Law," p. 824; Jerald Combs, *The History of American Foreign Policy: to 1920*, p. 7.

towards international law throughout the period from the Revolution up to the 1820s. For instance, it will show why in the wake of the 1790s—when the United States found itself under much pressure from the British and later the French—the government did not definitively bury its ambitions to promote liberal principles of the law of nations, but instead chose to fight for them, first through economic means and later even militarily. But this perspective will also be helpful in explaining more atavistic attitudes where the application of the law of nations was concerned in regards to territorial expansion and the position of the natives. Ideological differences about the law of nations also contributed to, or were the result of, party divisions in the early republic. But while there were frequently sharp disagreements over the means to defending principles of international law, there existed nonetheless a bipartisan consensus about their being part of the American founding creed. From a legal point of view, this argument will be pursued by tracing the linkages between the law of nations, the law of nature and the common law, and how their political and normative basis helped to entrench the law of nations as part of a constitutional framework.[15] Ultimately, the deeper roots of this normative edifice can be traced back to philosophical notions about how a newly constituted society should be organized, and interact with the rest of the world. The continuity between European and American thinking in this regard has been persuasively argued by J.G.A. Pocock, who held that the founding of the American republic constituted a 'Machiavellian moment' at which the key intellectual challenge that the founding generation faced was how to preserve virtue in an expanding and commercially-oriented republic.[16] In this quest, reference to the English common law as a repository of customary rules for organizing a society was only self-evident. Natural law served a similar purpose, albeit that its merits related more to its moral content, providing the Founding generation with guidance on framing new legal principles to be applied at home, but also in foreign relations.

Hence, this study is not meant to focus solely on doctrinal developments, but also on how these international legal ideas were applied in practice. In doing so, the idea is not to seek a monocausal explanation for the events and

---

15 See e.g. Charles Mullett, *Fundamental Law and the American Revolution, 1760–1776* (New York: Columbia University Press, 1933); Edward Corwin, "The "Higher Law" Background of American Constitutional Law," *Harvard Law Review* 42 nos. 2 and 3 (1929), pp. 149–185, 365–409 and Thomas Grey, "Origins of the Unwritten Constitution: Fundamental Law in American Revolutionary Thought" *Stanford Law Review* 30, no. 5 (1978), pp. 843–893.

16 J.G.A. Pocock, *The Machiavellian Moment: Florentine Political Thought in the Atlantic Republican Tradition* (Princeton: Princeton University Press, 1975), p. 462.

developments that are being chronicled here, but to shed more light on a dimension of foreign relations that has received relatively short shrift in studies of this kind so far. Therefore, if this study should succeed in illustrating an aspect of early American foreign policy which has mostly been neglected, it will be a useful contribution to the existing body of literature in this particular field.

In today's environment of academic specialization, it is not very common to pursue a joint treatment of developments in legal doctrine and how such ideas were applied in practice. In this instance however, such joint treatment seems eminently appropriate for various reasons. First of all, international law was a key instrument in foreign policy making in the early republic. While commerce was arguably the most important element in U.S. foreign relations in those days, as a policy instrument it proved to be a rather ineffectual one, invariably inflicting more harm at home than among the young republic's rivals.[17] With the military practically non-existent as a foreign policy instrument and a fledgling navy being at the country's disposition only since the early 1800s, the main instrument for the American government was the law of nations. In a way, this was not necessarily a bad thing for a nation that was founded on the basis of ideas, and for which the law of nations became a means for promoting its founding principles beyond its own shores. But most of all, a joint treatment is justified by the sheer fact that the first generation of American statesmen was exceptionally well versed in the law of nations, and actually made foreign policy with the great legal treatises right beside.[18] These treatises did not simply provide them with a set of legal rules to be applied in specific circumstances, but constituted 'bibles of statecraft'. Hence for this generation, there was little difference between thinking about international law and applying it, or between international law and international politics for that matter.

What is more, the linkage between law and policy is important with reference to the early republic because particularly for that period, a good argument can be made that foreign policy-making constituted a 'laboratory' in

17 See with respect to the trade embargoes of the early 1800s, Varg, *Foreign Policies of the Founding Fathers*, ch. 10–12; Tucker and Hendrickson, *Empire of Liberty*, and Lawrence Kaplan, "Jefferson, the Napoleonic Wars and the Balance of Power," *William and Mary Quarterly* 14, no. 2 (1957), pp. 196–217.

18 Good examples in this context are for instance the Nootka Sound crisis (1790) and the ratifications of treaties with revolutionary France in 1793, during which Jefferson set out his general views on international law and its sources (see further below, Chapter 5.1). Mark Janis noted that "[n]o group of America's leaders have [sic] ever been more mindful of the discipline [of international law] than were the Founding Fathers." *America and the Law of Nations 1776–1939* (Oxford: Oxford University Press, 2010), p. 24.

which approaches to the law of nations were being tried and tested. It is where law met practice. In the process, it will be shown that traditional political science cannot capture the subtle but crucial distinctions between Jeffersonians and Hamiltonians,[19] nor provide satisfactory explanations concerning international legal considerations. In the early period, linkages between legal and political exigencies were important because the nation's very existence needed to be assured and because the country wanted to protect its experiment in republican rule against 'pernicious influences from abroad.' From a legal point of view, this linkage is significant because it stresses the connection between the law of nations and the American constitution, which in some quarters was seen as a blueprint for a new international legal order.[20] In other words, in the context of the period studied here, the realm of foreign policy cannot be properly understood without considering domestic imperatives, which in turn shaped approaches to international law.

Given the potentially vast scope of this study, it is important to point out what this study does *not* purport to be. The emphasis is decidedly on the interdisciplinary nature of the topic, yet with a singular focus on developments pertaining to international law. Hence, the present study is not a history of early American foreign policy interspersed with occasional reflections on international law—in fact, many of the familiar events from the period will hardly be touched upon if at all, given the availability of much better treatments elsewhere. Also, it is not a comprehensive intellectual history of political or even legal ideas that went into the Constitution or early treatises on law. Finally, this study does not aspire to provide an exhaustive overview of Constitutional law on foreign affairs (i.e. relating to the separation of powers between government branches), but again, only incorporate those aspect which have a direct relevance for the main argument.

Chapter one will delve into the legal theories and systems that shaped the foundations on which American legal thinking were built. In the first part, the focus is on natural law, which in the 18th century was at the basis of both continental as well as the common law. Briefly, its evolution is being traced from its unusual Roman law origins through the era of Grotius to that of Vattel and Burlamaqui. The second part of the chapter will look at at the English common law tradition, and in particular how it related to international law. It will consider some doctrinal developments

---

19 A good example of a book that goes beyond the traditional realist-idealist dichotomy is Walter Russell Mead's *Special Providence: American Foreign Policy and how it Changed the World.* (New York: Alfred A. Knopf, 2001).

20 Onuf and Onuf, *Federal Union, Modern World*, pp. 142–213.

as well as some key court rulings that strongly influenced subsequent American legal thinking.[21] As such, this chapter should provide an overview of the tradition of international law that the Founding Fathers embraced and adapted to.

Chapter two focuses on legal theorizing in the colonial era and the drafting of the main documents straight after independence. The first part will deal in particular with the various theories on how the common law was introduced in the colonies, and the relationship between Britain and its overseas colonies in the context of what was called the 'imperial constitution.' In the second part, the focus will be on the drafting of the three main documents that were elaborated after independence, being the Declaration of Independence itself, John Adams' Model Treaty and the Articles of Confederation. Taken together, these documents reflect the aspirations and expectations the new country had with respect to international law, as well as the principles for its conduct on these matters.

Chapter three examines the new republic's experiences in managing foreign relations between 1776 and 1787, the year when the new constitution was adopted. The first section is devoted to a detailed study of the French alliance treaties of 1778, their consequences in terms of America's ability to live up to its own principles and its deeper involvement in the politics of balance of power with the main European powers. The close linkage between balance of power and the law of nations was regarded as a matter-of-fact, even if it was perceived with much scepticism from across the Ocean—as a principle which failed to maintain general peace among European powers.[22] The second part will look at how the new nation fared under the Articles of Confederation, focusing in particular on how its inability to enforce the law of nations at home imperilled the security and even existence of the fledgling nation, while at the same time highlighting some successes in treaties concluded.

The fourth chapter is devoted to explaining the American Constitution from the point of view of the law of nations. The first part looks at its genesis, examining how concerns about the enforcement of the law of nations influenced the drafting of the Constitution and analysing relevant legal provisions. The second part will provide a broader overview of early interpretations of these Constitutional provisions, in particular with reference to the *Federalist Papers*,

21 See e.g. Charles Lofgren, "War-Making under the Constitution: The Original Understanding" *Yale Law Journal* 81, no. 4 (1972), pp. 689–690.

22 See e.g. Lang, *Foreign Policy in the Early Republic*, pp. 142–145; Kaplan, "Jefferson, the Napoleonic Wars and the Balance of Power" and Detlev Vagts "The United States and the Balance of Power" *Journal of Politics* 3, no. 4 (1941), pp. 401–449.

as well as some of the early writings on the Constitution, including James Wilson's *Lectures on Law* and St. George Tucker's *View on the Constitution* in his edited version of Blackstone's *Commentaries*. This will help to explain and illustrate the relations between constitutional and international law, how the federal constitution came to be seen by some as a model for an alternative international legal order,[23] and how this affected legal thinking and possibly foreign policy-making.

The fifth chapter will look at international law and foreign policy during the "Federalist Era", which comprises the presidencies of Washington and Adams. This was a period of great political turbulence, during which the United States attempted to balance its obligations towards France against those it incurred towards Great Britain through the Jay Treaty in 1794. The first section will look at developments until the adoption of the Neutrality Proclamation,[24] which proved to be a decisive step away from the alliance with France. In addition, it will examine the two foreign policy approaches essentially crafted and developed by Alexander Hamilton and Thomas Jefferson, respectively Treasury Secretary and Secretary of State under George Washington. In particular, two different attitudes towards international law are identified with reference to Hamilton's and Jefferson's foreign policy perspectives, arguing that while their perspectives differed in their practical implementation and priorities, there existed agreement on the principal tenets of the law of nations as a cornerstone of America's founding ideology. The second part examines the period after the adoption of the Proclamation, and in particular the political conundrums emanating from concluding the Jay Treaty, which almost led to full-scale war with France at the end of the century.

The sixth chapter will consider law and policy making under the presidency of Thomas Jefferson. The first half will provide an introduction into Jefferson's thinking on the role of international law in foreign policy, and highlight some developments in relation to territorial expansion, the role of the native peoples, and how this affected the American calculus towards rights and obligations under the law of nations. The second part takes a closer look at maritime

23 Again, see Onuf and Onuf, *Federal Union, Modern World*, but see also David Hendrickson, *Peace Pact: The Lost World of the American Founding* (Lawrence, KS: University of Kansas Press, 2003), esp. ch. 4 (Pt 1).

24 See for example Wilhelm Grewe, *The Epochs of International Law* (Berlin/New York: Walter de Gruyter, 2000), pp. 389–394; Arthur Nussbaum, *A Concise History of the Law of Nations* (New York: Macmillan Press, 1954), p. 134; Lang, *Foreign Policy in the Early Republic*, pp. 117–118; and Sylvester, "International Law as Sword or Shield?", pp. 31–38.

issues, with a particular focus on defending and enforcing shipping rights, e.g. in terms of trade with the West Indies, and Haiti in particular, during the French Revolutionary wars, seizures of American ships and impressment of sailors and the actions against the Barbary pirates in the Mediterranean. The 1807–1809 Embargo crisis will serve as an illustration of the efficacy of defending neutral rights with economic means of coercion. In particular, this chapter will highlight the fact that different attitudes had developed as to adherence to the law of nations at sea and on land.

The final substantive chapter begins with a discussion on the onset of the War of 1812, and argues that in its essence, it was a war fought over recognition of asserted principles of the law of nations. In addition, it will consider various pronouncements by the Supreme Court that aimed at affirming continuing American adherence to the basic precepts of international law, though noting serious problems where it came to slavery and the slave trade. The second part takes a broader look, focusing on how Christian and civilizational notions influenced conceptions of international law, illustrated by studying the treatment of natives, the continuing quest for territorial expansion and the genesis of the Monroe Doctrine. This part in particular will provide more evidence for the existence of sharply diverging attitudes between international law at sea—which was very progressive—and on land, where the law was often blatantly disregarded or violated.

The conclusion will provide a retrospective on the period under investigation by way of studying some early major treatises on international law, those of chancellor James Kent and Henry Wheaton, as well as relevant sections from Joseph Story's *Commentaries*. Although the publication dates of these three treatises fall outside the scope of the period considered in this study, they provide appropriate *summae* of American thinking on international law reflecting on political developments up to the 1830s. More general conclusions will be drawn as to where American thinking on international law came from and where it was believed to be heading towards as the United States was on its way to becoming a world power.

Since historians, lawyers and social scientists never cease to invoke the wisdom of the Founding Fathers—therewith implying its continuing relevance today—it is hoped that any conclusions drawn here may help to advance our understanding of contemporary issues. This, in spite of the fact that in the conclusion to his article referred to above, Stewart Jay wrote that

> [n]otwithstanding the fascination we may feel for the events of the early Republic in regard to international relations, their contextual differences from world affairs today should lead us to view the various statements

> about the law of nations from that era as having no bearing on modern controversies.[25]

Of course, Jay is correct in stating that the law of nations in the late 18th century is qualitatively different from international law today; the same goes for the way the world is organized. But in spite of Jay's explicit admonition, this book aspires to have some relevance beyond the merely antiquarian.

---

25 Jay, "The Status of the Law of Nations in Early American Law", p. 849. Interestingly, Daniel Lang wrote however that "it is (...) possible to defend [the] continued relevance [of the Enlightenment theories of the early American statesmen] for present-day international relations." Daniel G. Lang, *Foreign Policy in the Early Republic*, p. 10.

CHAPTER 1

Antecedents of International Law in America

1.1 The Continental Tradition

Moving across the Atlantic, the first European colonists that came to America wished to make a fresh start and leave corrupt and duplicitous Europe behind them. Whether they succeeded is a different debate, but this spirit of drawing absolute and moral distinctions also came to distinguish American perspectives on the law of nations—its foundations, its utility and its application in foreign affairs. However, much of this traditional notion seems more folklore than actual reality. For instance, "[f]ar from seeking permanent separation from the Old World, the Puritans (…) aimed to establish a base from which to launch a counter-offensive across the Atlantic." As a result, "America was not the Puritans' promised land but a temporary refuge."[26] Yet, physical separation did not connote intellectual separation. In fact, the colonists took with them their European intellectual baggage and used their separation from the Old World to rethink their condition and how they wished to conduct relations with the outside world. Of course, in the first 150-odd years, this took place while the colonies were controlled by various European powers; initially the English, Swedish and Dutch, and later on, exclusively by the English. In that respect, intellectual developments in the colonies never took place in isolation, nor was the significance of the colonies as a trade hub in the British Empire never lost on its inhabitants. As a result, once the era of the American revolution arrived, the legal justifications for independence that had been proffered as well as the constitutional innovations subsequently proposed had their origins in European thinking. At the same time however, it can also be argued that separation and the spirit of the first settlers left their mark on how Americans would come to approach and interpret international law: partly as a body of 'fundamental principles' that ought to be obeyed up to the point where the new republic was prepared to commit to war to vindicate them, but also as a set of rules that provided a means for negotiating and consolidating America's independence. In order to better understand the underlying legal ideas, it is important to inquire into their provenance.

---

26 Kagan, *Dangerous Nation*, p. 8. In fact, as Kagan adds, "[the settlers] saw themselves [as] spreading European civilization, not escaping it." (p. 13).

 | DOI 10.1163/9789004305687_003

The purpose here is to investigate the notions that shaped the concept of the law of nations as understood by the generation of the Founding Fathers.[27] Indeed, the law of nations as it was known in the late 18th and early 19th centuries was in many ways qualitatively very different from what we consider to be international law today.[28] According to Dickinson, "the Law of Nations in the 18th century embraced a good deal more than the body of practice and agreement which later came to be called international law. (…) [I]t had been expounded as a universal law binding upon all mankind."[29] Van Vollenhoven noted that "it [was] possible for a sprightly-minded author like Hübner to write as late as 1759 that the Law of Nations of his day consists for seven eights of rules concerning ceremonial (…)."[30] Legal philosopher Martti Koskenniemi even argued that before the mid-point of the 19th century, one could not even speak of a recognisable body of literature that could be called international law; instead, there existed at best "a scattered series of inferences drawn by political and legal writers from general theories meant for domestic audiences."[31] Nevertheless, assuming that there did exist some international law tradition, the most important difference to note between now and the 18th

27 It is well-known for example that many of the Founding Fathers were well acquainted with the main literature on natural law. For instance, Alexander Hamilton, when recommending books for legal study to a Westchester farmer, counselled the following: "Apply yourself, without delay, to the study of the law of nature. I would recommend to your perusal, Grotius, Puffendorf, Locke, Montesquieu, and Burlemaqui. I might mention other excellent writers on this subject; but if you attend diligently to these, you will not require any others." See Alexander Hamilton, "The Farmer Refuted" (February 5, 1775), in Henry Cabot Lodge (ed.), *The Works of Alexander Hamilton,* (New York: G.P. Putnam's Sons, 1904), Vol. 1., p. 61.

28 In fact, the term "international law" itself was only coined in 1780 by the philosopher Jeremy Bentham in his *Introduction to the Principles and Morals of Legislation.* See discussed e.g. in Mark Janis, *The American Tradition in International Law* (Oxford: Clarendon Press, 2004), pp. 11–15.

29 Edwin Dickinson, "The Law of Nations as Part of the National Law of the United States" *University of Pennsylvania Law Review* 101, no. 1 (1952), pp. 26–27.

30 Cornelis Van Vollenhoven, The Three Stages in the Evolution of the Law of Nations, p. 4.

31 Martti Koskenniemi, "The Advantage of Treaties: International Law in the Enlightenment" *Edinburgh Law Review* 13 (2009), p. 30. Louis M. Sears however said quite the opposite, believing that "[b]y the close of the eighteenth century, the law of nations had acquired as much prestige as it could ever hope to secure without the support of its own guns and navies. It was the highest political expression of an age which believed in the perfectability of human relations through sheer intellect. (…) Nations broke treaties, to be sure, but they did not call them 'scraps of paper'." See Sears, "Thomas Jefferson and the Law of Nations" *The American Political Science Review* 13, no. 3 (August 1919), p. 379.

century is that in those days, it had a specific normative basis in natural law, and was often considered as its derivative. In a world in which there existed few 'binding' obligations to limit the authority of kings and princes to go to war, natural law was supposed to provide some limitations on the room for action of sovereigns. But a key issue with natural law was that its scope and content had always remained vague. Most of the time, this suited monarchs and other rulers just fine. At the time of the American Revolution, the authority of natural law was on the wane in Europe, and over the course of the 19th century, under the influence of scholars such as George Friedrich von Martens, Johann Kaspar Bluntschli and legal theorist John Austin, international law became increasingly more positivist; that is, based on treaty law and customary law without reference to higher norms whatsoever.

Investigating the nature of international law in 18th-century North America is a rather complex exercise. The goal would be to get a clear and consistent picture on first, how the law of nations was 'introduced' in the American colonies; and second, how it was subsequently integrated into the domestic legal system.[32] Based on these answers, we will make inferences about the role which the law of nations played in early American foreign relations. The answers to these questions are however not easily obtained. They require an investigation and evaluation of the interrelationships between natural law, the English common law and the law of nations, to which is added after 1787 a layer of constitutional law. The question is further compounded by the need to examine the role of the law of nations as a repository of normative ideas to be applied in the foreign policy arena, thus blurring the line between legal and moral norms. While this potentially complicates our ability to properly ascertain the role of international law in early American foreign policy, it does point to the fact that the law of nations as such served more than just an instrumental purpose.

While there are various ways to deal with this set of questions, the ideas that together shaped the concept of international law as understood by the Founding Fathers are examined here by separately looking at the continental[33] and common law traditions. This is not to imply that these two traditions had developed and evolved in isolation from each other—to the contrary. The main purpose for distinguishing between these two strands is to separately look at the body of law which gave rise to the law of nations itself—the continental tradition—and the body of law which helped introduce it to the American continent—the English

32 In modern international law, this is called municipal law.

33 With continental tradition, I denote the body of international law and its guiding principles as commonly understood and applied among Western European countries.

common law.[34] For our purposes, the importance of the continental tradition in international law lies specifically in the history of its doctrinal development, because it significantly helped to shape not just how Americans thought about the law, but also informed their international political relations. While today, law and politics are often seen as two separate realms, in the 18th century, they were deeply interwoven and therewith effectively inseparable. Natural law as the key normative underpinning of international law was taken for granted by most thinkers. This had however not always been the case. In order to better understand why and how the law of nations emerged, it is instructive to consider its development from the days of the Roman Empire, if only because the Founding Fathers themselves were invariably well versed in the classics and Roman law:[35]

> Like all educated people in the age of the Enlightenment, the thinking of the revolutionary generation was steeped in classical antiquity, though with a greater tilt towards the Roman than the Greek legacy. While they were generally best acquainted with historians, philosophers and the great poets including Plutarch, Thucydides, Polybius, Cicero, Vergil, Tacitus and Lucretius, they also used the great Roman lawyers Ulpian and Gaius, as well as Justinian's great *Corpus Juris Civilis* as point of reference.[36]

Jefferson even conceded "the superiority of the civil over the common law as a system of perfect justice."[37] It is therefore a good starting point for delving into the legal mindset of the generation that created the American republic.

While the concept of natural law already existed among the Greeks, it did not lie at the origins of the law of nations as it developed among the Romans.

34 As Jules Lobel noted: "International law was an important component of two sources of American notions of fundamental law: Enlightenment natural law thought and English common law conceptions." See Lobel, "The Limits of Constitutional Power: Conflicts between Foreign Policy and International Law" *Virginia Law Review* 71, no. 7 (October 1985), p. 1079.

35 Edward Dumbauld, "John Marshall and the Law of Nations" *University of Pennsylvania Law Review*, 104, no. 1 (1955), p. 38. Bederman said on this point that "[a]lthough it is by no means certain the Framers had in mind the Roman law concept of *jus gentium* when referring to the law of nations, this assumption has been commented upon by contemporary courts and scholars." David Bederman, *The Classical Foundations of the American Constitution: Prevailing Wisdom* (New York: Cambridge University Press, 2008), p. 172.

36 Quoted from Charles Mullett, "Classical Influences on the American Revolution" *Classical Journal* 35 (1939), pp. 93–94, cited in Bailyn, *Ideological Origins of the American Revolution* (Cambridge, MA: Belknap Press, Harvard University, 1992), p. 24.

37 Thomas Jefferson to John Tyler (June 17, 1812), in Albert E. Bergh (ed.), *The Writings of Thomas Jefferson* (Washington, DC: Taylor & Maury, 1907), Vol. 13, p. 166.

The earliest tenets of what came to be called *ius gentium* emerged in response to the need for Roman courts to create a legal basis upon which foreigners (or better, non-Roman citizens) could be judged, since they did not enjoy the rights and privileges that Romans did under the *ius civile*. To this end, the courts "were obliged to find certain principles and rules which could guide their action in the same way as the principles and rules of the pure Roman law guided them when dealing with citizens." For this purpose, they took "those general principles of justice, fair dealing, and common sense, which they found recognized by other peoples as well as their own, and by giving effect to those mercantile and other similar usages which they found prevailing among the strangers resident at Rome."[38] So, while *ius gentium* did recognize principles of equity, it was not considered to be coeval with natural law, since it remained based on practice. Also, while *ius gentium* as such could be considered a category of Roman law, it was never formally enacted in statutes.[39] Only in the days of the late Republic and the early Empire do *ius gentium* and *ius naturale* begin to approximate one another through the influence of the Stoic school, and in particular Cicero's thinking. The Stoics borrowed heavily from Greek moral philosophy, which they identified with the law of nature. Still, Cicero himself did not make the intellectual leap to link *ius gentium* to natural law. To him, *ius gentium* is "a part of the positive law, though much wider in its range than ius civile, whereas the Law of Nature is altogether an ethereal thing, eternal, unchangeable, needing no human authority to support it."[40] In a way, he sees it as a system of law by default: "Whatever we are bound, by the civil constitutions, to do to our citizens, we are not obliged, by the law of nations, to do the same to strangers; but whatever we are bound by this latter to do to others, the same we ought to do to our citizens also."[41]

---

38 James Bryce, *Studies in History and Jurisprudence*, Vol. II (New York: Oxford University Press, 1901), pp. 570–571.

39 James Bryce, *Studies in History and Jurisprudence*, p. 574.

40 James Bryce, *Studies in History and Jurisprudence*, p. 577. In the *Offices*, Cicero underlines the customary nature of the law of nations, which he calls "the universal law or consent of nations." See *De officiis*, Bk III, para 5, p. 122. "…natura, id est iure gentium…." Interestingly, the Loeb edition translates this passage as "…that is, by the common rules of equity." See Cicero, *De officiis* (tr. W. Miller, Cambridge: Harvard University Press, 1913) Bk III, para 5, at 23.

41 Cicero, *De officiis*, Bk III, para 18, p. 142. "Itaque maiores aliud ius gentium, aliud ius civile esse voluerunt, quod civile, non idem continuo gentium, quod autem gentium, idem civile esse debet."

The infusion of moral content into natural law was not the only contribution of the Stoics. They were also instrumental in developing the idea that the law of nature was created by a deity, which, in Christian times, became God.[42] However, this did not imply that natural law was not—or could not be—based on reason.[43] Stoic philosophers also developed the idea of a universal commonwealth—one which should be governed by a single body of law, for which *ius gentium* lend itself most conveniently.[44] And since this corpus was made up of generally agreed customs and principles of justice, "it became practically identical with the Law of Nature (…). In Justinian's *Institutes* the identification is complete."[45]

However, with the admixture of *ius gentium* and natural law, we have not yet identified the constitutive elements of the law of nations as it existed in the 18th century. For one, *ius gentium* did not provide rules for the interaction between territorial entities—again, it was part of Roman law and in terms of its content more of a private law character rather than of public law, as is the case today.[46] It was up to legal thinkers from Grotius onwards to start developing a concept of *ius inter gentes* that came to underpin the modern framework for interaction between states, otherwise known as the Westphalian order.

While he is not the most frequently cited lawyer by the generation of the Founding Fathers, Hugo Grotius must be regarded as the key figure in the

42 For instance, Cicero's concept of natural law has God as "its author, its promulgator, its enforcer." See *De Re Publica*, Bk III, para. 22. Quoted in Charles Mullett, *Fundamental Law and the American Revolution, 1760–1776* (New York: Columbia University Press, 1933), p. 15.

43 See e.g. Gaius, *Institutes*, Bk I, para. 1 "Nam (…) quod vero *naturalis ratio* inter omnes homines constituit, id apud omnes populos peraeque custoditur vocaturque ius gentium." (emphasis added). However, Bryce added, this is not the same as saying that natural reason could be considered as a source of *ius gentium*. He therefore deplores the phrase 'lost Code of Nature' used by Sir Henry Maine in *Ancient Law*. See *Studies in History and Jurisprudence*, p. 584, fn. 1.

44 See e.g. Ulpianus, *Digestae*, Bk I, sec 1, para. 1, at 4: "Ius gentium est, quod gentes humanae utuntur."

45 Bryce, *Studies in History and Jurisprudence*, p. 581. In fact, a few centuries before the *Corpus Juris Civilis* was published, the distinction between *ius gentium* and *ius civile* in the Roman Empire had disappeared because of the extension of Roman citizenship to all inhabitants of the Empire by emperor Caracalla (212–217 C.E.). See Ibid., p. 585. See also discussed in Edward Corwin, "The 'Higher Law' Background of American Constitutional Law" *Harvard Law Review* 42 (1928), pp. 163–164.

46 In spite of the fact that Roman lawyers considered that *ius gentium*, since it is based on generally recognized customs, should therefore be binding on all nations of the world. See Bryce, *Studies in History and Jurisprudence*, p. 603.

development of modern international law.[47] Born in 1583 in Delft in the Dutch Republic, Grotius is best known for his treatise on the law of nations called *De iure belli ac pacis* (*On the Laws of War and Peace*), which appeared in 1625. He is a pivotal thinker not only because his magnum opus appeared at the threshold of a new era in international history, but also because Grotius was personally involved in various episodes of his tumultuous era, both in the Dutch Republic and in France. This gave him a good sense of limits of the practical application of international law in the realm of politics, even if in his treatise, he made no direct references to current events, only arguing by analogy drawing on examples from classical antiquity. The transitional nature of Grotius' thinking is reflected in his concept of the law of nations. In the famous *Prolegomena*, he describes the law of nations as "that Law, which is common to many Nations or Rulers of Nations, whether derived from Nature, or instituted by Divine Commands, or introduced by Custom and tacit Consent."[48] At once, he acknowledges that while its source may be the law of nature (as in Justinian's *Institutes*), or even divine, he also deems state practice a source of law. At the same time, Grotius does not conceive of the laws of nature as naked rights to self-preservation. He posits the idea of sociability (derived from the Stoics), assuming that men have an interest in the preservation of society as a whole, and calling it the "Fountain of Right."[49]

The difficult move towards what came to be known as the secularization of the natural law origins of the law of nations[50]—and even towards a positivist conception of the latter—appears a few paragraphs later in the *Prolegomena*. Grotius starts out by noting that "the Law of Nature itself, (...) though it flows from the internal Principles of Man, may notwithstanding be justly ascribed to

---

47 Indeed, as Ward notes, "the philosopher of *Delft* rose like a star amid the surrounding darkness, and with an ability and happiness peculiar to himself, had at once the honour of inventing and bringing his system to perfection: For he gave the world a Treatise which has stood the test of time." A phrase which echoes Alexander Pope's epitaph to Newton: "Nature and nature's laws lay hid in night. God said: Let Newton be! And all was light." See Robert Plumer Ward, *An Enquiry into the Foundation and History of the Law of Nations in Europe*. (Dublin: P. Wogan, P. Byrne, W. Jones and J. Rice, 1795), Vol. II, p. 370.

48 Hugo Grotius, *The Rights of War and Peace* (Indianapolis: Liberty Fund, 2005), Prolegomena, para 1, p. 75.

49 Grotius, *The Rights of War and Peace,* Prolegomena, para 8, pp. 85–86.

50 Josef L. Kunz, "Natural-Law Thinking in Modern Science of International Law" *American Journal of International Law* 55, no. 4 (October, 1961), p. 951.

God, because it was his Pleasure that these Principles should be in us."[51] But then, Grotius starts to separate natural law from international law:

> But as the Laws of each State respect the Benefit of that State; so amongst all or most States there might be, and in Fact there are, some Laws agreed on by common Consent, which respect the Advantage not of one Body in particular, but of all in general. And this is what is called the Law of Nations, when used in Distinction to the Law of Nature.[52]

In spite of the transitional nature of Grotius' thinking, his work would be the touchstone both for continental jurists as well as for British lawyers, who would use his ideas to construct and justify a notion of "fundamental law" as a basis for the common law.[53]

For the revolutionary generation of American statesmen, Grotius was also important as a source on neutral rights and freedom of the seas. On the former, his ideas were still very much influenced by the notion of just war. "[I]t is the Duty of those that are not engaged in the War, to sit still and do nothing, that may strengthen him that prosecutes an ill Cause, or to hinder the Motions of him that hath Justice on his Side, as we have said before." However, if such strict neutrality proves impossible, he counsels neutral states "to behave themselves alike to both Parties; as in suffering them to pass through their Country, in supplying them with Provisions, and not relieving the Besieged."[54] On freedom of the seas, his best-known tract, *De Mare Liberum* (1609) seems to have been referred to very little; *De iure belli ac pacis* was the most important source here. Still, as a defender of the rights of an emerging nation and of maritime rights, the generation of the founders felt a natural affection for him. Indeed, Hamilton called him "that learned and persecuted friend of liberty, whose life and great talents were dedicated to the service of mankind, and who displayed so much ability and learning in defending the freedom of the seas and of commerce."[55]

---

51 Grotius, *The Rights of War and Peace,* Prolegomena, para 12. Indeed, in para 18, he adds that "the Mother of Natural Law is human Nature itself, which, though even the Necessity of our Circumstances should not require it, would of itself create in us a mutual Desire of Society." See also discussed in Wilhelm Grewe, *The Epochs of International Law* (Berlin/New York: Walter de Gruyter, 2000), pp. 191–192.

52 Grotius, *The Rights of War and Peace*, Prolegomena, para 18, p. 94.

53 See e.g. in Edward Corwin, "The "Higher Law" Background of American Constitutional Law" Pt. II, *Harvard Law Review* 42 (1929), p. 381.

54 Grotius, *The Rights of War and Peace,* Bk III, Ch. XVII, sec. 3, p. 1525.

55 Alexander Hamilton, "Camillus no. XXIX", in *The Works of Alexander Hamilton*, Vol. 6, p. 87.

On the development of doctrine, the other significant 17th-century lawyer is Samuel von Pufendorf. The first holder of a chair in 'the law of nature and of nations' at the University of Heidelberg in 1661, he conceived of a law of nations based on a Hobbesian concept of natural law. As Grewe wrote, for Pufendorf, "the law of nations was a part of natural law and States coexisted in a state of nature. Treaties and custom could not establish legal rules because they were not expressions of a will which was superimposed on the subjects of the law of nations."[56] Still, this should not be interpreted as implying that Pufendorf also shared Hobbes' view of the state of nature as a *bellum omnium contra omnes*. His initial premise is not very promising: "*Man* seems to be set in a *worse* condition than that of *Brutes*, that hardly any other Animal comes into the world in so great *weakness*; so that 'twould be a kind of Miracle, if any man should arrive at a mature Age, without the *aid* of somebody *else*."[57] But Pufendorf concluded from this that because of the need to cooperate, the state of nature is in fact peaceful.[58] And while Pufendorf pays lip-service to the idea that God is at the origin of the laws of nature,[59] he essentially believes that the law of nature derives from "the nature, condition, and desires of man himself."[60]

This reasoning has important consequences for the law of nations. Pufendorf is very categorical in subscribing to Hobbes' definition of the law of nations, who wrote that "because states, upon being constituted, take on the personal properties of men, the law, which we call natural when speaking of the duty of

56 Grewe, *The Epochs of International Law*, p. 354.

57 Samuel von Pufendorf, *The Whole Duty of Man According to the Law of Nature* [1673] (Indianapolis: Liberty Fund, 2003), p. 53 (emphasis in original).

58 See discussed in Albert de La Pradelle, *Maîtres et Doctrines du Droit des Gens* (Paris: Les Éditions Internationales, 1950), pp. 119–120. I am indebted to Martti Koskenniemi for pointing out to me this detail on Pufendorf. But see also discussed in Richard Tuck, *The Rights of War and Peace: Political Thought and the International Order from Grotius to Kant* (Oxford: Oxford University Press, 1999). pp. 150–151. Grewe said that "the differences between the theoretical foundations have to be kept in mind. For Pufendorf, the state of nature was a state of peace [and that] [n]atural law preserved its importance even after the establishment of the State." See Grewe, *The Epochs of International Law*, p. 354.

59 "Since He so formed the nature of the world and man that the latter cannot exist without leading a social life, and for this reason gave him a mind capable of grasping the ideas that lead to this end (…), it is surely to be recognised that He also willed for man to regulate his actions by that native endowment which God Himself appears to have given him (…). And since this end cannot be attained in any other way than by the observance of natural law, it is understood that man has been obligated also by the Creator to observe this law (…)." See Pufendorf, *De Jure Naturae et Gentium Libri Octo* (*On the Laws of Nature and Nations*, Oxford: Clarendon Press, 1934), Bk II, ch. 3, para. 20, pp. 217–218.

60 Pufendorf, *De Jure Naturae et Gentium Libri Octo*, Bk. II, ch. 3, para 14, p. 205.

individual men, on being applied to whole states and nations and peoples, is called the law of nations."[61] Separating himself from Grotius in an important respect, Pufendorf concludes that we do not "feel that there is any other voluntary or positive law of nations which has the force of a law, properly so called, such as binds nations as if it proceeds from a superior." Ultimately, there is hardly room for a distinct category of international law:

> Most of the matters which the Roman Jurisconsults and others refer to the law of nations (...) belong either to the law of nature or to the civil law of different nations, which law amongst nations agrees in such matters as do not otherwise depend on the universal reason that is common to all mankind. But no distinct branch of law can properly be constituted from these, since, indeed, those laws are common to nations (...) [because] they agree accidentally, due to the individual pleasure of legislators in different states.[62]

As we will see, Pufendorf's advocacy of this minimalist notion would not remain an exception, and in an important respect, paved the way for how the law of nations would come to be understood in the 18th century. Interestingly, while one modern historian of international law famously belittled Pufendorf's contribution by saying that he "did not add much to the science of international law,"[63] the first generations of Americans were much more in awe of his work.[64] One clear influence was on John Witherspoon, a representative of New Jersey and president of Princeton University, voiced a Pufendorfian view on the law of nations: "the law of nature and nations is nothing else but the law of general reason, or those obligations of duty from reason and conscience, on one individual to another, antecedent to any particular law derived from the social

61 Thomas Hobbes, *De Cive*, chap. XIV, paras 4–5, quoted in Pufendorf, *De Jure Naturae et Gentium Libri Octo*, Bk. II, ch. 3, para 23, p. 226. It should however be noted that Hobbes and Pufendorf disagree about the origin of the bindingness of natural law. For the former, it only becomes binding once it has been integrated into civil law, not merely by virtue of being of divine origin. See discussed in Jouannet, *Emer de Vattel et l'Émergence Doctrinale du Droit International Classique*, p. 43.

62 Pufendorf, *De Jure Naturae et Gentium Libri Octo*, Bk II, ch. 3, para. 23, pp. 226.

63 See Arthur Nussbaum, *A Concise History of the Law of Nations* (New York: The Macmillan Company, 1962), p. 150.

64 One American author of an introductory textbook on law that appeared in 1817 wondered out loud "[w]hat legal student, ambitious of deep and solid learning, would be willing to acknowledge an unacquaintance with the treatises "De Jure Belli ac Pacis," and "De Jure Gentium et Naturae?"" See David Hoffman, *A Course of Legal Study, Respectfully addressed to the Students of the United States* (Baltimore: Coale and Maxwell, 1836), p. 71.

compact, or even actual consent. On this account, it is called the law of nature(…); and because there are very rarely to be found any parties in such a free state with regard to each other, except independent nations, therefore it is also called the law of nations."[65] Apart from Pufendorf's international legal thought, his constitutional thinking, in particular as regards federal structures, would become an important point of reference in colonial debates about the role of the colonies in the British imperial order.[66]

Another important jurist for the Founding Fathers with respect to shaping modern notions of neutral rights was Cornelius van Bynkershoek, a judge in Dutch admiralty courts. He shared Grotius' general assertion of neutrality as implying "equality of treatment for both belligerents."[67] However, Bynkershoek further specifies his definition so as to leave little if no room at all to navigate between strict neutrality and alliance. As a result, he defined as neutral "those who belong to neither belligerent party and who owe no services to either party by treaty obligations. Those who have obligations are not mere neutral friends, they are allies."[68] Drawing on Livy, he concludes, "[neutrals] must in every way guard against interfering in the war, and against favouritism towards or prejudice against either belligerent."[69] Being a writer who is usually regarded as a precursor to the positivist thinkers of the 19th century,[70] Bynkershoek rejects the idea that just war thinking should affect neutrality considerations—a view to which Grotius had still adhered:

> In my judgement, the question of justice and injustice does not concern the neutral, and it is not his duty to sit in judgement between his friends who may be fighting each other, and to grant or deny anything to either belligerent through considerations of the relative degree of justice.[71]

---

65 John Witherspoon, "Speech in Congress" (January 8, 1778), in *Letters of Delegates to Congress*, Vol. 8, p. 555.

66 See e.g. as discussed in Alison Lacroix, "Drawing and Redrawing the Line: The Pre-Revolutionary Origins of Federal Ideas of Sovereignty." *Occasional Papers, University of Chicago* (2008), pp. 12–13.

67 See Thomas W. Balch, T., "The United States and the Expansion of the Law between Nations" *University of Pennsylvania Law Review* 64 (1915), p. 119.

68 Cornelius van Bynkershoek, *Quaestiones iuris publici libri duo* (The Classics of International Law, Oxford: Clarendon Press, 1930 [1737]), Bk. I, ch. 9, p. 60. See also discussed in Grewe, *The Epochs of International Law*, pp. 372–373.

69 Bynkershoek, *Quaestiones iuris publici libri duo*, Bk. I, ch. 9, p. 61.

70 See e.g. Nussbaum, *A Concise History of the Law of Nations*, pp. 167–172; Grewe, *The Epochs of International Law*, p. 357.

71 Bynkershoek, *Quaestiones iuris publici libri duo*, Bk. I, ch. 9, p. 61.

The situation is different, however, for allied states. If they seek to remain neutral between two allies who are at war (i.e. they are not neutrals in the sense of Bynkershoek's definition!), they are advised not to honor the obligations by sending troops to both sides "only to have them fight and slay each other." Instead, the country should rather pick sides on the basis of *justa causa*.[72]

This position had of course consequences for Bynkershoek's thinking regarding the freedom of the seas. For one, he agreed with the general principle found in the *Consolato del Mare*, a medieval corpus of rules regarding the laws of the sea, that "an enemy vessel when captured belongs to the captor, but the owners of neutral goods if present may compound for the purchase of the vessel and thus continue their voyage."[73] At the same time, Bynkershoek holds that "I cannot see why it should not be lawful to seize enemy goods found in neutral ships" after which neutral ships are released again.[74] In his discussion, he parts with the 'free ships, free goods rule' including the obligation by the captor to compensate the neutral freighter.[75] But even if Bynkershoek does not prove to be an unapologetic defender of the cause of neutrals, he was still popular among common law jurists because of his "plain and realistic character" appreciating his casuistic and positivist approach to legal matters.[76]

Before turning to Vattel, the most influential international legal thinker of the 18th century, it is worthwhile to briefly examine the ideas of two of his immediate predecessors, Wolff and Burlamaqui. Christian von Wolff was the most prodigious publicist of his era. A disciple of the philosopher Leibniz and a professor of natural law and the law of nations at the university of Halle, Wolff is best known for having revived the concept of *civitas maxima*, or society of states, with which he stands much closer to Grotius than to Pufendorf. Nevertheless, his point of departure, the state of nature, is conceptually much closer to Pufendorf. For instance, in the Prolegomena to the *Jus Gentium methoda Scientifica Pertractatum* (1749), he holds that "[s]ince nations are regarded as individual persons living in a state of nature, moreover, as men in a state of nature use nothing except natural law, nations also originally used none other than natural law; therefore the law of nations is originally nothing except the

72 Bynkershoek, *Quaestiones iuris publici libri duo*, pp. 62–63. Grewe finds this solution "not particularly logical", calling it a move towards a "discriminatory concept of war." See *The Epochs of International Law*, p. 374.

73 Bynkershoek, *Quaestiones iuris publici libri duo*, Bk 1, ch. 13, p. 85.

74 Bynkershoek, *Quaestiones iuris publici libri duo*, ch. 14, p. 88.

75 Bynkershoek, *Quaestiones iuris publici libri duo*, ch. 14, p. 88–89. See also discussed in Arthur Nussbaum, *A Concise History of the Law of Nations* (New York: The Macmillan Company, 1962), p. 170.

76 Nussbaum, *A Concise History of the Law of Nations*, p. 172.

law of nature applied to nations."[77] As such, the law of nature applied to nations constitutes what Wolff calls the necessary law of nations.

For the sake of promoting the common good, Wolff argues, nature has established a society among nations, called the *civitas maxima*.[78] At this point, he goes beyond Pufendorf in outlining three more types of international law. First, there is the voluntary law of nations, founded in the necessary law, followed by the stipulative law of nations (*jus pactitium*, i.e. treaty law), and by customary law, based on the tacit consent among nations. Taken together, these three bodies of law constitute the positive law of nations, since they all "spring from the will of nations."[79] Wolff even postulated the existence of an (albeit fictitious) *Rector civitatis maximae*, which was supposed to define "by the right use of reason what nations ought to consider as law among themselves."[80] Wolff assumed that by laying out his treatise in accordance with mathematical principles, his conclusions would have to be accepted as irrefutable. Unfortunately, his method of exposition also burdened his argument, which was subsequently deemed "too heavily based on rationalist constructions."[81] "In historical perspective" noted Nussbaum, "the treatise does not appear very important (...) offer[ing] little 'enlightenment' or ingenuity; essentially it is a stale residue of scholasticism."[82] Nevertheless, Wolff's work proved a key influence on that of the early Americans' most quoted jurist, Emer de Vattel.

Another author whose fame has faded into obscurity these days, but who was a particular favorite with some of the Founding Fathers is Jean-Jacques Burlamaqui, a Genevan lawyer and city councillor, praised as a "writer of great reputation on political law."[83] He is perhaps best known in American

77 Christian von Wolff, *Jus Gentium methoda Scientifica Pertractatum*, Prolegomena, para 3, p. 9.

78 "Civitas, in quam Gentes coiuisse intelliguntur, et cujus ipsae sunt membra, seu cives, vocatur Civitas maxima." Translated: "The State, into which nations are understood to have combined, and of which they are members or citizens, is called the supreme state." See Christian von Wolff, *Jus Gentium methoda Scientifica Pertractatum*, Prolegomena, para. 10, p. 13.

79 Christian von Wolff, *Jus Gentium methoda Scientifica Pertractatum*, Prolegomena, paras. 22–25, pp. 17–19.

80 Christian von Wolff, *Jus Gentium methoda Scientifica Pertractatum*, Prolegomena, para. 21, p. 17.

81 Grewe, *The Epochs of International Law*, p. 359.

82 Nussbaum, *A Concise History of the Law of Nations*, p. 156.

83 See Jonathan Elliot (ed.), *The Debates in the Several State Conventions of the Adoption of the Federal Constitution*, Vol. 4, p. 279.

constitutional history for having coined the phrase "pursuit of happiness,"[84] which was used by Jefferson in the Declaration of Independence.[85] Incidentally, the pursuit of happiness provides the very purpose of Burlamaqui's natural law theory. However, this is not to say that his theory is secular. He believes that through rational deduction, it becomes "unquestionable, that the will of the supreme Being is the efficient cause of the law of nature, and the source of the obligation from thence arising."[86] And like Grotius and Pufendorf, Burlamaqui also postulates a principle of sociability from which "all the laws of society, and all our general and particular duties towards other men, are derived."[87]

His ideas about the law of nations largely resemble those of Pufendorf. Assuming "that societies are considered as bodies, and receive the appellation of moral persons (…), the law of nations properly so called, and considered as a law proceeding from a superior, is nothing else, but the law of nature itself, not applied to men considered simply as such; but to nations, states, or their chiefs, in the relations they have together."[88] But while he dismisses the existence of voluntary law, calling it "destitute of all foundations,"[89] he grudgingly accepts that there may exist something like

> another law of nations, which we may call arbitrary and free, as founded only on an express or tacit convention; the effect of which is not of itself universal; being obligatory only in regard to those who have voluntarily submitted thereto, and only so long as they please, because they are always at liberty to change or repeal it. To which we must likewise add, that the whole force of this sort of law of nations

84 See Jean-Jacques Burlamaqui, *The Principles of Natural and Politic Law* [1747] (Indianapolis: Liberty Fund, 2006), Vol. I, Part I, ch. 5, pp. 65–66.

85 See discussed in Morton White, *The Philosophy of the American Revolution* (New York: Oxford University Press, 1978), pp. 162–164.

86 Burlamaqui, *The Principles of Natural and Politic Law,* Part II, ch. 4, p. 145. The divine basis of his theory of law greatly influenced James Wilson, not only in his "Considerations on the Nature and Extent of the Legislative Authority of the British Parliament" (1774), but also in the *Lectures of Law* (1790). Through the Considerations, Jefferson's Declaration was influenced by Burlamaqui. See Morton White, *The Philosophy of the American Revolution*, p. 37.

87 Burlamaqui, *The Principles of Natural and Politic Law*, Part II, ch. 4, p. 156.

88 Burlamaqui, *The Principles of Natural and Politic Law*, Part II, ch. 6, p. 174. See also discussed in Emmanuelle Jouannet, *Emer de Vattel et l'Émergence Doctrinale du Droit International Classique* (Paris: Editions A. Pedone, 1998), pp. 373–377.

89 Burlamaqui, *The Principles of Natural and Politic Law,* Part II, ch. 6, p. 176.

> ultimately depends on the law of nature, which commands us to be true to our engagements.[90]

Even if Burlamaqui's notion of international law is—like Pufendorf's—quite minimalist, this does not diminish the reach of its obligatory force. He says that "[t]he *Reason of state*, so often alleged to justify the proceedings or enterprises of princes, cannot really be admitted for this end [to pursue their own advantage to the prejudice of others], but inasmuch as it is reconcilable with the common interest of nations, or, which amounts to the same thing, with the unalterable rules of sincerity, justice, and humanity."[91]

By the second half of the 18th century, reason of state and balance of power thinking had reached their classical incarnation. In some way, it was not surprising that the minimalist notions of international law as espoused by Burlamaqui were sometimes regarded as adequately reflecting the state of the discipline, since there seemed to be few if any valid rules beyond the precepts of natural law. It was in this environment that in 1758, Emer de Vattel published his *Le Droit des Gens, ou Principes de la Loi Naturelle, appliqués à la conduite et aux affaires des nations et des souverains* (*The Law of Nations, or Principles of the Law of Nature, Applied to the Conduct and Affairs of Nations and Sovereigns*). Vattel hailed from Neuchâtel, a Prussian principality at the time. He was educated in the system of Pufendorf, and studied law under Burlamaqui in Geneva.[92] His seminal treatise, *The Law of Nations*, was initially intended to be an abridgement of Wolff's 1749 treatise.[93] It gained wide popularity, in particular in the United States, and was used as a textbook at for instance Dartmouth

---

90 Burlamaqui, *The Principles of Natural and Politic Law*, Part II, ch. 6, p. 177. Jouannet reads this as implying instead that Burlamaqui in fact attempts "de concilier à nouveau les thèses des uns et des autres" See *Emer de Vattel et l'Émergence Doctrinale du Droit International Classique*, p. 48.

91 Burlamaqui, *The Principles of Natural and Politic Law*, Part II, ch. 6, p. 175–176 (emphasis in original).

92 Nussbaum however notes that "Vattel's reasoning was aggravated by his lack of legal training" and that writing the book actually "required a familiarity with juristic methods and literature which he did not possess." See Nussbaum, *A Concise History of the Law of Nations*, p. 159.

93 In the case *Rutgers v. Waddington*, James Duane said that Vattel's treatise is "entitled to the highest admiration! He modestly takes Wolfius for his guide; but in numberless passages corrects, abridges and improves him." See *The Case of Elizabeth Rutgers v. Joshua Waddington*, August 7, 1786, Mayor's Court, New York (New York: Morrisania, 1866).

and the College of William and Mary until late into the 19th century.[94] As one historian wrote, it "enjoyed near-canonical status in Britain and the colonies."[95] Alexander Hamilton considered him "perhaps the most accurate and approved of the writers on the laws of nations."[96] Jefferson was even more lyrical, saying that in determining what the law ought to be, "let us appeal to enlightened and disinterested judges. None is more so than Vattel."[97] One reason for its popularity was that, unlike earlier works on international law, Vattel's was written in clear and crisp French (not Latin, as was customary), and was largely unburdened by references to classical authors (like the work of Grotius, Pufendorf and Wolff was).[98] What is more, Vattel was also appreciated because apart from being a theorist, he was an able chronicler of legal practice, making his treatise a useful handbook of statecraft. This may account for the fact that for the period up to 1820, he was the most cited lawyer in American courts.[99]

For the theory of international law, Vattel was instrumental as a synthesizer of the ideas of Pufendorf and Wolff by admitting of a law of nations based on

94 See Jesse Reeves, "The Influence of the Law of Nature upon International Law in the United States", pp. 551–552. Indeed, Hoffman said that, despite its shortcomings, "Vattel is generally a perspicuous and elegant writer; and this work contains so much useful matter, and is so universally read, that to be unacquainted with it would indicate either a want of industry, or an unwarrantable fastidiousness of opinion." Hoffman, *A Course of Legal Study*, p. 240. Henry Laurens, a one-time president of the Second Continental Congress from South Carolina, wished to "rather have" *two* copies of Vattel's *Law of Nations* instead of one. See Henry Laurens to William Alexander (November 29, 1778), in *Letters of Delegates to Congress*, Vol. 11, p. 266.

95 Eliga Gould, "Zones of Law, Zones of Violence: The Legal Geography of the British Atlantic, circa 1772" *William and Mary Quarterly* (3rd series) 60, no. 3 (July, 2003), p. 477.

96 Alexander Hamilton to George Washington (September 15, 1790), in Henry Cabot Lodge (ed.), *The Works of Alexander Hamilton,* (New York: G.P. Putnam's Sons, 1904), Vol. 4, p. 317.

97 Cited in Fenwick, "The Authority of Vattel", *American Political Science Review* 7, no. 3, 1913, p. 410.

98 Cornelis van Vollenhoven, a rather unsympathetic observer of Vattel, once famously sneered that "[t]he contrast between the old book by Grotius and the new one of 1758 is most briefly characterized by the christian names of either author; the Dutchman is called Hugh, a bluff and sturdy name; the other is called Eméric: the name of a balletmaster." However, he also had to concede that "[t]he most disheartening fact of all is that Vattel was enormously successful. The man, who was a thinker and a worker, could not hold a candle to Grotius, was so favoured by fortune that the second stage of the law of nations (+/– 1770–1914) may be safely called after him." See Cornelis van Vollenhoven, *The Three Stages in the Evolution of the Law of Nations* (The Hague, Martinus Nijhoff, 1919), pp. 4, 32.

99 See Edwin Dickinson, "Changing Concepts and the Doctrine of Incorporation." *American Journal of International Law* 26 (1932), p. 259, at fn. 132.

the law of nature, but also to recognize a voluntary law of nations. Interestingly, while Vattel's initial assumptions are strongly marked by natural law thinking, he gradually moves away towards a positivism that seriously questions the necessity and legitimacy of the law of nature. In his theory of obligations, this is not immediately evident, however. In an earlier essay written in 1747, Vattel discussed his views on the obligatory character of natural law, espousing a highly secular position. To him, natural law as such is founded on "*the essence and nature of man and things in general.*"[100] Very explicitly, Vattel eliminates God from the picture. Arguing that reason provides the epistemological basis for law, he says that "those who assign the instituting of natural law to the arbitrary will of God (...) must agree that God could only give laws suitable to the nature of things, and particularly to the essence and nature of man, whom he obstructs to observe them." He then goes on to conclude that

> But how will they know these most advantageous of laws? They will consider the nature of man and things, and they will see which laws are most appropriate to them. They are required to draw on the same sources as us. This is sufficient to show that natural law is founded on the essence and nature of things and of men in particular. Cicero recognized this when he said that law is established by nature: *natura ipsa constitutum est jus*.[101]

Subsequently, Vattel rejects the notion that obligations deriving from natural law could originate in the need to obey a superior, or that the character of the relationship between man and a superior which imposes this obligation. In fact, the motive for complying with legal norms derives from our concern regarding "our *well-being*, our *expediency*, our *advantage*";[102] in other words, self-interest. This then provides the starting point for his theory of international law, which is initially very Pufendorfian/Hobbesian. Arguing that nations unite "for the purpose of promoting their mutual safety and advantage by the joint efforts of their combined strength," he postulates that "nations or sovereign states are to be considered as so many free persons living together

100 Emer de Vattel, "Essay on the Foundation of Natural Law and on the First Principle of the Obligation Men find Themselves Under to Observe Laws", in Vattel, *The Law of Nations*, p. 748 (emphasis in original).

101 Vattel, "Essay on the Foundation of Natural Law and on the First Principle of the Obligation Men find Themselves Under to Observe Laws", p. 749.

102 Vattel, "Essay on the Foundation of Natural Law and on the First Principle of the Obligation Men find Themselves Under to Observe Laws", p. 753 (emphasis in original).

in the state of nature."[103] In this situation, the highest binding legal norms together constitute what Vattel calls the necessary (or natural) law of nations. This body of law is immutable and absolutely binding because it contains precepts based on the nature of man himself.

At the same time, because nature has put people in a mutual dependency, there arises a society of mankind for the purpose of their mutual preservation. From this society, Vattel derives a general law proscribing that "each nation is bound to contribute everything in her power to the happiness and perfection of all the others."[104] One interesting consequence of this is for example that "a nation is obliged to promote and carry a foreign trade" and that "a nation has a right to procure, at an equitable price, whatever articles it wants, by purchasing them of other nations who have no occasion for them."[105] While the idea of a society of mankind was obviously inspired by Wolff's ideal of a *civitas maxima*, Vattel did not follow Wolff in building on it. In the Preface to *The Law of Nations*, he writes that he does not "think the fiction of such a republic [the *civitas maxima*] admissible in itself, or capable of affording sufficiently solid grounds on which to build the rules of the universal law of nations which shall necessarily claim the obedient acquiescence of sovereign states."[106] The reason for this was simple: Vattel underlines this nature-given 'absolute independence' of all countries in noting that they are "naturally equal, and inherit from nature the same obligations and rights." He follows this by his well-known remark to the end that "[p]ower or weakness do not in this regard produce any difference. A dwarf is as much a man as a giant; a small republic is no less a sovereign state than the most powerful kingdom."[107]

---

103 Vattel, *The Law of Nations*, prelim, paras. 1–6, p. 67–68. He even goes on to literally paraphrase Hobbes by saying that "the *law of nations* is originally no other than the *law of nature applied* to nations." Ibid., p. 68.

104 Vattel, *The Law of Nations*, Prelim, para. 11, p. 73.

105 Vattel, *The Law of Nations*, Bk. I, ch. 8, p. 132, 133.

106 Vattel, *The Law of Nations*, Preface, p. 14. As Vattel wrote: "It is essential to every civil society (*civitati*) that each member have [sic] resigned a part of his right to the body of the society, and that there exist in it an authority capable of commanding all the members, of giving them laws, and of compelling those who should refuse to obey. Nothing of this kind can be conceived or supposed to subsist between nations. Each sovereign state claims and actually possesses an absolute independence on all the others (…) Now, although nature has indeed established a general society between mankind, by creating them subject to such wants as render the assistance of their fellow-creatures indispensably necessary to enable them to live in a manner suitable to men,—yet she has not imposed on them a particular obligation to unite in civil society, properly so called." Ibid.

107 Vattel, *The Law of Nations*, Prelim, para. 18, p. 75.

Yet, if all states are equal as sovereign states and are at the same time impelled to cultivate a society of mankind, there will be a need to elaborate concrete rules which all agree on so as to operationalize the natural law of nations. Here, Vattel borrows the notion of voluntary laws of nations—which are binding on all—from Wolff, which circumscribes the reach of the necessary law of nations. Another type of law, the conventional law of nations, i.e. treaty law, is only binding between the parties to an agreement. To some extent, so is the customary law of nations, which is founded on "a tacit convention of the nations that observe it towards each other."[108] Taken together, these three kinds of international law—voluntary, conventional and customary—constitute the positive law of nations. But while in Wolff, the positive law of nations existed largely only at the abstract level, it becomes much more concrete in Vattel, precisely because of Vattel's emphasis on the doctrine of state sovereignty.

Vattel's statism led him to reject the chimerical notion of the *civitas maxima*, but significantly, he maintained a residual notion of community called the society of mankind, characterized by certain shared values and a common understanding of the law of nations.[109] Taking into account the political realities of his day, he also demonstrates its existence from the fact that as a whole, "Europe forms a political system, an integral body, closely connected by the relations and different interests of the nations inhabiting this part of the world." This situation had developed since the Renaissance, when government representatives began to interact on a permanent basis through the establishment of embassies. These developments, Vattel says

> ma[d]e of modern Europe a kind of republic, of which the members—each independent, but all linked together by the ties of common interests—unite for the maintenance of order and liberty. Hence arose that famous scheme of the political balance, or the equilibrium of power; by which is understood such a disposition of things, as that no one potentate be able absolutely to predominate, and prescribe law to others.[110]

108 Vattel, *The Law of Nations*, Prelim, para. 25, p. 77.

109 See discussed in Jouannet, *Emer de Vattel et l'Émergence Doctrinale du Droit International Classique*, pp. 100–102.

110 Vattel, *The Law of Nations*, Bk III, ch. 3, para. 47, p. 496. Interestingly, Vattel praised England because it "has the glory of holding the political balance [preserving] it in equilibrium." Ibid., para. 48, p. 497.

It was inevitable that in attempting to reconcile the prerequisites of the balance of power and the necessary law of nations, incongruities would arise. One example is with respect to the right of a country to wage war. As a principle, says Vattel, "[t]he right of employing force, or making war, belongs to nations no farther than is necessary for their own defence and for the maintenance of their rights."[111] In terms of his just war theory, this excludes pre-emptive or preventive military operations: "it is a sacred principle of the law of nations, that an increase of power cannot, alone and of itself, give any one a right to take up arms in order to oppose it."[112] But, as is typical in Vattel's treatise, the necessity for self-preservation could trump this rule. As he says in the next paragraph: "where it is impossible or too dangerous to wait for an absolute certainty, we may justly act on a reasonable presumption."[113] And since states also have a duty to uphold the system as a whole, they are even obliged to intervene to help preserve other states.[114]

Similar ambiguities predominate in Vattel's discussion of the rights and duties of neutral states, a subject which was close to the hearts of the Founding Fathers. As a rule, neutral countries "by the law of nature nations are in a state of peace and have a right to remain so."[115] Therefore, if they wish to remain impartial, they should not provide any military assistance whatsoever to any belligerent state, although a treaty commitment to this end could be the sole exception.[116] At the same time, says Vattel, neutrals should "not refuse to one of the parties, on account of his present quarrel, what she grants to the other."[117] However, depending on the situation, realities prevail over principle. For instance, "if an unjust conqueror (...) makes me an offer of neutrality when he is able to crush me, what can I better do than accept it? I yield to necessity; and my inability discharges me from a natural obligation [to assist oppressed innocence]. The same inability would even excuse me from a perfect obligation

111 Vattel, *The Law of Nations*, Bk III, ch. 3, para. 26, p. 483.

112 Vattel, *The Law of Nations*, Bk III, ch. 3, para. 43, p. 492.

113 Vattel, *The Law of Nations*, Bk III, ch. 3, para. 44, p. 493.

114 Thus, says Vattel, "[e]very nation ought, on occasion, to labour for the preservation of others, and for securing them from ruin and destruction, as far as it can do this, without exposing itself too much. (...) It is in the interest of princes to stop the progress of an ambitious monarch who aims at aggrandising himself by subjugating his neighbours." See *The Law of Nations*, Bk II, ch. 1, para. 4, p. 263.

115 Jesse Reeves, "The Influence of the Law of Nature upon International Law in the United States" *American Journal of International Law* 31 (1935), p. 559.

116 Thomas Balch, "The United States and the Expansion of the Law between Nations", p. 119.

117 Vattel, *The Law of Nations*, Bk III, ch. 7, para. 104, p. 524.

contracted by an alliance. (…) Necessity, and the care of my own safety, absolve me from my engagements."[118]

Another telling example where Vattel's discussion becomes ambiguous is with regard to the right of innocent passage through neutral territory. Again, the general principle is that "[a]n innocent passage is due to all nations with whom a state is at peace. (…) But it rests with the sovereign of the country to judge whether the passage be innocent (…)."[119] Moreover, any party that wishes to obtain an innocent passage must request such with the sovereign. Still, this rule also knows an exception, namely in the case of 'extreme necessity.' In this case, for instance when "an army find themselves exposed to imminent destruction or unable to return to their own country unless they pass through neutral territories, they have a right to pass in spite of the sovereign, and to force their way, sword in hand." No right to be "mistress of [one's] own territory" is admitted in this case.[120] On the question of granting passage to just and unjust belligerents, Vattel also chooses necessity over principle. The general principle is that while "we are not bound to grant even an innocent passage except for just causes, we may refuse it to him who requires it for a war that is evidently unjust."[121] But notwithstanding the fact that "in assisting the unjust, we partake of his crime, and become, like him, guilty of injustice,"[122] Vattel assures us that "if it would be too dangerous for [a sovereign] to give a refusal [for passage], he is not obliged to draw down the impending evil on his own head (…) [for] to hazard the quiet and welfare of his people would be a very great breach of his duty."[123]

When discussing the voluntary law of nations as regards warfare, Vattel acknowledges the difficulty of respecting the importunities of natural law. Wondering how this can be enforced, he concludes that

> [e]very free and sovereign state has a right to determine, according to the dictates of her own conscience, what her duties require of her, and what she can or cannot do with justice. (…) If other nations take upon themselves to judge of her conduct, they invade her liberty, and infringe her most valuable rights (…)[124]

---

118 Vattel, *The Law of Nations*, Bk III, ch. 7, para. 107, p. 525.
119 Vattel, *The Law of Nations*, Bk III, ch. 7, para. 119, p. 534.
120 Vattel, *The Law of Nations*, Bk III, ch. 7, para. 122, p. 535.
121 Vattel, *The Law of Nations*, Bk III, ch. 7, para. 135, p. 541.
122 Vattel, *The Law of Nations*, Bk III, ch. 6, para. 83, p. 513.
123 Vattel, *The Law of Nations*, Bk III, ch. 7, para. 135, p. 541.
124 Vattel, *The Law of Nations*, Bk III, ch. 12, para. 188, p. 590. See also discussed in Fenwick, "The Authority of Vattel", pp. 401–402.

This is where the distinction between the necessary and voluntary law of nations comes to the fore. Since adherence to the former is up to "the conscience of the sovereigns," observance of the latter is only "recommend[ed] (...) for the common advantage of states." Consequently, "[t]hough the *necessary* law be the rule which [the sovereign] invariably observes in his own conduct, he should allow others to avail themselves of the *voluntary* law of nations."[125] Vattel then concedes that since the *causa justa* of a war cannot be ascertained by other states, justice should be sought on the basis of the "legality of the means in themselves."[126] Nevertheless, his defense of the voluntary law of nations as a basis for legitimating means of warfare does not instil much confidence. Rejecting Grotius' supposition that such rules are founded on "an actual consent on the part of mankind," Vattel holds that since they are derived from the law of nature, we should instead "presume their consent," whilst maintaining that the voluntary law of nations is "far from being a chimera, an arbitrary or groundless fiction."[127]

In spite of Vattel's struggling with providing a consistent account of international law, his work was by far the most influential in the late 18th and early 19th centuries.[128] For the early generations of American

125 Vattel, *The Law of Nations*, Bk III, ch. 12, para. 189, p. 590 (emphasis in original).

126 Vattel, *The Law of Nations*, Bk III, ch. 12, para. 189, p. 591. Vattel already alluded to this idea in the Preliminaries: "Each nation in fact maintains that she has justice on her side in every dispute that happens to arise: and it does not belong to either of the parties interested, nor to other nations, to pronounce a judgment on the contested question. The party who is in the wrong is guilty of a crime against her own conscience: but as there exists a possibility that she may perhaps have justice on her side, we cannot accuse her of violating the laws of society." See *The Law of Nations*, Prelim, para. 21, p. 76.

127 Vattel, *The Law of Nations*, Bk III, ch. 12, para. 192, p. 592–593. Jouannet however rejects such a sceptical reading of Vattel on this point, arguing that "[a]yant pour objet de préserver l'intéret général de la société des Nations dans le respect de la liberté et l'égalité des États, le droit des gens volontaire est en effet le seul apte à permettre une application satisfaisante des règles juridiques en évitant que dégénèrent les situations conflictuelles." Consequently, Vattel, in desiring to serve both international stability and justice, concluded, says Jouannet, that "la fonction pacifiste, et donc stabilisatrice du droit naturel, n'est assuré que par la neutralisation de sa fonction de maintien de la justice." See *Emer de Vattel et l'Émergence Doctrinale du Droit International Classique*, p. 229. See also discussed, in a more 'traditionally' critical fashion, in Tim Hochstrasser, *Natural Law Theories in the Early Enlightenment* (Cambridge: Cambridge University Press, 2000), pp. 180–182.

128 According to Hochstrasser, the "dramatic series of concessions to empirical political reality, together with the systematic aspirations of the treatise, and the author's lucid style ensured a wide readership of *Le Droit Des Gens*." Indeed, "Vattel told professional diplomats what they wanted to hear with the aid of everyday political examples." See *Natural*

statesmen he became particularly appealing because of his support for English constitutional principles, his advocacy of democracy as well as federalism. On the first point, Vattel praised England for its "admirable constitution" which enabled its citizens to contribute to its glory: "Happy constitution! which they did not suddenly obtain: it has cost rivers of blood; but they have not purchased it too dear. (…) [It is] a monument capable of teaching kings how glorious it is to rule over a free people!"[129] As we will see below, it is not over these principles that the political leaders of the colonies quarrelled.

Vattel proved to be a strong defender of democratic principles.[130] First of all, he emphatically affirms that "[t]he prince derives his authority from the nation; he possesses just so much of it as they have thought proper to intrust him with."[131] At the same time, neither the prince nor the legislature (which in Vattel may be one and the same)[132] have the right to alter or abolish the fundamental laws of the state, since these "limit and regulate" the extent of the power of the sovereign.[133] However, in Lockean fashion, Vattel also argues that when a tyrant becomes insupportable, there is "no reason why the nation should not curb [him], pronounce sentence on him (…) and withdraw itself from his obedience." This could become the case when "a prince attacks the constitution of the state."[134] As such, Vattel can certainly be regarded as a true inspiration for the American and French revolutions.[135]

Finally, as to federations, he appears to believe they are "a sure mode of preserving the equilibrium, and maintaining the liberty of nations,"[136]

Law Theories in the Early Enlightenment, p. 182. See also Jesse Reeves, who called his work "the latest and most popular if not the most authoritative of the Continental writers." See "The Influence of the Law of Nature Upon International Law in the United States" *American Journal of International Law* 3, No. 3 (1909), p. 549.

129 Vattel, *The Law of Nations*, Bk I, ch. 3, para. 24, p. 90.

130 Even if he never mentions the word 'democracy' explicitly.

131 Vattel, *The Law of Nations*, Bk I, ch. 4, para. 45, p. 100.

132 Vattel, *The Law of Nations*, Bk I, ch. 4, para. 34, p. 95.

133 Vattel, *The Law of Nations*, Bk I, ch. 4, paras. 34, 46–47, p. 95, 101.

134 Vattel, *The Law of Nations*, Bk I, ch. 4, para. 51, p. 104. But see also ibid., para. 54, pp. 110–112.

135 Jouannet, *Emer de Vattel et l'Émergence Doctrinale du Droit International Classique*, p. 339.

136 Vattel, *The Law of Nations*, Bk III, ch. 3, para. 49, p. 498. Vattel appears not to sharply distinguish between federation and confederation, since when sovereign and independent states decide to unite in a "perpetual confederacy", they will together constitute a "federal republic." See *The Law of Nations*, Bk I, ch. 2, para. 10, p. 84.

albeit clearly implying that the society of mankind falls well short of what could be called a confederation. The model that he sketched for federal republics became an important starting point for the drafting of the Articles of Confederation: "[S]everal sovereign and independent states may unite themselves together by a perpetual confederacy, without ceasing to be, each individually, a perfect state."[137] Like Pufendorf, Wolff and Burlamaqui, Vattel recognizes that there is an intimate connection between domestic constitutional orders and the international legal order. This is only one way in which theories about the law of nations were important in the debates about the constitution in the United States between 1776 and 1787.

As a whole, the continental tradition of the law of nature and nations provided an indispensable repository of knowledge of international law; one which the early republic had to rely on to ensure its survival; and one from which "[t]he early generation of American statesmen had drunk deeply."[138] As a contemporary author, William Bradford, a Philadelphia attorney, put it in a letter to Madison: "Vattel, Barlemaqui, Locke & Montesquie[u] seem to be the standar[d]s to which [Congress] refer either when settling the rights of the Colonies."[139] As such, the continental tradition provided the bulk of the philosophical input where American conceptions of the law of nations were concerned. But in the struggle for independence and in thinking about constitutional principles for incorporating the law of nations into their domestic legal system, the Americans would inevitably rely on the legacy of the British common law tradition.[140]

1.2 The Common Law Tradition

In the 1764 case *Triquet v. Bath*, William Murray, better known as Lord Mansfield, famously declared that "the law of nations was to be determined from the practice of nations and also from the authority of Grotius, Barbeyrac, Bynkershoek, Wicquefort and others, there being no English writer of prominence

137 Vattel, *The Law of Nations*, Bk I, ch. 1, para. 10, p. 84. See also Gordon Wood, *The Creation of the American Republic 1776–1787* (New York: W.W. Norton, 1972) p. 355.

138 David Hendrickson, "International Law in Times of Empire" *Proceedings of the American Society of International Law* 99 (2005), p. 308.

139 Bradford to Madison (October 17, 1774). Quoted in David Armitage, *The Declaration of Independence, A Global History* (Cambridge/London: Harvard University Press, 2007), p. 41.

140 See discussed in e.g. Raoul van Caenegem, *An Historical Introduction to Western Constitutional Law* (Cambridge: Cambridge University Press, 1995), p. 171.

upon the subject."[141] As we will see below, this is not to say that English law had nothing to say about international legal issues. Moreover, Mansfield's contention would be gainsaid in his own times by authors such as Blackstone and Rutherforth. Also, by discussing the common law tradition separately from developments on the continent is not to say that there had been no cross-channel influences. For instance, there are various commonalities between the ways in which Roman law and the common law evolved in their early days. Also, there are similarities in how principles of *ius gentium* developed in Roman courts and how English courts shaped understandings of the law of nations from the late Middle Ages onwards. In the 18th century, therefore, "English lawyers (...) were perfectly ready to draw on Continental writings."[142] The development of English law—and its ideas about international law—was therefore never a purely insular matter.

For our purposes, the issue here is to analyse how Parliament and courts defined concepts of international law in the context of the English legal system. After all, while the first generations of American statesmen took recourse to the continental treatises on the law of nations to proclaim or defend their rights abroad, it was in the context of the common law—as introduced in the colonies—that the law of nations became anchored in American law. As Picciotto summarized the point: "[In the 18th century], the view prevailed that International Law consisted of the principles of natural justice; as the Common Law was similarly regarded, [therefore] it was an easy conclusion that International Law was part of the Common Law."[143] Looking at developments in England will thus help us in understanding the status that Americans attributed to the law of nations, and what role it played in securing independence in 1776 and in consolidating it subsequently. For Americans, the substance of the common law was useful for instance with respect to commerce and navigation, and this was another reason why British common law—being the law of a seafaring nation—served their interests well.[144] Considering these

141 *Triquet v. Bath,* 7 Burr. 1478, 96 Eng. Rep. 273, 97, Eng. Rep. 936 (1764). Quoted in Reeves, "The Influence of the Law of Nature upon International Law in the United States.", p. 548.

142 Nussbaum, *A Concise History of the Law of Nations*, p. 161.

143 Cyril M. Picciotto, *The Relation of International Law to the Law of England and the United States of America* (London: McBride, Nast & Co, 1915), p. 107.

144 As Peter Stephen Duponceau noted, "the law of nations, the law merchant, the maritime law, the constitution and even the religion of the kingdom [of England], are considered to be parts of and parcels of the *common law*. It pervades everything, and everything is interwoven with it. (...)" See *A Dissertation on the Nature and Extent of the Jurisdiction of the Courts of the United States.* (Philadelphia: Abraham Small, 1825), p. viii (emphasis in original).

parts of the law of nations as part of the law of the land gave American courts a chance to interpret these laws from their own vantage point.

It is sometimes assumed that the common law, by dint of its reliance on custom and precedence, developed in entire detachment of natural law ideas. The opposite is the case however. Already since the middle ages, continental ideas began to penetrate the English legal system. As one British lawyer said, "the law of nature [was] a familiar idea and a guiding principle among lawyers and judges [which] may even be said to be the source and spring of the common law."[145] This development already began with Henry de Bracton, a 13th-century jurist under Henry III, who was among the first English lawyers to distinguish between *ius naturale* and *ius gentium*.[146] He has been credited with making the connection between common law and Roman and continental ideas about a "higher law."[147] This would become known as fundamental law in the early United States, which was to be "tremendously influential upon the generation that framed the American constitution."[148] The reason for exploring these connections is because it will help us to understand how the law of nations was conceived of in England, given that it was obviously not introduced as a legal category by way of natural law. In that sense, international law in England is more closely associated with customary law—like in Roman law—than was the case in 17th-century Europe.

The two most significant court cases to be looked at here are *Calvin's Case*[149] and *Dr. Bonham's Case*.[150] A decision in the first case was rendered in 1608, and was considered pivotal by late 18th-century Americans because of its pronouncements on the applicability of the common law outside of Britain and on the nature of the British constitution. The case revolved around the issue whether or not subjects of the Scottish King James VI who were born after he acceded to the English throne as James I,[151] could hold land both in Scotland and England, since they were now subject to a king who ruled over two territories. Because of the extraterritorial implications of the case, it also briefly touched upon the law of nations.

---

145 Richard O'Sullivan, " Natural Law and Common Law" *Transactions of the Grotius Society* 31 (1945), p. 119.

146 O'Sullivan, "Natural Law and Common Law", p. 123.

147 Edward Corwin, "The 'Higher Law' Background of American Constitutional Law" *Harvard Law Review* 42 (1928), pp. 172–173.

148 Suzanna Sherry, "The Founders' Unwritten Constitution" *The University of Chicago Law Review* 54, no. 4 (1987), p. 1129.

149 See 7 Coke report 1a, 77 ER p. 377, 1608.

150 See 8 Coke report 107a, 114a C.P., 1610.

151 Which is why the case is also known as that of the *Post-natii*.

The Lord Chief Justice at the English Court of the Common Pleas, Sir Edward Coke, called "a 'framer' of the English constitution,"[152] ensured the fame of this case because of his unequivocal statements to the end that "the law of nature was part of the law of England." Both in the colonial era and after the Revolution, his digest of English case law was considered as authoritative among American lawyers and statesmen, and were studied by Jefferson and Story, among others. Coke conceived of the law of nature as "that which God at the time of creation of the nature of man infused into his heart, for his preservation and direction; and this is *lex aeterna,* the Moral Law, called also the Law of Nature."[153] What is more, he attributed it a superior status in the English legal system, his argument being that:

> First, That the ligeance or faith of the Subject is due unto the King by the Law of Nature: Secondly, That the Law of Nature is part of the Law of England: Thirdly, That the Law of Nature was before any Judicial or Municipal Law: Fourthly, That the Law of Nature is Immutable.[154]

The consequence was that with respect to the colonies, there was a continuing need for the King to supervise the royal charters because the laws created under them needed to be consistent with English law, as well as with the law of nature.[155] Coke himself did not directly address the international law implications. This was left to Thomas Egerton, Lord Ellesmere, in a speech on the case. He was of the opinion that "the Common Law of England is grounded upon the law of God, and extends itself to the original law of nature and the universal law of nations."[156] But he limited its application by defining it as "the fundamental laws of (…) the realms of Christian kingdoms and empires."[157] It therefore appears that Ellesmere

---

152 Daniel Hulsebosch, "The Ancient Constitution and the Expanding Empire: Sir Edward Coke's British Jurisprudence." *Law and History Review* 21, no. 3 (2003), p. 444.

153 *See* 7 Coke Report 13 *a, 77 ER p. 392.* On this point, he also relies on his readings of Henry de Bracton, *De Legibus et Consuetudinibus Angliae* (?1230); John Fortescue, *The Governance of England* [1885], and Christopher St. Germain's *Doctor and Student* (1518).

154 See 7 Coke Report 12 a, 77 ER p. 391. See also discussed in Corwin, "The "Higher Law" Background of American Constitutional Law", p. 369.

155 See discussed in Ken Macmillan, *The Atlantic Imperial Constitution: Center and Periphery in the English Atlantic World* (London: Palgrave Macmillan, 2011), pp. 16–17.

156 See "Speech of the Lord Chancellor…touching the Post-Nati," in Louis A. Knalfa, *Law and Politics in Jacobean England: The Tracts of Lord Chancellor Ellesmere,* (Cambridge: Cambridge University Press, 2008), p. 216.

157 Ellesmere MS 1763, Huntington Library, CA, Quoted in Kelly De Luca, "Lord Chancellor Ellesmere and the Law of Nations" Paper read at St. Catherine's College, Oxford, July 3, 2007, p. 4. Retrieved from <http://www.law.harvard.edu/programs/ames_foundation/BLHC07/De Luca BLHC Paper.pdf>.

did not think that the law of nations was a sub-category of the common law, but only shared particular commonalities with it.

The other great case of the day came two years later. *Dr. Bonham's Case* concerned the imprisonment for practising medicine without a license as required of one Thomas Bonham by the Royal College of Physicians on the basis of a claimed authority granted by Parliamentary statute. Presiding as the chief judge, Edward Coke seized the opportunity to declare the supremacy of the common law over statutory law:

> And it appears in our books that in many cases the common law will controul acts of parliament, and sometimes adjudge them to be utterly void: for when an act of parliament is against common right and reason, or repugnant, or impossible to be performed, the common law will controul it, and adjudge such act to be void.[158]

This quotation has often been advanced to demonstrate that Coke believed in the common law as being part of fundamental law.[159] However, Gough concludes that in this instance, Coke "was not really appealing to any 'fundamental, higher, or natural law' [or] propounding a theory of unconstitutional legislation, but only one of strict statutory interpretation."[160] This is however not to say that Coke did not believe in the idea of fundamental law, as we saw in *Calvin's Case*. Edward Corwin saw it as the starting point of a momentous shift within English law towards natural law:

> In the great constitutional struggle with the Stuarts [the receptive and candid attitude towards natural law ideas] enabled Coke to build upon Fortescue, and it enabled Locke to build upon Coke. It made allies of sixteenth century legalism and seventeenth century rationalism, and the alliance then struck has always remained, now more, now less vital, in American constitutional law and theory.[161]

---

158 See 8 Coke Report, 117b–188b, quoted in John W. Gough, *Fundamental Law in English Constitutional History* (Oxford: Clarendon Press, 1961), p. 32.

159 Stimson says that "the closest Coke ever came to defining the fundamental common law conceptually was to call it 'the absolute perfection of reason'." Quoted from Edward Coke, *Second Part of the Institutes of the Laws of England*, p. 179, in Shannon Stimson, *The American Revolution in the Law: Anglo-American Jurisprudence before John Marshall* (Princeton, NJ: Princeton University Press, 1990), p. 18.

160 Gough, *Fundamental Law in English Constitutional History*, p. 40.

161 Corwin, "The 'Higher Law' Background of American Constitutional Law", p. 370. Indeed, while in England, the verdict in this case met with strong criticism, allegedly leading to

In the latter half of the 18th century, two other cases were ruled on which contained important reflections on the status of the law of nations in English law. In *Triquet v. Bath*, the presiding Chief Justice, Lord Mansfield, whilst quoting Lord Talbot, declared that "the law of nations, in its full extent was part of the law of England [and] was to be collected from the practice of different nations, and the authority of writers."[162] A few years later, Mansfield repeated his point, and drew the obvious conclusion with respect to the legal position of statutory law—consistent with Coke's dictum in *Dr. Bonham*: "the law of nations is part of the common law of England. And the Act of Parliament 7 Anne c. 12 did not intend to alter, nor can alter the law of nations."[163]

All of this demonstrates that natural law as a component or foundation for common law and as a means for interpreting obligations under the law of nations was generally accepted in England. Simultaneously, a shift towards a positive law of nations still met with resistance in some quarters. A typical example of this is the *Institutes of Natural Law*, a treatise written by a professor at Cambridge, Thomas Rutherforth. It had first appeared in 1750 and was delivered as a series of lectures at Cambridge University as a commentary on Grotius' *De iure belli ac pacis*. His book shows that in mid-1700s England, natural law continued to captivate the thinking of leading jurists, and as a result found a willing audience as well in the American colonies, including future chief justice John Marshall.[164]

The most problematic issue for Rutherforth is Grotius' definition and justification of positive law. Rutherforth criticises him for assuming that the law of nations "is a system (...) which derives its authority from the positive consent

---

Coke being dismissed from the court, it nevertheless had significant influence in the American colonies.

162 See *Triquet v. Bath*, at 936. Quoted in Mark Janis, *The American Tradition in International Law*, p. 14. On this occasion, Lord Mansfield apparently quoted from *Barbuit's Case* (1737) Forr 280; 25 ER 777. However, E. Adair notes that "[s]imilarities in arrangement and wording make it almost certain that the editor of Talbot's cases in adding the note was merely copying Lord Mansfield's remarks in Triquet v. Bath." See "The Law of Nations and the Common Law in England: A Study of 7 Anne cap. 12" *Cambridge Historical Journal* 2, no. 3 (1928), p. 296.

163 See *Heathfield v Chilton* (1767) 4 Burrow 2016, referring to an act concerning ambassadorial privileges, which was declaratory with respect to the status of *jus gentium* in the common law. Quoted in Gough, *Fundamental Law in English Constitutional History*, p. 208–209.

164 "This digest of Grotius was one of the few law books in Marshall's library." See Edward Dumbauld, "John Marshall and the Law of Nations" *University of Pennsylvania Law Review*, 104, no. 1 (1955), p. 38.

of all, or of most nations." In Rutherforth's view, given that there is a "union between all nations" and that "nature has made a connexion between all mankind, (…) all nations, when we consider them as so many collective persons, are obliged to observe the same law of nature."[165] But, so Rutherforth argues, this connection between nations cannot be the basis of a positive law of nations, the reason being that there is no overarching legislative power amongst the nations. What is more, since the only difference between the law of nature and the law of nations is that the former applies to individuals and the latter to collectives, there is no qualitative difference between the two. *A fortiori*, treaty-making is also not an element of positive law, since it is based on an act of consent.[166] Likewise, customary international law also cannot be admitted as an instance of positive law, the argument being that "a law, that does not appear, is in effect, a law that does not exist."[167] In effect, Rutherforth wants to close the door to positive law altogether:

> It may be necessary here to caution the reader against imagining, that a law of nations, which is purely positive, might be established, if not by the constant and uninterrupted practice, yet by the approved practice of nations. (…) If there is any such law, it must have been introduced and established by mere usage (…) but we have already observed that (…) no such usage is to be found.[168]

Rutherforth, being more of a moral philosopher than a legal scholar, unfortunately does not take the opportunity to discuss the interrelationship between the common law and the law of nations, in spite of his extensive discussion of various sub-fields of civil law.[169] But, while given his non-legal background he could perhaps not be taken as seriously as a scholar of international law, his insistence on natural law likely contributed to his relative popularity among the early American statesmen.

Other British thinkers also entertained doubts about the viability of an independent and obliging international law. The philosopher David Hume

165 Thomas Rutherforth, *Institutes of Natural Law; Being the Substance of a Course of Lectures on Grotius' De iure belli ac pacis* (Baltimore, MD: William and Joseph Neal, 1832), ch. 9, p. 483.
166 Rutherforth, *Institutes of Natural Law*, ch. 9, p. 484.
167 Rutherforth, *Institutes of Natural Law*, ch. 9, p. 485.
168 Rutherforth, *Institutes of Natural Law*, ch. 9, pp. 487–488.
169 In fact, he does not mention the common law once, nor does he appear to discuss the English legal system at all.

wrote for instance that "though the morality of princes has the same extent, yet it has not the same force as that of private persons, and may lawfully be transgressed from a more trivial motive."[170] Another famous Scot, Adam Smith, concluded that the problem lay in a lack of enforceability. In his *Lectures on Jurisprudence*, he prefaced his discussion of international law with the remark that "with respect to the laws of nations, we can scarce mention any one regulation which is established with the common consent of all nations, and observed as such at all times. This must necessarily be the case, for where there is no supreme legislative power nor judge to settle differences, we may always expect uncertainty and irregularity."[171] His account is also remarkable for its low threshold for declaring war. For instance, encroachments on property, non-servicing of debt repayments or insults to the sovereign would be "reasonable" justifications for going to war.[172]

The most popular of English legal scholars in late 18th-century America was however Sir William Blackstone. As Mark Janis said, "Blackstone's rendering of the law of nations was the first great British intellectual legacy to American international lawyers."[173] Like the authors discussed above, Blackstone grounded his legal thinking in the law of nature. His celebrated treatise, the *Commentaries on the Laws of England* (1765–1769) constituted the first systematic modern treatment of English law.[174] As a result, the *Commentaries* went on to become the most influential source on the common law in the late 18th and early 19th century and together with Vattel's *The Law of Nations*, formed the bedrock of American legal thinking in that era. Simply put, "[the] *Commentaries* should be regarded as the baseline, or shared starting-point, of American legal thought."[175]

---

170 David Hume, *A Treatise of Human Nature* (New York: Oxford University Press, 1978) Bk. III, pt. 2, ch. 11 (On the Law of Nations), in *The Philosophical Works of David Hume* (Edinburgh: Adam Black and William and Charles Tait, 1826), Vol. 2, pp. 352–353.

171 Adam Smith, *Lectures on Jurisprudence* (Indianapolis: Liberty Fund, 1982), p. 545.

172 Smith, *Lectures on Jurisprudence*, pp. 545–546. On neutral shipping, Smith repeated the standard rule: "A neutral bottom will not however protect the goods of the enemy, nor does the hostility of the bottom, so to speak, forfeit the goods of the neutral power." See Ibid., p. 550.

173 Mark Janis, *The American Tradition of International Law* (Oxford: Clarendon Press, 2004), p. 4.

174 For instance, Jefferson praised the *Commentaries* as "the last perfect Digest of both branches of the law," but famously added that he disliked Blackstone's Toryism, which led to "honeyed Mansfieldism." Edward Dumbauld, *Thomas Jefferson and the Law*, pp. 9–10.

175 Albert Alschuler, "Rediscovering Blackstone" *University of Pennsylvania Law Review* 145, No. 1 (1996), p. 2.

Not surprisingly, in the introduction to the *Commentaries*, Blackstone emphasizes the pivotal role of natural law. First of all, he points out that its origin is divine, saying that "[t]his will of his maker is called the law of nature."[176] Secondly, he defines the scope of its obligatory nature in Ciceronean fashion. Being "co-eval with mankind and dictated by God himself," natural law "is of course superior in obligation to any other. It is binding over all the globe, in all countries, and at all times: no human laws are of any validity, if contrary to this; and such of them as are valid derive all their force, and all their authority, mediately or immediately, from this original."[177] In order for humans to 'find' this law, we need to apply right reason. But, says Blackstone, since human reason is often defective, we need the "benign interposition of divine providence" to guide us in these efforts. As a result, he concludes that the law of nature and the law of revelation underpin all human laws, none of which "should be suffered to contradict these."[178]

Given these foundations, what is it that gave rise to the law of nations, and how does it relate to natural law? In Blackstone's view, the main impetus behind this was the fact that "man was formed for society."[179] Consequently,

> as it is impossible for the whole race of mankind to be united in one great society, they must necessarily divide into many; and form separate states, commonwealths, and nations; entirely independent of each other, and yet liable to a mutual intercourse. Hence arises a third kind of law to regulate this mutual intercourse, called "the law of nations;" which, as none of these states will acknowledge a superiority in the other, cannot be dictated by either; but depends entirely upon the rules of natural law, or upon mutual compacts, treaties, leagues, and agreements between these several communities: in the construction also of which compacts we have no other rule to resort to, but the law of nature; being the only one to which both communities are equally subject: and therefore the civil law very justly observes, that *quod naturalis ratio inter omnes homines constituit, vocatur jus gentium*.[180]

176 William Blackstone, *Commentaries on the Laws of England* (Oxford: Clarendon Press, 1765–1769), Introduction, p. 40.

177 Blackstone, *Commentaries*, Introduction, p. 42.

178 Blackstone, *Commentaries*, Introduction, p. 43.

179 He relies on this point on Pufendorf.

180 Blackstone, *Commentaries*, Introduction, Sec. 2, p. 43. The translation of the Latin is "That which constitutes natural reason among men is called the law of nations." (own translation).

With this description, Blackstone takes a mainstream position going back via Burlamaqui to Pufendorf and Grotius, and actually appears to be ignoring the positivist move made by Vattel a decade earlier. This becomes even clearer at the point where he discusses the law of nations more in detail, and suggests a possible definition:

> The law of nations is a system of rules, deducible by natural reason, and established by universal consent among the civilized inhabitants of the world; in order to decide all disputes, to regulate all ceremonies and civilities, and to insure the observance of justice and good faith, in that intercourse which must frequently occur between two or more independent states, and the individuals belonging to each. This general law is founded upon this principle, that different nations ought, in time of peace, to do one another all the good they can; and, in time of war, as little harm as possible, without prejudice to their own real interests.[181]

In the last part of his definition, Blackstone alludes to what Pufendorf (and Vattel!) considered a natural duty to assist other countries. Notable in this definition is the reference to "natural reason" as the basis of the law of nations. Blackstone introduces this idea because no state "will allow a superiority in the other (...)" and because of that, rules of international law had to "necessarily result from those principles of natural justice, in which all the learned of every nation agree (...)."[182] He also admits that mutually acceptable rules can follow from "mutual compacts or treaties between the respective communities." However, these compacts or treaties are predicated upon "the law of nature and reason, being the only one in which all the contracting parties are equally conversant, and to which they are equally subject."[183]

Hence, for Blackstone, natural law is a necessary basis for the law of nations lending authority to treaties and mutually agreed upon rules. How then does the law of nations relate to the common law? On this point, Blackstone is very succinct:

> [T]he law of nations (wherever any question arises which is properly the object of it's jurisdiction) is here adopted in it's full extent by the common

181 Blackstone, *Commentaries*, Bk IV, Ch. 5, p. 67, where he quotes from Montesquieu, *De L'Esprit des Lois*, Bk. I, ch. 3: "Le droit des gens est naturellement fondé sur ce principe: que les diverses nations doivent se faire, dans la paix, le plus de bien, et, dans la guerre, le moins de mal qu'il est possible, sans nuire à leurs véritables intérêts."

182 Blackstone, *Commentaries*, Bk IV, Ch. 5, pp. 67–68.

183 Blackstone, *Commentaries*, Bk IV, Ch. 5, p. 68.

> law, and is held to be a part of the law of the land. And those acts parliament, which have from time to time been made to enforce this universal law, or to facilitate the execution of it's decisions, are not to be considered as introductive of any new rule, but merely as declaratory of the old fundamental constitutions of the kingdom (…).[184]

The reason why Blackstone asserts that neither Parliament nor the King[185] can actually change the law of nations is because it is partly predicated on natural law (natural reason), and because it belongs to the common law. It was regarded as the customary law of the land, and "governed the jurisdiction and modes of proceeding of English courts," including admiralty, maritime and ecclesiastical courts.[186] As such, the common law was known as *lex non scripta*, or unwritten law, and was regarded as a touchstone for Parliamentary legislation,[187] albeit not in a concrete fashion.[188] This distinction between written and unwritten law—*lex scripta* and *lex non scripta*—would later be adopted by American jurists as well, and led to a debate about which law prevailed. According to Blackstone, in Britain, the common law did not trump acts of Parliament: "where the common law and a statute differ, the common law gives place to the statute."[189]

On the substance of the law of nations Blackstone is less comprehensive. Of the many sub-fields in international law, he discusses mercantile law, maritime

---

184 Blackstone, *Commentaries*, Bk IV, Ch. 5, p. 68.

185 "[I]n England no royal power can introduce a new law, or suspend the execution of the old." See Blackstone, *Commentaries*, Bk IV, Ch. 5, p. 68.

186 Anthony Bellia and Bradford Clark, "The Federal Common Law of Nations" *Columbia Law Review* 109 (January, 2009), pp. 12–13.

187 With respect to the unwritten laws of England, Tucker distinguished between what he called *jus commune* and the *jure coronae*, the prerogatives of the crown. Together these constituted the "common law, *generally* so called." See St. George Tucker, "Of the Unwritten, or Common Law of England; And Its Introduction into, and Authority Within the United American States", in *View of the Constitution of the United States with Selected Writings,* ed. Clyde N. Wilson (Indianapolis: Liberty Fund 1999), p. 217 (emphasis in original).

188 As Wood wrote, "[a]lthough the idea of fundamental law or natural law underlying all governmental actions and positive law was scarcely forgotten (…), by the last quarter of the eighteenth century it seemed clearer than ever before to most Englishmen that all such moral and natural law limitations on the Parliament were strictly theoretical, without legal meaning, and relevant only in so far as they impinged on the minds of the lawmakers." Wood, *Creation of the American Republic*, p. 260.

189 Blackstone, *Commentaries*, Introd., Sec. III, p. 89. See also discussed in Anthony Bellia and Bradford Clark, "The Federal Common Law of Nations" *Columbia Law Review* 109 (January, 2009), pp. 12–13.

law, the rights of embassy and piracy in some detail. Since all of these are relevant issues in the context of our discussion, they will be highlighted briefly.

For a country that depended so much on foreign commerce, it is not surprising that the 'law merchant' has had a long history in the English legal tradition. As a number of court cases attest, at the end of the 17th century, "it had been (…) absorbed [into the common law as to] its application to foreign trade without losing its distinctive character as a species of *jus gentium*."[190] This appears to be a typical development in English law: since the common law is by its very nature unwritten law and based on customs, it facilitates the integration of universally accepted customs into its corpus of rules. This state of affairs is well reflected by Blackstone himself, who wrote that: "the affairs of commerce are regulated by a law of their own, called the law merchant or lex mercatoria, which all nations agree in and take notice of. And in particular the law of England does in many cases refer to it, and leaves the causes of merchants to be tried by their own peculiar customs (…)."[191]

A similar symbiosis occurred with respect to maritime law. Here too, English courts had developed the law as a part of English law, while at the same time claiming to be administering principles of the law of nations. Lord Mansfield, "whose masterly acquaintance with the law of nations," as Blackstone said, "was known and revered by every state in Europe,"[192] had made the point in 1759: "the maritime law is not the law of a particular country, but the general law of nations."[193] On this matter, Blackstone noted that British admiralty courts have jurisdiction for all issues arising at sea, also when beyond the limits of the common law. With respect to the overseas colonies, Blackstone wrote that "[a]ppeals from the vice-admiralty courts in America, and our other plantations and settlements, may be brought before the courts of admiralty in

190 Edwin Dickinson, "The Law of Nations as Part of the National Law of the United States", p. 27.

191 Blackstone, *Commentaries*, Bk I, Ch. 7, p. 265.

192 Blackstone, *Commentaries*, Bk. III, Ch. 5, p. 70. Lieberman noted that because of Mansfield's acquaintance with the law of nations, he was able to draw "upon foreign legal sources for his commercial law rulings (…)," which he largely developed as a branch of the English common law. See discussed in David Lieberman, *The Province of Legislation Determined* (Cambridge: Cambridge University Press, 1989), pp. 112–113.

193 See *Luke v. Lyde,* 2 Burr 882; 97 ER 614, quoted in Dickinson, "The Law of Nations as Part of the National Law of the United States", p. 28. See also Lauren Benton, who noted that "[b]y its very nature, the ocean has seemed to demand the mutual recognition of legal norms derived from natural law or other law standing outside the control of polities." Benton, *A Search for Sovereignty: Law and Geography in European Empires, 1400–1900.* (New York: Cambridge University Press, 2010), p. 105.

England, as being a branch of the admiral's jurisdiction, though they may also be brought before the king in council."[194] But while the courts are free to apply the common law or principles of international law in the case of English vessels, they do not have this choice in the case of prize vessels taken at time of war, "this being a question between subjects of different states, it belongs entirely to the law of nations, and not to the municipal laws of either country, to determine it."[195] In this respect, Picciotto said that judge William Scott, Lord Stowell, a prominent English lawyer, believed that prize court jurisdiction is "something quite distinct from that of an ordinary Municipal Court, (…) administering something which was not English Law, but a kind of *jus gentium* or Common Law of civilised nations."[196] In the case *Walsingham Packet*, the court explicitly declared itself "properly and directly a Court of the law of nations only, and not intended to carry into effect the Municipal Law of this or any other country."[197]

As to the rights of ambassadors, Blackstone remarks that these are "established by the law of nations, and are therefore matter of universal concern." As such, he adds, "the common law of England recognizes them in their full extent." This view has been amply borne out by *Barbuit's Case, Triquet v. Bath* and *Heathfield v. Chilton*. The practical reasons for integrating this body of law into the common law had become obvious by the mid-18th century, a time when infringements on ambassadorial (and by extension, sovereign) privileges, had come to be considered a very serious matter.[198]

---

194 Blackstone, *Commentaries*, Bk III, Ch. 5, p. 70.

195 Blackstone, *Commentaries*, Bk III, Ch. 5, p. 70.

196 As based on the *Maria* case (1 Rob. 340, 1799). See Cyril M. Picciotto, *The Relation of International Law to the Law of England and the United States of America* (London: McBride, Nast & Co, 1915), p. 28.

197 See 2 Rob. 77 (1799), cited in Picciotto, *The Relation of International Law to the Law of England and the United States of America*, p. 29. Picciotto noted here that consequently, these courts did not take cognizance of alleged violations of British laws, even if brought to the court by British subjects. This position he considers to represent "the climax of the tendency to exalt International at the expense of Municipal Law." Ibid, p. 30.

198 Blackstone, *Commentaries*, Bk IV, Ch. 5, p. 71; see also Bk. I, ch. 7, pp. 246–249. In stressing the seriousness of violating prerogatives of ambassadors, he said that in accordance with English statute law, "all process[es] whereby the person of any ambassador, (…) may be arrested, (…) shall be utterly null and void; and that all persons prosecuting, soliciting, or executing such process[es], being convicted by confession or the oath of one witness, before the lord chancellor and the chief justices, or any two of them, shall be deemed violaters of the laws of nations, and disturbers of the public repose." Ibid., Bk IV, Ch. 5, pp. 71–72.

The last topic on the law of nations that Blackstone discussed was piracy. It is an issue that had been dealt with in the context of international law since the days of the Roman Empire. Blackstone therefore uses the old expression *hostis humani generis*, and argues that in terms of the law, it is still a valid one.[199] Noting that "the crime of piracy, or robbery and depredation upon the high seas, is an offence against the universal law of society," pirates themselves have by committing this act "renounced all the benefits of society and government and has reduced [themselves] afresh to the savage state of nature, by declaring war against all mankind, all mankind must declare war against [them]."[200] While piracy was originally prosecuted by admiralty courts on the basis of civil law, since Henry VIII this was done on the basis of the common law, irrespective of the nationality of the pirates. Again, given the fluidity between the common law and the law of nations, this was only a natural development to occur.

More in general, Blackstone adds a possibly significant comment at the end of his discussion, saying that there are only three issues "in which the statute law of England interposes, to aid and enforce the law of nations, as a part of the common law; inflicting an adequate punishment upon offences against that universal law, committed by private persons." These are breaches of faith, violations of ambassadorial rights and piracy.[201] Was this further evidence that all other matters of international law were already absorbed into the common law, and therefore did not need further enactment into English law? Or were these provisions only introduced so as to ensure *individual* criminalization of certain offences against the law of nations? The issue raises a larger question about the content of the law of nations, at least with respect to how this was understood in the United Kingdom. What complicated matters in Britain was the fact that in the common law tradition, no sharp distinction existed between public and private law. What is more, "[t]he universal law was law for individuals no less than for states. As such, it was concerned somewhat indiscriminately with matters between individuals, between individuals and states, and between states."[202]

As a consequence, doubts have been raised about the extent to which the law of nations was genuinely integrated into the common law. Lords Ellesmere

199 According to Blackstone, this term apparently originated with Edward Coke, though it was used before him by Bartolus, going back to Cicero. See Dickinson, "The Law of Nations as Part of the National Law of the United States", p. 29.

200 Blackstone, *Commentaries,* Bk. IV, Ch. 5, p. 72.

201 Blackstone, *Commentaries*, Bk IV, Ch. 5, p. 69, 74.

202 Dickinson, "The Law of Nations as Part of the National Law of the United States," pp. 26–27.

and Mansfield, and Blackstone's pronouncements notwithstanding, E.R. Adair had argued that before the enactment of the Act of Anne in 1709 (7 Anne cap. 12), at least with respect to the diplomatic immunity of ambassadors, the law of nations had not been integrated into the common law. The Act itself was, in Lord Talbot's words, "only declaratory of the antient universal *jus gentium*."[203] He concluded that "[t]he assertions that Lord Mansfield made in 1764 [that the law of nations is part of the law of the land] were radically unsound; today they would not be wholly true, for even if the wit of man could decide beyond cavil what constituted international law, it would still not be in its entirety part of the common law of England."[204]

Thus, the record on the status of international law within the British realm in the late 18th century is not clear-cut. In some areas, it is well advanced, and can find support in various court decisions. Other areas are much less developed, and raise the question whether jurisdiction by British courts can be assumed by way of natural law, via the common law or even by virtue of being a separate subject matter within English law. As Ramsey noted, "the eighteenth-century law of nations defies easy description."[205] It is remarkable how pervasive natural law appears to be in a country that is ruled by a system of laws based on custom and precedent. This is not to say that there were no authors who explicitly acknowledged the existence and validity of positive international law. For instance, James Mackintosh, a Scottish author, wrote in 1799 that instead of being based on natural law principles, "the law of nations has, in many of its parts, acquired among European ones much of the precision and certainty of positive law (...)."[206] The American colonists, however, were faced with a complicated and at times confusing legal legacy, which they had to grapple with both when they struggled for their rights to be respected under the common law, and when they began to formulate their rights and obligations under the law of nations after independence.

---

203 See *Barbuit's Case* (1737) Forr 280; 25 ER 777. With reference to a comment by Lord Ellenborough in the case *Viveash v. Becker* (1814) 3 M and S 284. Picciotto said that the Act was declaratory of the common law as well. See *The Relation of International Law to the Law of England and the United States of America*, pp. 79–80.

204 Adair, "The Law of Nations and the Common Law in England", p. 297.

205 Michael Ramsey, *The Constitution's Text in Foreign Affairs* (Cambridge, MA: Harvard University Press, 2007), p. 346.

206 James Mackintosh, "A Discourse on the Law of Nature and Nations", in *Vindiciae Gallicae and Other Writings on the French Revolution* (Indianapolis: Liberty Fund, 2006), p. 344.

CHAPTER 2

The Move Towards Independence

2.1 The Colonies and the British Imperial Constitution

It is seldom acknowledged that the American Revolution was the result of a legal dispute between the colonies and the metropolis. In part, this also explains why the Revolution was not 'revolutionary' in the sense that the American colonists were intent from the very beginning to rid themselves of their British overlords. Rather, their respect and even reverence for English political and legal institutions made that declaring independence was certainly not the inevitable or only possible outcome. Many members of the founding generation were reared in the works of Coke and Blackstone, some by professors like George Wythe at William and Mary.[207] Intellectually, the eventual struggle came to center on natural rights, one reason being that uncertainty had persisted about which rights—if any—American colonists could claim as British overseas subjects under the common law. For our purposes, this debate is relevant because it concerns the introduction or 'reception' of the English legal tradition in the colonies as well as the shape of what came to be called the 'imperial constitution,' both of which had a significant influence on how the law of nations was conceived of in the colonies—and subsequently incorporated into the legal system of the independent United States.

In the discussions that ensued in the latter half of the 18th century, one of the key issues in determining the status of the law in the colonies was the basis on which the colonies themselves were established. Some modes of acquisition provided more rights for overseas communities—whether colonists or natives—than others, which explains why this otherwise rather abstruse and complex debate was conducted in vigorous fashion. Among the main theories that the colonists discussed were conquest, discovery and cession.

Traditionally, the British government based its claims to possession of its American colonies on the basis of conquest, principally because this ensured that they would be under direct control of the Crown, giving it wide powers, "enabl[ing it] to assert unlimited rights to grant [or repeal] concessions (…)."[208]

---

207 Among his students, Wythe could count James Monroe and John Marshall; his most famous student being Thomas Jefferson. See, for a fuller treatment of the Wythe-Jefferson relationship, Edward Dumbauld, *Thomas Jefferson and the Law* (Norman, OK: Univ. of Oklahoma Press, 1979).

208 Anthony Pagden, "Law, Colonization, Legitimation, and the European Background' in Michael Grossberg and Christopher Tomlins, *The Cambridge History of Law in America (1580–1815)* (New York: Cambridge University Press, 2008), p. 14.

 | DOI 10.1163/9789004305687_004

The argument had some credence given that the British government had issued charters in the 16th century to take possession of swaths of land in North America whereby the existing population was either to be expelled or subdued.[209] However, in the late 18th century, this theory faced the problem that not all thirteen colonies had been acquired through conquest, and that their juridical status differed between them.[210] Back in the 17th century, the British government had tried to resolve this legal confusion as to the status of the colonies, adopting a series of Navigation Acts between 1651 and 1696 with the aim to create a structure resembling the Spanish Council of the Indies. This was meant to extend direct rule by the Crown over all the colonies, to which end previous royal charters establishing colonies were revoked.[211] The thirteen colonies were to be regrouped into four vice-royalties, only one of which was eventually created, the Dominion of New England (combining the present New England with New Jersey and New York). However, the Dominion ceased to exist in the wake of the Glorious Revolution.[212]

The conquest argument was upheld in the English courts, and had one important consequence for the colonists, namely that they could not enjoy established freedoms under the common law as their brethren in England did. This conclusion followed from *Calvin's Case*. In this case, Edward Coke, presiding as Lord Chief Justice, held that "the king-in-council had jurisdiction over all inhabitants in those other dominions but that his common law courts did not."[213] With respect to the case of conquest, he added that "if a Christian King should conquer a kingdom of an Infidel, and bring them under his subjection, there *ipso facto* the Laws of the Infidel are abrogated, for that they be not only against Christianity, but against the Law of God and of Nature."[214] However, it could not be assumed that in lieu, "the common law and liberties of Englishmen were exported to the king's other dominions,"[215] since Coke famously opined that "the common law meddles with nothing that is done

209 See e.g. discussed in Blake Watson, "John Marshall and Indian Land Rights: A Historical Rejoinder to the Claim of "Universal Recognition" of the Doctrine of Discovery," *Seton Hall Law Review*, 36, no. 2, (2006), pp. 526–527.

210 Pagden, "Law, Colonization, Legitimation, and the European Background," p. 2.

211 Pagden, "Law, Colonization, Legitimation, and the European Background," p. 13.

212 Pagden, "Law, Colonization, Legitimation, and the European Background," p. 14.

213 Hulsebosch, "The Ancient Constitution and the Expanding Empire," p. 457.

214 *Calvin's Case*, in 7 Coke reports 1a, 77 ER p. 377, 1608. In general, there was often a link made between rights of conquest and justifications based in Christianity. See e.g. Blake Watson, "John Marshall and Indian Land Rights: A Historical Rejoinder to the Claim of "Universal Recognition" of the Doctrine of Discovery," *Seton Hall Law Review*, 36, no. 2, (2006), p. 486.

215 Hulsebosch, "The Ancient Constitution and the Expanding Empire," p. 458.

beyond the seas."[216] What is more, there also existed a notion that Britain's transatlantic colonies were "beyond the line," constituting a "zone of conflicting laws where Britons were free to engage in forms of violence that were unacceptable [within Europe]."[217] In other words, even if the common law had reached the shores of America, its validity and applicability was highly questionable, and so was that of the law of nations.[218]

Yet, the idea that the common law had migrated along with the English settlers to America found support in an opinion by an associate of the Privy Council, Richard West, which the American colonists evoked on a number of occasions. In 1720, he suggested that "let an Englishman go where he will, he carries as much of law and liberty, as the nature of the thing will bear." To be unequivocal, West added that "the Common Law of England, is the Common Law of the Plantations, and all statutes in affirmance of the Common Law passed in England, antecedent to the settlement of a colony, are in force there, unless there is some private Act to the contrary."[219] Even more interesting, the Royal Proclamation of 1763—which served to establish new governments in the colonies—had it that the governors and the peoples in the colonies were summoned "to make, constitute and ordain laws, statutes and ordinances (...) as near as be, agreeable to the laws of England."[220]

216 Robert C. Johnson, et.al., *Commons Debates* 1628 (New Haven: Yale University Press, 1977–1983), Vol. 3, p. 487, quoted in Daniel J. Hulsebosch, "The Ancient Constitution and the Expanding Empire: Sir Edward Coke's British Jurisprudence," *Law and History Review,* Vol. 21, no. 3, p. 439.

217 Eliga Gould, "Zones of Law, Zones of Violence: The Legal Geography of the British Atlantic, circa 1772" *William and Mary Quarterly* (3rd series) 60, no. 3 (July, 2003), p. 474.

218 As Gould said, "[t]heoretically, the law of nations was universal, with rules as binding in the woodlands of North America as the at the center of Europe. In practice, the international customs and conventions of Europe often possessed less authority in the wider Atlantic." See Gould, "Zones of Law, Zones of Violence: The Legal Geography of the British Atlantic, circa 1772," p. 479.

219 See Mr West's opinion, in *Opinions of Eminent Lawyers on Various Points of English Jurisprudence* (London: Reed and Hunter, 1814), Vol. 1, p. 194–195, quoted in Hulsebosch, "The Ancient Constitution and the Expanding Empire," p. 474. Interestingly, the Supreme Court echoed this view in an 1815 case, saying that "we take it to be a clear principle that the common law in force at the emigration of our ancestors is deemed the birthright of the colonies unless so far as it is inapplicable to their situation or repugnant to their other rights and privileges." *Town of Pawlet v. Clark* 13 U.S. (9 Cranch), 292 (1815) at 333.

220 Gould, "Zones of Law, Zones of Violence: The Legal Geography of the British Atlantic, circa 1772," p. 498. Remarkably, the Proclamation inadvertently (?) appeared to borrow from the 1754 Albany Plan of Union, which had called for "laws [to be] made (...) as near as may be, agreeable to the laws of England."

Nevertheless, this viewpoint was not shared by the most eminent of 18th-century English lawyers, Sir William Blackstone. He continued to uphold Coke's standpoint on the matter, arguing that only "if an uninhabited country be discovered and planted by English subjects, [will] all the English laws [be] immediately there in force." *Ipso facto*, this was not the case for "conquered or ceded countries." As Blackstone said,

> OUR American plantations are principally of this latter sort, being obtained in the last century either by right of conquest and driving out the natives (with what natural justice I shall not at present enquire) or by treaties. And therefore the common law of England, as such, has no allowance or authority there; they being no part of the mother country, but distinct (though dependent) dominions.

Interestingly, Blackstone added that, while the theory claimed that the colonies are only subject to the Crown, they are also "subject however to the control of the parliament; though (like Ireland, Man, and the rest) not bound by any acts of parliament, unless particularly named."[221] This theory was not universally shared however. Vattel's opinion was closer to that of the colonists,[222] and St. George Tucker, America's most important interpreter of Blackstone, rejected Blackstone's position as a whole: "[n]ow the British emigrants by whom the colonies were settled were neither a conquered nor a ceded people, but free citizens of that state, by which, the conquest was made, or, to which, the territory was ceded (…)." As a result, he concluded, "[w]hat is here said by Mr. Blackstone, cannot, therefore, be applicable to any colony, which was settled by English emigrants, after the Indian natives had ceded, or withdrawn themselves from, the territory."[223]

---

221 William Blackstone, *Commentaries on the Laws of England* (Oxford: Clarendon Press, 1765–1769), Introd., sec. 4, pp. 105–106.

222 "When a nation takes possession of a distant country, and settles a colony there, that country, though separated from the principal establishment, or mother-country, naturally becomes a part of the state, equally with its ancient possessions. Whenever therefore the political laws, or treaties, make no distinction between them, every thing said of the territory of a nation, must also extend to the colonies." Vattel, *The Law of Nations*, Bk. 1, ch. 19, para 210, p. 217. See also discussed in L.C. Green, and Olive Dickason, *The Law of Nations and the New World* (Calgary: The University of Alberta Press, 1989), pp. 73–79.

223 Tucker admits that the conquest-argument could possibly be applied to New York, which were ceded by the Dutch to the English in 1663. St. George Tucker, "Of the Unwritten, or Common Law of England; And Its Introduction into, and Authority Within the United American States," in *View of the Constitution of the United States with Selected Writings*, ed.

Given that the conquest theory granted the colonists no basic rights under the common law and at best only limited measures of autonomy, they felt more inclined on advancing a different theory, namely that of discovery and settlement; a theory which had much currency in Catholic countries.[224] This mode of acquisition entailed that land discovered in North America could be considered *res nullius*.[225] One reason for resorting to claims of discovery is that it was a means to seek equivalence between Spanish and English claims. Under Elizabeth and after, this was done by framing royal charters in the same way as the Papal bulls that justified Spanish claims.[226] One of the attractions of this theory was that it "justified and explained [according to many] the development of common law institutions abroad better than Coke's theory of conquered lands,"[227] the reason being that "settlers capable of establishing regular governments and systems of law had an unambiguous right to occupy underdeveloped land."[228] Since the charters were modelled on Papal bulls, the latter's Roman law language also helped to shape ideas about the law of nations in America.[229] In an ironic twist, the theory of discovery was used against the Spanish by the British in the sense that the related doctrine of effective

---

Clyde N. Wilson (Indianapolis: Liberty Fund 1999), p. 214. Indeed, dislike of Blackstone was quite virulent in some quarters. For instance, James Wilson, in *Chisholm*, called him a supporter of "a plan of systematic despotism." Jefferson even thought that Hume and Blackstone "have done more towards the suppression of the liberties of man than all the millions of men in arms of Bonaparte (…)." See quoted in Albert Alschuler, "Rediscovering Blackstone" *University of Pennsylvania Law Review* 145, No. 1 (1996), pp. 10–11.

224 For instance, Vitoria had claimed, on the basis of Justinian's *Institutes*, that "natural reason admits the title of the first occupant to that which previously had no owner." See John B. Moyle (ed.), *Institutes of Justinian* (Oxford: Clarendon Press, 1906), Bk. II, tit. 1, para. 12, p. 37. However, elsewhere, Vitoria drew on Justinian to claim that it is "a universal rule of the law of nations that whatever is captured in war becomes the property of the conqueror." From Vitoria, *On the Indians Lately Discovered*, quoted in Christopher Tomlins, *Freedom Bound: Law, Labor, and Civic Identity in Colonizing English America, 1580–1865* (Cambridge: Cambridge University Press, 2010), pp. 105–106.

225 Hulsebosch, "The Ancient Constitution and the Expanding Empire," p. 471.

226 Ken Macmillan, *Sovereignty and Possession in the English New World: The Legal Foundations of Empire, 1576–1640*, (Cambridge: Cambridge University Press, 2006), pp. 106–107.

227 Hulsebosch, "The Ancient Constitution and the Expanding Empire," p. 471.

228 Gould, "Zones of Law, Zones of Violence: The Legal Geography of the British Atlantic, circa 1772," p. 499.

229 Macmillan, *Sovereignty and Possession in the English New World*, p. 107. At the same time, Macmillan writes that in terms of legal doctrine, "[e]ven by the end of the sixteenth century, discovery was a comparatively new terminology for Europeans, as it had a dubious place in Roman law and was still building consensus within the *ius commune* and the *ius gentium*." See ibid., p. 181.

occupation was used "to subvert Spanish claims to territory not directly under Spain's control [which helped to] differentiate Britain's "libertarian" imperial project from what the British came to regard as Spanish Empire dependent on excessive force and conquest."[230] The obvious problem with the discovery theory was of course that North America was already inhabited when the Europeans arrived. But at least, in the eyes of the colonists, deriving rights of occupation from discovery seemed morally more acceptable than basing them on conquest, and amounted to a denial of empire-seeking. This was also more reassuring because "imperial conquests" raised the specter of corruption at home.[231] Still, the early jurists of the age also knew that "of all the claims to sovereignty made by the European powers in America, discovery had, in what by Marshall's day had become known as international law, been the one discredited most easily."[232]

Another potentially more convincing theory which was posited was based on the idea of improvement. It is an idea that makes both arguments based on conquest *and* discovery more palatable, since it justifies occupation and possession on the basis of natural law. One consideration was that moral equivalence with divine justifications for conquest which were associated with Catholic countries was therewith avoided.[233] Also, establishment of a civil society in *terra nullius* could even supply a legitimate right to sovereignty.[234]

---

230 Eliga Gould, "Entangled Histories, Entangled Worlds: The English-Speaking Atlantic as a Spanish Periphery" *The American Historical Review* 112, no. 3 (2007), p. 771.

231 J.G.A. Pocock, *The Machiavellian Moment: Florentine Political Thought in the Atlantic Republican Tradition* (Princeton: Princeton University Press, 1975), p. 510. However, Pocock also adds, reassuringly, that "[e]ven if empire must ultimately corrupt, there was a historical *anakuklosis* whereby liberty-loving warriors—Greeks, Romans, and Goths—won empires by their virtue and held them so long as it lasted. This (…) helps explain the freedom with which Americans of the early national period spoke of the "empire" which was to be theirs in the Ohio and Mississippi valleys. An empire compatible with virtue was a concept very necessary to them if they were to accept themselves as what they were by the circumstances of their foundation and prehistory." Ibid., p. 511.

232 Pagden, "Law, Colonization, Legitimation, and the European Background," p. 16.

233 As Voltaire said in his *Dictionnaire Philosophique*: "On demande ensuite s'il y a eu quelque justice à massacrer en Amérique dix ou douze millions d'hommes désarmés? on répond qu'il n'y a rien de plus juste et de plus saint, puisqu'ils n'étaient pas catholiques, apostoliques et romains." (Article droit naturel).

234 Another legal notion that was often refereed to in this context was the Roman law category of prescription. This notion permitted "long-term de facto occupation to be recognized as de iure as conferring retrospective rights of property and of jurisdiction." Pagden notes that even if strictly speaking, this was a civil law category, among English lawyers, it

The argument was most prominently articulated by John Locke, who said that man had a duty to "make use of [the commons, i.e. uncultivated parts of the Earth] to the best advantage of Life and convenience,"[235] and that to this end,

> God and his reason commanded him to subdue the earth, i.e. improve it for the benefit of life, and therein lay out something upon it that was his own, his labour. He that, in obedience to this command of God, subdued, tilled, and sowed any part of it, thereby annexed to it something that was his property, which another had no title to, nor could without injury take from him.[236]

This line of thinking was deployed against the native population since the early 17th century, by which time "the natives were accorded rights of sovereignty regardless of their incivility, infidelity, and inhospitability, [but] their unwillingness to put the land to agricultural use meant that they further betrayed the laws of God and nature."[237] Following independence, this argument would continue to be part of the legal arsenal that the new nation would use vis-à-vis the native population. Vattel summarized these various ideas and placed this idea in an international legal context:

> But it is questioned whether a nation can, by the bare act of taking possession, appropriate to itself countries which it does not really occupy, and thus engross a much greater extent of territory than it is able to people

"was also widely held to be a part of the Law of Nations." See Pagden, "Law, Colonization, Legitimation, and the European Background," pp. 22–23.

235 Locke, *Second Treatise of Government*, para 26. but see Tuck for a discussion how Locke at this point in fact attempted to respond to Pufendorf, who denied in his *Elementa* that there could be such a thing as a natural right to private property. The consequence of this was, says Tuck, that "the native peoples of America had as good property rights in their ancestral forests as the Europeans had in their ancestral farmlands, and that the colonizing projects were morally highly dubious." See Tuck, *The Rights of War and Peace: Political Thought and the International Order from Grotius to Kant* (Oxford: Oxford University Press, 1999), pp. 173–174.

236 John Locke, *Second Treatise of Government*, paras. 26, 32, in *The Works of John Locke*, Vol. 4, pp. 353, 356.

237 Ken Macmillan, *Sovereignty and Possession in the English New World: The Legal Foundations of Empire, 1576–1640* (Cambridge: Cambridge University Press, 2006), p. 9. See also discussed in Craig Yirush, *Settlers, Liberty, and Empire: The Roots of Early American Political Theory, 1675–1775* (New York: Cambridge University Press, 2011), p. 13.

> or cultivate. It is not difficult to determine, that such a pretension would be an absolute infringement of the natural rights of men, and repugnant to the views of nature, which, having destined the whole earth to supply the wants of mankind in general, gives no nation a right to appropriate to itself a country, except for the purpose of making use of it, and not of hindering others from deriving advantage from it. The law of nations will therefore not acknowledge the property and sovereignty of a nation over any uninhabited countries, except those of which it has really taken actual possession, in which it has formed settlements, or of which it makes actual use.[238]

James Wilson, who is among the great legal minds of the early republic, used precisely this argument in the years before independence, saying that the American colonists had earned their rights under the law of nature because "[p]ermitted and commissioned by the crown, they undertook, at their own expense, expeditions to this distant country, took possession of it, planted it, and cultivated it. Secure under the protection of their king, they grew and multiplied, and diffused British freedom and British spirit, wherever they came."[239]

Still, the most popular theory of territorial acquisition held by colonists in the 18th century was that of cession or purchase, since it allowed them the strongest claim to governing their own lands independent from the Crown in London. Indeed, since the very founding of the New England colonies, land had been bought from the Indians since it helped establish strong claims against their Dutch neighbors, who engaged in the same practice.[240] But while in the 17th century, Roger Williams, the well-known pastor from Salem, had still been expelled from Massachusetts Bay Colony for insisting that only purchase could establish a valid title to lands belonging to the natives,[241] the purchase argument had become dominant over the course of the 18th century. Importantly, cession entailed that the colonists had legitimately purchased land from the Indians, implying that the latter had originally disposed of it.

---

238 Emer de Vattel, *The Law of Nations*, Bk. I, ch. 18, para. 208, pp. 214–215. The obligation to cultivate the land under the law of nature was already defined in Bk I, ch. 7, para. 81, p. 129.

239 James Wilson, "Considerations on the Nature and Extent of the Legislative Authority of the British Parliament, 1774." in *The Collected Works of James Wilson*, Vol. 1, p. 24.

240 Blake Watson, "John Marshall and Indian Land Rights: A Historical Rejoinder to the Claim of "Universal Recognition" of the Doctrine of Discovery," *Seton Hall Law Review* 36, no. 2, (2006), p. 533.

241 See discussed in e.g. Blake Watson, "John Marshall and Indian Land Rights: A Historical Rejoinder to the Claim of "Universal Recognition" of the Doctrine of Discovery," *Seton Hall Law Review* 36, no. 2, (2006), pp. 487–498.

What also made this theory attractive is that cession and purchase arguments ran counter to Catholic claims for occupying new land. Vattel's support for this line of reasoning ensured "near-universal acceptance"[242] of his views on territorial acquisition amongst American colonial leaders.

This argument was relied on by Samuel Adams, a political thinker from Massachusetts and one of the principal leaders of the Revolution, who used it to turn the distinction between King and Crown against Britain. With reference to Coke, Grotius and Pufendorf, he claimed that while "the King had an absolute right in himself to dispose of the land (…) our ancestors considered the land, which they took possession of in America, as out of the bounds of the kingdom of England, and out of the reach and extent of the laws of England." Moreover, since the original colonists had acquired the land from the King through grants, title had been unequivocally established in favor of the colonists through land purchases, so Adams concluded:

> How much clearer then, in natural reason and equity, must our title be, who hold estates dearly purchased at the expense of our own, as well as our ancestors' labor, and defended by them with treasure and blood.[243]

That there existed a strong tendency to avoid and even reject Lockean arguments based on cultivation of land was demonstrated in a remarkable 1775 letter by Edward Bancroft to Benjamin Franklin. Bancroft rejected wholesale "those pretensions on which Former Popes availing themselves of the ignorance and Superstition then prevailing over all Europe, arrogantly assumed a right to dispose of the Persons and Countries of unbelieving Nations in Asia, Africa and America," adding with a sneer that this is "a right which is now universally

---

242 David Hendrickson, *Union, Nation or Empire: The American Debate over International Relations, 1789–1941* (Lawrence, KS: University Press of Kansas, 2009), p. 148. Vattel had written that "in establishing the obligation to cultivate the earth, (…) nations cannot exclusively appropriate to themselves more land than they have occasion for, or more than they are able to settle or cultivate. Their unsettled habitation in those immense regions cannot be accounted a true and legal possession; and the people of Europe (…) were lawfully entitled to take possession of it, and settle it with colonies. (…) [W]e cannot help praising the moderation of the English puritans who first settled in New England; who, notwithstanding their being furnished with a charter from their sovereign, purchased of the Indians the land of which they intended to take possession." See Vattel, *The Law of Nations*, Bk. I, ch. 18, para. 209, pp. 216–217.

243 Samuel Adams, "The House of Representatives of Massachusetts to the Governor" (March 2, 1773), in *The Writings of Samuel Adams* (New York: G.B. Putnam & Sons, 1906), Vol. 2, pp. 441–442.

ridiculed by all whose minds are emancipated from the shackles of superstitious prejudice." Instead, he proposed that

> the aborigines of America being the Primitive Occupiers of that Continent, and having obtained the possession of it, from the Creator and most rightful disposer of the Earth, without that injustice and violence by which other Nations have frequently acquired their Territories, were by the Laws of Nature and Nations justly intituled [sic] to the full and Absolute Dominion and Property of that Continent.[244]

Such an argument would in fact leave the cession theory as the only one under which the colonists could have acquired land from the natives. Understandably, this argument was not made just out of selfless but also for strategic purposes. Emphasizing the need to "exterminate this Error in America" forever, Bancroft added that it will also help to forestall "that endeavours will be used to excite the Indians of America, to butcher the Inhabitants of the Colonies, to the end, that by an accumulation of distress and Carnage, they may the sooner be reduced to submission."[245]

However, the British did not accept the cession theory. In the 1763 Royal Proclamation, issued in the wake of the Seven Years' War and dealing with territorial acquisitions in North America,[246] they declared explicitly that "great

244 Edward Bancroft to Benjamin Franklin (August 7, 1775), in *The Papers of Benjamin Franklin*, Vol. 22, pp. 149–150. In the 17th century, Roger Williams, one of the founders of Rhode Island, had advanced similar ideas, claiming that the Indians were the "true owners of the soil." See George G. Wilson, "International Law and the Constitution" *Boston University Law Review* 13 (1933), p. 235, 253. Even earlier, Vitoria had already disposed of the argument that natives could not possess land because of their being heathens: "barbarians in question [the Indians] cannot be barred from being true owners, alike in public and in private law, by reason of the sin of unbelief or any other mortal sin (…)." Quoted from Francisco de Vitoria, *De Indis Noviter Inventis*, Sec. I, paras. 19, 24, in L.C. Green and Olive Dickason, *The Law of Nations and the New World* (Calgary: The University of Alberta Press, 1989), p. 40.

245 Edward Bancroft to Benjamin Franklin (August 7, 1775), in *The Papers of Benjamin Franklin*, Vol. 22, pp. 149–150.

246 Pagden, "Law, Colonization, Legitimation, and the European Background," p. 25. Elsewhere, Pagden noted that "[w]hen the Royal Proclamation of 1763 [spoke of] what it described significantly as "the several Nations or Tribes of Indians" living in the lands west of the Appalachians as "under our Sovereign Protection and Dominion," it was not, as some later commentators have suggested, setting those "nations" on the road to eventual independence. It was merely trying to limit the power of the settlers." See Pagden, "Fellow Citizens and Imperial Subjects: Conquest and Sovereignty in Europe's Overseas Empires" *History and Theory*, 44, No. 4, (Dec., 2005), p. 45.

Frauds and Abuses have been committed in purchasing Lands of the Indians, to the great Prejudice of our Interests, and to the great Dissatisfaction of the said Indians." Consequently, "no private Person do presume to make any purchase from the said Indians of any Lands reserved to the said Indians, within those parts of our Colonies where, We have thought proper to allow Settlement (...)."[247] Thus, the British continued to rely as before on the conquest theory.

With their variations, the different theories about territorial acquisition sometimes blended into one another, as it became difficult to distinguish whether a right to land was based on natural rights, inherent rights as Englishmen, cultivation of the land, or charters or royal decrees. Gradually, the discussion about which rights the colonists could claim to possess began to be conducted in a different context, away from the modes of establishment of the colonies towards the nature of the imperial constitution itself. The rights question became more focused on the division of power between the Crown, the Westminster parliament and the various colonial assemblies.

Up into the 1760s, there existed a general understanding on both sides of the Atlantic about the prerogatives of the Crown and Parliament. For Lord Mansfield for instance, the position of the colonies within the empire was beyond dispute. "[T]he British Legislature, as to the power of making laws, represents the whole British Empire, and has authority to bind every part, and every subject without the least distinction, whether such subjects have the right to vote, or whether the law binds places within the realm or without."[248] It was therefore argued at the time that the colonists needed no actual representation in Parliament since they were 'virtually represented.' Around 1765, colonial representatives acknowledged their "due subordination (...) to the crown and parliament," and only admitted limitations to Parliament's authority insofar as to ensure they could continue "with the enjoyment of [their] essential rights as freemen and as British subjects."[249] However, this was in fact the last time that such a consensus existed. The occasion for which the representatives had assembled in 1765 happened to be the Stamp Act Congress, which discussed the recently passed Stamp Act—which introduced a tax on stamped paper used for official purposes—and led to more vociferous debates

247 Interestingly, the Proclamation also declared that "such Parts of Our Dominions and Territories as, not having been ceded to or purchased by Us, are reserved to [the Indians], or any of them, as their Hunting Grounds."

248 See Thomas C. Hansard, *The Parliamentary History of England*, XVI, p. 174 (Feb 24, 1766), quoted in Adams, *Political Ideas of the American Revolution*, p. 24.

249 Adams, *Political Ideas of the American Revolution*, p. 22–23.

in the colonies about the imperial constitution, the rights of the colonists and the place of the common law.

The discussion on the imperial constitution came to revolve around the question whether there could be shared authority within the empire, and what authority the colonial assemblies could claim to possess. This question had arisen largely as a result of changing British policy following the Seven Years' War. After 1763, the government in London sought to change the imperial constitution in the direction of a more centralized polity. However, as Greene has noted, this "directly challenged the colonies' autonomy over their local affairs and, by subjecting the colonies to legislation and other directives to which the settler populations had not given their consent, called into question settler claims to a British identity and their rights as Britons to enjoy Britain's traditional liberties." Hence, a debate was precipitated in the colonies that would eventually lead to independence.[250]

In 1764, Richard Bland, a Virginia planter who was a member of the Continental Congress, set out some ideas in an ingenious pamphlet towards a solution to the problem of—as it became known—*imperium in imperio*, the question being whether it was possible for the colonies to have a large measure of autonomy while being part of the British Empire. Bland made a distinction between *internal* and *external* government, which he borrowed from Jean-Jacques Burlamaqui, arguing that internal laws exclude "all power derogatory to their dependence upon the mother kingdom." Consequently, he added, "[i]n every instance, therefore, of our *external* government we are and must be subjects to the authority of the British Parliament, but not in others; for if the Parliament should impose laws upon us merely relative to our *internal* government, it deprives us, as far as those laws extend, of the most valuable part of our birthright as Englishmen."[251] In his more famous 1766 pamphlet, *An Inquiry into the Rights of the British Colonies*, he would further elaborate on this theme, arguing that only the authority of the King goes beyond Westminster, and that Parliament's prerogatives are correspondingly limited.

Bland's was not the only conservative-leaning voice in the colonies in the late 1760s. Another was that of John Dickinson from Pennsylvania, called the "Penman of the Revolution" and later a member of the 1787 Constitutional Convention. In his 1768 *Letters from a Farmer in Pennsylvania*, he discussed the powers of a legislature in an imperial constitution, distinguishing between

250 Jack Greene, "Colonial History and National History: Reflections on a Continuing Problem," *William and Mary Quarterly*, 3rd Series, Vol. 64, no. 2 (2007), p. 242.

251 Richard Bland, "The Colonel Dismounted, or the Rector Vindicated" (1764), quoted in Bailyn, *Ideological Origins of the American Revolution*, pp. 210–211.

the position of a legislature of an empire and of a nation. In the words of Bernard Bailyn, he found that "[o]ver the American colonies, Parliament must have all the power, but only the power, necessary to maintain the essential connections of empire (...)."[252] So, Dickinson was arguing that there could only be limited independence for the colonies. At the time, his line of thinking "represented a radical challenge to the metropolitan belief in Parliament's supremacy over the whole empire."[253]

James Otis, a conservative Massachusetts lawyer and coiner of the phrase "No taxation without representation," focused on Parliament's role with respect to protecting the rights of the colonists.[254] He believed that Parliament was the highest power in the imperial system, and that as a consequence, its acts could never be in contravention of the common law, or of previous court decisions.[255] In his 1764 pamphlet *The Rights of the British Colonies Asserted and Proved*, he contended that the colonists were entitled to "as ample rights, liberties, and privileges as the subjects of the mother country are and in some respects to more. (...) Should the charter privileges of the Colonists be disregarded or revoked, there are natural, inherent, and inseparable rights as men and citizens that would remain."[256] Thus, Parliament had an absolute duty to uphold and preserve the "natural, inherent and inseparable rights" of the colonists, and could never overturn these. But because of Otis' moderate outlook, he "tore his mind to pieces" in choosing between the more conservative views of Coke and the more progressive ones of Vattel. Ultimately, he chose Coke over Vattel, and therewith, historian Gordon Wood said, "miss[ed] the Revolution."[257]

Other pamphleteers had fewer intellectual difficulties with abandoning the idea that Parliament could exercise any power whatsoever over the affairs of the colonies.[258] Among the first voices in this chorus was none other than

252 Bailyn, *Ideological Origins of the American Revolution*, p. 216.

253 Greene, "Law and the Origins of the American Revolution." p. 465.

254 John Adams called Otis "a great master of the laws of nature and nations. He had read Pufendorf, Grotius, Barbeyrac, Burlamaqui, Vattel, Heineccius, and in the civil law, Domat, Justinian, and upon occassions, consulted the *Corpus Juris* at large." Adams also quoted a maxim of his, being that "a lawyer ought never to be without a volume of natural or public law, or moral philosophy, on his table or in his pocket." Adams to Hezekiah Niles (14 January, 1818), in *The Works of John Adams*, Vol. 10, p. 274.

255 Bailyn, *Ideological Origins of the American Revolution*, pp. 176, 179–180.

256 Quoted in Corwin, "The "Higher Law" Background of American Constitutional Law," p. 399.

257 Wood, *Creation of the American Republic*, p. 9.

258 The idea that the authority of Parliament could be abjured was countenanced by Locke in his *Second Treatise* (paras. 149, 222). Blackstone however denied its practicability—an

Benjamin Franklin's, who had argued already in the 1760s that the colonies constituted separate states within the British Empire, and that the authority of Parliament did not extend to them, since this was not prescribed in their respective charters.[259] Another example is that of John Adams, at the time a member of the Massachusetts General Court (the state legislature) and involved in the famous debate with governor Thomas Hutchinson over the authority of Parliament over the colonies.[260] In his 1763 essay series called *Novanglus*, Adams strenuously resisted the notion that Parliament had any such authority:

> By the law of God, in the Old and New Testament, it has none; by the law of nature and nations, it has none; by the common law of England, it has none, for the common law, and the authority of parliament founded on it, never extended beyond the four seas; by statute law it has none, for no statute was made before the settlement of the colonies for this purpose; and the declaratory act, made in 1766, was made without our consent, by a parliament which had no authority beyond the four seas.[261]

In a subsequent pamphlet, he denied that "the best writers on the law of nations" have it that colonies automatically become part of the mother country, noting that "there is nothing in the law of nations, which is only the law of

---

opinion not shared by Wilson—holding that "[i]t must be owned that Mr Locke, and other theoretical writers, have held, that "there remains still inherent in the people 'a supreme power to remove or alter the legislative, when they 'find the legislative act contrary to the trust reposed in them: 'for when such trust is abused; it is thereby forfeited, and de-"volves to those who gave it." But however just this conclusion may be in theory, we cannot adopt it, nor argue from it, under any dispensation of government at present actually existing." Blackstone, *Commentaries*, Bk. I, Ch. 2; James Wilson, *Lectures on Law*, Ch. 5, in *The Collected Works of James Wilson*, Vol. 1, p. 441. See also discussed in Gough, *Fundamental Law in English Constitutional History*, pp. 189–191 and Jack Greene, *The Constitutional Origins of the American Revolution.* (New York: Cambridge University Press, 2011), pp. 126–129.

259 Carl Becker, *The Declaration of Independence*, p. 101–105.

260 For a detailed account of the legal arguments raised in this debate, see Alison Lacroix, "Drawing and Redrawing the Line: The Pre-Revolutionary Origins of Federal Ideas of Sovereignty." *Occasional Papers, University of Chicago* (2008). Underlining the momentousness of the debate, she notes that "the [final] proposal [made by the Council, which opposed governor Hutchinson] laid the foundation for American federalism's parallel arrangement of national and state legislatures." Ibid., p. 25.

261 John Adams, "Novanglus, Addressed to the Inhabitants of Massachusetts Bay, no. III," in *The Works of John Adams*, Vol. 4, pp. 37–38.

right reason applied to the conduct of nations, that requires that emigrants from a state should continue, or be made, a part of the state."[262] In practice, the various colonial assemblies had for quite some time enjoyed a measure of autonomy, even if on matters of foreign affairs they deferred to the Crown.[263] But because of the *de facto* independence of the assemblies, James Iredell, a future Supreme Court justice, rejected arguments about the impossibility of having multiple legislatures with separate powers within one polity or empire, saying that "the great solecism of an *imperium in imperio* argument is (…) not at all applicable to our case, though it has been so vainly and confidently relied on."[264] This of course also took care of the 'virtual representation' argument, since the colonists were no longer interested even in actual representation in Parliament.[265]

By the second half of the 18th century, the colonial assemblies had "through precedent and custom been able to establish their authority and status as local parliaments (…) and the primary guardians of the colonists' inherited rights as Englishmen" which included the right not to be taxed without their consent.[266] What is more, the assemblies were asserting their rights based on the fact that "their Power or Authority [derived] from the common Custom and Laws of England…."[267] In the same vein, while citing Edward Coke, the

262 John Adams, "Novanglus, Addressed to the Inhabitants of Massachusetts Bay, no. VII," in *The Works of John Adams,* Vol. 4, p. 102 Adams responded here directly to a claim made by Daniel Leonard (nom de plume: *Massachusettensis*), who argued that "The colonies are a part of the British empire. The best writers upon the law of nations tell us, that when a nation takes possession of a distant country, and settles there, that country, though separated from the principal establishment, or mother country, naturally becomes a part of the state, equal with its ancient possessions."

263 Martin Flaherty, "History Right? Historical Scholarship, Original Understanding and Treaties as "Supreme Law of the Land" 99 *Columbia Law Review,* no. 8 (1999), p. 2116.

264 See James Iredell, "Address to the Inhabitants of Great Britain" (1774), quoted in Bailyn, *Ideological Origins of the American Revolution,* p. 224–225.

265 One pamphlet argued in fact that this formula could only apply to residents of Britain, and not of the colonies. See Becker, *The Declaration of Independence*, pp. 87–89.

266 Greene, "Law and the Origins of the American Revolution." p. 450.

267 Quoted from Joseph Murray, *Mr. Murray's Opinion Relating to the Courts of Justice in the Colony of New York* (1734), cited in Greene, "Law and the Origins of the American Revolution." p. 451. Jack Greene concluded that in fact, "the diminution of demands for explicit guarantees of English laws in the colonies after 1730 strongly suggests that provincial and local courts had by that time effectively established the customary rights of the colonists in this broad area." See Greene, "Law and the Origins of the American Revolution." in Michael Grossberg and Christopher Tomlins, *The Cambridge History of Law in America (1580–1815)* (New York: Cambridge University Press, 2008), p. 449.

colonists argued that, since the law of nature is part of the common law,[268] and that this only required obedience to the sovereign, they were not answerable to the British parliament, but only to the king.[269] James Wilson put it—with reference to Blackstone—very simple, saying that "[the law of nature] must control every political maxim: it must regulate the legislature itself."[270] Hence, if a legislature would act in contravention with the law of nature, citizens would have the right to ignore these acts. Another example in case from as late as 1775 comes from Alexander Hamilton—albeit with reference to *Calvin's Case*, and not *Dr. Bonham*:

> The law of nature, and the British constitution, both confine allegiance to the person of the king, and found it upon the principle of protection. We may see the subject discussed at large in the case of Calvin. The definition given of it by the learned Coke is this: "Legiance is the mutual bond and obligation between the king and his subjects; whereby subjects are called his liege subjects, because they are bound to obey and serve him; and he is called their liege lord, because he is bound to maintain and defend them." Hence it is evident, that while we enjoy the protection of the king it is incumbent upon us to obey and serve him, without the interposition of parliamentary supremacy.[271]

Thus, the colonists had arrived at a point at which "they had agreed that, if the indivisibility of sovereignty required that Parliament had either total authority

268 Indeed, one colonial writer put it thus in the early 18th century: "the Common Law, takes in the Law of Nature, the Law of Reason and the revealed Law of God; which are equally binding, at All Times, in All Places and to All Persons." D. Dulany, "The Right of the Inhabitants of Maryland to the Benefit of English Laws." (Annapolis, 1728) Quoted in Jules Lobel, "The Limits of Constitutional Power: Conflicts between Foreign Policy and International Law" *Virginia Law Review* 71, no. 7 (October 1985), p. 1082.

269 Mullett, *Fundamental Law and the American Revolution*, p. 46. However, Coke's dictum in the famous case of *Dr. Bonham* did not amount to declaring the common law or fundamental law as a "higher law," or as a touchstone for evaluating the constitutionality of legislation. Therefore, "Coke had meant only that the courts would interpret statutes "in such a way as not to conflict with those accepted principles of reason and justice which (…) were presumed to underlie all law" [and] that the courts were to construe statutes so as to bring them into conformity with recognized legal principles." Bailyn, *Ideological Origins of the American Revolution*, p. 177.

270 James Wilson, "Considerations on the Nature and Extent of the Legislative Authority of the British Parliament, 1774." in *The Collected Works of James Wilson*, Vol. 1, p. 5.

271 Alexander Hamilton, "The Farmer Refuted" (February 23, 1775), in *The Works of Alexander Hamilton* (New York: G.P. Putnam's Sons, 1904), Vol. 1, p. 68.

over the colonies or none, it had none. The colonies, they argued, were separate states, each with its own sovereign legislature."[272]

In Britain, however, the idea that sovereignty could be divided was categorically denied.[273] In his *Commentaries*, Blackstone had already written that in Britain, like in all independent countries, "there is and must be in all of them a supreme, irresistible, absolute, uncontrolled authority, in which the *jura summi imperii*, or the rights of sovereignty, reside."[274] And this authority was the King-in-Parliament.[275] As the famous lexicographer Dr. Samuel Johnson said: "In sovereignty, there are no gradations."[276] The question of sovereignty became very pointed in the years leading up to independence and explained why, as Wood noted, "[t]he doctrine of sovereignty almost by itself compelled the imperial debate to be conducted in the most theoretical terms of political science."[277] In that respect, as Hartog once remarked, "the members of North's cabinet well knew, [that] the claims made by the American Revolutionaries were often better—that is, better rooted in constitutional history and practice—than those initiated by Parliament after 1763."[278]

What was also noticeable was that before 1765, the conflict was between the assemblies and the Crown; after that year, it was between the assemblies and Parliament. Interestingly, up to the adoption (and subsequent repeal) of the Stamp Act, Parliament had in fact rarely interfered in colonial legislation. At best, it had nullified statutes adopted by local legislatures, but never imposed legislation itself. In effect, this meant that while the colonists "did not deny that the British Parliament possessed of right a general legislative jurisdiction

272 Jack Greene, "The Background of the Articles of Confederation," *Publius* 12, No. 4 (1982), p. 38.

273 See e.g. discussed in Anthony Pagden, "Fellow Citizens and Imperial Subjects: Conquest and Sovereignty in Europe's Overseas Empires" *History and Theory*, 44, No. 4, (Dec., 2005), p. 42ff.

274 William Blackstone, *Commentaries on the Laws of England* (Oxford: Clarendon Press, 1765–1769), Introduction, p. 49.

275 See also discussed in Craig Yirush, *Settlers, Liberty, and Empire: The Roots of Early American Political Theory, 1675–1775* (New York: Cambridge University Press, 2011), p. 47. Pagden, drawing on the legal ideas of Sir Henry Maine, traces this notion back to the Roman Empire, saying that the king acted as a proprietor. See Pagden, "Fellow Citizens and Imperial Subjects: Conquest and Sovereignty in Europe's Overseas Empires" *History and Theory*, pp. 40–42.

276 See his pamphlet "Taxation no Tyranny" (March 8, 1775).

277 Wood, *Creation of the American Republic*, p. 345.

278 Hendrik Hartog, "Review, Peripheries and Center: Constitutional Development in the Extended Polities of the British Empire and the United States, 1607–1788 by Jack P. Greene." *William and Mary Quarterly*, 3rd Series, Vol. 45, No. 4 (1988), p. 774.

over them,"[279] their issues were over representation, but perhaps more importantly, over its authority with regard to interpreting the common law. Behind the constitutional question of empire, the primordial issue had now become to ensure that the colonists' rights under the common law would be respected and protected; and in the face of British denials that the common law extended overseas, they increasingly resorted to natural law arguments to make their case.[280] This development was not universally welcomed in the Continental Congress, where some feared that resorting to references to natural law amounted to seeking extra-constitutional reasons that would precipitate a split between the colonies and the center.[281]

The move in this direction occurred as a result of fusing continental with British legal thought,[282] and did therefore not constitute a revolutionary turn as such. The first element of this move was that in the colonies, "[natural law philosophy] was also identified with the immemorial rights of Englishmen as declared by Coke and Blackstone."[283] When combined with the thinking of prominent continental legal philosophers, this helped to shape what Haines called a "philosophical mould [in which] Grotius, Pufendorf, Burlamaqui, and Vattel and some of the characteristic ideas of Coke's *Second Institute* and of Blackstone's *Commentaries* [were injected so as to create] a unique form of natural law, supposed to be universal in its applications."[284] Hence, the common law came to be regarded in the colonies as the key element of what later legal historians called fundamental law and which was famously called

279 Carl Becker, *The Declaration of Independence, A Study in the History of Political Ideas* (New York: Vintage Books, 1970), p. 91.

280 Becker, *The Declaration of Independence*, pp. 81–86.

281 See discussed in e.g. Barry Alan Shain, "Rights Natural and Civil in the Declaration of Independence," in Barry Alan Shain (ed.), *The Nature of Rights at the American Founding and Beyond* (Charlottesville: University of Virginia Press, 2007), p. 137.

282 Wood described this as follows: "Mingled with their historical citations were repeated references to the natural-law writings of the Enlightenment philosophers and the common-law writings of English jurists—both contributing to a more obviously rational, rather than experiental, understanding of the nature of politics. (…) It seemed indeed a peculiar moment in history when all knowledge coincided, when classical antiquity, Christian theology, English empiricism, and European rationalism could all be linked. (…) They represented to eighteenth-century Americans the experience and reason of the western world." Wood, *Creation of the American Republic*, pp. 8–9.

283 Charles Haines, *The Revival of Natural Law Concepts* (Cambridge, MA: Harvard University Press, 1930), p. 56. See also J.G.A. Pocock, *The Machiavellian Moment: Florentine Political Thought in the Atlantic Republican Tradition* (Princeton: Princeton University Press, 1975), pp. 340–341.

284 Haines, *The Revival of Natural Law Concepts*, p. 56.

"a brooding omnipresence in the sky" by Oliver Wendell Holmes. It was seen as something antecedent to any constitution, which "drew its content from sources other than enactment, whether usage or custom, or reason and natural justice."[285] The prevailing idea about law thus became that, as Wood summarized, "[it] was basically what the principles of right reason declared to be law, the codification of which was hardly inclusive."[286]

For the colonial assemblies, the most important task was to ensure respect for the common law rights of the colonist and to protect these against potential encroachments. This was partly to be achieved by grafting a legal edifice on the basis of natural law. But another key element here was to enshrine their rights in constitutional documents. In itself, this move towards constitutionalization helped to create a clearer distinction between superior and secondary laws. At the time, the British constitution, while *as a whole* informed by fundamental law, constituted an "assemblage of laws, customs and institutions [forming a] general system; according to which the several powers of the state are distributed, and their respective rights are secured to the different members of the community."[287] The colonial constitutions distinguished certain fundamental rights, and elevated them into non-derogable rights. In the process, the assemblies therewith became "the principal interpreters of the fundamental laws they sat under (…)."[288] This development had an attendant consequence, being that the nature of Parliament's legislation came to be perceived differently. As Wood described it:

---

285 Thomas Grey, "Origins of the Unwritten Constitution: Fundamental Law in American Revolutionary Thought" *Stanford Law Review* 30 (1978), p. 850. See also Jules Lobel, "The Limits of Constitutional Power: Conflicts between Foreign Policy and International Law" *Virginia Law Review* 71, no. 7 (October 1985), p. 1078. Bailyn noted that "[t]he common law tradition was important for the founding generation not because it would "in itself determine the kinds of conclusions men would draw in the crisis of the time," but because "it was a repository of experience in human dealings embodying the principles of justice, equity, and rights; above all, it was a form of history—ancient, indeed immemorial, history (…) [which] helped explain the movement of events and the meaning of the present." Notwithstanding the myriad internal contradictions the common law and its study gave rise to, it "stood side by side with Enlightenment rationalism in the minds of the Revolutionary generation." Bailyn, *Ideological Origins of the American Revolution,* p. 31.

286 Wood, *Creation of the American Republic*, p. 295.

287 See Charles Inglis, "True Interest of America," quoted in Wood, *Creation of the American Republic*, p. 261; see also discussed in Bailyn, *Ideological Origins of the American Revolution,* pp. 67–69 and 175–176.

288 Wood, *Creation of the American Republic*, p. 274.

> Parliament (...) had in truth become the sovereign lawmaker of the realm, whose power, however arbitrary and unreasonable, was uncontrollable. Parliament could now actually create new law whose binding force came not from its intrinsic justice and conformity to the principles of the common law, but from its embodiment of the will of the social constituents of the nation or from simply its sovereign authority. This new parliamentary law was now, as it had not been in medieval times, considered to be manifestly distinct and separate from the customary common law, whose binding force came not from enactment but, as Blackstone said, from long and immemorial usage preserved in the law books and court decisions from ancient times.[289]

Hence, if parliamentary law was no longer based on common law precepts, then this emboldened the colonists' claims to defend their constitutional and natural rights under the common law through their own assemblies. However, this constitutional development in Britain itself—which resulted in strengthening the position of Parliament—also helped to bring the key question about independence a little closer. As John Phillip Reid has written, "once Parliament asserted the authority by promulgating statutes intended to legitimize the right to legislate, the British imperial constitution was forever changed, and Americans either had to concede the right or either leave the empire."[290] On the whole, this turn towards constitutionalization would come to mark the key distinction between American law and the legal system that existed under the British imperial constitution. What is more, its renewed emphasis on natural law would also contribute to shaping how the law of nations would be perceived, interpreted and applied later on in the early republic.

The early 1770s saw a sharpening of the positions taken on the American side, signaling that the tide had irrevocably shifted to the detriment of the more moderate voices. Thus, John Dickinson's reasoning, which allowed for a limited role for Parliament and had been very influential in the late 1760s, had now been eclipsed,[291] and so had James Otis'. The general consensus had definitively shifted towards the idea that, as Benjamin Franklin said, between the several parts of the empire, there exists "only a Connection, of which the King is the common Link."[292] Indeed, it has been said that When Franklin, who for

289 Wood, *Creation of the American Republic*, pp. 264–265.

290 John Phillip Reid, *Constitutional History of the American Revolution: The Authority to Legislate* (Madison: University of Wisconsin Press, 1986), p. 5.

291 Bailyn, *Ideological Origins of the American Revolution*, pp. 222–224.

292 Benjamin Franklin to Matthew Wheelock (London, 1770). "Reflections, Moral and Political" in *The Papers of Benjamin Franklin*, Vol. 17, p. 393. Quoted in Greene, "Law and the Origins of the American Revolution." p. 477.

years had thought about and sought accommodation Britain, had "abandoned the prospect of peacefully ending the Imperial Crisis, a major milestone on the part towards American independence had been passed."[293] James Wilson drew the same conclusion in an influential pamphlet four years later.[294] In fact, colonial agents had been bypassing Parliament for a time now, issuing appeals directly to the King, under the assumption "that the king was the only proper link between America and England."[295] "The result" says Wood,

> was a fundamental shift in the American position. (…) The Americans in effect accepted the irresistible logic of the concept of legislative sovereignty and turned it against the British to justify their legislatures' independence from all parliamentary control. Their connection with the British Empire, it was now claimed, was solely through the King, in his personal not his political capacity, said John Adams, for it was with the natural person of the King that the American people had made their several contracts.[296]

Thus, the debate was on to search for a new model for imperial relations,[297] whereby most ideas veered in the direction of a federation.[298] In recognition of the fact that the chasm was widening, colonial representatives had started to organise themselves to coordinate their actions through the establishment of a Continental Congress. The first of these met in the fall of 1774, while its second—and more significant—incarnation was assembled from May 1775 until the ratification of the Articles of Confederation.[299]

---

293 Leonard Sadosky, *Revolutionary Negotiations: Indians, Empire and Diplomats in the Founding of America* (Charlottesville: University of Virginia Press, 2010), p. 64.

294 "The only dependency which [the colonies] ought to acknowledge is a dependency on the crown." James Wilson, "Considerations on the Nature and the Extent of the Legislative Authority of the British Parliament", in *The Collected Works of James Wilson* (Indianapolis: Liberty Fund, 2007) Vol.1, p. 28. See also Bailyn, *Ideological Origins of the American Revolution*, p. 225.

295 Kaplan, *Colonies into Nation*, p. 57.

296 Wood, *Creation of the American Republic*, p. 352.

297 See for a discussion of the different ideas Randolph Greenfield Adams, *Political Ideas of the American Revolution* (Durham, NC: Trinity College Press, 1922), pp. 16–18.

298 Kaplan, *Colonies into Nation*, p. 79.

299 It is important to understand that the Congress did not approximate a legislative body, but was rather a deliberative body of state representatives, and therefore more like a permanent diplomatic conference in the mould of the Dutch States-General in the time of the Republic.

During the early stages of the Second Continental Congress, various plans were mooted for reaching accommodation with Britain so as to resolve the constitutional crisis. One of the most ambitious and concrete plans was a "Plan of Union by Admitting Representatives from the American Colonies and from Ireland into the British Parliament," which was found among the manuscripts of Benjamin Franklin. It proposed, among other things, to set up a "limited supreme legislature"[300] for the empire as a whole. Another intermediate solution was presented four years later by Joseph Galloway, a loyalist and member of the Continental Congress from Pennsylvania who fled to England in 1778 never to set foot on American soil thereafter. His Plan of Union included establishing a colonial parliament and a Grand Council to have "authority over civil, criminal and commercial affairs of America and with the right of veto over Parliament's legislation affecting the colonies."[301] Both plans took some inspiration from the 1707 Act of Union between England and Scotland, whereby the Scottish and Westminster Parliaments were merged to form a single parliament for all of Great Britain, with its seat in Westminster. The Crowley proposal built more specifically on Franklin's earlier Albany Plan of 1754. But this plan, partly drafted in response to a switch in allegiance of the Iroquois league to the French side, had proved to be too far ahead of its time, as Franklin admitted that it was "impracticable to obtain a joint agreement of all the colonies to an [*sic*] union."[302] The period between 1765–75 was clearly more promising in that regard and witnessed other proposals beyond the Crowley and Galloway plans. One of these came from Thomas Pownall, a governor of Massachusetts,[303] while another, even more radical idea, came from Stephen Hopkins, a Rhode Island politician and chancellor of the precursor to Brown University, who suggested a constitutional framework that would assume equality among the constituent parts of the empire.[304]

---

300 Adams, *Political Ideas of the American Revolution*, pp. 35–36. The authorship of this plan is usually attributed to Thomas Crowley (c. 1713–1787), an English Quaker emigré.

301 Kaplan, *Colonies into Nation*, p. 78.

302 Benjamin Franklin, "Reasons and Motives for the Albany Plan of Union," in *The Papers of Benjamin Franklin*, Vol. 5, pp. 397ff. As Hendrickson said, "[i]t had become a maxim among imperial officials that the American colonials were incapable of united effort." So ironically, in 1754, the union failed to transpire not because of American mistrust of the English, but because of mutual mistrust among the colonies. See Hendrickson, *Peace Pact*, p. 84. See also Jack Greene, "The Background of the Articles of Confederation," *Publius* 12, No. 4 (1982), p. 18.

303 Adams, *Political Ideas of the American Revolution*, p. 31. Pownall's plan was similar to that of Franklin, and proposed an imperial federation with American representation in Parliament in London.

304 Stephen Hopkins, *The Rights of the Colonies Examined* (Providence, RI, 1765), quoted in Greene, "Law and the Origins of the American Revolution." p. 458.

Up to 1774–1775, many colonial leaders still assumed that the constitutional crisis could be resolved through some kind of compromise, and believed that Britain would eventually abandon its inflexible stance. One avenue to achieve a solution was thought to be by way of a treaty. Indeed, John Adams wrote in *Novanglus* that the colonies could be united to the motherland through something akin to a treaty of commerce "in perpetual league and amity," which "the colonies would readily enter into (…), provided their other liberties were inviolate."[305]

At this point, some British Parliamentarians were already prepared to accept American independence, the most celebrated example being Edmund Burke, the Anglo-Irish philosopher. In his 1774 "Speech on American Taxation," he called upon Parliament to let the Americans go, unwilling to propose an intermediate solution: "[S]eek peace and ensue it; leave America, if she has taxable matter in her, to tax herself. I am not here going into the distinctions of rights, nor attempting to mark their boundaries. I do not enter into these metaphysical distinctions; I hate the very sound of them."[306] He went on to sketch his own views on how the British imperial constitution worked. Prefacing his remarks by saying that "I look (…) on the imperial rights of Great Britain, and the privileges which the Colonists ought to enjoy under these rights, to be just the most reconcilable things in the world," he offered the following analysis:

> The Parliament of Great Britain sits at the head of her extensive Empire in two capacities: one as the local legislature of this island, providing for all things at home, immediately, and by no other instrument than the executive power. The other, and I think her nobler capacity, is what I call her imperial character; in which, as from the throne of heaven, she superintends all the several inferior legislatures, and guides and controuls them all, without annihilating any. As all these provincial legislatures are only co-ordinate with each other, they ought all to be subordinate to her; else they can neither preserve mutual peace, nor hope for mutual justice, nor effectually afford mutual assistance. (…) But in order to enable

305 John Adams, "Novanglus, Addressed to the Inhabitants of Massachusetts Bay, no. VII," in *The Works of John Adams,* Vol. 4, p. 114. See also discussed in Onuf and Onuf, *Federal Union, Modern World: The Law of Nations in an Age of Revolutions 1776–1814* (Madison, WI: Madison House, 1992), pp. 109–111.

306 Edmund Burke, "Speech on American Taxation," in *Select Works of Edmund Burke* (Indianapolis: Liberty Fund, 1999) Vol. 1, p. 154.

> Parliament to answer all these ends of provident and beneficent superintendence, her powers must be boundless.[307]

Notwithstanding Burke's opinion and the still existing and mutually acknowledged connection through the King, the colonies had enjoyed "*de facto* independence" for quite some time already,[308] and months even before the Declaration of Independence, "[v]irtually every colony functioned as an independent state, in control of its political and military establishment."[309] Years later, James Madison pointed to such constitutional issues as the cause of the Revolution:

> The fundamental principle of the Revolution was, that the Colonies were co-ordinate members with each other and with Great Britain, of an empire united by a common executive sovereign, but not united by any common legislative sovereign. The legislative power was maintained to be as complete in each American Parliament, as in the British Parliament. And the royal prerogative was in force in each Colony by virtue of its acknowledging the King for its executive magistrate, as it was in Great Britain by virtue of a like acknowledgement there. A denial of these principles by Great Britain, and the assertion of them by America, produced the Revolution.[310]

This overview of matters suggests that, had Britain acquiesced in the fact that the empire would henceforth be structured like "a loosely federated empire of independent states"[311] as it had *de facto* become, the Revolution might have been averted after all. The salient issue was that colonial parliaments wanted

---

307 Edmund Burke, "Speech on American Taxation," in *Select Works of Edmund Burke* (Indianapolis: Liberty Fund, 1999) Vol. 1, pp. 156–157.

308 Pagden, "Law, Colonization, Legitimation, and the European Background," in Michael Grossberg and Christopher Tomlins, *The Cambridge History of Law in America (1580–1815)* (New York: Cambridge University Press, 2008), p. 31.

309 Don Higginbotham, "War and State Formation in Revolutionary America," in Eliga Gould and Peter Onuf (eds.), *Empire and Nation: The American Revolution in the Atlantic World* (Baltimore/London: The Johns Hopkins University Press, 2005), p. 58.

310 See James Madison, "Report on the Resolutions (House of Delegates, session of 1799–1800)," in *Writings*, Vol. 6, p. 373.

311 Ellen H. Pearson, "Revising Custom, Embracing Choice: Early American Scholars and the Republicanization of the Common Law," in Eliga Gould and Peter Onuf (eds.), *Empire and Nation: The American Revolution in the Atlantic World* (Baltimore/London: The Johns Hopkins University Press, 2005), p. 94.

to be able to operate independently from Westminster, and to reserve the right to decide themselves about the question what legal system to adopt and to enforce, as well as how to interpret it. Interestingly, this outcome aptly reflects the different constitutional implications that follow from contrasting English versus continental legal thinking. While under the common law, divided sovereignty was very problematic, there was a long-standing tradition in European thought that supported confederal constitutional models.[312]

What was certain was that the colonists wanted to receive a system of law which expressed fundamental ideas about liberty and individual rights, and in that regard, there was nothing unusual in that they chose to adopt the English common law as their law.[313] After all, their differences with Britain were not about the common law as such, but rather about how it was interpreted, and by whom. When the Continental Congress adopted a "Declaration of Rights of the Colonies" in 1774, it declared *inter alia* "[t]hat the respective colonies are entitled to the common law of England, and (…) [t]hat they are entitled to the benefit of such of the English statutes as existed at the time of their colonization; and which they have, by experience, respectively found to be applicable to their several local and other circumstances."[314] In spite of Coke and

---

312 See discussed in Alison Lacroix, "Drawing and Redrawing the Line: The Pre-Revolutionary Origins of Federal Ideas of Sovereignty," *Occasional Papers, University of Chicago* (2008), pp. 11–13.

313 As Roger Sherman said, "The Colonies adopt the common law, not as the common law, but as the highest reason." See John Adams, "Debates," in *The Works of John Adams*, Vol. 2, p. 371. Bailyn wrote in this context: "Belief that a proper system of laws and institutions should be suffused with, should express, essences and fundamentals—moral rights, reason, justice—had never been absent from English notions of the constitution. But not since the Levellers had protested against Parliament's supremacy in the mid-seventeenth century had these considerations seemed so important as they did to the Americans of the mid-eighteenth century." Bailyn, *Ideological Origins of the American Revolution,* p. 69. See also Helen Keller, *Rezeption des Völkerrechts* (Berlin: Springer Verlag, 2003), pp. 83–84.

At the same time, Wood noted that while American demands for freedom are often couched in legal language, there existed a long-standing distrust towards lawyers, who were held responsible "for everything that was wrong in the society." As a result, there was a desire for codification or rationalization of the law system, to make it more comprehensible. Thus, when the states became independent, they invariably adopted the common law but at the same time aimed at systematizing and simplifying it. Many of these attempts at reform failed however. See Gordon Wood, *Empire of Liberty: A History of the Early Republic, 1789–1815* (New York: Oxford University Press, 2009), p. 403, 404–405.

314 "Declaration of Rights and Grievances" (October 14, 1774), *Journals of the Continental Congress*, Vol. 1, p. 69.

Blackstone, eminent jurists such as James Wilson and St. George Tucker reaffirmed that the common law was effectively introduced to America by dint of consent and choice, a view for which they found some support in Blackstone.[315] Later documents sometimes espouse different theories, but do not question the notion that the common law was in force in the respective colonies. Thomas Jefferson was very explicit in his support of this idea, saying that "[t]o suppose this branch of law, not existing in our code, would shake the foundation of our whole legal system."[316] Later, in 1799, he wrote that "[t]he common law (…) which was not in force when we landed here, (…) continued to be our law, because the nation continued in being, & because though it changed the organs for the future declarations of its will [i.e. Congress], it did not change its former declarations that the common law was it's law."[317] Alexander Hamilton also had no doubts on this question, writing in *Camillus* no. XX (1795) that

> The United States, when a member of the British Empire, were, in this capacity, a party to that law, and not having dissented from it, when they became independent, they are to be considered as having continued a party to it. The common law of England, which was and is in force in each of these States, adopts the law of nations, the positive equally with the natural, as a part of itself.[318]

This did not necessarily mean that the common law as it was in force in England was going to be substantively the same in the United States. As St. George Tucker wrote, it would be "in vain [to] attempt, by a general theory, to establish an [sic] uniform authority and obligation in the common law of

315 Ellen H. Pearson, "Revising Custom, Embracing Choice: Early American Scholars and the Republicanization of the Common Law," p. 102–104. For instance, Tucker held that "without recurring to the authority of the writers on the law of nations," it could be concluded that "[t]he laws of the parent state would from this circumstance acquire a tacit authority, and reception in all cases to which they were applicable [of which] the colonists themselves could be the only competent judges." See St. George Tucker, "Of the Unwritten, or Common Law of England; And Its Introduction into, and Authority Within the United American States," in Clyde N. Wilson (ed.), *View of the Constitution of the United States with Selected Writings* (Indianapolis: Liberty Fund 1999), p. 319.

316 Thomas Jefferson, "Second Report of the Conference Committee" (January 9, 1778), in *The Works of Thomas Jefferson*, Vol. 2, p. 315.

317 Thomas Jefferson to Edmund Randolph (August 18, 1799), in *The Works of Thomas Jefferson*, Vol. 9, pp. 75–76.

318 Hamilton, "Camillus no. XX," in *The Works of Alexander Hamilton.* (New York: G.P. Putnam's Sons, 1904), Vol. 5, p. 436.

England, over the American colonies, at any period between the first migrations to this country, and that epoch, which annihilated the sovereignty of the crown of England over them."[319] But between the colonies, there were also differences to be reckoned with. As James Madison wrote:

> But whether it be understood that the original colonists brought the law with them, or made it their law by adoption, it is equally certain that it was the separate law of each colony within its respective limits, and was unknown to them as a law pervading and operating through the whole as one society. It could not possibly be otherwise. The common law was not the same in any two of the Colonies, in some the modifications were materially and extensively different. There was no common legislature by which a common will could be expressed in the form of a law; nor any common magistracy by which such a law could be carried into practice.[320]

One reason for the divergences in the application of the common law across the colonies had to do with the customary nature of the common law, which permitted it to develop in different directions in each of the colonies.[321] Thus, it appears that there is no single satisfactory theory on how the common law was introduced in the American colonies. Paraphrasing Adam Ferguson, it may have been more the result of human action than of human design.

Still, while the common law could admit of local differences, this was not the case with the law of nations, the uniform application of which across the colonies would become one of the key issues in the struggle for independence and its consolidation after the issuance of the famous Declaration of July 4, 1776.[322] The Declaration and the Articles of Confederation—the country's first

319 St. George Tucker, Blackstone's *Commentaries*, at 405. Quoted in Morton Horwitz, *The Transformation of American Law, 1780–1860* (Cambridge, MA: Harvard University Press, 1977), p. 11. Madison wrote in this regard that "[i]n the state prior to the Revolution, it is certain that the common law, under different limitations, made a part of the colonial codes." See James Madison, "Report on the Resolutions" (February 7, 1799), in *The Writings of James Madison*, Vol. 6, p. 373.

320 James Madison, "Report on the Resolutions" (February 7, 1799), in *The Writings of James Madison*, Vol. 6, p. 373.

321 Ellen H. Pearson, "Revising Custom, Embracing Choice: Early American Scholars and the Republicanization of the Common Law," in Eliga Gould and Peter Onuf (eds.), *Empire and Nation: The American Revolution in the Atlantic World* (Baltimore/London: The Johns Hopkins University Press, 2005), p. 94.

322 The act of declaring independence had already been taken by Congress by way of a resolution on July 2nd. The Declaration itself was adopted two days later.

constitution—would provide the first indications as to how the newly-born state would position itself in the international legal system. As to the law of nations itself, a significant discrepancy emerged between ability and ambition, between living up to the law and the promotion of new principles, something for which the Founding Fathers displayed an early zest.

2.2 Independence, Union, and the Law of Nations

When the momentum towards independence began to swell, anxiety arose among the leaders of the Continental Congress as to which steps to take and in which sequence. Indeed, for several years, there had been a debate whether union should precede independence, or the other way round. Both sides had their merits. For if union should precede independence, this provided a better guarantee that the states would stay together, and less chance that they would be split apart by the British. On the other hand, some states did not want to unite unless there was a prior declaration of independence. Early opponents of union such as John Dickinson at first made union "hostage to a prior decision on independence." However, in early 1776 they changed their position, now "ma[king] independence hostage to union."[323] Insisting on this position, Dickinson refused to sign the Declaration of Independence. A principal objective for union and independence was to secure foreign assistance in the struggle against Britain, and both were considered prerequisites to obtaining such assistance.

In practice, this debate had an ambiguous outcome. For while the Articles of Confederation are generally regarded as the first constitution—having been adopted after the Declaration of Independence—there had been a prior unifying initiative, namely the adoption of so-called "Articles of Association," which constituted an an agreement between the thirteen colonies for the purpose to "obtain redress of (…) grievances, which threaten destruction to the lives liberty, and property of his majesty's subjects, in North-America." It was adopted on October 20, 1774 but despite its appearance, hardly amounted to a 'constitutional' document, although it did contain some interesting provisions which suggested confederal powers. Rather, the Articles were more concerned with specificities as to the imposition of a trade embargo against Britain. Thus, while "avowing our allegiance to his majesty, our affection and regard for our fellow-subjects in Great-Britain and elsewhere," the first Continental Congress —which adopted the Articles—declared that in order to counter the "ruinous

323 Hendrickson, *Peace Pact*, p. 123.

system of colony administration" in place since 1763, "a non-importation, non-consumption, and non-exportation agreement" is to be instituted, which, if "faithfully adhered to, will prove the most speedy, effectual, and peaceable measure" to alleviate the distress.[324]

The Articles did not create new political bodies; the Continental Congress remained the only common institution in the colonies. However, they did provide for the establishment of certain committees, which were "attentively to observe the conduct of all persons touching this association." Any individual violators of the agreement were to be "universally condemned as the enemies of American liberty; and thenceforth [the states pledged to] break off all dealings with him or her." What is more, the colonies also agreed that "we will have no trade, commerce, dealings or intercourse whatsoever, with any colony or province, in North-America, which shall not accede to, or which shall hereafter violate this association, but will hold them as unworthy of the rights of freemen, and as inimical to the liberties of their country."[325] In this way, the Association constituted in several aspects an embryonic form of the later Confederation; "a first, limited step toward American nationhood,"[326] although it should be said that the Association was certainly not generally regarded like that by all participants at the time. Breaking the bond of allegiance with Britain and the King was not among its objectives.

The Association would however remain short-lived, being in force for hardly a year while open warfare had broken out by April of 1775. For the colonies to take on the world's mightiest empire certainly did not affect the resolve of its leadership; however, they did realize that no war could not be won without outside support. Thus, while there existed much apprehension about creating formal treaty links with European powers, it was also quickly realized that there was no real alternative available. At the same time, all previous discussions about independence and union and which should precede were now drawn into the vortex, demanding a swift but comprehensive solution. A year into the war, Congress decided to address all three questions at once. To this end, Richard Henry Lee of Virginia put forward a resolution which declared, *inter alia*,

324 "Articles of Association" (October 20, 1774), in *Journals of the Continental Congress*, Vol. 1, p. 76.

325 "Articles of Association" (October 20, 1774), in *Journals of the Continental Congress*, Vol. 1, p. 79.

326 Don Higginbotham, "War and State Formation in Revolutionary America," in Eliga Gould and Peter Onuf (eds.), *Empire and Nation: The American Revolution in the Atlantic World* (Baltimore/London: The Johns Hopkins University Press, 2005), p. 59.

- [t]hat these United Colonies are, and of right ought to be, free and independent States, that they are absolved from all allegiance to the British Crown, and that all political connection between them and the State of Great Britain is, and ought to be, totally dissolved.
- That it is expedient forthwith to take the most effectual measures for forming foreign Alliances.
- That a plan of confederation be prepared and transmitted to the respective Colonies for their consideration and approbation (…)[327]

Drafting a declaration of independence was the first task taken to hand, famously to be undertaken by Thomas Jefferson, representative of Virginia. While the eventual Declaration is best known for espousing "self-evident" truths about human equality, inalienable rights and the pursuits of life, liberty and happiness,[328] it was "framed in the universal law of nations,"[329] and primarily meant to inform the world about the new country's intent to become a member of the society of nations with all appurtenant rights. J.G.A. Pocock wrote that the Declaration was "a document performed in the discourse of *jus gentium* rather than *jus civile*,"[330] stressing the extent to which the document was actually concerned with the wider world.

This comes immediately to the fore in the very first paragraph, which made clear—albeit implicitly—that the newly-formed United States not only wished to assert its rights under the law of nations, but also to assume its obligations. Thus, at the outset, the country declares its intention to be "assume[d] among

327 Resolution introduced by Richard Henry Lee (June 7, 1776), *Journals of the Continental Congress*, Vol. 5, p. 425.

328 A very contentious issue that the drafting committee dealt with was slavery. In an early draft, Jefferson had taken up a paragraph in which he reprobated the British for permitting this to take place in the empire: "He waged cruel war against human nature itself, violating its most sacred rights to life and liberty in the persons of a distant people who never offended him, captivating and carrying them into slavery in another hemisphere, or to incur miserable death in their transportation thither." Not surprisingly, southern delegates decided that this passage had to be scrapped.

329 Mark Janis, *America and the Law of Nations 1776–1939* (Oxford: Oxford University Press, 2010), p. 26.

330 John Pocock, "Political Thought in the English-speaking Atlantic: The Imperial Crisis," in Pocock (ed.), *The Varieties of British Political Thought, 1500–1800* (Cambridge, 1995), p. 281 (emphasis in original). Quoted in David Armitage, *The Declaration of Independence, A Global History* (Cambridge, MA: Harvard University Press, 2007), p. 65. Armitage himself noted that after independence, the document came to be seen as an expression of positive international law. See ibid., pp. 87–88.

the powers of the earth, the separate and equal station to which the Laws of Nature and of Nature's God entitle them." At the same time, it also believed that it owed "a decent respect to the opinions of mankind" in explaining the reasons why the nation decided to abjure its bonds with Britain and why it was entitled to be a recognized independent member of the international community. In terms of entitlements to rights, the final paragraph of the Declaration says very explicitly "that these united colonies are (…) Free and Independent States [and] (…) have the full power to levy war, conclude peace, contract alliances, establish commerce and do all other acts and things which Independent States may of right do."[331] Hence, in issuing the Declaration, the Continental Congress wanted to leave no doubt that it was "America's intention to be included within the family of nations."[332] What is more, in its framing, the Declaration appears to owe much to Vattel. For him, independence was a key precondition for entry into international society as an accepted and recognized entity. Only sovereign states could be regarded as "moral persons [living] together in a natural society subject to the law of nations." In order to remain respected as a member of international society, Vattel said that "it is sufficient that nations conform to what is required of them by the natural and general society, established among mankind."[333]

The salience of the law of nations found not only expression in the Declaration's concrete goals, but also in its exposition. For instance, the Declaration said that Britain had actually "waged war" against the colonies, thereby framing the issue and the justifications for proclaiming independence in the language of the laws of war, which helped the colonists to create distance between themselves and the motherland.[334] A few years later, Abigail Adams would write that one day,

331 U.S. Declaration of Independence, para. 35.

332 Douglas Sylvester "International Law as Sword or Shield?' pp. 9–10. In another article, Dumbauld said that the phrase "a decent Respect to the Opinions of Mankind" constituted "an express acceptance of the binding force of international law." See Edward Dumbauld, "Independence under International Law" p. 425. According to Janis, it signalled the need "to justify its actions on the international stage by reference to neutral principles of international law and morality." Janis, *America and the Law of Nations 1776–1939*, p. 26.

333 Vattel, *On the Law of Nations*, Preface, p. 15. See quoted in Armitage, *The Declaration of Independence*, pp. 39–40.

334 As Reginald Stuart said on this point: "[t]he *jus ad bellum* provided a moral sanction which admirably suited the American situation, even though the Revolutionary leaders did not cite it directly." Reginald Stuart, *War and American Thought from the Revolution to the Monroe Doctrine.* (Kent, OH: Kent State University Press, 1982), p. 21. He added that "[indeed] legists and philosophers all agreed that defensive wars needed no justification." Ibid. Even so, the British always maintained that they in fact fought the war "to uphold the law of nations in both Europe and America." See discussed in Eliga Gould, *Among the*

"Britain will Rue the Day that in Breach of the Law of Nations, she fell upon their defenceless dominions, and drew upon her (…) the combined force of all the Neutral Powers,"[335] suggesting that the conflict between Britain and the colonies was to be seen as an 'international' one. David Armitage affirmed this perspective when he said that the third group of charges listed in the Declaration belonged to "the realm of the law of nations."[336] Among the complaints enumerated were that the King "has plundered our seas, ravaged our Coasts, burnt our towns, and destroyed the lives of our people." In addition, he had "constrained our fellow Citizens taken Captive on the high Seas to bear Arms against their Country." What is more, in violation of the existing laws of war, the King "endeavoured to bring on the inhabitants of our frontiers, the merciless Indian Savages, whose known rule of warfare, is an undistinguished destruction of all ages, sexes and conditions." The implication was that by using Indian tribes to do his bidding, "the king had effectively placed the colonies "beyond the line" of civilized practice in warfare."[337] It was perhaps another way for Britain to show that it was not prepared to accept American independence, ensuring that no recognition could be derived from abidance by the international laws of war.[338]

While the Declaration proclaimed the independence of the American people, this did not necessarily mean that the *country* as such had now become independent. In fact, said St. George Tucker, "when the American states declared themselves independent of the crown of Great-Britain, each state from that moment became sovereign, and independent, not only of Great-Britain, but of all other powers, whatsoever. (…) From that moment there was no common law among them but the general law of nations, to which all civilized nations conform."[339] Joseph Story shared Tucker's views.[340] And one

---

Powers of the Earth: The American Revolution and the Making of a New World Empire. (Cambridge, MA: Harvard University Press, 2013), pp. 80–81.

335 Abigail Adams to John Adams (April 23, 1781), in *Adams Family Correspondence* (ed. L.H. Butterfield et al.), Vol. 4, p. 104. Quoted in Armitage, *The Declaration of Independence,* p. 47.

336 Armitage, *The Declaration of Independence*, p. 55.

337 Armitage, *The Declaration of Independence*, p. 56.

338 In contrast, the Americans demonstrated through the language of the Declaration that they wished to declare "their faith in the laws of war." John Fabian Witt, *Lincoln's Code: The Laws of War in American History* (New York: The Free Press, 2012), p. 15ff.

339 St. George Tucker, "Of the Unwritten, or Common Law of England; And Its Introduction into, and Authority Within the United American States' in Clyde N. Wilson (ed.), *View of the Constitution of the United States with Selected Writings* (Indianapolis: Liberty Fund 1999), p. 227–228.

340 "Whatever political relation existed between the American colonies antecedent to the Revolution, as constituent parts of the British empire, or as dependencies upon it, that

Pennsylvanian minister later declared that "[t]he Declaration of Independence, though it annulled the power of Britain over the colonies, established no superintending government in its room; and each colony became a free and independent state."[341] The Declaration is indeed unequivocal on this point, saying that "We, therefore, the Representatives of the united States of America, in General Congress, Assembled, appealing to the Supreme Judge of the world for the rectitude of our intentions, do, in the Name, and by Authority of the good People of these Colonies, solemnly publish and declare, That these United Colonies are, and of Right ought to be *Free and Independent States*."[342] Still, James Wilson read this very passage differently, inferring from the phrase 'United Colonies' that "they were independent, not *individually* but *Unitedly* and that they were confederated as they were independent, States." Hamilton agreed with Wilson, and "denied the doctrine that the States were thrown into a State of Nature." From the point of view of international law, it is very significant that he believed that "the Confederacy could be dissolved by partial infractions of it."[343] To add to the weight of the Declaration, some states integrated it into their state legislation to give it the force of law, whilst signalling their sense of independence.

Still, the Declaration on its own could therefore not have been enough to establish the independence of the United States. Equally important was the key issue of recognition. Thomas Pownall, for one, an Englishman sympathetic to the American cause and a former governor of Massachusetts, did not think

---

relation was completely dissolved, and annihilated from that period. From the moment of the Revolution they became severally independent and sovereign slates, possessing all the lights, jurisdictions, and authority, that other sovereign states, however constituted, or by whatever title denominated, possess; and bound by no ties, but of their own creation, except such, as all other civilized nations are equally bound by, and which together constitute the customary law of nations" Joseph Story, *Commentaries on the Constitution of the United States* (Boston: Hilliard, Gray and Co./Cambridge: Brown, Shattuck and Co., 1833), p. 283.

341 Alexander Addison "Analysis of the Report of the Committee of the Virginia Assembly" (1800), in Donald Lutz and Charles Hyneman, *American Political Writing During the Founding Era: 1760–1805* (Indianapolis: Liberty Fund, 1983), p. 1078. At the same time, he hastened to add that "The declaration of Independence, which raised the United States to the rank of a nation, gave to any government, which the people of the United States should establish with the charge of common defence and foreign intercourse, all the rights which the law of nations gives to every sovereign government." Ibid., p. 1070.

342 Emphasis added. See also discussed in Armitage, *The Declaration of Independence*, pp. 17–19.

343 "Journal of the Constitutional Convention of 1787" (June 19th, 1787) in *The Writings of James Madison*, Vol. 3, p. 225.

that the Declaration of Independence was enough to establish the country as a full member of the society of nations: "It is not sufficient that the United States feel that they are sovereign" he said, in a 1780 pamphlet,

> until they *lift up on high a Standard to the Nations,* it will remain an abstract idea, as a Theory in the World at large. This Sovereign must come forward amongst the Nations, as an active Existing Agent, a Personal Being, standing on the same ground as all other Personal Sovereigns. Its (…) claims to, and exercise of, the Rights of the Law of Nations, must have their full and free scope in act and deed: wherever they come forward, their Standard and Flag, the ensign of the Majesty of their Sovereignty, must be erected, and its Rights and Privileges established amongst the Nations of the Earth (…).[344]

The question of recognition under international law was one which in modern times European states rarely had to grapple with before. For them, this meant balancing legal against strategic imperatives. The French republic, which sensed a strategic advantage in recognizing American independence, did so explicitly when it signed the treaties of alliance and commerce in 1778. As a result, when its trade with the newborn republic was interfered with by the British, the French framed the issue as one concerning the law of nations.[345] The British obviously disagreed, and argued that had another country's colony revolted, France would not have acquiesced in accepting its independence.[346] In response, the French government said that the independence of the Dutch republic provided a precedent here, since the English Queen had recognized Dutch independence from Spain long before Spain had accepted it. But in the process, France had created a precedent that would be followed throughout the 19th century; that is, to extend recognition on the basis of effective

344 Thomas Pownall, *A Memorial, Most Humbly Addressed to the Sovereigns of Europe, on the Present State of Affairs between the Old and the New World.* (London, J. Debrett, 1780), pp. 129–130 (emphasis in original).

345 Wilhelm Grewe, *The Epochs of International Law*, p. 347. As a consequence of independence, the French government pointed out in a memorandum that henceforth, and for their purposes, the laws of war were deemed to apply between the British and the United States. See Ernest Nys, *Les États-Unis et le Droit des Gens* (Bruxelles: Bureau de la Revue, 1909), p. 68.

346 A memorandum to this end was drawn up by none other than Edward Gibbon. See Henry Wheaton, *History of the Law of Nations in Europe and America* (New York: Gould & Banks, 1845), p. 291–292.

independence.[347] For the United States, it was in most if not all respects a matter of course that full sovereign independence started with the proclamation of the Declaration. As justice Samuel Chase said in *Ware v Hylton*, it is "the established doctrine of the United States that its independence originated from and commenced with the declaration of Congress on 4 July, 1776, and that no other period can be fixed on for its commencement, and that all laws made by the legislatures of the several states after the Declaration of Independence were the laws of sovereign and independent governments."[348]

The fact that the Declaration was steeped in natural rights doctrine and stressed what later came to be called ideas of American exceptionalism did not imply that the United States wished to separate itself from European or world affairs. On the contrary: one of the purposes of the Declaration was "to create the legal basis necessary to form alliances with European powers."[349] In that respect, it was a clear repudiation of the main ideas that Thomas Paine had expressed in *Common Sense*, which called for a complete rupture of connections between the new world and the old.[350] The Founders, who were apparently of a much more realistic stock, were neither convinced of the desirability of such a course, nor of its feasibility. Instead, they concluded that only if the United States was to fully engage in foreign affairs and fight for its rights did it have a realistic chance of survival. This is why, upon independence, they "began a foreign policy in order to establish themselves as a nation."[351]

For all intents and purposes, it can be said that the Founders took a legalistic approach to establishing ties to foreign nations, namely by way of treaties of amity and commerce. John Adams even once wrote that "[t]he colonies were considered formerly, both here and at home, as allies rather than subjects" by way of "a treaty of commerce, by which distinct states have been cemented together, in perpetual league and amity."[352] However, this is

347 Wilhelm Grewe, *The Epochs of International Law*, p. 348.

348 *Ware v. Hylton*, 3 U.S. (3. Dall.), 199, 1796, at 225. In this case, which is also known as the British Debt case, the Supreme Court heard a claim by a representative of a British claimant for recovery of debts owed to him by a Virginian, which the latter refused to service due to a Virginia statute that considered that claims held against enemy aliens do not need to be repaid. The Court decided that this issue was covered by a provision in the Treaty of Paris, which took precedence over and nullified the Virginia statute.

349 Robert Kagan, *Dangerous Nation*, p. 42.

350 See discussed in Felix Gilbert, *To the Farewell Address*, pp. 37–38, 42–43.

351 Kagan, *Dangerous Nation*, p. 42.

352 John Adams, "A Dissertation upon Seekers" and "Novanglus, Addressed to the Inhabitants of the Colony of Massachusetts Bay, no. VII' in *The Works of John Adams*, Vol. 2, p. 172, and Vol. 4, p. 114.

not to say that there were no objections against treaties as instruments of foreign relations. Especially in the 18th century, many thinkers considered treaties to be "temporary armistices" (Rousseau) or even "preparations for treason" (Raynal).[353] Early American statesmen often shared these sentiments, but thought that by exclusively pursuing *commercial* engagements, they would be able to avoid duplicitous political entanglements. Indeed, treaties could be used as law-making instruments, and therewith, "they stood opposed to the perversion of law in Parliamentary statutes [which had deprived] colonists of their rights."[354] What is more, treaties also had the virtue of being based on mutual interests and consent, and were therefore more respectful of basic rights. As the Onuf brothers said, "[t]reaties were the basic instruments through which the rights of nations were recognized and confirmed, the fundamental acts that created international society."[355] Hence, it was hoped that, with only a few peaceful commercial treaties, the United States would be able to serve its purposes for establishing relations with overseas countries.[356]

In order to set out the desired parameters, Congress decided to have a model treaty drafted; one which should reflect American ideals and interests. Ideologically, there existed a strong disinclination towards military ties. So when John Adams was appointed to a committee to draft this model treaty—which also included the likes of John Dickinson and Benjamin Franklin—he set out a few ground rules:

> 1. No political connection. Submit to none of her authority; receive no governors or officers from her. 2. No military connection. Receive no troops from her. 3. Only a commercial connection; that is, make a treaty to receive her ships into our ports; let her engage to receive our ships into her ports; furnish us with arms, cannon, saltpetre, powder, duck, steel.[357]

353 Felix Gilbert, "The "New Diplomacy" of the Eighteenth Century" *World Politics* 4, no. 1 (1951), p. 8.

354 Peter Onuf and Nicholas Onuf, *Federal Union, Modern World*, p. 108.

355 Peter Onuf and Nicholas Onuf, *Federal Union, Modern World*, p. 109.

356 In fact, noted Perkins, the initial belief was among some that "[f]ive or six commercial agreements with major powers (…) should be about the limit." See Perkins, *The Creation of a Republican Empire* (Cambridge and New York: Cambridge University Press, 1993), Vol. 1, p. 77.

357 John Adams, "Notes of Debates in the Continental Congress, in 1775 and 1776" in *The Works of John Adams*, Vol. 2, pp. 488–489.

On September 17, the committee presented its draft to Congress.[358] While the Plan has often been praised for its overtly liberal approach in modern terms—for instance insisting on a most-favored nations clause—it also reflected a difficult compromise between different political factions. As Varg said, "[t]he attitude of each was that no other should have at its disposal a political structure for imposing its will on other groups."[359] But beyond the political differences, there was a strong belief among some of the Founders, including Adams and Madison, that there existed an inherent connection between commerce and peace, and that "a commercial system of freedom and equality (…) would eliminate all cause for tension and political conflicts."[360] However, this view was not shared by Hamilton and Jefferson. Both thought that commerce was a major factor for conflict, but drew different conclusions on how to approach this issue. In Pocock's words, Hamilton "was opting for dominion and expansion (…). There would be war, and there must be strong government."[361] Jefferson, however, feared that such an outcome would only help feed corruption at home. His inclination was thus rather to ensure that agriculture should continue to dominate economic activity in the new republic.[362]

Nevertheless, the intertwined nature of commerce of peace made that the Model Treaty was also to contain provisions related to warfare, at least in relation to the protection of mutual trade relations. For instance, articles III and IV required the signatories "to protect and defend all Vessels, and the Effects" of each other's inhabitants. More in particular, the treaty also demanded the contracting parties to protect each other's vessels against attacks by pirates, specifically from the Barbary states (article V and VI). Article VII went even further, requiring that "[i]f, in Consequence of this Treaty, the King of Great Britain,

---

358 For a thorough analysis of the sources which Adams used, and the contributions of Franklin, see Gregg Lint, "John Adams on the Drafting of the Treaty Plan of 1776" *Diplomatic History* 2, No. 3 (1978), pp. 313–320.

359 Paul Varg, *Foreign Policies of the Founding Fathers* (Baltimore, MD: Penguin Books, 1972), p. 21.

360 Felix Gilbert, *To The Farewell Address* (Princeton, NJ: Princeton University Press, 1961), pp. 51–52. See also Gordon Wood, *Empire of Liberty: A History of the Early Republic, 1789–1815* (New York: Oxford University Press, 2009), p. 191.

361 J.G.A. Pocock, *The Machiavellian Moment: Florentine Political Thought in the Atlantic Republican Tradition* (Princeton: Princeton University Press, 1975), p. 531.

362 See discussed in e.g. Robert Tucker and David Hendrickson, *Empire of Liberty: The Statecraft of Thomas Jefferson* (New York: Oxford University Press, 1992), pp. 30–31. As Secretary of State, Jefferson would basically toe the same line as Hamilton. As president, he attempted to avert or confront conflict by reducing commercial intercourse by way of embargoes.

should declare War, against the most Christian King, the said United States shall not assist Great Britain, in such War, with Men, Money, Ships, or any of the Articles in this treaty denominated Contraband Goods." In effect, this provision required the United States to stay neutral in various respects.[363]

Beyond this, the United States wished to make a number of additional demands from their future treaty partner—which was to be France. Among these were that no one was supposed to conquer any part of North America, from Labrador all the way south to Florida,

> it being the true Intent and meaning of this Treaty, that the said United States, shall have the sole, exclusive, undivided and perpetual Possession of the Countries, Cities, and Towns, on the said Continent, and of all Islands near to it, which now are, or lately were under the Jurisdiction of or Subject to the King or Crown of Great Britain, whenever they shall be united or confederated with the said United States.

But this was not all. The United States also wanted to ensure that American citizens enjoyed the same rights as Frenchmen in the West Indies should France manage to conquer them from the British (article X–XII), and demanded that French fishers stay out of fishing grounds claimed by the United States, on a reciprocal basis.[364] In general, most provisions are concerned with maritime rights, reflecting the preoccupations of the fledgling republic. It centered on the 'free ships shall make free goods' stipulation of article XXVI, albeit that James Wilson noted that "[t]his [was] to be obtained if possible, but not to be insisted on so as to break off the Treaty."[365]

Historian Reginald Horsman called the Model Treaty a "supremely confident document [which] reveal[ed] the optimism with which John Adams and his American compatriots viewed the prospects of the infant nation at the time of its birth."[366] Lawrence Kaplan was more cynical, noting that "[t]he Plan of 1776

363 The version of the Plan of Treaties printed in the *Journals of the Continental Congress* makes reference to France and the French King because it did not use the original copy, which only makes reference to parties [A.] and [B.] See Vol. 5, p. 579.

364 Although the version of the Plan of Treaties on the Avalon project website does include this article (as number x), this is not the case in the online version of the *Journals of the Continental Congress*, where such a provision is wholly absent. Though Avalon claims to base itself on the *Journals*, they might have drawn from a different version, unknown to me.

365 *Journals of the Continental Congress*, Vol. 5, p. 585.

366 Reginald Horsman *The Diplomacy of the New Republic, 1776–1815* (Arlington Heights, Ill.: Harlan Davidson, 1985), p. 11.

[could be seen as] the mouthings of colonial bumpkins innocent of the realities of international politics, or empty bravado of a frightened government pinning its hopes on impossible dreams to divert itself from its perils."[367] But despite the grandiose demands the Americans planned to make on the French, the Plan of Treaties did become the basis for negotiating the treaties of alliance with France two years later, which would perhaps surprisingly come to include many of its provisions.

Yet, Adams' exertions in drafting of the Model Treaty paled in comparison to those needed to draft the Articles of Confederation and Perpetual Union, the constitutional document which was to forge the states together to create a single union. As it was, the Declaration of Independence constituted only "a pledge that [the states] would see each other through the making of the union and the winning of independence, but it was not an achievement of either."[368] What had emerged from the colonial era was in effect a state system whereby "there was no common law amongst [the states] but the general law of nations."[369] To move from this state-of-nature condition to actual union was therefore the way to avoid the spectre of continual war that had dogged Europe for centuries. In rethinking their governmental structures, American statesmen reached for their copies of Vattel, Burlamaqui and other authorities on legal matters. In 1775, Benjamin Franklin thankfully acknowledged the receipt in December of three copies of Vattel, which "came to us in good season, when the circumstances of a rising State made it necessary frequently to consult the law of nations."[370] It testifies to the fact that these authorities were frequently referred to, and that Vattel in particular "had a very appreciable influence in shaping the attitude of the United States to the Law of Nations from their very beginning as a confederation (…) until the adoption of the present Constitution."[371]

---

367 Kaplan, *Colonies into Nation*, p. 91.

368 Hendrickson, *Peace Pact*, p. 126. In fact, he described it metaphorically as follows: "Because the confederation had not yet been made, July 4, 1776, may perhaps best be regarded not as their day of betrothal but as their night of forbidden passion, a glorious consummation of the warm embraces of the previous two years yet an act that fell well short of a regular marriage."

369 St. George Tucker, "Of the Unwritten, or Common Law of England' in *Blackstone's Commentaries*, Vol. 1, p. 407.

370 Jesse Reeves, "The Influence of the Law of Nature upon International Law in the United States." *American Journal of International Law* 31 (1935), p. 552.

371 Thomas W. Balch, "The United States and the Expansion of the Law between Nations" *University of Pennsylvania Law Review* 64 (1915), p. 116.

The drafting of the Articles was not without precedent. In the years leading up to the severance from Britain, colonial leaders had put significant thought into the reshaping of relations between the states. Benjamin Franklin, for instance, had studied the constitutional structure of the Holy Roman Empire when he visited the universities of Göttingen and Halle over the course of a journey across Germany in 1766.[372] This had helped him in the colonial debates about reforming the British imperial constitution, but also proved to be useful in thinking about a new constitution for the confederation.[373] For this exercise, his point of reference was the Albany Plan of Union, the drafting of which he had been extensively involved in. In 1775, Franklin submitted a plan to Congress which was very revelatory of the ambitions he foresaw for the young country. The name he had devised for this association was "The United Colonies of North America." Each of the colonies was entitled to "enjoy and retain as much as it may think fit of its own present Laws, Customs, Rights, Privileges, and peculiar Jurisdictions within its own Limits; and may amend its own Constitution as shall seem best to its own Assembly or Convention."[374] A subsequent article pointed out that authority in foreign affairs was to reside with the Confederal government, not with the states: "No Colony or Colonies without the Consent of the (union) [United States assembled,] shall send any Embassy to or receive any Embassy from or Enter into any treaty [Convention] or Conference with the King or Kingdom of Great Brittain or any foreign prince." This is also expressed in the eighteenth article, which states that "The (Congress) [United States assembled shall] have the sole & Exclusive power & right of Determining on [Peace and] war." One element from Franklin's draft which was resurrected in Dickinson's later plan was contained in article 12 [XIV] "A perpetual alliance offensive & Defensive is to be Entered into by the (whole union) [United States assembled] as soon as may be with the Six nations & all other [neighboring] nations of Indians." Altogether, this plan was 'realistic' in that it put more emphasis on legislative rather than executive

372 See e.g. in Jürgen Overhoff, *Benjamin Franklin: Erfinder, Freigeist, Staatenlenker* (Stuttgart: Klett-Cotta, 2006) and Overhoff, "Benjamin Franklin, student of the Holy Roman Empire: his summer journey to Germany in 1766 and his interest in the empire's federal constitution" in Paul Kerry and Matthew Holland (eds.), *Benjamin Franklin's Intellectual World* (Madison: Fairleigh Dickinson University Press, 2012), pp. 77–88.

373 In the *Federalist Papers*, Madison had written that the Empire failed to arrest internal conflict because it was "incapable of regulating its own members, insecure against external dangers and agitating with unceasing fermentations in its own bowels." Madison, *The Federalist Papers*, no. XIX, pp. 165–166.

374 Benjamin Franklin, "Proposed Articles of Confederation" (July 21, 1775), in *The Papers of Benjamin Franklin*, Vol. 22, p. 120ff.

responsibilities for common tasks, such as defense; i.e. the General Council would have less executive power than Congress would have had. In addition, because the states had grown much closer together over the past two decades, the chances of a plan of union to be passed by Congress were much greater than at the time of the Albany Plan.[375]

But in spite of the fact that Franklin's proposal was now closer to mainstream thinking, it was still deemed too premature by Congress, and not taken into consideration. When a year later, the Continental Congress had to take up the question of union, the chairmanship of the drafting committee of the Articles of Confederation was left to John Dickinson, a member who had been sceptical about independence all along. As things went, Dickinson proved not to be the person whose views best chimed with the times. In August, 1776, he already resigned, having become increasingly ignored by Congress and his friends.[376] Nevertheless, Dickinson's first draft of the Articles would prove to be very significant. As a basis for union, he proposed to the states to unite on the following basis (draft article two):

> The said Colonies unite themselves (into one Body politic) so as never to be divided by any Act whatever (of the Legislature of any Colony or Colonies, or of the Inhabitants thereof), and hereby severally enter into a firm League of Friendship with each other, for their Common Defence, the Security of their Liberties, and their mutual & general Wellfare, binding the said Colonies (and all the Inhabitants, & their Posterity,) to assist one another (with their Lives and Fortunes) against all Force offered to or Attacks made upon them or any of them, on account of Religion, Sovereignty, Trade, or any other Pretence whatever, (and faithfully to observe and adhere to all & Singular the Articles of this Confederation).[377]

The final draft of the Articles would instead in a more succinct manner declare that

> The said States hereby severally enter into a firm league of friendship with each other, for their common defense, the security of their liberties, and their mutual and general welfare, binding themselves to assist each other, against all force offered to, or attacks made upon them, or

375 See further discussed in Hendrickson, *Peace Pact*, pp. 119–121.

376 Hendrickson, *Peace Pact*, pp. 128–129.

377 "Draft Articles of Confederation" (June 17-July 1?, 1776), in *Letters of Delegates to Congress*, Vol. 4, p. 233.

> any of them, on account of religion, sovereignty, trade, or any other pretense whatever.

While the idea that the confederation would constitute a "firm league of friendship" was maintained, the name of the confederation, "the United States of America," left little doubt as to the intended closeness of the bond, particularly when compared with Franklin's "United Colonies of North America" proposed only a little over a year before. It is interesting on this point to note that Franklin's ambition to see the new nation expand from north to south was preserved in the Articles of Confederation by privileging the admission of Canada to the confederation, and, conditionally, that of other colonies.[378] Still, some ambiguity remained in the provisions regarding the rights to engage into compacts with other states, domestic or foreign. Thus, article VI of the Articles said that "No State, *without the consent of the United States in Congress assembled,* shall send any embassy to, or receive any embassy from, or enter into any conference, agreement, alliance or treaty with any King, Prince or State (...)." (emphasis added) The same applied to what could be called domestic alliances, something which today would be considered a curiosity: "No two or more States shall enter into any treaty, confederation or alliance whatever between them, *without the consent of the United States in Congress assembled,* specifying accurately the purposes for which the same is to be entered into, and how long it shall continue." (emphasis added) While such provisions potentially open up the prospect for discord within the confederation, Hendrickson assures us that since the consent of Congress would be needed, "the renunciation of [the power to unilaterally conclude treaties and alliances] by the states was pretty much complete."[379] With its focus on the duties of the states, the Articles of Confederation hold the middle between a constitution and a treaty of alliance. As Helfman wrote, "it was more a diplomatic document than a political one, exclusively governing the conduct of the states without touching upon the rights and obligations of their citizens."[380] Indeed,

378 See Article IX: "Canada acceding to this confederation, and adjoining in the measures of the United States, shall be admitted into, and entitled to all the advantages of this Union; but no other colony shall be admitted into the same, unless such admission be agreed to by nine States." Hendrickson however notes that "the desire [to incorporate Canada into the union] owed more to security considerations than territorial cupidity." Still, after 1779, this desire soon started to slide as a strategic objective, also because general Washington saw it as inimical to the interests of the south. See *Peace Pact*, p. 189.

379 Hendrickson, *Peace Pact*, p. 130.

380 Tara Helfman, "The Law of Nations in *The Federalist Papers.*" p. 116.

Madison is on record having said that the Confederation was governed by the principles of the "civil law on treaties."[381]

As such, the powers of Congress were to be relatively strong. Article IX, which enumerated its powers, determined that it would have "the sole and exclusive right and power of determining on peace and war," which followed from the general prohibition contained in article VI, stipulating that "[n]o State shall engage in any war without the consent of the United States in Congress assembled, unless such State be actually invaded by enemies, (...) and the danger is so imminent as not to admit of a delay till the United States in Congress assembled can be consulted." What is more, the power of Congress was further strengthened by the fact that a qualified majority vote rule applied on the major issues regarding war and peace, alliances, treaties and national defense including the military and navy. Agreement by nine out of the thirteen states was sufficient for Congress to take decisions. All of this makes that article two, which insisted that "Each state retains its sovereignty, freedom, and independence, and every power, jurisdiction, and right, which is not by this Confederation expressly delegated to the United States, in Congress assembled," needed not to be regarded as a serious check on the authority of Congress. Indeed, David Hendrickson argues that this article was "supremely unimportant and simply restat[ing] the intention of the congress with respect to the sources and limits of its authority."[382]

Another important aspect in this context is that "the United States in Congress assembled" is not to be regarded as a body similar to the Continental Congress (i.e. a conference of sovereign representatives) or as a parliamentary legislature, but rather as a "deliberating Executive assembly," similar to the position of the States-General in the Netherlands in the 17th century.[383] In other words, the Articles provided for an executive, albeit not with a single head. The continuing precariousness of the United States throughout the 1780s helped to increase the calls for a more singular executive, one that could take decisive action when needed without prior assent by as assembly. Although the Articles were eventually agreed upon in November 1777, it nevertheless

381 *Elliot's Debates*, Vol. 1, p. 424.

382 Hendrickson, *Peace Pact*, p. 134. He adds that this kind of division of powers was very common in the 18th century: "This was also the language of Burlamaqui, Vattel, Pufendorf, and Montesquieu, who each had written in a similar vein: when several commonwealths joined together in a confederate republic or firm league of friendship, they surrendered only that portion of their sovereignty, freedom and independence which they had expressly committed to their common councils." See ibid.

383 Hendrickson, *Peace Pact*, p. 136.

took another four years before they would be ratified by all of the thirteen states. In the meantime, the Continental Congress, which, after independence, had "essentially [become] an international congress in which the participants gained experience in negotiation,"[384] continued to be the only common body in charge of all principal issues on foreign relations.

Legally speaking, the status of the United States was very fragile, and it was not evident beyond all doubt that upon independence, the law of nations had been adopted unequivocally. Still, there is quite some evidence that suggests that international law was incorporated either by virtue of independence, or by way of the common law.[385] For the first view, support can be found in *Ware v. Hylton*, an early Supreme Court case in which James Wilson delivering a court opinion said that "[w]hen the United States declared their independence, they were bound to receive the law of nations, in its modern state of purity and refinement."[386] Further support came from Alexander Hamilton, who added that "the modern law of Nations [is] by adoption that of the U[nited] States."[387] In view of the above, a distinguished 20th century observer, Edwin Dickinson, concluded that "there [existed] as little doubt among men of legal learning in America as in England that the Law of Nations was adopted in its full extent as part of the law of the land."[388]

384 George G. Wilson, "International Law and the Constitution" *Boston University Law Review* 13 (1933), p. 238.

385 Louis Henkin, "International Law as Law of the United States' *Michigan Law Review* 82, no. 5/6 (May, 1984), pp. 1555–1556. Describing the first view, Henkin wrote that "[i]n the eighteenth century, the law of nations was part of the law of England, and English law, including the law of nations, applied in the colonies. With American independence, the law of England in the colonies (including the law of nations), was "received" as common law in the United States." The other view holds that international law was adopted "by implication from [American] independence, by virtue of international statehood. (...) [F]rom our beginnings, (...) courts have treated international law as incorporated and applied it as domestic law." See ibid.

386 *Ware v. Hylton* 3 U.S. (3 Dall.), 199 (1796), at 281.

387 Alexander Hamilton, "To Defence, no. XX' in Harold Syrett and James Cooke, (eds.) *The Papers of Alexander Hamilton* (New York: Columbia University Press, 1961–1987), Vol. 19, p. 332. See also Hamilton, "Camillus no. XX' in *The Works of Alexander Hamilton.* (New York: G.P. Putnam's Sons, 1904), Vol. 5, p. 421. In fact, Hamilton claims that the law of nations was adopted both by way of the common law and as a result of independence. See *infra*, p. 160.

388 Edwin Dickinson, "The Law of Nations as Part of the National Law of the United States" *University of Pennsylvania Law Review* 101, no. 1 (1952), p. 34. Incidentally, Dickinson quoted here almost verbatim a statement by Charles Lee, who opined that "the law of nations in its fullest extent [is] part of the law of the land." See Charles Lee, "Territorial

With respect to the common-law argument, support can be found in the 1784 New York appeals court case *Rutgers v. Waddington*, in which judge James Duane declared that "by our excellent constitution, the common law is declared to be part of the law of the land; and the *jus gentium* is a branch of the common law."[389] He concluded that "it is time that the law of nations and the nature and effect of treaties should be understood: And in the infancy of our republic, every proper opportunity should be embraced to inculcate a sense of national obligation, and a reverence for institutions, on which the tranquillity of mankind, considered as members of different states and communities so essentially depends."[390] Yet, one of the most important lawyers in the new republic, St. George Tucker, held an opposite view. His argument was that between 1776–1787 the individual colonies largely functioned as independent states, and that they had not received the common law—and therewith the law of nations—at the federal level. "First," he said,

> [t]he articles of confederation, were not agreed upon, nor ratified, till several years after the states became independent. Secondly, when agreed upon, and ratified, they contained an express declaration, in conformity to the law of nations, "that each state retains its sovereignty, freedom and independence, and every power, jurisdiction, and right, which is not thereby expressly delegated to the United States in congress assembled." Thirdly, that no power is therein delegated to congress, whereby that body was authorised to introduce, or to establish the common law, or

---

Rights—Florida" (January 26, 1797), in Benjamin Hall (ed.), *Official Opinions of the Attorneys General of the United States* (Washington DC: R. Farnham, 1852), Vol. 1, p. 69.

389 *Rutgers v. Waddington*, p. 23. The preceding paragraph makes clear that Duane speaks here about the Articles of Confederation, and not the New York State Constitution, since the question concerned was "whether these states are not bound by the *customary and voluntary laws of nations*." Jules Lobel wrote that with the adoption of the common law, the new nation had also adopted the law of nations since "the law of nations reflected universal reason and custom and thus was part of the law of nature and the common law." See Lobel, "The Limits of Constitutional Power: Conflicts between Foreign Policy and International Law" *Virginia Law Review* 71, no. 7 (October 1985), p. 1082. Stimson affirms that incidentally, the New York State Constitution of 1777 also recognized "the law of nations as part of the common law." Shannon Stimson, *The American Revolution in the Law: Anglo-American Jurisprudence before John Marshall* (Princeton, NJ: Princeton University Press, 1990), p. 113.

390 *Rutgers v. Waddington*, p. 46. See discussed in its contemporary context in Gordon Wood, *The Creation of the American Republic 1776–1787* (New York: W.W. Norton, 1972) pp. 457–459.

> statutes of England, or of any other country or nation, in the United States, as the general law of the land, therein.[391]

Hence, the only way in which it could be maintained that the law of nations was introduced in the United States up to 1787 was through the adoption of the common law by the respective states after 1776.[392] As will be readily understood, this did not obviate the need for consistent and uniform application of the law by and throughout the new union as a whole.

Still, the apparent absence of a 'constitutional' basis for adopting the whole or part of international law did not stop the Continental Congress from taking measures in conformity with the law in order to protect vital national interests. Already in 1775, Congress authorized the capturing of British vessels involved in the fight against the colonies, and permitted the establishment of prize courts (which would replace English prize courts on American soil) whilst prohibiting privateering—the practice of private vessels raiding enemy ships on the basis of letters of marque—without Congressional approval.[393] In 1779, Congress even adopted a resolution to declare that "Congress (...) will cause the law of nations to be most strictly observed" and that it will act as an instance of last resort, enabling it "to preserve the Law of Nations inviolate."[394] More in general, it appeared that there existed a natural tendency towards accepting international law as it stood in practice and as reflected by the great treatises of writers on the law of nations, even if it could not formally be integrated into a federal system of law. After all, as Stewart Jay noted, the founders respected these treatises as being "the same sources who had an established place in the intellectual foundation of the Revolution's ideology of natural rights."[395]

The Declaration of Independence and the Model Treaty spoke a different language still. They exuded a strong sense of confidence in the future, and in the law of nations as an instrument not only to protect America's interests, but

---

391 St. George Tucker, "Of the Unwritten, or Common Law of England' in *Blackstone's Commentaries*, Vol. 1, p. 408.

392 Bellia and Clark note that upon independence, eleven states adopted 'receiving statutes' so as to incorporate the common law as state law. New Jersey did so through a provision in its state constitution of 1776 while in Connecticut, the judiciary applied the common law as part of its unwritten constitution. See Anthony Bellia and Bradford Clark, "The Federal Common Law of Nations" *Columbia Law Review* 109 (January, 2009), p. 29.

393 Henry Bourguignon, "Incorporation of the Law of Nations during the American Revolution—The Case of the San Antonio" *American Journal of International Law* 71 (1977), p. 271.

394 Resolution adopted in May, 1779, in *Journals of the Continental Congress*, Vol. 14, p. 635.

395 Stewart Jay, "The Status of the Law of Nations in Early American Law," p. 824.

also to promote a new vision on conducting international relations. However, the realm of theory proved to be different from that of reality. While Americans had a penchant for adopting and expressing themselves in the neat language of Vattel, the raw realities of applying the law of nations in international politics remained often governed by the arbitrary sentiments of the great powers. As Eliga Gould wrote: "Although neither Vattel nor his many admirers would have expressed the point quite so baldly, the law of nations was more or less whatever Europe's imperial powers collectively said it was."[396] What is more, the period between 1776–1789 demonstrated that neither America's own constitutional foundations, nor its international legal commitments, could be relied upon. Partly as a result of the legal uncertainties that the domestic structure engendered, the early republic went through a very dangerous dozen-odd years, during which its very existence was seriously challenged. Ultimately, it took a dramatic departure from principle to save the revolution: concluding a military alliance with France.

396 Eliga Gould, "On the Margins of Europe: The Law of Nations in the Western Atlantic, circa 1755" (paper presented at the conference *The Law of Nations and the Early Modern Atlantic World*, Chicago, February 24, 2009), p. 6.

CHAPTER 3

The Struggle to Consolidate the Republic

3.1 The French Alliance and the Balance-of-Power

In the first years after independence, the idea that the law of nations could be reformed in a new direction was very much a key aspect of American foreign policy, in spite of the perilous condition in which the country found itself. With that came a rejection of theory of balance-of-power politics as practised by the European powers of the *ancien régime*. As Lawrence Kaplan said, the early American statesmen shared "the *Weltanschauung* of the philosophes" in that "[they] assailed power politics and the traditional statecraft that served only dynastic interests. To them the balance-of-power was wasteful and destructive as well as immoral, and the system of alliances a conspiracy against the natural order."[397] This idea was also nourished by older isolationist notions, which had always constituted a prominent intellectual current in the American colonies. "It centered on the idea that America possessed an innocence and a superiority that must remain isolated from the corrupting influence of Europe."[398] The Founders thus invariably shared the assessment of Montesquieu, who wrote about balance-of-power in the following terms:

> A new distemper has spread itself over Europe, infecting our princes, and inducing them to keep up an exorbitant number of troops. It has its redoublings, and of necessity becomes contagious. For, as soon as one prince augments his forces, the rest of course do the same; so that nothing is gained thereby but the public ruin. Each monarch keeps as many armies on foot as if his people were in danger of being exterminated; and they give the name of peace to this general effort of all against all.[399]

Indeed, the colonists had denounced the settlements of Utrecht (1713) and Aix-la-Chapelle (1748) precisely because these perpetuated a balance-of-power situation in North America, while the colonists wanted to conquer French

---

397 Lawrence Kaplan, *Colonies into Nation: American Diplomacy 1763–1801* (New York: Macmillan Company, 1972), p. 93.

398 Kaplan, *Colonies into Nation*, p. 17.

399 Charles Louis de Secondat, Baron de Montesquieu, "Of the Augmentation of Troops," *The Spirit of the Laws*, Vol. 1, Bk XIII, Ch. 17, in *The Complete Works of M. de Montesquieu* (London: T. Evans, 1777), pp. 287–288.

 | DOI 10.1163/9789004305687_005

territories in the north so as to prevent such conditions from obtaining in their part of the world.[400]

Still, it was clear for all to see that the United States was going to be a strategic player in the European balance-of-power—whether it liked it or not. As French foreign minister Étienne-François, Duc de Choiseul famously said in 1759, "the true balance-of-power really resides in commerce and in America."[401] Similar awareness existed on the American side, where John Adams wrote in a letter to Patrick Henry that "[a] connection with America must in the future decide the Ballance [sic] of Maritime Power in Europe."[402] That events in America and Europe were closely interconnected became palpably clear when none other than George Washington was involved in a battle in the forests of Ohio that would ignite the French and Indian Wars in 1754, which in turn precipitated the Seven Years' War (1756–1763), arguably the world's first global conflict. When in the course of the war, the French lost the city of Québec to the British, foreign minister Choiseul presciently foresaw that this "could lead to the removal of Britain herself from the continent." This was because he believed that "Americans no longer needed British protection, and were convinced that the balance of dependence had shifted to the favor of the colonies."[403] This is at least part of the explanation for the expansionist inclinations of the colonists, which their European adversaries understood all too well. Hence, when the British had decided after the siege of Québec in 1759 not to hold on to French Canada, the reason was that they wished to maintain it as a counterbalance to the colonies.[404] As a result, when Benjamin Franklin

400 Robert Kagan, *Dangerous Nation: America's Foreign Policy from its Earliest Days to the Dawn of the 20th Century* (New York: Vintage Press, 2007), pp. 21–22 and 28–29.

401 G. de Raxi de Flassan, G., *Histoire Générale et raisonnée de la Diplomatie Francaise*, 2nd ed., Vol. IV, Paris 1811, p. 413. Quoted in Felix Gilbert, *To The Farewell Address: Ideas of Early American Foreign Policy* (Princeton, NJ: Princeton University Press, 1970), p. 106. Étienne-Francois is not to be confused with his cousin César Gabriel de Choiseul, who succeeded him as minister of foreign affairs in 1761, and then stepped down again in favor of Étienne-Francois in 1766.

402 James Hutson, "Intellectual Foundations of Early American Diplomacy," *Diplomatic History* 1, no. 1 (1977), p. 12.

403 Lawrence Kaplan, *Colonies into Nation: American Diplomacy 1763–1801* (New York: The Macmillan Company, 1972), p. 3.

404 John Mitchell however dismissed such thinking out of hand: "The opinion of some lame or designing politicians, who pretend to tell us that it is in the interest of Great Britain to allow France a considerable power in America, in order to keep the British colonies in subjection! This is surely the first time that any one ever imagined it, to be the interest of Britain to aggrandize the power of France (…)." See "The Contest in America Between Great Britain and France, with its Consequences and Importance (…)" (published

submitted a proposal for total security on the North American continent, it was dismissed as ridiculous.[405]

In traditional accounts of early American history, the generation of the Founding Fathers has sometimes been portrayed as either ignorant about balance-of-power politics, of using it for defensive posturing only, or both.[406] For instance, historian Felix Gilbert once wrote that "it was difficult [for Americans] to comprehend the importance of the power factor in foreign relations."[407] From this point of view, it was only natural that they would use international law as a defensive means to protect their interest. A typical example in this vein is Stewart Jay's argument that "the primary consideration that forced the United States to pay respect to the law of nations was the country's weakness in relation to the European powers."[408] More recently, this view was reiterated by Robert Kagan, who wrote:

> The statesmen of the founding era (...) were practical idealists. (...) They viewed alliances as necessary but dangerous. They denigrated so-called power politics and claimed an aversion to war and military power. They extolled the virtues of commerce, where Americans competed on a more equal plane. They appealed to international law as the best means of regulating the behaviour of nations, knowing that they had no other means of constraining the great empires of Britain and France.[409]

---

anonymously, London, 1757) quoted in Alfred Vagts, "The United States and the Balance-of-Power" *The Journal of Politics* 3, no. 4 (November 1941), p. 410.

Edward Corwin even noted that France might have chosen not to support the Americans, for "by leaving England her non-rebellious provinces in North-America, a certain portion of her strength and attention would be permanently diverted from the European balance to the maintenance of a minor balance in the Western Hemisphere." Corwin, "The French Objective in the American Revolution." *The American Historical Review* 21, no. 1, (October 1915), p. 44.

405 Kagan, *Dangerous Nation*, p. 29.

406 See e.g. Gilbert, *To the Farewell Address*, p. 17; Paul Varg, *Foreign Policies of the Founding Fathers*, pp. 3–4. For contrarian views, see Kagan, *Dangerous Nation*, pp. 56–57; Douglas Sylvester, "International Law as Sword or Shield?" *NYU Journal of International Law and Politics* 32, no. 1 (1999), pp. 37–38.

407 Gilbert, *To the Farewell Address*, p. 17.

408 Stewart Jay, "The Status of the Law of Nations in Early American Law," *Vanderbilt Law Review* 42 (1989), p. 839. In the same vein, see Edwin Dickinson, "Changing Concepts and the Doctrine of Incorporation," *American Journal of International Law* 26, no. 2 (1932).

409 Kagan, *Dangerous Nation,* p. 57. Elsewhere, however, Kagan claims that "Americans understood the intricacies of the European balance-of-power, and how to exploit it to their advantage." See ibid., p. 59.

What is more, it has also been said that "[o]n the North American continent, law and power were sharply contrasted, irreconcilable with each other."[410] In that respect, the thinking in the colonies was almost the reverse of that on the continent, where, in the 18th century, the operation of international law was predicated on balance-of-power mechanisms. The apparent ability of balance-of-power politics to prevent any state from seeking hegemony on the continent was often hailed as testimony to Enlightenment progressivism. David Hume even believed that checking countries with universalist pretensions could help to change their behaviour. He therefore concluded that because "[e]normous monarchies are, probably, destructive to human nature," the balance-of-power as a means to preserving the peace was ineluctably "founded (…) on common sense and obvious reasoning."[411] But no matter the rationality and efficacy of the balance-of-power being able to maintain the peace, this was always going to be a very fragile condition; the best illustration being a verse from Alexander Pope, that paragon of the British Augustan Age:

> Now Europe's balanced, neither side prevails;
> For nothing's left in either of the scales.[412]

But while in the first part of the 18th century, there was still believed to be a link between balance-of-power and the law of nations,[413] these became increasingly dissociated during the French Revolutionary wars, when the breakdown of the European system came to be blamed on balance-of-power and alliance politics.[414] In the process, confidence on both sides of the Atlantic in the ability of international law—seen as a mere companion to balance-of-power—to preserve stability and peace was also seriously shaken. One scholar even wrote that in the latter half of the 18th century, "there was no international law generally recognized. (…) There was no one system of law universally recognized, but there were a confusion of feudal customs complicated

410 Gilbert, *To the Farewell Address*, p. 17.

411 David Hume, "Of the Balance-of-Power," in *Essays Moral, Political, Literary* (Indianapolis: Liberty Fund 1987), pp. 340, 337. See also discussed in Daniel Lang, *Foreign Policy in the Early Republic*, pp. 37–41.

412 Alexander Pope, "The Balance of Europe" (1711).

413 For instance, Vattel wrote that, on the basis of just war doctrine, "there cannot exist a doubt, that if a formidable potentate certainly entertains designs of oppression and conquest (…) the other states have a right to anticipate him." See Vattel, *The Law of Nations* (Indianapolis: Liberty Fund, 2008), Bk. III, para. 49, p. 498.

414 In 1829, Arnold Heeren still held that this link existed. See *History of the Political System of Europe and Its Colonies* (New York: S. Butler & Son, 1829), p. 12.

with all the subtleties of Roman jurisprudence. But nothing was sacred (…) Not even the most explicit treaty arrangements need be honored."[415] Thus, if international law was in disarray and the maintenance of peace was to depend on balance-of-power machinations, many Americans confidently concluded that "the European diplomatic system was fundamentally flawed."[416]

Yet, instead of rejecting wholesale European traditions in law and politics, early American statesmen sought to reform the system. Partly, this was because the Founders were quite familiar with the operation of the balance-of-power, and appreciated its merits too. Both John Adams and Thomas Jefferson had a good and realistic understanding of it. As one scholar said, "[i]n the New World Americans preferred hegemony to a balance-of-power, but in the Old World they knew a balance served their interests well."[417] One should also note the familiarity of American political leaders with political theorists such as Algernon Sidney and Viscount Bolingbroke,[418] whose views on balance-of-power from an English (that is, an aloof maritime power) perspective shaped those of for example John Adams and Alexander Hamilton. Even more so, they intended to use it to their advantage as much as possible. As James Hutson argued, between 1776 and the early 1790s, there existed a consensus in that "American leaders operated in foreign politics according to the assumptions of power politics (…). They believed (…) that it was their duty to manipulate it for the country's advantage [and that] the possession of military power was justifiable and necessary because it helped to preserve the peace."[419]

But in promoting a balance-of-power, the early statesmen did not have in mind to continue the old militaristic policies of their European counterparts. So, if balance-of-power politics were going to persist, the least American statesmen wanted was to reform it in such fashion as to make it serve the cause of

---

415 Francis Ruddy, *International Law in the Enlightenment: The Background of Emmerich de Vattel's Le Droit des Gens* (Dobbs Ferry: Oceana Publications, 1975), pp. 42–43.

416 Peter Onuf and Nicholas Onuf, *Federal Union, Modern World: The Law of Nations in an Age of Revolutions, 1776–1814* (Madison, WI: Madison House Publishers, 1993), p. 166.

417 Robert Kagan, *Dangerous Nation*, p. 59. See also Felix Gilbert, *To the Farewell Address*, p. 86, 89.

418 Hutson, "Intellectual Foundations of Early American Diplomacy" p. 14.

419 Hutson, "Intellectual Foundations of Early American Diplomacy" p. 18. In his article, Hutson citicises the then-mainstream opinion as articulated by Felix Gilbert that the early American statesmen were intent on shaping a new world order based on commerce in the mould of Enlightenment thinking. David Fitzsimons however finds that "the refutation of Gilbert and idealistic internationalism fails to hold up to scrutiny." See Fitzsimons, "Tom Paine's New World Order: Idealistic Internationalism in the Ideology of Early American Foreign Relations." *Diplomatic History* 19, no. 4 (September 1995), p. 570.

peace. Broadly envisaged, they "sought to create a balance-of-power system predicated on free trade and commercial arrangements [underpinned by] the doctrine of neutral rights."[420] This last point in particular was to become a cornerstone of early U.S. foreign policy, which not only furnished America with a measure of respectability among the European great powers, but also with its first authentic contribution to the development of doctrine and practice in international law. It is thus in the realm of the law of nations that the United States began a new approach as well; a passive approach would not do. The Model Treaty in particular provided a blueprint of what the country eventually hoped to achieve. To push these ideas forward, the founders had to use international law as an 'offensive tool' as well. Thus, the 'conventional' notion that international law was only used as a shield does not appear to comport with the actual historical record. Rather than merely being used as a shield, "[the law of nations] was used just as often as a sword to achieve specific policy goals."[421]

While many of the early American statesmen possessed first-rate legal minds and a well-tuned political acumen, few if any among them were able to combine America's idealist aspirations with the hard-headed realist necessities of statecraft in their thinking and diplomacy like Benjamin Franklin. He was sent to France at the end of 1776 in order to start negotiations on a treaty of alliance with Louis XVI. Being the most famous American in the world, and with many years of experience having lived in Europe, he was best placed to fulfil this assignment.[422] While in Paris, Franklin had to contend with one of the most cunning diplomats of his era, French foreign minister Comte de Vergennes, trying to balance America's obvious weakness as a new country against France's anxiety about strengthening its position vis-à-vis Britain in the hegemonic struggle for colonial overlordship. Franklin knew he was in for a tough test, given that, as Bemis wrote,

> European diplomacy in the 18th century was no gentle craft. The chancelleries of the powers acted according to the unblushing principles of Machiavelli—that the attainment of a good end justified the use of any means, however dirty. (…) It was a world of the survival of the strongest, or of the weak only with the assistance of the strong bought at a heavy price. (…) No ruler trusted another, not even a blood relative and treaty

420 Sylvester, "International Law as Sword or Shield?" pp. 42–43.

421 Sylvester, "International Law as Sword or Shield?" p. 7.

422 See for a colourful account of Franklin's stay in Paris, Stacy Shiff, *A Great Improvisation: Franklin, France, and the Birth of America* (New York: Henry Holt, 2005).

> ally. No government could rely on the fulfillment of a treaty, unless by calculating it to be the interest of the obligated party.[423]

For Franklin, this was however no reason to shrink from his duties, for he "could not have been more Machiavellian, shrewder in playing both ends off against the middle, or more skilful in exploiting the balance-of-power. (…)." And as a result of Franklin's nonchalant behaviour in dealing with diplomatic issues, he "strengthened France's support of America while it inhibited Britain's war effort."[424] In fact, almost all of his diplomatic correspondence had often been passed on to London by secret agents before the French government had had a chance to take note of it.[425] While Franklin's counterparts in Paris, John Adams and Arthur Lee, were aghast about his careless attitude, it did serve American purposes in that it permitted the English to know how closely the Americans coordinated their moves with the French, which made them more reluctant to get involved in a war with France. At one point, Franklin got into a discussion with Adams about whether America should try to remain neutral, or whether it should conclude a full-blown alliance with France. For Franklin, the latter was the only viable option. For Adams, a much more principled man, this position was very hard to accept. The clash between Franklin and Adams was therewith not simply one between different interpretations of what constituted America's 'national interest,' but also a personal one. In general, Franklin's disposition towards politics cannot be said to have been an ideological one. Even if he often professed his allegiance to higher principles and shared the objectives of the Model Treaty, his attention was always fixated on how America's best interest could be served given the political circumstances.[426] Famously, he said of Adams that "he means well for his Country, is always an honest Man, often a Wise one, but sometimes and in some things absolutely out of his Senses."[427]

The Americans and the French had obviously very different objectives in mind for entering into an alliance, the conclusion of which would be contingent on the immediate course of the war. In fact, while the French could simply

423 Samuel Flagg Bemis, *The Diplomacy of the American Revolution* (New York: D. Appleton Century, 1935), p. 13.

424 Bernard Bailyn, *Realism and Idealism in American Diplomacy: The Origins. Homage to Felix Gilbert* (1905–1991). (Princeton, NJ: Institute for Advanced Study, 1994), p. 13.

425 From a discussion with Gregg Lint.

426 Gerald Stourzh, *Benjamin Franklin and American Foreign Policy* (Chicago: University of Chicago Press, 1954), p. 235.

427 Benjamin Franklin to James Lovell (July 22, 1783), in *The Papers of Benjamin Franklin*, Vol. 40, p. 86.

have let the British struggle with the insurgency in North America, Vergennes' objective was not "the continuance of peace with Great Britain, but a chance to meet that power, on better than even terms, in a war for the recovery of French power and prestige [lost after the 1763 Peace of Paris]."[428] Given their key role in the Atlantic trade, American merchantmen believed that anti-British European powers would swiftly come over to the American side. For instance, Thomas Paine expected that "[t]he weapons of commercial opportunity which would flow from a declaration of independence would permit diplomatists to secure such foreign assistance as might be necessary."[429] This was however too starry-eyed a view. Instead, as Horsman said, "[the] United States discovered that rather than welcoming American trade with open arms, most European countries were wary of doing anything that would offend powerful Great Britain until they were sure that the American colonies would offer more than token resistance to British force."[430] While the French were thus interested in escalating the conflict, and indeed had provided secret arms shipments to the American rebels since 1776,[431] they operated in a more circumspect mode with respect to concluding formal ties with the self-declared independent nation. One reason why France adopted a wait-and-see approach is because while it supported the rebellion for strategic aims, it did not necessarily share the principles underpinning the struggle, which of course included the idea that a monarch could be deposed when not respecting a people's 'self-evident rights.'

The idea of concluding an alliance with France even pre-dated the revolution itself. Already in 1774, the French chargé d'affaires in London reported to Paris that the American insurgents were interested in creating such an alliance, or to receive assistance from the French.[432] In order to get the best concessions as possible from the French, Franklin kept a negotiation channel open with the British. It would only be after the Continental army's victory at Saratoga in December 1777 that Vergennes felt the time had arrived to offer the Americans a treaty of alliance. Britain's efforts to come to an understanding with its rebelling overseas possession put further pressure on

428 Bemis, *The Diplomacy of the American Revolution*, p. 20.

429 Kaplan, *Colonies into Nation*, p. 90.

430 Horsman, *The Diplomacy of the New Republic, 1776–1815*, p. 17.

431 As an example, in order to shield the role of the government from the British, a company was created as an intermediary called Roderigue Hortalez and Company, led by the well-known playwright Caron de Beaumarchais. See Jonathan Dull, *A Diplomatic History of the American Revolution* (New Haven and London: Yale University Press, 1985), pp. 61–63.

432 Samuel F. Bemis, *The Diplomacy of the American Revolution* (New York: D. Appleton Century, 1935), p. 19.

France, compelling it to conclude the treaty of alliance. Any attempts by the British to make last-minute overtures to the Americans—offering acceptance of independence in exchange of abjuring the alliance treaty—were now met with derision.[433] The moment had simply passed, as Franklin implicitly told a British agent: "[W]e are bound by Ties, stronger than can be formed by any Treaty, to fight against you with them, as long as the War against them shall continue."[434]

The American delegation that was to negotiate with the French was instructed by the Committee of Secret Correspondence, which was in charge of foreign relations on behalf of Congress between November 1775 until 1781, to conclude only a trade treaty, not a military alliance. It should be remarked here that the word 'alliance' had in fact a different meaning in the 18th century as opposed to today, as some scholars have noted. For instance, diplomatic historian Alexandre DeConde wrote that the concept "did not yet definitely carry the modern connotation of a military-political commitment. At the time, in keeping with past usage, many American statesmen saw little distinction between the treaty of alliance and that of commerce." In fact, DeConde adds, "[o]ftentimes they referred to both collectively as either the treaty of alliance or the treaty of commerce," hence, not even distinguishing between the two.[435] Gilbert noted the same, saying that the term was used in a "loose way" by the Americans.[436] The Model Treaty was to serve as the blueprint for the alliance. For its author, John Adams, it was clear that 'alliance' was not to imply a military connection: "I am not for soliciting any political connection, or military assistance, or indeed naval, from France. I wish for nothing but commerce, a mere marine treaty with them."[437] When discussing treaties of alliance with France, he pointed out the dangers of taking sides at a time of instability in Europe. For Adams, the point was "to avoid all Alliance which might embarrass Us in after times and involve us in future European wars [and to] place [France] on a more equal footing with England, for the protection of her foreign possessions (…)."[438] Commerce in combination with neutrality was in the best interest of the United States, Adams felt. These "negotiations with France," he said,

433 See Hendrickson, *Peace Pact*, p. 166.

434 Benjamin Franklin to William Pulteney (March 30, 1778), in *The Papers of Benjamin Franklin*, Vol. 26, p. 195ff.

435 Alexandre Deconde, *Entangling Alliance: Politics and Diplomacy under George Washington* (Durham: Duke University Press, 1958), p. 7.

436 Gilbert, *To the Farewell Address*, p. 46.

437 John Adams to John Winthrop (June 23, 1776), in *The Works of John Adams*, Vol. 9, p. 409.

438 John Adams, "Autobiography," in *The Works of John Adams*, Vol. 2, p. 516.

> ought (...) however, to be conducted with great caution, and with all the foresight we could possibly obtain; that we ought not to enter into any alliance with her, which should entangle us in any future wars in Europe; that we ought to lay it down, as a first principle and a maxim never to be forgotten, to maintain an entire neutrality in all future European wars; that it never could be our interest to unite with France in the destruction of England, or in any measures to break her spirit, or reduce her to a situation in which she could not support her independence. On the other hand, it could never be our duty to unite with Britain in too great a humiliation of France; that our real, if not our nominal, independence, would consist in our neutrality. If we united with either nation, in any future war, we must become too subordinate and dependent on that nation, and should be involved in all European wars, as we had been hitherto; that foreign powers would find means to corrupt our people, to influence our councils, and, in fine, we should be little better than puppets, danced on the wires of the cabinets of Europe.[439]

For these reasons, Adams argued, America "ought to confine [itself] strictly to a treaty of commerce; that such a treaty would be an ample compensation to France for all the aid we should want from her."[440] But in spite of France's eventual generosity towards the United States, a military alliance *was* to be part of the treaties to be signed on February 6, 1778. As one author said with some understatement, "the commissioners and the nation alike recognized that their world of 1778 was something less than ideal."[441]

With some exceptions, the first treaty—on amity and commerce—"conformed almost identically with the articles of the "Plan of 1776" laid down by the Continental Congress in the original instructions to the Commissioners of France."[442] The issues agreed upon included, among others, a most-favored nation clause (article II); a pledge to protect each others' vessels on sea (articles VI and VII); a pledge by the French king to use his good offices in order to obtain protection against Barbary Pirates (article VII) and a pledge on the American side not to infringe of French fishing rights off the coast of Newfoundland (article X). The key principle of 'free ships, free goods' was incorporated into article XXV. The treaty was most detailed on the point of defining contraband (article XXVI) and commercial shipping rights in times of

439 John Adams, "Autobiography," in *The Works of John Adams*, Vol. 2, p. 505.

440 John Adams, "Autobiography," in ibid., p. 505.

441 Kaplan, *Colonies into Nation*, p. 116.

442 Bemis, *The Diplomacy of the American Revolution*, p. 61.

war. What the treaty reflected was that the American perspective on commerce was "vastly different from the outlook prevailing in European courts" in that it was "pointedly 'liberal' rather than 'mercantilist.'—in favor of removing the fetters and restraints on commerce (…)."[443]

The entry into force of the accompanying treaty of alliance was made contingent on the outbreak of war between France and Great Britain. In that event, both countries pledged to make it "a common cause." War was considered to have broken out "either by direct hostilities" or if Britain would "hind[er France's] commerce and navigation, in a manner contrary to the Rights of Nations."[444] As the objective of the treaty, article II declared the following: "The essential and direct End of the present defensive alliance is to maintain effectually the liberty, Sovereignty, and independance absolute and unlimited of the said united States, as well in Matters of Gouvernement as of commerce." Based on this wording, John Adams argued that it would only apply for the duration of the war against the English. Article XI however suggested otherwise:

> The two Parties guarantee mutually from the present time *and forever*, against all other powers, to wit, the united states to his most Christian Majesty the present Possessions of the Crown of France in America as well as those which it may acquire by the future Treaty of peace: and his most Christian Majesty guarantees on his part to the united states, their liberty, Sovereignty, and Independence absolute, and unlimited, as well in Matters of Government as commerce and also their Possessions, and the additions or conquests that their Confederation may obtain during the war, from any of the Dominions now or heretofore possessed by Great Britain in North America, conformable to the 5th & 6th articles above written, the whole as their Possessions shall be fixed and assured to the said States at the moment of the cessation of their present War with England. (my emphasis)

Article XII stipulated in addition that "if such rupture shall not take place, the mutual obligations of the said guarantee shall not commence, until the moment of the cessation of the present War between the united states and England shall have ascertained the Possessions." But while the duration of the treaty remained perhaps ambiguous, the American commissioners were able

443 David Hendrickson, *Peace Pact: The Lost World of the American Founding* (Lawrence, KS: University of Kansas Press, 2003), p. 164.

444 See Preamble, *Treaty of Alliance*, February 6, 1778.

to extract further concessions in addition to those they obtained in the treaty on amity and commerce. For instance, they secured a promise (article VI) that France would not seek to reconquer British territory in North America, which should be left for the Americans to conquer at some point.[445] The preceding article already contained the possibility for the United States to enlarge its territory should it succeed in conquering any areas held by the British.

In order to encourage unity of action between the alliance partners, they agreed in article VIII that "Neither of the two Parties shall conclude either Truce or Peace with Great Britain, without the formal consent of the other first obtain'd; and they mutually engage not to lay down their arms, until the Independence of the united states shall have been formally or tacitly assured by the Treaty or Treaties that shall terminate the War." Shortly after the conclusion of the treaties, the British had attempted to come to an accommodation with the Americans through a last-ditch effort by the so-called Carlisle commission, which offered a repeal of the war measures of 1763 and home rule. However, their delegation arrived too late, allowing Congress to ratify the treaties of amity, commerce and alliance on May 4, 1778, which they did with great joy.

When signing the Treaties of Alliance with the stroke of a quill, it looked like the United States therewith consigned its high-minded approach to the law of nations to a lower plan—a "radical departure" from established principles.[446] But having to accept a military alliance with a major European power, and thus to 'entangle' itself in overseas affairs, did not stop Americans from continuing to work towards a wider acceptance of principles such as 'free ships, free goods' and neutral rights—and least of all Benjamin Franklin. Interestingly, according to Gerald Stourzh—who wrote one of the standard studies on his foreign policy—Franklin "never did care much for legal arguments in international relations." His approach being rather "careless" with regard to the law, what mattered to him was that "its spirit was observed."[447] In the early 1780s, he became one of America's strongest advocates for reforming the law of nations. But Franklin's approach towards international law cannot solely—if at all—be ascribed to an idealist outlook. In fact, Franklin may have thought reform of the law of nations a necessity for the United States to become a full member of the community of nations.[448]

---

445 See also in Bemis, *The Diplomacy of the American Revolution*, p. 47.

446 Paul Varg, *Foreign Policies of the Founding Fathers*, p. 24.

447 Gerald Stourzh, *Benjamin Franklin and American Foreign Policy* (Chicago: University of Chicago Press, 1954), p. 219.

448 I am indebted to Joyce Chaplin for this observation.

One possibility for reform appeared to come when in 1780 Catherine II of Russia announced the creation of a League of Armed Neutrality,[449] which was to unite all neutral powers and their friends in an attempt to force the British Navy to accept neutral shipping rights and to undo the 'Rule of 1756,' which determined that trade between neutrals and belligerent states was allowed in wartime as it was in peacetime, but that new direct trade between an enemy states and its colonies would be subject to seizure.[450] According to the *Consolato del Mare*, which was largely adhered to in the late 18th century, neutral goods on enemy ships were not subject to capture, while enemy goods on neutral ships were. Both Bynkershoek and Vattel reaffirmed this position.[451]

---

449 The contemporary author William Duane summarized its principles as follows: 1. That it shall be lawful for any ship whatever, to sail freely from one port to another, or along the coasts of the powers at war. 2. That all merchandize and effects, belonging to the subjects of powers at war, and shipped in neutral vessels, shall be entirely free; excepting contraband goods, (cannon, mortars, musquets, pistols, flints, matches, gunpowder, sulphur, saltpetre, pikes, swords, saddles, or other articles positively forming munitions or implements of war.) 3. That, to ascertain what constitutes the blockade of any place or port, it is to be understood to be in such a predicament, when the assailing power has taken such a station, as to expose to imminent danger, any ship or ships, that should attempt to enter or depart. 4. That no neutral ship shall be stopped without a material and well grounded cause; and in such cases justice shall be done them, without loss of time; and, besides indemnifying, each and every time, the party aggrieved by being stopped without sufficient cause ; satisfaction shall also be given to the power, whose flag may be thus insulted. 5. That all decisions in cases of capture, shall be determined by the principles here laid down. See William Duane, *The Law of Nations, Investigated in a Popular Manner* (Philadelphia, William Duane, 1809), p. 23.

450 Remarkably, Britain did at one point agree to its principles, as the prime minister wrote in 1782: "His majesty therefore, *accepts as the basis* of a separate peace with Holland, *a free navigation according to the principles* demanded by her imperial majesty, in her *declaration* (of armed neutrality) of February 26, 1780." See note sent by prime minister Charles James Fox to Catherine of Russia (date unknown, 1782?), quoted in Duane, *The Law of Nations, Investigated in a Popular Manner*, p. 24 (emphasis in original). On the history of neutrality in the 18th century, see, *inter alia*, Kulsrud, Carl J., *Maritime Neutrality to 1780. A History of the Main Principles Governing Neutrality and Belligerency to 1780* (Boston: Little, Brown, and Company, 1936).

451 Bynkershoek said that "[i]n consulting reason, I cannot see why it should not be lawful to seize enemy goods found in neutral ships, for this is only taking what belongs to the enemy and falls to the victor by the laws of war." Cornelius van Bynkershoek, *Quaestiones iuris publici libri duo* (The Classics of International Law, Oxford: Clarendon Press, 1930 [1737]), Bk. I, ch. 14. According to Vattel, "If we find an enemy's effects on board a neutral ship, we seize them by the rights of war: but we are naturally bound to pay the freight to

The United States followed this practice in its Admiralty Courts.[452] Up to 1780, Franklin also defended this position,[453] and even communicated this to Vergennes.[454] Instead of rejecting the offer to join the League of Armed Neutrality, the United States instead tried strenuously to join it. At the urging of John Adams and Benjamin Franklin, Congress adopted a resolution on October 5, 1780 accepting the armed neutrality principles, declaring that "all Neutral vessels have by the Law of Nations a right to navigate freely to and from the ports and on the coasts of powers at war, when not prohibited by treaty or municipal law."[455] The resolution was subsequently countenanced by the Federal Court of Appeals.[456] In early March of 1781, John Adams formally requested admission of the United States to the league of Neutrals; a request which had to be rebuffed given that the United States was of course still at war with Britain. The prospects for a League defending neutral rights made Franklin's hopes for reform suddenly soar. Henceforth, Franklin believed, the 'free ships, free goods' rule would rapidly take root among European powers:

> All the neutral states of Europe seem at present disposed to change what had before been deemed the law of Nations, to wit, that an Enemy's Property may be taken wherever found and to establish a Rule that free Ships Shall make free Goods. This rule is in itself so reasonable, and of a nature to be so beneficial to mankind that I cannot but wish it may become general. And I make no doubt but that the Congress will agree to it in as full an extent as France and Spain.[457]

---

the master of the vessel, who is not to suffer by such seizure." Vattel, *The Law of Nations*, Bk III, ch. 7, para. 115, p. 532.

452 William Carpenter, "The United States and the League of Neutrals of 1780" *American Journal of International Law* 15, no. 4 (July 1921), pp. 515–516.

453 See a letter to Charles Dumas (April 23, 1780): "[T]here being Yet no treaty between Holland and America to that purpose, I apprehend that the Goods being declared by the Captain to be English, a neutral ship will not protect them the Law of Nations governing in this Case, as it did before the Treaty above mentioned." See also quoted in Stourzh, *Benjamin Franklin and American Foreign Policy*, p. 228.

454 Franklin indicated that, until "a Treaty was enter'd into [which stipulated that "free Ships should make free Goods," the old Law of Nations took Place, by which the Property of an Enemy was deem'd good Prize wherever found." Franklin to Vergennes (June 18, 1780), in *The Papers of Benjamin Franklin*, Vol. 32, p. 552.

455 *Journals of the Continental Congress*, Vol. XVIII, p. 865.

456 *Miller v. The Ship Resolution* 2 U.S. (2 Dallas) 1, 1781.

457 Franklin to John Torris (May 30, 1780), in *The Papers of Benjamin Franklin*, Vol. 32, p. 443. But see also his letter to Samuel Huntington (May 31, 1780): "[W]hatever may formerly have been the Law of Nations, all the Neutral Powers at the Instance of Russia, seem at

What is more, Franklin also had good hope that the United States would follow suit, given that

> it is likely to become henceforth the Law of Nations, that *free Ships make free Goods.* England does not like this Confederacy. I wish they would extend it still farther, and ordain that unarm'd Trading Ships, as well as Fishermen and Farmers, should be respected, as working for the common Benefit of Mankind, and never be interrupted in their Operations even by national Enemies: but let those only fight with one another whose Trade it is, and who are armed and paid for the Purpose.[458]

Ultimately, however, the United States never became a member. While the United States continued to respect the League's principles, its rationale for joining disappeared once the peace treaty was signed in 1783. In steering a true neutral course, Hamilton and Madison now thought that, in the words of the latter, it would be "unwise to become a party to a confederacy which might thereafter complicate the interests of the United States with the politics of Europe."[459] This view was reflected in a resolution[460] adopted by Congress on

---

present disposed to change it, and to inforce the Rule that *free Ships shall make free Goods,* except in the Case of Contraband. Denmark, Sweden and Holland have already acceded to the Proposition, and Portugal is expected to follow. France and Spain in the Ansrs. have also expressed their Approbation of it. I have therefore instructed our Privateers to bring in no more neutral Ships, as such Prizes occasion much Litigation, and create ill Blood." In ibid., Vol. 32, p. 448.

458 Franklin to Robert Morris (June 3, 1780), in *The Papers of Benjamin Franklin*, Vol. 32, p. 466. In a letter a few days earlier, Franklin wrote that "But it is a critical time with respect to such cases, for whatever may formerly have been the law of nations, all the neutral powers, at the instance of Russia, seem at present disposed to change it, and to enforce the rule that free ships shall make free goods, except in the case of contraband. Denmark, Sweden, and Holland have already acceded to the proposition, and Portugal is expected to follow. France and Spain, in their answers, have also expressed their approbation of it." See Franklin to the President of Congress (May 31, 1780), in *The Revolutionary Diplomatic Correspondence*, Vol. 3, p. 745.

459 "Proceedings of Congress as to Russian Mission" (May 21, 1783), in *The Revolutionary Diplomatic Correspondence of the United States*, Vol. 6, p. 438. See also discussed in Theodore Lyman, *The Diplomacy of the United States* (Boston, MA: Wells and Lilly, 1828), pp. 357–358.

460 The resolution declared that "the true interest of the States requires that they should be as little as possible entangled in the politics and controversies of European nations (…)." See "Report of a Committee to Congress" (June 12, 1783), in *The Revolutionary Diplomatic Correspondence*, Vol. 6, p. 482.

June 12 and vindicated soon thereafter when the Armed Neutrals "abandoned (…) the creed which they had sought to enforce by arms [when they became belligerents]."[461] Franklin himself saw the League as a good instrument for the promotion of peace, though he did not seem to believe in a peacetime alliance. In other words, anything approximating collective security could only be brought about through a uniting of states against a common enemy, rather than that states decided to organise for the sake of the preservation of future peace out of their own volition.[462]

The failure of the League and America's non-participation did not dent Franklin's hopes for the future. In a 1782 letter, he demonstrated a strong faith in the ability of the law of nations to become more humane by degrees:

> I go with you as far as you go, in Proposals for diminishing the Occasions & Mischiefs of War, & perhaps a little farther.—By the Original Law of Nations, War & Extirpation was the Punishment of Injury. Humanizing by degrees, it admitted Slavery instead of Death. A farther Step was, the Exchange of Prisoners instead of Slavery. Another, to respect more the property of private Persons under Conquest, & to be content with acquir'd Dominion. Why should not this Law of Nations go on improving? Ages have interven'd between its several Steps; but as Knowledge of late encreases rapidly, why should not those Steps be quicken'd?[463]

In listing concrete ways in which this could be achieved, he suggested that in wartime farmers and fishermen, merchants and artists should receive protection. At the same time, he also argued that "Hospitals of Enemies should be unmolested."[464] Franklin had hoped to include provisions to protect these categories of people in the peace treaty with the British, including an article which would prohibit the capture of merchant ships and their cargo by warships:[465]

> If War should hereafter arise between Great Britain and the United States, which God forbid, the Merchants of either Country, then residing in the

461 Carpenter, "The United States and the League of Neutrals of 1780," p. 522.

462 Stourzh, *Benjamin Franklin and American Foreign Policy*, p. 224.

463 Franklin to Benjamin Vaughan (July 10, 1782), in *The Papers of Benjamin Franklin*, Vol. 37, pp. 608–610. Incidentally, the need for adequate treatment of prisoners of war had been acknowledged in the case *Respublica v. Chapman* 1 U.S. (Dall.) 53 (Pa. 1781), at 59.

464 Franklin to Benjamin Vaughan (July 10, 1782), in *The Papers of Benjamin Franklin*, Vol. 37, pp. 608–610.

465 Nys, *Les États-Unis et le Droit des Gens*, p. 71.

> other, shall be allowed to remain 9 Months to collect their Debts and settle their Affairs, and may depart freely carrying of all their Effects without Molestation, or Hindrance. And all Fishermen, all Cultivators of the Earth, and all Artizans, or Manufacturers unarmed and inhabiting unfortified Towns, Villages or Places, who labour for the common Subsistence and Benefit of Mankind, and peaceably follow their respective Employments, shall be allowed to continue the same, and shall not be molested by the Armed Force of the Enemy, in whose power by the Events of War, they may happen to fall; but if any thing is necessary to be taken from them for the use of such Armed Force, the same shall be paid for at a reasonable price. And all Merchants, or Traders with their unarmed Vessels employed in Commerce, exchanging the Products of different places and thereby rendering the Necessaries, Conveniences and Comforts of human Life more easy to obtain and more general, shall be allowed to pass freely unmolested. And neither of the Powers, Parties to this Treaty shall grant, or issue any Commission to any private armed Vessel, empowering them to take or destroy such trading Ships, or interrupt such Commerce.[466]

What is more, he also made a hardly veiled plea to end privateering: "The practice of robbing Merchants on the High Seas, a remnant of the ancient Piracy, tho't it may be accidentally beneficial to particular Persons, is far from being profitable to all engaged in it, or to the Nation that Authorizes it. (…) A just Punishment [would be appropriate for] their having wantonly and unfeelingly ruined many honest innocent Traders and their Families, whose Subsistence was employed in serving the common Interests of Mankind."[467] It is interesting to note on this point that in the early days of the Revolution, American ships had actually engaged in seizing neutral ships, as well as enemy ships within sight of neutral shorelines. The practice had even been sanctioned by Congress in April 1776.[468] When this led to various breaches of the law of nations and letters requesting American vessels to respect the law had no tangible effect,[469] a proclamation was issued in May 1778 calling upon armed

---

466 Franklin, "Observations on War Privateering" (unpublished, January 14, 1781), in *The Papers of Benjamin Franklin*, Vol. 38, p. 607.

467 Franklin, "Observations on War Privateering" (unpublished, January 14, 1781), in ibid., p. 607.

468 See *Journals of the Continental Congress*, Vol. 4, p. 253.

469 "Franklin, Deane and Lee to Captains of American Armed Vessels" (November 21, 1777) and "Arthur Lee to the Committee on Foreign Affairs" (November 27, 1777), in *The Revolutionary Diplomatic Correspondence*, Vol. 2, p. 425, 431.

American vessels to desist from capturing neutral ships or to capture enemy ships within neutral water, and therewith to pay "a sacred regard to the rights of neutral powers and the usage and custom of civilized nations."[470]

The decisive battle of the Revolutionary war came in October, 1781, when a Franco-American army led by general Washington defeated the British under Lord Cornwallis at Yorktown. French assistance had made a vital difference on the battlefield. The French had been generous with the new United States because they hoped to win the sympathy of neutral powers on the continent so as to prevent an extension of the war onto the European mainland.[471] But France's generosity was not repaid in kind by the Americans. To their credit, the Americans never seriously entertained British proposals to come to a reconciliation with their former colonies. For instance, the British proposed a plan in 1780 consisting of a series of treaties to be concluded between Great Britain, the United States and Ireland, which they rebuffed.[472] But at the same time, whilst "betraying in spirit if not in letter, the alliance with France,"[473] they continued peace negotiations with the British without keeping the French informed. The reason for this lay in suspicions some Americans had about the larger French objectives in connection to the alliance.[474] So when the preliminary articles of the treaty of peace with Britain were signed on November 30, 1782, and the definitive treaty on September 3, 1783,[475] Vergennes felt offended as a result of having been kept in the dark on these developments. But he was not in the position to punish the Americans by downgrading or breaking relations with them. Because of their insistence on the French ties, the Americans were able to obtain very generous peace terms from the British, who had hoped therewith to create a wedge between the United States and France—to no avail however.[476] Irony had it that in the year before the conclusion of the

470 "A Proclamation" (May 9, 1778), in *Journals of the Continental Congress*, Vol. XI, p. 486.

471 Bemis, *The Diplomacy of the American Revolution*, p. 65.

472 Together they were to form an empire with a common defense policy, with a "representative of the crown" to function more like an ambassador than like a governor. See discussed in Adams, *Political Ideas of the American Revolution*, pp. 59–60.

473 Bradford Perkins, *Cambridge History of American Foreign Relations*, Vol. 1, p. 44.

474 Deconde, *Entangling Alliance*, p. 9.

475 Contrary to diplomatic practice at the time, the British negotiator, David Hartley, was instructed to sign both copies of the document first, while normally each party has the right to sign its own copy first. This amounted to "a supreme symbol of American inferiority." See Kaplan, *Colonies into Nation*, p. 188.

476 At the same time, however, John Jay contemplated to break off relations with France in exchange for a generous peace treaty with the British. See Hendrickson, *Peace Pact*, pp. 195–196.

peace treaty, Britain had a very pro-American government, led by the Earl of Shelburne. While conceding the inevitability of American independence, Shelburne—a patron of political economist Adam Smith—would have liked to conclude a commercial treaty with the Americans, also as a means to restoring good mutual relations. But understandably, the political climate which prevailed at the time in Britain made this course an impossible one to pursue. Notwithstanding the failure to conclude this treaty, early American diplomacy could consider the 1783 treaty with Britain a great success:[477] "With all its shortcomings the treaty with Great Britain represented a magnificent piece of statecraft whereby a weak republic acquired independence and an empire of its own."[478] Hamilton saw the peace of 1783 as an opportunity to renounce the French treaties so as "to prevent our being a ball in the hands of European powers, bandied against each other at their pleasure."[479] But America's position in the balance-of-power had enabled it in the end to promote its international law agenda as well, most conspicuously with respect to France. As DeConde concluded, "[a]s it was, and as it was to be again and again in American history, the American nation at its birth profited from the complications of European diplomacy."[480]

Still, the arrival of peace did not herald an age of disinterested detachment from world affairs, far from it. Instead, the following years would demonstrate that "the American Revolution, originally an internal Anglo-American controversy which had degenerated into a limited war, gradually became merely a phase in a war of international scope."[481] But even if the revolution looked more like a sideshow as seen from the European side of the Atlantic, which would soon see itself be convulsed by the French revolutionary and subsequently Napoleonic wars, for the United States it was the beginning of what John Quincy Adams in his commencement address at Harvard in 1787 called the "critical period," the roughly three decades after independence when the new nation had to prove its strength and integrity, being pulled at both from

477 Interestingly, Benjamin Franklin advocated the idea of a "Family compact between England, France and the United States," in order for the latter to be able to "unit[e] in perpetual peace her father and her husband." See Franklin to David Hartley (October 16, 1783), quoted in Gerald Stourzh, *Benjamin Franklin and American Foreign Policy* (Chicago: University of Chicago Press, 1954), p. 218.

478 Kaplan, *Colonies into Nation*, p. 142.

479 Hamilton to Washington (March 24, 1783), in *The Works of Alexander Hamilton*, Vol. 9, p. 327.

480 Deconde, *Entangling Alliance*, p. 10.

481 Henry Blumenthal, *France and the United States, Their Diplomatic Relations, 1789–1914* (Chapel Hill: The University of North Carolina Press, 1970), p. 6.

from the inside as well as the outside. The young nation showed much promise, which was also evident to overseas observers. As the Spanish ambassador to France, Conde de Aranda noted: “This federal republic is born a pigmy. A day will come when it will be a giant, even a colossus, formidable in these countries. (…) In a few more years we shall watch with grief the tyrannical existence of this same colossus.”[482]

3.2 Foreign Relations under the Articles of Confederation

The ultimate failure of the Articles of Confederation was due to certain defects inherent in the Articles themselves. But the treaty obligations the United States assumed helped to expose them for all to see. With no other treaty did this become more apparent than with the Treaty of Paris of 1783. If the ability of honor treaty obligations is the test of a constitution, then the struggle of the Confederation in upholding its part of the bargain with Britain is emblematic for the period between 1781 and 1787. By insisting on its rights under the treaty, Britain helped to expose the flaws and weaknesses of the new nation’s constitutional construct as well as its still fledgling sense of nationhood. It was a set of challenges the government in Philadelphia was forced to address, and which it did quite successfully, given the circumstances. Ironically, the ‘price’ it had to pay was the need to craft a new constitution, one which would ensure that the country would act in unison in its external affairs, and which unequivocally established the country as a single entity under international law.

Seven years after the Declaration of Independence, and two years into the new Confederation—which had entered into force in 1781 after the final ratification by Maryland—the sense of individual statehood had by no means been extinguished yet. As Varg noted, “[a] nationalistic spirit (…) underla[id] the struggle among local sovereignties.”[483] And despite the generosity displayed by the British with respect to the terms of peace, various states failed to live up to their obligations under its provisions. The most problematic proved to be article VI, which stipulated that “Congress shall earnestly recommend it to the legislatures of the respective states to provide for the restitution of all estates, rights, and properties, which have been confiscated belonging to real British subjects.” In addition, it was agreed that “all persons who have any interest in

---

482 Quoted in Kaplan, *Colonies into Nation*, p. 168.

483 Paul Varg, *Foreign Policies of the Founding Fathers*, p. 51.

confiscated lands, either by debts, marriage settlements, or otherwise, shall meet with no lawful impediment in the prosecution of their just rights." Behind this was the fact that many states wanted to have loyalists expelled from their jurisdictions. This was for instance the case in New York State, where the state assembly attempted to expropriate and confiscate land held by Loyalists, and to prosecute them, to the point of declaring them aliens. Alexander Hamilton considered such measures to be in violation of articles V and VI of the 1783 Treaty. In his *Phocion* letters, he pointed out that such behaviour could have serious consequences: "Breach of treaty on our part will be a just ground for breaking it on theirs. The treaty must stand or fall together. The wilful breach of a single article annuls the whole."[484] Madison shared Hamilton's assessment: "If we consider the federal Union as analogous not to the Social compacts among individual men, but to the conventions among individual States, What is the doctrine resulting from these conventions? Clearly, according to the Expositors of the law of Nations, that a breach of any one article by any one party, leaves all the other parties at liberty, to consider the whole convention as dissolved, unless they choose rather to compel the delinquent party to repair the breach."[485] What is more, this attitude on the part of the states seriously affected the ability of the country as a whole to engage in bilateral relations. As Hamilton would later write in *Federalist* paper no XXII:

> No nation acquainted with the nature of our political association would be unwise enough to enter into stipulations with the United States, by which they conceded privileges of any importance to them, while they were apprised that the engagements on the part of the Union might at any moment be violated by its members.[486]

Similar concerns were shared in 1786 by Hamilton's New York counterpart, John Jay, who stressed that the credibility and ability of a country to engage in relations with other countries depended on faithful adherence to the law of nations. To ensure uniform applicability, it was intolerable that individual states engage in breaches of treaties concluded by the federal authorities:

---

484 Alexander Hamilton, "To the Considerate Citizens of New York, on the Politics of the Times, in Consequence of the Peace" (1784), in *The Works of Alexander Hamilton*, Vol. 4, p. 242. See also discussed in Tara Helfman, "The Law of Nations in *The Federalist Papers*," pp. 113–115.

485 "Journal of the Constitutional Convention of 1787" (June 19th, 1787) in *The Writings of James Madison*, Vol. 3, p. 210.

486 Alexander Hamilton, *Federalist Papers* no. XXII, p. 177.

> The rights to make war, to make peace, and to make treaties, appertaining *exclusively* to the national sovereign, that is, to Congress, your secretary is of opinion that the thirteen state legislatures have no more authority to exercise the powers, or pass acts of sovereignty on those points, than any thirteen individual citizens. To execute the laws, or exercise the rights of war against a national enemy, belongs only to the national sovereign, or to those to whom the national sovereign may constitutionally delegate such authority. So that whatever right each state, individually considered, may have to sequester or confiscate the property of their own proper citizens, yet with respect to the common enemy of the nation, they can separately do no act of national sovereignty.[487]

In a report to Congress, Jay gave an extensive assessment of the deficiencies of American practice in regards to the 1783 treaty:

> We have deliberately and dispassionately examined and considered the several facts and matters urged by Britain as infractions of the treaty of peace, on the part of America; and we regret that, in some of the states, too little attention appears to have been paid to the publick faith pledged by that treaty. Not only the obvious dictates of religion, morality and national honour, but also the first principles of good policy, demand a candid and punctual compliance with engagements constitutionally and fairly made. Our national constitution having committed to us the management of the national concerns with foreign states and powers, it is our duty to take care that all the rights which they ought to enjoy within our jurisdiction, by the laws of nations and the faith of treaties, remain inviolate. (…) When therefore a treaty is constitutionally made, ratified and published by us, it immediately becomes binding on the whole nation, and superadded to the laws of the land, without the intervention of state legislatures. (…) Hence it is clear, that treaties must be implicitly received and observed by every member of the nation; for as state legislatures are not competent to the making of such compacts or treaties, so neither are they competent, in that capacity, authoritatively to decide on or ascertain the construction and sense of them.

487 "Report of Secretary Jay on Mr. Adams' letter of 4th March 1786," in *The Diplomatic Correspondence of the United States* (United States Dept. of State, Washington DC: Blair & Rives, 1837), Vol. 5, p. 29.

What is more, Jay believed that interpretation of a treaty should be left to appropriate courts, and not in the hands of legislatures:

> In cases between individuals all doubts respecting the meaning of a treaty, like all doubts respecting the meaning of a law, are in the first instance mere judicial questions; and are to be heard and decided in the courts of justice having cognizance of the causes in which they arise, and whose duty it is to determine them according to the rules and maxims established by the laws of nations for the interpretation of treaties. From these principles it follows of necessary consequence, that no individual state has a right, by legislative acts, to decide and point out the sense in which their particular citizens and courts shall understand this or that article of a treaty. It is evident that a contrary doctrine would (...) prove no less inconvenient in practice than it is irrational in theory; for in that case, the same article of the same treaty might by law be made to mean one thing in New Hampshire, another thing in New York, and neither the one nor the other of them in Georgia.

In order to resolve this situation, Jay proposed for Congress to adopt a resolution which would declare "that such of the acts or parts of acts of the legislature of this state as are repugnant to the treaty of peace between the United States and his Britannick majesty, or any article thereof, shall be and hereby are repealed."[488] Hence, it was apparent to all that honoring its legal obligations was among the paramount interests of the country. John Adams expressed a consensus view when he said that "[i]f we establish the principle, that we have a right to depart from the treaty in one article, because they have departed from it in another, they will certainly avail themselves of the same principle, and probably extend it as much farther." He added that escalation was possible because "their sense of justice is less, and their opinion of their own power, however ill-founded, is greater."[489] Jay put it a little more bluntly: "it would be in the power of a particular State, by injuries and infractions of treaties, to involve the whole Confederacy in difficulties and War."[490]

---

488 *Secret Journals of the Acts and Proceedings of Congress* (Boston: Thomas Wait, 1821), Vol. 4, pp. 330–337.

489 John Adams to John Jay (April 24, 1785), in *The Works of John Adams*, Vol. 8, p. 237.

490 John Jay, "Report to Congress" (October 13, 1786), in *Journals of the Continental Congress*, Vol. 31, p. 869. See also discussed in Mark Janis, *America and the Law of Nations 1776–1939* (Oxford: Oxford University Press, 2010), p. 34.

The states' refusal to abide by agreements concluded at the federal level and to cooperate with the central government made it impossible for the latter to raise enough revenues to service American debts to the English. In response, they refused to vacate forts held along the northern border, which remained occupied until well into the early 1790s. Moreover, the failure by the United States to repay its debts gave the creditor even "a just cause for armed intervention" under prevailing international law.[491] What is more, the lack of financial means hampered efforts to raise a military force to protect the western borders of Ohio, where Indian tribes were straddling into American territory.[492] The situation was indeed so dire that the Confederation was threatened with being torn apart through secessions. Not only did western and eastern interests clash, a north–south rift also appeared more likely. Silas Deane, a former Connecticut delegate to the Continental Congress and the nation's first diplomat as envoy to France, sensed that the idea was gaining ground that the union was only a result of contingency and convenience for the purpose of prosecuting the war, and that it could soon dissolve absent a common purpose: "That union which subsisted between the several States during the war, but especially that between the Northern and Southern states, was in too great degree an union from the necessity of time, from the war existing in the country. (…) Hence men of observation and of cool reflection in America (…) wish to see the whole of them divided into two new confederations, the Northern and the Southern."[493]

The same issues were at stake with respect to Indian tribes living in the border areas. While Congress was in charge of commerce with the Indian tribes, the states retained effective control within their territories. Thus, "[i]n practice any state could render meaningless the authority of the Articles by imposing its own laws on Indians within the state's jurisdiction. Congress therefore was no more able to make meaningful agreements with Indians than it could with the British (…) even though Indian problems were intimately linked to foreign relations (…)."[494] In order to upend ambiguity about the status of treaties with Indian tribes and who could conclude them,[495] from the 1770s to the 1790s, both the Continental Congress and the government considered agreements

---

491 Frederick Marks, *Independence on Trial: Foreign Affairs and the Making of the Constitution* (Wilmington, DE: Scholarly Resources, 1986), p. 45.

492 Rakove, "Confederation and Constitution," in Michael Grossberg and Christopher Tomlins, The Cambridge History of Law in America (1580–1815) (New York: Cambridge University Press, 2008) p. 495.

493 Silas Deane to Caron de Beaumarchais (April 2, 1784), in *The Deane Papers*, Vol. 5, p. 287.

494 Kaplan, *Colonies into Nation*, p. 166.

495 This related to the fact that rather than an agreement between two sovereign entities, treaties could also be understood as mere 'contracts' or 'acts of negotiation.' See discussed in James Lengel, "The Role of International Law in the Development of Constitutional

with Indian tribes as treaties governed by the law of nations, on the basis of equality.[496] Indeed, the ones sent by Washington to the Senate in 1789 constituted "the first treaties ever submitted [which] were drawn up in regular treaty form and were acted upon in the same manner as other treaties."[497] But in spite of the agreements, not even Indian tribes were always prepared to remain within the new union. The Iroquois for instance, who had been loyal to the British, attempted to flee across the border north into Canada. So in various respects, centrifugal forces were palpably present. As Marks concluded: "the leaders of the frontier were looking to the future, and the future appeared not to lie with the United States."[498]

One of these frontiers was the Mississippi. It had become so as a result of the 1783 peace treaty, which had effectively doubled the territory of the United States following the cession by Great Britain of all the land between the Proclamation line of 1763—which settled the borders between the colonies and Indian lands—and the Mississippi river.[499] It was the main barrier on the way to westward expansion which would take some twenty years for the United States to cross. Indeed, access to the Mississippi had existential value, giving rise to the claim that "by the law of nations, the United States, holding the upper portion of the river, and possessing a territory of such immense extent, had a right to the navigation of the river, as an outlet created by Providence itself."[500]

Jurisprudence in the Supreme Court: The Marshall Court and American Indians," *The American Journal of Legal History* 43, no. 2 (1999), pp. 122–123.

496 Hermes, "The Law of Native Americans, to 1815," p. 52. For instance, treaties were concluded with the Delawares (1778); the Chickasaw (1782); the Six Nations (1784); the Wyandot and Cherokee (1785); the Chocktaw, Chickasaw and Shawnee (1786) and again with the Wyandot and Six Nations in 1789.

497 George G. Wilson, "International Law and the Constitution" *Boston University Law Review* 13 (1933), p. 251.

498 Frederick Marks, *Independence on Trial*, p. 36.

499 The natives were however not permitted to exercise their rights to this land. On the basis of rights deriving from conquest coupled with security imperatives, the Americans argued that they now possessed valid title to all land between the east coast and the Mississippi. See Stourzh, *Benjamin Franklin and American Foreign Policy*, p. 221. A right which, incidentally, Spain rejected. See Katherine Hermes, "The Law of Native Americans, to 1815," in Michael Grossberg and Christopher Tomlins, *The Cambridge History of Law in America (1580–1815)* (New York: Cambridge University Press, 2008), pp. 54–55.

500 See William H. Trescot, *The Diplomatic History of the Administrations of Washington and Adams, 1789–1801.* (Boston: Little, Brown and Co, 1857), p. 228. Indeed, the North Carolina delegation in Congress sponsored a motion which "[r]esolved that the United States have a clear, absolute and unalienable Claim to the free Navigation of the River Mississippi, which Claim is not only supported by the express Stipulations of Treaties, but by the great Law of Nature." See *Journals of the Continental Congress*, Vol. 34, p. 493.

What is more, the 1783 peace treaty had stipulated that navigation of the Mississippi would remain open in perpetuity for both Great Britain and the United States, in spite of the fact that the mouth of the river was in Spanish hands.[501] Spain was however not party to the decisions taken in Paris, and was by no means prepared to acquiesce in an agreement it had had no part in.

The problems for the United States started with the fact that Britain had signed a separate peace treaty with the Iberian kingdom in which it ceded the Floridas to Spain whilst leaving its boundaries indeterminate. As a result, "[t]he new expanded boundaries of the United States, from the Mississippi to the Atlantic, from the Great Lakes to Florida, were all subject to differing interpretations by the affected parties."[502] The United States came to share its entire western and southern borders with Spain. For all of the War of Independence, Spain had proved to be a reluctant ally, only being nominally on the side of the Americans by virtue of a family pact between the Bourbon kings, Louis XVI and Charles III. In 1779, Vergennes had tried to bring Spain into the 1778 agreement with the United States,[503] but foreign minister Floridablanca had rejected the French invitation. Still, Spain did join the war against Britain in 1779, albeit while withholding recognition. The Spanish ambassador in Paris, Conde de Aranda, was in fact very eager for a conflict with Great Britain, believing that an independent United States posed a lesser danger to Spanish possessions than a united British Empire would.[504] But when Spain and the United States found each other on opposite sides of the Mississippi after the war for independence, the Americans sought an agreement that would ensure their right to navigate the river down to its mouth, upon which "Spain's capricious fingers rested."[505] Up to the days of the revolution, Spain—being in possession of

---

501 What is more, adds Kaplan, both countries had also agreed on a secret article according to which the boundary between the United States and Florida be drawn at the Yazoo river, but that if Britain would return Florida to Spain, the border would be drawn much further south, along the 31st parallel. See *Colonies into Nation*, p. 167.

502 Kaplan, *Colonies into Nation*, p. 148.

503 This was by virtue of article X, which invited other countries to join the alliance, and which was primarily aimed at Spain.

504 Bemis, *The Diplomacy of the American Revolution*, p. 42.

505 Reginald Stuart, *United States Expansionism and British North America, 1775–1871* (Chapel Hill and London: The University of North Carolina Press, 1988), p. 3. In a secret treaty agreed on November 3, 1762, concluded between France and Spain, the former agreed to cede New Orleans and Louisiana to the court at Madrid as a way to compensate for Spain's cession of the Floridas to Britain, which was agreed upon in a treaty that same day. See Nys, *Les États-Unis et le Droit des Gens*, p. 104.

Louisiana—had to allow British ships to navigate the Mississippi.[506] During the war, it became Spain's objective to prevent the United States from getting a foothold on the river, with support from France.[507] As Bemis summarized the issue: "Spain was consistently opposed to any approach to the settlements of territory of the United States to the Mississippi, and the efforts of Spanish diplomacy (…) were directed toward keeping the United States away from the river."[508] Thus, when in 1781 John Jay communicated to Floridablanca a decision by Congress to recognize Spain's rights to navigation on the Mississippi below the 31st parallel in exchange for an agreement of alliance, the latter rejected the offer, which was then swiftly withdrawn by Jay.[509] To demonstrate its resolve, Spain decided in 1784 to prohibit free navigation by American ships on the Mississippi altogether.[510]

When Don Diego de Gardoqui, the new Spanish envoy, arrived in the United States in 1785 to negotiate a trade treaty with the Americans, he was not to concede them a right to free navigation of the Mississippi. In return for an agreement, Gardoqui asked his interlocutor, John Jay, that the Americans renounce any claims to navigation of the Mississippi for thirty years.[511] Spain felt to be in a strong enough position to ignore American demands based on the 1783 and '63 treaties. Nevertheless, Jay was in fact open to such a concession, believing that in time, the United States would obtain its rights to the Mississippi anyway, and because the agreement would have provided for a full-blown treaty of commerce and *alliance*, including a mutual guarantee of each other's territory in North America.[512] However, when he requested Congress to

---

506 As a result of the Treaty of Paris of 1763, whose article vii provisioned that "it is agreed, that (…) the navigation of the river Mississippi shall be equally free, as well to the subjects of Great Britain as to those of France, in its whole breadth and length, from its source to the sea, and expressly that part which is between the said island of New Orleans and the right bank of that river, as well as the passage both in and out of its mouth."

507 In September 1782, the senior clerk at the French Foreign Ministry, Joseph-Mathias Gérard de Rayneval, sent a memorandum on the issue to Secretary of Foreign Affairs John Jay. In it, he declared that "[a]s to the course and navigation of the Mississippi, they follow with the property, and they will belong, therefore, to the nation to which the two banks belong [i.e. Spain, and possibly England]." Thus, "the United States of America can have no pretensions to it, not being masters of either border of this river." See Rayneval to Jay (September 6, 1782), in *Revolutionary Diplomatic Correspondence*, Vol. 6, p. 27.

508 Bemis, *The Diplomacy of the American Revolution*, p. 95.

509 Kaplan, *Colonies into Nation*, p. 136.

510 Kaplan, *Colonies into Nation*, p. 167.

511 Horsman, *The Diplomacy of the New Republic, 1776–1815*, p. 35. See also discussed in Kaplan, *Colonies into Nation*, pp. 170–172.

512 Samuel F. Bemis "John Jay," in Samuel F. Bemis (ed.), *The American Secretaries of States and their Diplomacy* (New York: Albert A. Knopf, 1927), Vol. 1, pp. 242–243.

change his instructions accordingly, an uproar ensued. Because of strong opposition in Congress, and because of the impending Constitutional Convention in 1787, the draft treaty was never even submitted. On this episode, Madison admitted later that while he understood the logic of Jay's position, he did not agree with it.[513]

This episode only served to underline the weakness of the United States when negotiating in peacetime one-on-one with a European power, even a secondary power like Spain. In terms of future expansion, however, the young republic found that "no European power posed a greater threat (…) or cast in sharper relief its post-independence vulnerability to foreign powers than Spain."[514] Most certainly, for as long as European powers possessed footholds on the American continent, the United States would inevitably remain entangled in European affairs. In this environment, the ability of the United States to conclude any kind of agreement was seriously impaired, and "prevented American diplomats from negotiating the commercial treaties that would constitute a more civilized system of alliances."[515] For while in 1783, prime minister Lord Shelburne had expressed interest in getting a commercial treaty with the United States,[516] the new Pitt government took a much tougher line, trying to exclude the United States from the profitable trade with the British West Indies, and issued a number of Orders in Council to that end. Parliament dared to be so bold because the United States was very weak politically and economically. As the Earl of Sheffield, a member of the House of Commons, dismissively noted: "We might as reasonably dread the effects of combinations among the German as among the American states, [because like the Germanies] no treaty can be made with the American states that can be binding on the whole

513 James Madison, "Speech in the Virginia Assembly" (June 13, 1788), in *The Writings of James Madison*, Vol. 5, pp. 181–182.

514 Eliga Gould, "Entangled Histories, Entangled Worlds: The English-Speaking Atlantic as a Spanish Periphery" *The American Historical Review* 112, no. 3 (2007), pp. 780–781.

515 Peter Onuf and Nicholas Onuf, *Federal Union, Modern World: The Law of Nations in an Age of Revolutions 1776–1814* (Madison, WI: Madison House, 1992), p. 94.

516 Kaplan, *Colonies into Nation*, p. 158. David Hartley even "went so far as to recommend a common citizenship for the two peoples." Ibid. During the negotiations, Jay, fearing a possible separate agreement between Britain and France, offered to Shelburne that the Americans abrogate the treaty of alliance with France. Jonathan Dull, *A Diplomatic History of the American Revolution* (New Haven and London: Yale University Press, 1985), p. 148. This effort was incidentally thwarted as a result of French interference, which led to the dissolution of the negotiation committee. I am indebted to Gregg Lint for this point.

of them."[517] Besides this, the British felt they did not really need a trade agreement with the United States; they expected commercial relations between the United States and the United Kingdom inevitably to resume in any event.

Notwithstanding the grave difficulties, Congress adopted a resolution in 1784 calling on ministers resident in Europe to commence negotiations on treaties of commerce with a very liberal import. In the subsequent instructions, they were asked to work towards concluding treaties in the spirit of the 1776 Plan of Treaties, whose central objective was, after all, "to keep America out of European struggles and to secure for her peace and freedom by making all European powers interested partners in American trade."[518] As John Adams said pithily: "the business of America with Europe was commerce, not politics or war."[519] In fact, Americans believed that "access to American markets [would be in] itself sufficient inducement for the European powers to support the American cause."[520] But while the American approach to foreign relations must have seemed quite naïve in the eyes of the heads of European chancelleries,[521] the United States would prove to be remarkably successful in achieving commercial agreements with various European countries. In a number of them, the principle of 'free ships, free goods' was enshrined: with the Dutch Republic in 1782, Sweden in 1783, Prussia in 1785 and with Morocco in 1786. It led Jefferson to say in 1787 that because of American efforts and the influence of the Armed Neutrality principles, the notion of 'free ships, free goods' could "be considered now as the law of nations."[522] For the moment however, this proved to be a premature if not altogether chimerical assertion.

On the issue of contraband goods, the United States inaugurated a new policy with the ratification of the treaty with The Netherlands in 1783. Previously, it had simply accepted the law as it stood, but now, the United States decided to accept only a limited list of goods that constituted contraband, implying that any other goods fell outside of the list. Also, no definition was incorporated. This became a template for all subsequent treaties.[523] More

517 Quoted in Kaplan, *Colonies into Nation*, p. 161.

518 Felix Gilbert, *To the Farewell Address*, p. 55.

519 Adams to Robert Livingston (February 5, 1783), in *The Works of John Adams*, Vol. 8, p. 35.

520 Onuf and Onuf, *Federal Union, Modern World*, p. 106.

521 Gilbert Chinard, "Les Origines Historiques de la Doctrine de l'Isolement aux États-Unis" *Recueil des Cours* 59, no. 1, p. 264.

522 Jefferson to Burrill Carnes (September 22, 1787), in *The Writings of Thomas Jefferson*, Vol. 6, p. 318.

523 Lint, "Early American Conceptions of International Law," pp. 66–67. For instance, the treaty with Prussia stipulated in article 13 that in the event one of the contracting parties would be engaged in war, "no (…) articles [i.e. arms, ammunition & military stores of

in general, "by defending a strict construction of contraband and blockade [the United States] was promoting principles of international law that strengthened all maritime states, not exclusively the fledgling United States."[524]

The most remarkable treaty became that with Prussia, which included provisions guaranteeing freedom of worship and conscience (article XI); respecting of neutral rights of the other party in case of war (article XII); protection for "cultivators of the earth (…) whose occupations are for the common subsistence and benefit of mankind" (article XXIII) and most remarkably, basic protections for prisoners of war (article XXIV). Jefferson was very proud of this and similar treaties because he believed that they would lead to a "free intercommunication of happiness" between nations.[525] The handiwork of Franklin lay behind many of these provisions, which constitute a late monument to Enlightenment thinking.[526] Inspired by the principles of the Armed Neutrality league, these treaties appeared to herald a new era in international law. As James Duane noted: "Upon the strength of these notorious and universally interesting transactions, writers date the commencement of the modern laws of nations from the year 1780, in which they took place. Since that year, *twenty-eight* treaties have been ratified, containing and confirming the principles of the armed neutrality and to *three* of these England was a party." And, Duane added, even if Russia and the United States both concluded a treaty which negated the principles of the armed neutrality, "the principles and sentiments of both states remained unchanged, as the subsequent policy and conduct of both have gloriously established."[527]

The zeal to push liberal principles of international law also found expression in the area of fisheries, in particular with respect to fishing grounds off the

---

every kind] carried in the vessels, or by the subjects or citizens of one of the parties to the enemies of the other, shall be deemed contraband, so as to induce confiscation or condemnation and a loss of property to individuals." The single exception to this general rule was that vessels and goods could be temporarily held for the purpose of preventing undue damage to be suffered should it have proceeded, subject to "reasonable compensation." Ernest Nys notes that this idea had been developed by the Prussian state jurist Samuel Cocceji in the 1740s. See Nys, *Les États-Unis et le Droit des Gens*, p. 74.

524 Kaplan, *Colonies into Nation*, p. 94.

525 Quoted in Stephen Rosen, "Alexander Hamilton and the Domestic Uses of International Law," *Diplomatic History* 5, no. 3 (1981), pp. 184–185.

526 See, for a detailed discussion of Franklin's contribution to humanizing warfare, John Fabian Witt, *Lincoln's Code: The Laws of War in American History* (New York: The Free Press, 2012), pp. 43–47.

527 Duane, *The Law of Nations, Investigated in a Popular Manner*, pp. 24–25 (emphasis in original).

coast of Newfoundland. In a letter written to Franklin, Robert Livingston set out the basis for American rights to fishing in that particular area. First of all, fishermen had enjoyed such rights at the time of the British Empire, and since "the oppressions of Great Britain forced us to a seperation (sic)," these rights cannot now be considered abridged. Secondly, Livingston sought a justification on the basis of international law. With implicit reference to Grotius and Locke, he argued that

> provided we do not come within such distance of the coasts of other powers as the law of Nations allows them to appropriate, is the right which Nature gives to all Mankind to use its common Benefits, so far as not to exclude others. The Sea cannot in its nature be appropriated. No Nation can put its mark upon it, Tho' attempts have sometimes been made to set up an Empire over it, they have been considered as unjust usurpations, and resisted as such in turn by every Maritime Nation in Europe.[528]

His position was backed up by Congress, which declared in 1782 that, while respecting Britain's maritime zone of three leagues measured from the shoreline, there existed "a common right of taking fish [that] cannot be denied to them without a manifest violation of the freedom of the seas, as established by the law of nations, and the dictates of reason; according to both which the use of the sea, except such parts thereof as lie in the vicinity of the shore, and are deemed appurtenant thereto, is common to all nations (…)."[529]

But American efforts in promoting principles of international law and commerce were not limited to European powers only. In search for new trade opportunities, the young country made a foray into the Mediterranean given that Britain had effectively shut the United States out of the West Indies, and had no access to the Mississippi.[530] At that time, however, the Mediterranean

---

528 Robert Livingston to Franklin (January 7, 1781), in *The Papers of Benjamin Franklin*, Vol. 36, p. 390. In fact, he added that "[t]his Subject is treated so much at large by Grotius and Vattel that I do not think it necessary to detail [further] Arguments (…)." Ibid.

529 *Secret Journals of the Acts and Proceedings of Congress* (Boston: Thomas Wait, 1821), Vol. 3, pp. 156–157.

530 Other early contacts were established with Canton, China in 1784–1785, and further trade missions were undertaken with Manila, Java (Batavia), India, the Arabian peninsula and the east coast of Africa, with consuls being appointed in Calcutta, Canton and Batavia up to 1807. See Samuel F. Bemis, *Diplomatic History of the United States* (New York: Henry Holt and Co., 1936), pp. 341–343. For the connection with China, see e.g. Teemu Ruskola, "Canton is not Boston: The Invention of American Imperial Sovereignty" *American*

was plagued by pirates emanating from the so-called Barbary states, the Ottoman vassal states along the southern rim of the sea. In order to negotiate an end to the seizing of American vessels, the United States assembled a committee consisting of Adams, Franklin and Jefferson to talk to the beys, or local leaders. But instead of arriving at a solution, the state of Algiers, feeling confident as a result of a recently concluded treaty with Spain, declared war on the United States.[531] In response, Jefferson called upon other European nations to join the United States in combating piracy in the Mediterranean through a league of nations, but his proposal fell on deaf ears.[532] Jefferson then took the opportunity to plead for the building of an American navy in order to solve the issue with military means if necessary; a proposal which was rejected by Jay due to lack of funds.[533] Jay's own proposal to impose tariffs or embargoes against countries that were on good terms with the Barbary pirates from Algiers also failed due to Congress' incapacity to enforce its will.[534] In the end, only the Moroccan sultan responded positively to the American overture, and a treaty was concluded with the Maghreb country in 1786, a landmark treaty with a non-Christian power which included a most-favored-nation clause as well as recognition for neutral rights.[535]

Quarterly 57, no. 3 (2005), pp. 859–884. Gordon Wood even notes that between 1795–1805, American trade with India exceeded that of all European countries with the subcontinent! See Gordon Wood, *Empire of Liberty: A History of the Early Republic, 1789–1815* (New York: Oxford University Press, 2009), p. 623.

531 Marks, *Independence on Trial*, p. 38.

532 Louis Sears, "Thomas Jefferson and the Law of Nations" *The American Political Science Review* 13, no. 3 (August 1919), pp. 392–393. In 1785, Richard Henry Lee inquired with the Marquis de Lafayette about French interest in combating piracy in the Mediterranean: "Will it not happen, during the reign of this glorious monarch, that those lawless pirates, upon the African coast of the Mediterranean, will be compelled, by some proper system, to respect the rights of men, and the laws of nations, instead of receiving annual stipends for not doing what it is really infamous to do? I mean roaming about to injure, oppress, and destroy, their unoffending fellow creatures. Among the many leagues that are formed, why may not one be made for the purpose of protecting the rights of humanity?" Richard Henry Lee to Marquis de Lafayette (October 30, 1785), in *Letters of Delegates to Congress*, Vol. 22, p. 713.

533 Don Higginbotham, "War and State Formation in Revolutionary America," in Eliga Gould and Peter Onuf (eds.), *Empire and Nation: The American Revolution in the Atlantic World* (Baltimore/London: The Johns Hopkins University Press, 2005), p. 66.

534 Ramsey, *The Constitution's Text in Foreign Affairs*, p. 43. Because amendment of the Articles required unanimity, no amendments were ever passed, and consequently, Congress never passed any measures imposing tariffs or imposts on foreign trade.

535 Marks, *Independence on Trial*, p. 40.

Still, all of this diplomatic activity could not conceal the fact that when it came to upholding the law of nations at home, the United States faced very serious problems. First of all, it took four years for the Articles of Confederation to enter into force. As a result, up to the final ratification, the authority of Congress could only be considered political, and not constitutional.[536] Until 1781, the Committee on Foreign Affairs created by the Second Continental Congress was responsible for foreign relations. But even when the Articles came in force, the states continued to claim jurisdictional powers in adjudicating the law of nations.[537] An example in case is the negotiations between Vergennes and Benjamin Franklin from 1782 to 1784 on a consular convention.[538] The initial draft emphasized the sovereignty of the separate states instead of that of the confederation as a whole with its reference to the "Thirteen States of North America."[539] It was one of the reasons why John Jay, Secretary of Foreign Affairs, recommended Congress not to ratify the convention. What is more, Jay was actually opposed to the conclusion of such treaties, and deemed that Franklin had overstepped his mandate.[540] In 1788–1789, the treaty was re-negotiated by Thomas Jefferson, and this time it would refer to the "United States of America."

In the early years of the Confederation, the government had sincerely tried to ensure adherence to and enforcement of international law. For instance, the American commissioners in Paris issued a letter to their captains and commanders "to warn and request [them] not to commit any Violation of the Laws of Nations." Instead, the commissioners implored them to

> confine yourselves to the capture of the Enemys Vessels when not within the protection of a neutral River, Fort or Coast, and of all others whatsoever that shall be carrying Soldiers, Arms, Ammunition, Provisions, or other contraband Goods, to any of the British Armies, or Ships employed

536 As Rakove explained, "the state legislatures were to act as administrative auxiliaries of Congress, while Congress itself was less a legislative body than a collective form of executive power (…)." See Jack Rakove, "Confederation and Constitution," in Michael Grossberg and Christopher Tomlins, *The Cambridge History of Law in America (1580–1815)* (New York: Cambridge University Press, 2008), p. 489.

537 Douglas Sylvester, "International Law as Sword or Shield?" p. 18.

538 Samuel F. Bemis, *A Diplomatic History of the United States* (New York: Henry Holt and Co., 1936), p. 83.

539 Deconde, *Entangling Alliance*, p. 22.

540 Deconde, *Entangling Alliance*, p. 24. For a full assessment of Jay's record under the Confederation, see John Kaminski, "Honor and Interest: John Jay's Diplomacy during the Confederation" *New York History* 83, no. 3 (2002), pp. 293–327.

> against the united States. In every other Case you will respect the rights of neutrality, from which you expect Protection, and treat all neutral Ships, with the utmost kindness and Friendship, for the honour of your Country and of yourselves.[541]

It led Benjamin Franklin to exclaim that "I do not wish to see a New Barbary rising in America, and our long extended Coast occupied by Piratical States."[542] Following the case *Ross v. Rittenhouse,*[543] in which the Pennsylvania state court ruled against the Continental Congress in a privateering case, Congress created a Court of Appeals for Prize Cases in May 1780—which, incidentally, did little to mitigate Congress' plight.[544] Further attempts by Congress to induce more respect for the law of nations included an Ordinance adopted in 1781 which declared that "[t]he rules of decision in the several courts shall be the resolutions and ordinances of the United States in Congress assembled, public treaties when declared to be so by an act of Congress, and the law of nations, according to the general usages of Europe. Public treaties shall have the preeminence in all trials."[545] In a case before the Federal appeals court, *Miller v. The Ship Resolution,* the judge suggested that the law of nations should prevail over domestic statutes: "[t]he municipal laws of a country cannot change the law of nations, so as to bind the subjects of another nation."[546] In his second *Phocion* letter, Alexander Hamilton also pleaded for strict adherence to international law: "having taken our station among nations and having claimed the benefit of the laws which regulate them, [we] must in our turn be bound by the same laws."[547]

In the state courts the difficulties of ensuring uniform application and enforcement were very apparent. For instance, in the 1784 case *Rutgers v. Waddington*—in which Hamilton established his reputation as a lawyer—judge

541 "The American Commissioners to Commanders of American Armed Vessels" (November 21, 1777), in *The Papers of Benjamin Franklin,* Vol. 25, p. 174.

542 Franklin to David Hartley (May 8, 1788), in *The Papers of Benjamin Franklin,* Vol. 39, p. 443.

543 2 U.S. (Dallas) 11, 1792.

544 See discussed in Sylvester, "International Law as Sword or Shield?" pp. 13–17 and discussing the similar *San Antonio* case, Henry Bourguignon, "Incorporation of the Law of Nations during the American Revolution—the Case of the San Antonio" *American Journal of International Law* 71, no. 2 (April 1977), pp. 270–295.

545 *Journals of the Continental Congress* (Dec. 4, 1781), Vol. 21, p. 1158.

546 *Miller v. The Ship Resolution* 2 U.S. (2 Dallas) 1, 1781.

547 Alexander Hamilton, "To the Considerate Citizens of New York, on the Politics of the Times, in Consequence of the Peace" (1784), in *The Works of Alexander Hamilton,* Vol. 4, p. 278.

James Duane held that while the legislature could not enact a law in derogation of the natural law of nations, it could do so in contradiction of the voluntary laws of nations, i.e. treaty law.[548] Another case in which the difficulties of enforcing the law of nations was a major issue was the *Longchamps* affair. This case concerned an physical attack on the French consul-general in Philadelphia, Francois Barbé-Marbois, in May of 1784 by a French resident in the same city, Charles de Longchamps. The judge in the case, Thomas M'Kean, invoking Lord Mansfield, quoted him almost verbatim on the applicability of the law of nations: "[t]his law, in its full extent, is part of the law of this State, and is to be collected from the practice of different Nations, and the authority of writers."[549] However, even if the case concerned a foreign official, there were doubts in some corners about the applicability of the law of nations: "Longchamps has been convicted of the notable infraction &c but no sentence had been passed when he left Philadelphia", Francis Dana said, adding that "[i]t seems their judges, bar and all agreed in opinion, that the Laws of Nations applicable to the subject are to be considered as the Law of the Land. Of this I yet have my doubts."[550] Still, the case was decided with reference to international law, and in the fall of 1784, Longchamps was sentenced to be imprisoned for two years and to pay a fine of $200. The French however continued to insist that Longchamps be extradited. As a result of this demand, tensions between France and the United States, which had been heightened in any event after the 1783 peace treaty, further increased. Among the solutions that were suggested to rectify the situation was the creation of a federal court with standing to try cases concerning the law of nations and to enforce compliance with its

---

548 Jules Lobel, "The Limits of Constitutional Power: Conflicts between Foreign Policy and International Law" *Virginia Law Review* 71, no. 7 (October 1985), p. 1086. Judge Duane was indeed very much in awe with the law of nations, saying that "now since we are placed in a new situation, as one of the nations of the earth, it is become an indispensable obligation. We profess to revere the rights of human nature; at every hazard and expence we have vindicated, and success fully established them in our land! And we cannot but reverence a law which is their chief guardian—a law which inculcates as a first principle—that the amiable precepts of the law of nature, are as obligatory on nations in their mutual intercourse, as they are on individuals in their conduct towards each other; and that every nation is bound to contribute all in its power to the happiness and perfection of others! What more eminently distinguishes the refined and polished nations of Europe, from the piratical states of Barbary, than a respect or a contempt for this law." See *Rutgers v. Waddington*, pp. 21–22.

549 1 U.S. 111 (Dall.), at. 116.

550 Francis Dana to Elbridge Gerry (June 28, 1784), in *Letters of Delegates to Congress*, Vol. 21, p. 702.

provisions among the states.[551] But by the summer of 1785, the French king had decided to drop the extradition request, which helped to close the matter.

The affair proved to have some important long-term repercussions, if only because it had generated further debate about the extent to which international law was applicable in the United States, and whether the states and/or the federal government were responsible for enforcing it. One of the outgrowths of the case was the enactment of the Alien Tort Claims Act, which provided that "district courts shall have original jurisdiction of any civil action by an alien for a tort only, committed in violation of the law of nations or a treaty of the United States." Thus, the *Longchamps* affair turned out to be very consequential for the further development of international law in the early United States.[552] It prompted Peter Stephen DuPonceau, a French linguist and jurist living in the United States, to declare that "this affair is one of those which interests every sovereign and every community, and will make a remarkable era in the history of the Law of Nations."[553] For the more immediate future, *Longchamps* was the legal equivalent of the Shay's rebellion that drove concerns about the law of nations in shaping the new Constitution.

At the time of the Confederation, the United States was arguably at its lowest ebb. Surely, the new nation sought to benefit from the protections afforded by appealing to the law of nations, and the central government in particular. As Hendrickson said, "[t]he restraints that [the law of nations] did mandate, (…) were barriers that mostly favored the interests of the weak confederation among the American states, and were certainly useful in rallying other

551 *Journals of the Continental Congress*, Vol. 31, p. 497. See also Rowe and Knott, "The Longchamps Affair," p. 214.

552 One contemporary scholar concluded however that "the importance of the Longchamps affair has been exaggerated" because ultimately the case had been resolved satisfactorily and because there had never been a real risk of war between France and the United States. Also, even if prosecution under the law of nations had not been available, Longchamps could still have been sentenced and convicted under the common law, he argues. See J. Andrew Kent, "Congress's Under-Appreciated Power to Define and Punish Offenses Against the Law of Nations" *Texas Law Review* 85 (2006–2007), pp. 874–880. It seems however that this reading of the case is too much coloured by the author's perspective in trying to explain developments from the point of view of the creation of the law of nations clause in Art. 1, sec. 8, cl. 10. Indeed, the author seems to admit as much when he said that "even though the incident was largely a dispute about extradition, (…) the Founders still might have wanted to ensure that future incidents of this kind would be within the judicial and prosecutorial purview of the national government." Ibid, p. 880.

553 *Freeman's Journal*, 4 August 1784, quoted in Rowe and Knott, "The Longchamps Affair," p. 219.

European powers against the imperious acts of Great Britain."[554] But while the Confederation managed to conclude a series of favorable trade agreements with overseas powers, it failed in its efforts to enforce the law of nations at home. Not only did Congress fail to give effect to various treaties, the political strength of the states bred an "unwillingness to accept the law of nations, as understood by Europe, or to force acceptance of that tradition, with modifications, upon America's thirteen states."[555] Most of the early American statesmen were aware that the day of reckoning could not be far off if the situation would endure in the same fashion. It was clear that while the country had now been independent for about ten years, the American project had certainly not been consolidated yet, and could still be extinguished should one of the great European powers find a reason to do so. "The record of the Confederation", said Lawrence Kaplan, "was inevitably one of failure in this critical area [of foreign relations] which in turn led to a contempt and hostility for the United States in all the courts of Europe."[556] In the end, the Founders had to become Framers, and bequeath the country a new constitutional basis that would ensure its survival.

554 David Hendrickson, *Peace Pact: The Lost World of the American Founding* (Lawrence: University Press of Kansas, 2003), p. 54.

555 G.S. Rowe and Alexander W. Knott, "The Longchamps Affair (1784–1786), The Law of Nations, and the Shaping of Early American Foreign Policy," *Diplomatic History* 10, no. 3 (July, 1986), pp. 199–200.

556 Kaplan, *Colonies into Nation*, p. 149.

CHAPTER 4

The Federal Constitution and the Law of Nations

4.1 The Law of Nations and the Framing of the Constitution

Most accounts of the early history of the United States point to political and constitutional weaknesses of the Confederation as the main impetus for the convening of the Constitutional Convention in Philadelphia in May of 1787, without explicitly emphasizing the importance of issues regarding the enforcement of the law of nations. Many of the Founders identified these as the principal reason why the Confederation did not work. As the previous chapter attempted to show, conflicts over international law in many instances precipitated and exacerbated divisions between the states. Many of these disputes stemmed from questions about jurisdiction and the right to interpret—or even to enforce—the law of nations, and furthered the sense of autonomy among the individual states. In the months leading up to the famous Convention, many of the senior American statesmen had expressed themselves on the state of the union and the need for drastic reform, underlining the need for the new country to be able to better respect and enforce the laws of nations.

Arguably the best-known of the tracts written in this period is James Madison's *Vices of the Political System of the United States*. If the conclusion of various favorable treaties might have inspired confidence about the future of the union among some, Madison pointed out that such confidence was misplaced, being very concerned about the efficacy of the union up to that point. The main problem was, said Madison, that the states had not faithfully fulfilled their obligations under the law of nations, noting that:

> Accordingly not a year has passed without instances of them in some one or other of the States. The Treaty of Peace—the treaty with France—the treaty with Holland have each been violated. (…) The causes of these irregularities must necessarily produce frequent violations of the law of nations in other respects. As yet foreign powers have not been rigorous in animadverting on us. This moderation, however cannot be mistaken for a permanent partiality to our faults, or a permanent security against those disputes with other nations, which being among the greatest of public calamities, it ought to be least in the power of any part of the community to bring on the whole.[557]

557 James Madison, "Vices of the Political System of the United States" (April 23, 1787), in *The Writings of James Madison* (New York: G.P. Putnam's Sons, 1900), Vol. 2, p. 362. In the

 | DOI 10.1163/9789004305687_006

According to Madison, the states had neglected their duties in accordance with the law because ignoring or trespassing on the law carried no sanctions to be imposed by the central authorities:

> A sanction is essential to the idea of law, as coercion is to that of Government. The federal system being destitute of both, wants the great vital principles of a Political Constitution. Under the form of such a Constitution, it is in fact nothing more than a treaty of amity of commerce and of alliance, between so many independent and Sovereign States. From what cause could so fatal an omission have happened in the articles of Confederation? From a mistaken confidence that the justice, the good faith, the honor, the sound policy, of the several legislative assemblies would render superfluous any appeal to the ordinary motives by which the laws secure the obedience of individuals: a confidence which does honor to the enthusiastic virtue of the compilers, as much as the inexperience of the crisis apologizes for their errors. (...) Even during the war, when external danger supplied in some degree the defect of legal & coercive sanctions, how imperfectly did the States fulfil their obligations to the Union? In time of peace, we see already what is to be expected. How indeed could it be otherwise?

Another reason Madison proffered in explaining the failures to enforce the law was that some states felt that the burden of adherence to the law of nations was shared unequally. Because non-compliance with the law could bring economic benefits, voluntary adherence to the law could not be relied upon. The states were no angels, Madison could have said:

> In the first place, every general act of the Union must necessarily bear unequally hard on some particular member or members of it. Secondly the partiality of the members to their own interests and rights, a partiality which will be fostered by the Courtiers of popularity, will naturally exaggerate the inequality where it exists, and even suspect it where it has no existence. Thirdly a distrust of the voluntary compliance of each other may prevent the compliance of any, although it should be the latent disposition of all. Here are causes & pretexts which will never fail to render federal measures abortive. If the laws of the States, were merely

Federalist Papers, James Madison wrote that "[the Articles of Confederation] contain no provision for the case of offences against the law of nations; and consequently leave it in the power of any indiscreet member to embroil the confederacy with foreign nations." Madison, *The Federalist Papers*, no. XLII, p. 274.

> recommendatory to their citizens, or if they were to be rejudged by County authorities, what security, what probability would exist, that they would be carried into execution?[558]

The quasi-anarchical condition that existed under the Articles between the states led to the ultimate consequence that it "provided [the states] the ground on which, by the law of nations, they might make war against each other."[559] One could perhaps say that if anything was deemed an entangling alliance in those days, this did not involve France or any other country, but the confederated states themselves, bound together by mutual obligations that few states fully trusted the other states to faithfully abide by. Yet internal differences had to be overcome if the United States was to be a credible member of the community of civilized nations. Constitutionally speaking, this problem was exacerbated as a result of the failure of the Articles to delegate sufficient powers to the Congress.[560] As Hamilton summarized the point in the *Federalist*: "The Treaties of the United States, under the present constitution [the Articles of Confederation], are liable to the infractions of thirteen different legislatures, and as many different courts of final jurisdiction, acting under the authority of those legislatures. (…) Is it possible that foreign nations can either respect or confide in such a government?"[561]

For the Founders, the task was to find a *via media* between universal empire and anarchy. History had taught them that on a continental scale, only a monarchical system could keep the peace while federal systems could only work on a small scale;[562] notions which Jefferson hoped "will be exploded by experience."[563] Indeed, they recognized that there had never been a serious attempt at forging a state on a continental scale. Even if the Europeans referred to their continent as a "kind of republic," as Vattel put it, it did not approximate a republic in the sense of the peace plans of Henri IV or Abbé de St. Pierre. Some of the examples that informed the thinking of the early American

558 James Madison, "Vices of the Political System of the United States" (April 23, 1787), in *The Writings of James Madison* (New York: G.P. Putnam's Sons, 1900), Vol. 2, p. 364.

559 Hendrickson, *Peace Pact*, p. 216.

560 Ramsey, *The Constitution's Text in Foreign Affairs*, p. 33 (emphasis in original).

561 Alexander Hamilton, *Federalist* no. XXII, p. 183.

562 See e.g. Montesquieu, *The Spirit of Laws*, Bk. VIII, ch. 20; and Jean-Jacques Rousseau, *Du Contrat Social*, Bk. III, Chs. 4, 6.

563 Thomas Jefferson to M. d'Ivernois (February 6, 1795), in *The Works of Thomas Jefferson*, Vol. 8, p. 165.

statesmen were the Dutch and Swiss confederations,[564] whose histories reflected many aspects of the American experience.

The guiding principle of the *via media* that was sought happened to be the idea of an internal balance of power. Hendrickson wrote that "in contrast with either the dreaded spectre of universal monarchy or the no less distasteful prospect of utter anarchy, [the balance of power] might still be held up as a progressive principle and be closely identified with the public law of Europe." The problem with it was however that "there lay alongside this perception considerable anxiety over the operation of the balance in practice."[565] The solution was to be a calibrated system based on balance-of-power principles, what came to be called 'checks and balances.'

That the Confederation had lacked such equilibrating instruments was widely acknowledged during the first days of the Philadelphia Convention, which opened on May 25, 1787.[566] A typical expression of sentiments was that of Edmund Randolph, a future Attorney-General from Virginia who became caught between Hamilton and Jefferson when in Washington's first cabinet. At the Convention, he listed among the defects of the confederation that

> [it] produced no security agai[nst] foreign invasion; congress not being permitted to prevent a war nor to support it by th[eir] own authority—Of this he cited many examples; most of which tended to shew, that they could not cause infractions of treaties or of the law of nations, to be punished: that particular states might by their conduct provoke war without controul (…).[567]

He reiterated the point that the Confederation was incapable of enforcing the law among its constituent entities, which would make military conflict inevitable: "[i]f a State acts against a foreign power contrary to the laws of nations or violates a treaty, [the Confederation] cannot punish that State, or compel its obedience to the treaty. It can only leave the offending State to the operations

564 See e.g. James Madison, "Of Ancient and Modern Confederacies," in *The Writings of James Madison*, Vol. 2, pp. 375–379; Alexander Hamilton, "The Continentalist no. 11" (July 19, 1781), in *The Works of Alexander Hamilton*, Vol. 1, pp. 252–253. Vattel also named them as examples. See *The Law of Nations*, Bk 1, ch. 2, para. 10, p. 84. See also Hendrickson, *Peace Pact*, pp. 47–48.

565 Hendrickson, *Peace Pact*, p. 44.

566 In fact, the very term "Convention" reflects the fact that the meeting constituted a gathering of representatives from sovereign states.

567 Edmund Randolph (May 29, 1787), in Max Farrand (ed.), *The Records of the Federal Convention of 1787*, Vol. 1, p. 19.

of the offended power. It therefore cannot prevent a war."[568] For the domestic order, the conclusion had to be that if the Articles were merely a treaty among independent states, then any violation of the law of nations by one state could have led to the other states declaring the Confederation be dissolved, in accordance with the law of treaties.[569] Madison thus wanted to ensure that the newly drafted Constitution "exclude[d] such an interpretation."[570]

To create something more than just a treaty between the states required a move towards a federal constitutional framework. The understanding of the Founders in this respect was more complicated than today, because they looked at both constitutional and international legal constructs, and referred to "the web of treaties, laws, and restraints that was to govern the relations of civilized states."[571] This is another reason why for them "[t]he place of foreign policy and the management of diplomacy were important issues (…), even if they were not central to the worries of the nation at large."[572] As a result, foreign affairs would play a much more significant role in the provisions of the Constitution than is perhaps otherwise appreciated. Simultaneously, it underscores the fact that in the 18th century, "[d]omestic law and international law were not [regarded as] two separate bodies of law, but simply two branches of the law of nature."[573] Because no fewer than thirty-five out of the fifty-five of the attendees in Philadelphia were lawyers, it was no surprise that in searching for organizing principles, the framers were drawn to the law of nations, given "its origin in natural law, [its] attitude toward the rule of law in domestic society [and] as the foundation of their rights."[574] Hence, there was no shortage on ideas on how to conceive of a legal framework that would ensure respect for the law of nations as well as means to enforce it.

---

568 Edmund Randolph (May 29, 1787), in Max Farrand (ed.), *The Records of the Federal Convention of 1787*, Vol. 1, pp. 24–25.

569 William Paterson (June 19, 1787), in Max Farrand (ed.), *The Records of the Federal Convention of 1787*, Vol. 1, pp. 314–315.

570 James Madison (July 23, 1787), in Max Farrand (ed.), *The Records of the Federal Convention of 1787*, Vol. 2, p. 93.

571 Hendrickson, *Peace Pact*, pp. 22–23.

572 Kaplan, *Colonies into Nation*, p. 186.

573 Jules Lobel, "The Limits of Constitutional Power: Conflicts between Foreign Policy and International Law" *Virginia Law Review* 71, no. 7 (October 1985), p. 1079. See also Elisabeth Zoller, "Aspects Internationaux du Droit Constitutionnel: Contribution à la Théorie de la Fédération d'États" *Recueil des Cours* 294 (2002), p. 76.

574 Gregg Lint, "The American Revolution and the Law of Nations 1776–1789" *Diplomatic History* 1, no. 1 (1977), p. 21.

The first article of the Constitution enumerated the powers of Congress. Since it established that Congress should provide for the "common defense" of the country, and was assigned the power to declare war (Art. 1, sec. 8, cl. 11), it was also granted the power to "define and punish Piracies and Felonies committed on the high Seas, and Offenses against the Law of Nations." This clause is in fact the only one in the Constitution which explicitly mentioned the law of nations. The word 'define' may perhaps seem strange in relation to the law of nations, a point which James Wilson made at the Convention. He found that "[t]o pretend to *define* the law of nations which depended on the authority of all the Civilized Nations of the World, would have a look of arrogance. That would make us ridiculous."[575] Wilson was answered by fellow Pennsylvanian Gouverneur Morris—widely credited with having written the Constitution's famous preamble—who retorted that on many occasions, "the law of nations [is] often too vague and deficient to be a rule."[576]

With the authority to define international law also came the power to punish offences. That Congress was granted this power is not astounding; the reason for its significance lies in the fact that, as Blackstone wrote, such offences against international law were "principally incident to whole states or nations: in which case recourse can only be had to war (…) neither state having any superior jurisdiction to resort to force upon earth for justice."[577] Hence, if recourse to war was seen as a legitimate means for settling disputes on international legal questions, the Framers wished to ensure that the power to declare war was put in the hands of a deliberative body like Congress, and not in that of the executive or judiciary. Together with this power came related responsibilities including the issuing of "Letters of Marque and Reprisal and [to] make Rules concerning Captures on Land and Water" (Article 1, sec. 8, cl. 11), stipulations which were meant to end the practice of privateering, at least as practised by the states (see also Art. 1, sec. 10, cl. 1).

The power to conclude treaties, which had caused so much confusion under the Articles of Confederation, was further centralized. It came to be shared by

575 James Wilson (September 14, 1787), in Max Farrand (ed.), *The Records of the Federal Convention of 1787*, Vol. 2, p. 615.

576 Gouverneur Morris, in Max Farrand (ed.), *The Records of the Federal Convention of 1787*, Vol. 2, p. 615. On a later occasion, Marshall commented on this article by saying that "[it] can never be construed to make to the Government a grant of power, which the people making it do not themselves possess." See John Marshall, "Speech of March 4, 1799" in Joseph Gales (ed.), *Annals of Congress, or the Debates and Proceedings in the Congress of the United States* (1789–1824). (Washington: Gales and Seaton, 1834–1856), Vol. 10, p. 607.

577 William Blackstone, *Commentaries on the Laws of England* (Oxford: Clarendon Press, 1765–69), Bk IV, Ch. 5, p. 67.

Congress and the President. The rule became that the latter has the power, "by and with the Advice and Consent of the Senate, to make Treaties, provided two thirds of the Senators present concur" (Art. 2, sec. 2, cl. 2). At the same time, the states were prohibited from "enter[ing] into any Treaty, Alliance, or Confederation" (Art. 1, sec. 10, cl. 1). Even though this terse language seems to foreclose any room for manoeuvre on the part of the states, the third clause opens up some room, suggesting that "No State shall, without the Consent of Congress, (...) enter into any Agreement or Compact with another State, or with a foreign Power, or engage in War, *unless actually invaded, or in such imminent Danger as will not admit of delay.*" (emphasis added). This language is reminiscent of that in article VI of the Articles of Confederation, and is one of the few treaty-like elements that survived into the Constitution.[578] Still, Madison believed that no longer, "treaties might be substantially frustrated by regulations of the States (...)."[579]

The powers of the president were not formally enumerated. But his capacity to initiate the conclusion of treaties was important because, as Onuf and Onuf argue, treaties "constituted the crucial mechanism for elaborating and extending the law of nations."[580] Another important provision concerned the President's obligation to "preserve, protect and defend the Constitution of the United States," which could either be read to imply including the law of nations or not. What remained unclear was whether in light of the fact that the power to declare war was bestowed upon Congress, the president would be left with "the power to repel sudden attacks," as Madison wrote.[581] The documentary evidence for this assertion is not unambiguous.[582]

The stipulations with respect to the judicial branch are more specific. There was general consensus that determinations concerning the law of nations had to be delegated to a centralized judicial body. Prior to the Convention, George

578 Another such element was considered in relation to treason committed by individuals, one proposal being "wherever any State entered into Contest with the General Governmt. that during such Civil War, the general Law of Nations, as between Independant States should be the governing rule between them." However, in the spirit of creating a new compact, this idea was rejected. See Max Farrand (ed.), *The Records of the Federal Convention of 1787*, Vol. 3, p. 158–159.

579 James Madison, *The Federalist Papers*, no. XLII, p. 273.

580 Peter Onuf and Nicholas Onuf, *Federal Union, Modern World: The Law of Nations in an Age of Revolutions 1776–1814* (Madison, WI: Madison House, 1992), p. 108.

581 James Madison (August 17, 1787), in Max Farrand (ed.), *The Records of the Federal Convention of 1787*, Vol. 2, p. 318.

582 Charles Lofgren, "War-Making under the Constitution: The Original Understanding" *Yale Law Journal* 81, no. 4 (1972), pp. 675–676.

Mason wrote for instance that among the leading ideas to be discussed was the need "to establish a judiciary system with cognizance of all such matters as depend upon the law of nations (…)."[583] To this end, the New Jersey plan, which was introduced by William Paterson, emphasized the need for federal jurisdiction with respect to violations of treaty law or the law of nations, and proposed the establishment of a supreme tribunal at the federal level.[584] James Madison however rejected the plan, among other reasons because in his estimation, it did not provide for sufficiently broad federal jurisdiction to prevent the country from falling victim to war.[585] He implored the Convention to adopt a more robust proposal:

> Will it prevent the violations of the law of nations & of Treaties which if not prevented must involve us in the calamities of foreign wars? The tendency of the States to these violations has been manifested in sundry instances. The files of Congress contain complaints already, from almost every Nation with which treaties have been formed. Hitherto indulgence has been shewn to us. This cannot be the permanent disposition of foreign nations. A rupture with other powers is among the greatest of national calamities. It ought therefore to be effectually provided that no part of a nation shall have it in its power to bring them on the whole. The existing Confederacy does not sufficiently provide against this evil. The proposed amendment to it does not supply the omission. It leaves the will of the States as uncontrouled as ever.[586]

One plan that proposed just such a wide jurisdictional margin was the Pinckney plan, which would grant jurisdiction on "all questions wherein questions shall arise (…) on the law of nations, or general commercial or marine laws," to be treated by a "federal judicial Court."[587] The proposal had its origins in a discussion in Congress in 1786, which considered a proposition allowing for "a federal

583 George Mason to Arthur Lee (May 21, 1787), in Max Farrand (ed.), *The Records of the Federal Convention of 1787*, Vol. 3, p. 24.

584 William Paterson (June 15, 1787), in Max Farrand (ed.), *The Records of the Federal Convention of 1787*, Vol. 1, p. 244. See also discussed in Edwin Dickinson, "The Law of Nations as Part of the National Law of the United States," p. 37.

585 Anthony Bellia and Bradford Clark, "The Federal Common Law of Nations" *Columbia Law Review* 109 (January, 2009), p. 38.

586 Madison, "Journal of the Constitutional Convention of 1787" (June 19, 1787) in *The Writings of James Madison*, Vol. 3, pp. 211–212.

587 July 24–26, 1787, in Max Farrand (ed.), *The Records of the Federal Convention of 1787*, Vol. 2, p. 136.

Court" to serve as an appeals court "in all Causes wherein questions shall arise on the meaning and construction of Treaties entered into by the United States with any foreign power, or on the Law of Nations (...)."[588] The fact that the proposal was resubmitted by a southern representative demonstrated that there existed "an impressive measure of agreement at the outset that the Law of Nations and treaties must be subjects (...) of a paramount national concern."[589]

But in spite of the apparent consensus, the Convention resolved on July 18th on a more ambiguous formulation, namely "[t]hat the jurisdiction of the national Judiciary shall extend to cases arising under laws passed by the General Legislature, and to such other questions as involve the National peace and harmony."[590] In its final draft, the Constitution would provide that the power of the judicial branch extend to

> all Cases, in Law and Equity, arising under this Constitution, the Laws of the United States, and Treaties made, or which shall be made, under their Authority;—to all Cases affecting Ambassadors, other public Ministers and Consuls;—to all Cases of admiralty and maritime Jurisdiction (...) (Art. 3, sec. 2).

This formulation ensured that all matters which were deemed crucial as regards enforcement of international law would come under the purview of the court, and also covered criminal and civil cases.[591] One can clearly trace the influence of the common law system in this provision through its explicit mentioning of such areas as admiralty and maritime law, and the fact that it also covers civil cases, recognizing the fact that the common law does not distinguish sharply between public and private law. Interestingly, the inference that the common law as such could therewith be considered as a source of law at the federal level became a highly contested one, as the second part of this chapter will demonstrate. Another issue was that without an explicit mentioning of the law of nations as such, no applicability of customary international law could be implied, thus leaving at least part of the law of nations outside the

588 *Journals of the Continental Congress* (August 7, 1786), Vol. 31, p. 497.

589 Edwin Dickinson, "The Law of Nations as Part of the National Law of the United States," *University of Pennsylvania Law Review* 101, no. 1, (October 1952), p. 37.

590 Madison, "Journal of the Constitutional Convention of 1787" (July 26, 1787) in *The Writings of James Madison*, Vol. 4, p. 157.

591 Edwin Dickinson, "The Law of Nations as Part of the National Law of the United States," *University of Pennsylvania Law Review* 101 (1952), p. 793.

jurisdiction of the federal courts. Nevertheless, Sprout concluded that at least, "there seems to be sufficient grounds (sic) to infer that the phraseology of the Constitution was intended to provide the judiciary with the requisite authority to apply rules drawn from international law, as they would municipal law."[592]

That the omission of the law of nations was not unintentional becomes clear when examining article six of the Constitution. Reiterating the need for citizens and the states to honor their wartime debt obligations to British parties, it sets out that "All Debts contracted and Engagements entered into, before the Adoption of this Constitution, shall be as valid against the United States under this Constitution, as under the Confederation." More important for this discussion is the second clause, which came to be called the 'Supremacy Clause.' It provides that

> [t]his Constitution, and the Laws of the United States which shall be made in Pursuance thereof; and all Treaties made, or which shall be made, under the Authority of the United States, shall be the supreme Law of the Land; and the Judges in every State shall be bound thereby, any Thing in the Constitution or Laws of any State to the Contrary notwithstanding.

As such, this provision is arguably the single most important stipulation on the status of the law of nations under the federal Constitution. It only deems treaties to be part of "the supreme law of the land." The phrase "Laws of the United States" could not be read to include the customary law of nations,[593] if only because such laws ought to have been made in their pursuit.[594] At face value, the clause appears to suggest that the Constitution

---

592 Harold Sprout, "Theories as to the Applicability of International Law in the Federal Courts of the United States" *American Journal of International Law* 26, no. 2 (April 1932), p. 282.

593 Anthony Bellia and Bradford Clark, "The Federal Common Law of Nations" *Columbia Law Review* 109 (January, 2009), p. 35.

594 Jordan Paust rejects this reading, claiming that the phrase "in pursuance of" can mean "consistent with the Constitution," and could therefore also include the customary law of nations, adding that "customary international law, to be supreme law of the land, must be consistent with the Constitution." Interestingly, this wording appears to suggest that if customary international law is *not* consistent with the Constitution, it will not be 'supreme law of the land.' In support, Paust cites the case *United States v. Robins* (27 F. Cas. 825 (1799)), in which the counsel argued that if a treaty was "contrary to the Constitution," it was not made "in pursuance thereof." See Jordan Paust, "In Their Own Words: Affirmations of the Founders, Framers and Early Judiciary Concerning the Binding Nature of the Customary Law of Nations" *U.C. Davis Journal of International Law and Policy* 13, no. 2, pp. 252–253. A similar argument had been made earlier by Louis Henkin, who suggested

has equal status to laws passed by Congress as well as treaties. Constitutional scholar Michael Glennon embraces a different understanding, arguing that 'supreme' should be understood as meaning that "[t]he Constitution is the most supreme law, prevailing over all treaties (...) and principles of federal and state common law,"[595] a position that was earlier espoused by Louis Henkin.[596] This would be correct when considering that in the 18th century, "a constitution as such was not itself seen as positive, enacted law but rather as a declaration of first principles" in the sense of codified natural law.[597] Even if the Constitution does not explicitly set out natural law principles, it could still have had the status of such a charter inspired by the language of natural law.

The ambiguities that Article six and other provisions of the Constitution contained made that the question regarding primacy between federal law and international law remained unresolved in the final text of the Constitution. During some of the ratification debates in the various states, some delegations attempted to introduce language to eliminate such ambiguities. For instance, at the Pennsylvania ratifying convention, a proposal had been mooted to the end "that no treaty which shall be directly opposed to the existing laws of the United States in Congress assembled, shall be valid until such laws shall be repealed, or made conformable to such treaty; neither shall any treaties be valid which are in contradiction to the constitution of the United States or

---

that cases arising under international law are "cases arising under (...) the laws of the United States" [and] that principles of international law as incorporated in the law of the United States are "Laws of the United States." See Henkin, "International Law as Law in the United States," *Michigan Law Review* 82, no. 2 (1984), p. 1560. Note however that Henkin never explicitly mentions customary law but refers to principles of international law. Bellia and Clark therefore seem to be correct in rejecting Paust's reading, which would also be more logical given that the Supremacy Clause speaks about laws "which shall be made," a phrase which only seems to make sense in conjunction with "in pursuit of" rather than with "be consistent with."

595 Michael Glennon, *Constitutional Diplomacy* (Princeton, NJ: Princeton University Press, 1990), p. 247.

596 Louis Henkin, "International Law as Law in the United States" *Michigan Law Review* 82, no. 2 (1984), pp. 1562–1563. Henkin noted that, since since laws and treaties (which have equal status) are "inferior" to the Constitution, "[i]t is not unconstitutional for Congress to enact law inconsistent with a treaty of the United States," nor is it unconstitutional for the President to make a treaty that contradicts an earlier act of Congress. See ibid., p. 1563. Of course, even if this poses no problems under U.S. Constitutional law, it does have consequences for the U.S. as a reliable party under international law.

597 Suzanna Sherry, "The Founders' Unwritten Constitution," *The University of Chicago Law Review* 54, no. 4 (1987), p. 1146.

the constitutions of the several states." This suggestion did however not garner a majority.[598] A similar sentiment was voiced by William Grayson, an Oxford-trained lawyer and future senator from Virginia, who was concerned that if the United States were to subscribe to the general law of nations, it could possibly surrender rights that it would have a claim to under its own set of laws. But even if he acknowledged "the existence of a general law of nations" he maintained that therewith "as a principle, nations can, as well as individuals, renounce any particular right." Fellow Virginian George Nicholas answered however that "there was no such thing as a particular law of nations, but that the law of nations was permanent and general. It was superior to any act or law of any nation; it implied the consent of all, and was mutually binding on all, being acquiesced in for the common benefit of all."[599] The debate was also waged in North Carolina, where one participant noted that "although treaties are mere conventional acts between the contracting parties, yet, by the law of nations, they are the supreme law of the land to their respective citizens or subjects. All civilized nations have concurred in considering them as paramount to an ordinary act of legislation."[600]

Moreover, the ambiguities also served to perpetuate concerns that violations of the law of nations could have grave consequence in the years to come. As John Jay wrote in the *Federalist* no. III, "The JUST causes of war, for the most part, arise either from violation of treaties or from direct violence. America has already formed treaties with no less than six foreign nations, and all of them, except Prussia, are maritime, and therefore able to annoy and injure us. She has also extensive commerce with Portugal, Spain, and Britain, and, with respect to the two latter, has, in addition, the circumstance of neighborhood to attend to." For sure, he added, the new government could not prevent war in all circumstances, but it could certainly help to limit and mitigate its occurrence: "it appears evident that [observance of the law of nations] will be more perfectly and punctually done by one national government than it could be either by thirteen separate States or by three or four distinct confederacies."[601] What is more, Jay concluded, "as either designed or accidental violations of treaties

---

598 See "Dissent of the Minority of the Pennsylvania Convention" (December 18, 1787), in Bernard Bailyn, The *Debate on the Constitution*, Vol. 1, p. 534. An almost verbatim amendment was suggested in North Carolina on August 1, 1788. See Jonathan Elliot (ed.), *The Debates in the Several State Conventions on the Adoption of the Federal Constitution*, Vol. 4, p. 246.

599 *Elliot's Debates*, Vol. 3 (June 18, 1788), pp. 505–506.

600 *Farrand's Records*, Vol. 3, p. 347.

601 John Jay, *The Federalist Papers*, no. III, p. 95.

and the laws of nations afford JUST causes of war, they are less to be apprehended under one general government than under several lesser ones, and in that respect the former most favors the SAFETY of the people."[602]

In terms of contractual obligations, the Constitution was an unprecedented achievement, succeeding in welding together different states and creating an effective central government invested with real powers of enforcement. As one scholar said, it acknowledged that "the Framers recognized that the law of nations governing treaties also governed the replacement of the Articles with the Constitution."[603] Indeed, it is even said that "the law of nations governed the Constitution's construction (…)."[604] Among other things, this move annulled the possibility of resort to the *exceptio non adimpleti contractus*, according to which a violation on the part of one party of the contract permits the other side(s) to renounce their obligations under the contract.[605] As such, the Constitution entailed a "paradigm shift," from balance of power to federal union,[606] creating a 'peace pact' on a par with for instance the settlements of 1648, 1814–15 and 1919. What made the American example so unique was that, as Golove and Hulsebosch said, the "revolutionary situation forced [the Founders] to contribute to the very definition of "civilized" statehood. They did so by designing a republican Constitution that tried to balance the twin revolutionary goals of popular sovereignty and international recognition."[607]

Not only had the Founders defied Montesquieu, Rousseau and others by creating a republic on a continental scale, they had therewith also devised a system for the maintenance of peace that could possibly serve an an example for the other side of the Atlantic. James Wilson compared the Constitution

602 John Jay, *The Federalist Papers*, no. III, p. 96.

603 Francisco F. Martin, *The Constitution as Treaty: The International Legal Constructionalist Approach to the U.S. Constitution* (New York: Cambridge University Press, 2007), pp. 4–5.

604 Martin, *The Constitution as Treaty*, p. 8. See also Elisabeth Zoller, "Aspects Internationaux du Droit Constitutionnel: Contribution à la Théorie de la Fédération d'États" *Recueil des Cours* 294 (2002), p. 109. Bederman said that "[i]n the Constitution, the Framers enshrined a recognition of the new nation's dependence on international law (…)." David Bederman, *The Classical Foundations of the American Constitution: Prevailing Wisdom* (New York: Cambridge University Press, 2008), p. 172.

605 Elisabeth Zoller, "Aspects Internationaux du Droit Constitutionnel: Contribution à la Théorie de la Fédération d'États" *Recueil des Cours* 294 (2002), p. 83.

606 Hendrickson, *Peace Pact*, p. 24.

607 David Golove and Daniel Hulsebosch, "A Civilized Nation: The Early American Constitution, The Law of Nations and the Pursuit of International Recognition," Public Law and Legal Theory Research Paper Series, working paper no. 10–58. *New York University School of Law* (2010), p. 146.

with the great peace plan of the Duc de Sully in the 16th century, saying that the United States had now "accomplished, what the great mind of Henry IV of France had in contemplation, a system of government, for large and respectable dominions, united and bound together in peace, under a superintending head, by which all their differences may be accommodated, without the destruction of the human race!"[608] With his typical idealist flourish, Benjamin Franklin used the same reference when wondering "why you might not in Europe carry the Project of good Henry the 4th into Execution, by forming a Federal Union and One Grand Republick of all the different States and Kingdoms by means of a like Convention; for we had many Interests to reconcile."[609]

Of course, the country was only at its inception, but it proved to be an intriguing exercise in statecraft. Hendrickson concluded that "North America, then, was a laboratory in international cooperation, a working out of the peace plan tradition in European thought."[610] The years following its adoption would take the project out of the laboratory, so to speak, where it would be tested in real-world circumstances. The country ultimately withstood its rendez-vous with reality, even if its independence "remained defeasible" until the end of the War of 1812, after which it could breathe more comfortably.[611] In various respects, the United States owed its survival and subsequent expansion due to its largely successful recourse to the law of nations.

4.2 The Constitution from an International Legal Perspective

The new federal constitution inaugurated many fresh debates on the status it attributed to the law of nations; sometimes prompted by current events, and sometimes as a result of scholarly reflections on the law. As the first part of this chapter demonstrated, many of these discussions began in the

---

608 Wilson, "Remarks of James Wilson in the Pennsylvania Convention to Ratify the Constitution of the United States," in *Collected Works of James Wilson*, Vol. 1, p. 282.

609 Benjamin Franklin to Rodolphe-Ferdinand Grand (October 22, 1787), in *The Papers of Benjamin Franklin*, Vol. 45, p. 229.

610 David Hendrickson, "Independence and Union: Foundations of American Internationalism" *Orbis* 49 (Winter 2004), p. 46.

611 David Golove and Daniel Hulsebosch, "A Civilized Nation: The Early American Constitution, The Law of Nations and the Pursuit of International Recognition," p. 111.

context of the debates over the ratification of the Constitution. Many questions remained on the application and enforcement of international law in the context of the new Constitution. Soon after the entry into force of the Constitution, two subsequent enactments helped to further frame the issue: the Judiciary Act of 1789 and the Bill of Rights—the first ten amendments to the Constitution—which entered into force in 1791.

At the broadest level, legal thinkers revisited the debate concerning the introduction of the law of nations in the United States as a means to understanding how it fitted in the new Constitutional construct; not just in terms of its actual text, but also in relation to natural law and the rights and obligations that derived from it. Among the most important authors to broach this subject was James Wilson. A signer of the Declaration of Independence, delegate in Philadelphia in 1787 and regarded as the most learned of the Founding Fathers, Wilson's views were strongly influenced by natural law thinking. In this respect, he was opposed to the secularization of natural law at the hands of Grotius and some of his successors, believing that it would undermine the binding nature of the law of nations. In his *Lectures on Law*, published in 1790, he reproached Grotius for basing the law of nations on the principle of universal consent. "The consequence of this is," says Wilson, "that the law of nations would be obligatory only upon those by whom the consent was given, and only be reason of that consent."[612] The law of nations would lose most of its obligatory character, an unacceptable result to him: as a part of the law of nature, he argues that "[t]he law of nations (...) is of obligation indispensable [because it is] of origin divine."[613] The reason for grafting the law of nations (and, *ipso facto*, the law of nature) once again on a religious foundation is because, so Wilson believes "[a] human source leads to passive obedience and to tyranny."[614] Intellectually speaking, religion as a basis for natural law was not problematic since the latter was regarded as revelatory of a rational religion.

---

612 James Wilson, "Lectures on Law," in *The Collected Works of James Wilson* (Indianapolis: Liberty Fund, 2007), Vol. 1, p. 528.

613 James Wilson, "Lectures on Law," in *The Collected Works of James Wilson*, Vol. 1, p. 527. Elsewhere in the *Lectures*, he added that "Our knowledge of moral philosophy, of natural jurisprudence, of the law of nations, must ultimately depend, for its first principles, on the evidence and information of the moral sense." See in ibid., Vol. 2, p. Ch. XIII, p. 803.

614 Jesse Reeves, "The Influence of the Law of Nature upon International Law in the United States" *American Journal of International Law* 31 (1935), p. 553. What may perhaps be behind this view is that, in Wilson's day, as we have seen before, (secularized) international law was regarded by some as apologetic, enabling worldly rulers to interpret it in any fashion they desired, and that this had gravely damaged the authority of international law.

In addition, there was also a more ideological, or political, reason for this preference, since the assertion of an authority above that of worldly sovereigns could be a means for controlling balance-of-power politics.[615]

At the same time, Wilson does not argue that the entire body of the law of nations is governed by divine obligation. Thus, one of the reasons for his opposing secular natural law is because he intends to sharply distinguish between divine and human laws. He therefore had wished that the part of the law of nations that was devised by humans—the voluntary law of nations, i.e. treaty law and customary law—had been "designated by an appropriate name."[616] For laws drawn up by humans, Wilson's starting point was one of the principles of the American Revolution, namely rule based on the consent of the governed.

> Now that the will of a superiour is discarded, as an improper principle of obligation in human laws, it is natural to ask — What principle shall be introduced in its place? In its place I introduce — the consent of those whose obedience the law requires. This I conceive to be the true origin of the obligation of human laws.[617]

Herewith, Wilson also defined the extent to which individuals (and countries) could modify their obligations under international law. "By a treaty, the voluntary or positive law of nations may be altered so far as the alteration shall affect *only* the contracting parties. But it is equally true, that no state or states can, by treaty or municipal laws, alter or abrogate the law of nations any farther."[618] This is a result of the fact that the voluntary law of nations was governed by the law of nature, whose obligation is "universal, indispensable, and unchangeable."[619] As a judge on the Supreme Court, Wilson was able to directly influence American legal doctrine as to the application of the law of nations within its own jurisdiction. Even if inadvertently, Wilson's

615 Sylvester, "International Law as Sword or Shield?," p. 65.

616 Wilson, "Lectures on Law," in *The Collected Works of James Wilson,* Vol. 1, p. 529.

617 Wilson, "Lectures on Law," in ibid., p. 494.

618 James Wilson, "A Charge Delivered to the Grand Jury in the Circuit Court of the United States for the District of Virginia" (May 1791), in *The Collected Works of James Wilson*, Vol. 1, p. 333. This position was confirmed in the case *Ross v. Rittenhouse* 2 U.S. 160 (Dall.) 1792, at 162 ("the municipal law of the country [can] facilitate or improve the execution [of the law of nations] provided the great universal law remains unaltered.") See also discussed in Sylvester, "International Law as Sword or Shield?," pp. 13–16.

619 Wilson, "Lectures on Law," in *The Collected Works of James Wilson,* Vol. 1, p. 529.

legal philosophy helped to lift international law on a higher level in the early United States.[620]

At first glance, the Constitution did not give explicit sanction to the idea that the law of nations *as a whole* had become part of the law of the land, let alone belong to the category of superior law. Only treaties had been explicitly granted a status equal to laws passed by Congress, while the phrase "law of nations" was only mentioned once explicitly. One way to make the argument in favor of international law was to assume it was incorporated on the basis of being fundamental law. As Jules Lobel summarized the main point: "[t]he theoretical underpinnings of the Constitution, its text, and the ratification debates all reflect the contemporary understanding that the law of nations, as a part of the fundamental law of nature, implicitly limited the foreign affairs powers granted by the new constitution."[621] This view is reflected in the philosophy of James Wilson, who wrote that the people could not grant authority to the federal government to violate fundamental principles of international law: "[W]hen I say that, in free states, the law of nations is the law of the people; I mean that as the law of nature (…) it is indispensably binding upon the people, in whom the sovereign power resides."[622] As a result, there existed a moral obligation on the part of all branches of the government to abide by the law of nations. Hamilton hinted at such a kind of reasoning when he said that

> [i]t is evident, however, that parts of [the Constitution of the United States] use a language which refers to former principles. (…) Not even the Legislature of the Union can change it. (…) Such is the general tenor of the Constitution of the United States, that it evidently looks to antecedent

620 Randolph C. Adams, "The Legal Theories of James Wilson" *University of Pennsylvania Law Review and American Law Register* 68, no. 4 (June 1920), p. 350.

621 Jules Lobel, "The Limits of Constitutional Power: Conflicts between Foreign Policy and International Law" *Virginia Law Review* 71, no. 7 (October 1985), p. 1090. Elsewhere, he added that "during the first twenty years of American independence, jurists and statesmen established that fundamental international law principles reflecting the law of nature were inviolate and binding on the political branches of government." See ibid., p. 1095.

622 James Wilson "Lectures on Law" ch. 4, in *The Collected Works of James Wilson*, p. 532. See also Paust, who concluded that "the people could not delegate to the U.S. Congress, federal executive, or the states a power that they themselves did not possess to violate or compromi[se the law of nations]." Jordan Paust, "In Their Own Words: Affirmations of the Founders, Framers and Early Judiciary Concerning the Binding Nature of the Customary Law of Nations" *U.C. Davis Journal of International Law and Policy* 13, no. 2, p. 211.

> law. What is, on this point, the great body of the common law? Natural law and natural reason applied to the purposes of society. What are the English courts now doing but adopting natural law?[623]

In a charge to a grand jury in North Carolina in 1794, James Iredell made this argument even more explicitly: "[t]he common law of England, from which our own is derived, fully recognizes the principles of the law of nations (...). Even the Legislature (...) is bound by the dictates of moral duty to the rest of the world, in no instance to transgress them, although if it in fact doth so, it is entitled to actual obedience within the sphere of its authority."[624] Lobel concluded from this that "for most of the judges and scholars at the time (...) law and morality were closely connected."[625]

But rather than directly positing natural or fundamental law as the basis for the application of the law of nations under the new Constitution, some early American jurists and statesmen did so indirectly by introducing the common law as providing such a basis. Indeed, the federal courts tried early on to invoke common law jurisdiction in considering crimes under the law of nations and breaches of neutrality, mostly in relation to piracy. Many prominent lawyers, among them Iredell, Wilson and Marshall (all of whom were Federalists), agreed with that approach. For instance, in *Talbot v. Janson*, Iredell explicitly held that the "law of nations is (...) a part of the common law."[626] In the early 19th century, one member of the House said, reflecting on sources of law, that "[t]he judges of the United States have generally held that the Constitution of the United States was predicated upon existing common law. Of the soundness of that opinion I have never had a doubt. I should scarcely go too far where I to say, that stripped of the common law, there would be neither Constitution, nor government."[627] In conclusion, many early jurists and statesmen agreed with the notion that, as Glennon put it, "[t]he courts' authority to apply international

623 Hamilton, "Speech in the Case of Harry Croswell" (1804), in *The Works of Alexander Hamilton,* Vol. 8, pp. 420–421.

624 James Iredell, "A Charge Delivered to the Grand Jury for the District of North Carolina" (June 2, 1794), in Griffith McRee, (ed.), *Life and Correspondence of James Iredell* (New York: D. Appleton and Company, 1858), vol. 2, p. 423.

625 Jules Lobel, "The Limits of Constitutional Power: Conflicts between Foreign Policy and International Law" *Virginia Law Review* 71, no. 7 (October 1985), p. 1090.

626 See 3 U.S. 3 (Dallas), 133, 1795, at 161.

627 Speech of Mr Bayard, Debates on the Judiciary, House of Representatives, 1802, quoted in J. Whitla Stinson, "The Common Law and the Law of Nations under the Federal Constitution" *California Law Review* 9 (September, 1921), p. 472–473.

law thus derived from English common law, incorporated into the law of the United States."[628]

Opinions to the contrary are however equally abundant. St. George Tucker conceded that together with other bodies of law, the common law could only be considered as the law of the land insofar as it could serve as a rule of decision, by analogy, and "whenever the written law is silent":

> the law of nations, the common law of England, the civil law, the law maritime, the law merchant, or the *lex loci,* or law of the foreign nation, or state, in which the cause of action may arise, or shall be decided, must in their turn be resorted to as the rule of decision, according to the nature and circumstances of each case, respectively. So that each of these laws may be regarded, so far as they apply to such cases, respectively, as the law of the land.[629]

The *ratio decidendi* of the 1788 case *Miller v. Hall* suggested a similar reasoning, albeit that it did not proclaim such foreign laws to be the law of the land in the United States: "It is true, that the laws of a particular country, have in themselves no extra-territorial force, no coercive operation; but by the consent of nations, they acquire an influence and obligation, and, in many instances, become conclusive throughout the world. Acts of pardon, marriage, and divorce, made in one country, are received and binding in all

628 Michael Glennon, *Constitutional Diplomacy* (Princeton, NJ: Princeton University Press, 1990), p. 257.

629 St. George Tucker, "Of the Unwritten, or Common Law of England," in *Blackstone's Commentaries*, Vol. 1, p. 430. Elsewhere, Tucker added that: "To controversies between citizens of different states; and between citizens of any state and the subjects or citizens of foreign states. (…) In these cases, the municipal law of the place where the cause of controversy arises, whether that be one of the United States, or Great Britain, France, Spain, Holland, Hamburg, or any other country; or the general law of merchants; or, the general law of nations according to the nature and circumstances of the case, must be the rule of decision, in whatever court the suit may be brought. Thus if a bond be given in Philadelphia, the rate of interest must be settled according to the laws of Pennsylvania. If a bill of exchange be drawn in Virginia, the rate of damages must be settled by the law of that state. If in England, Hamburg, or Cadiz, the custom of merchants in those places, respectively, must govern. If a ransom bill be drawn at sea, the law of nations in that case must be consulted. If the controversy relate to lands, the law of the state where the lands lie must be referred to; unless the lands be claimed under grants from different states; in which case the territorial rights of each state must be inquired into. The same must be done, in the last case which remains to be noticed." See ibid., p. 421.

countries."[630] Tucker himself therefore drew the conclusion that "to infer from hence, that the common law of England is the general law of the United States, is to the full as absurd as to suppose that the laws of Russia, or Germany, are the general law of the land (…)." With respect to the Constitution, Tucker's opinion was clear. Having established that "the common law of England, and every statute of that kingdom, (…) were brought over to America, by the first settlers of the colonies," he nevertheless concluded that "the authority and obligation of the common law and statutes of England, as such in the American states, must depend solely upon the constitutional or legislative authority of each state." The result was that there could not be a federal common law:

> [T]he present constitution of the United States, [never authorized] the federal government, or any department thereof, to declare the common law or statutes of England, or of any other nation, to be the law of the land in the United States.[631]

James Madison fully shared Tucker's assessment, formulating his point of view over the course of a dispute concerning the Alien and Sedition Acts,[632] which

630 *Miller v. Hall*, 1 U.S. 229 (Dall.), 1788, at 232. Discussing rules concerning captures, justice Marshall said in *The Nereide* that "Congress has not left it to this department to say whether the rule of foreign nations shall be applied to them, but has by law applied that rule. If it be the will of the government to apply to Spain any rule respecting captures which Spain is supposed to apply to us, the government will manifest that will by passing an act for the purpose." Interestingly, he added, apparently with reference to Randolph's 1792 statement, that "[t]ill such an act be passed, the Court is bound by the law of nations which is a part of the law of the land." See 13 U.S. (9 Cranch), 1815, at 423. See also discussed in Edward Dumbauld, "John Marshall and the Law of Nations" *University of Pennsylvania Law Review* 104, no. 1 (1955), pp. 50–51 and *Camp v. Lockwood* 1 U.S. 393 (Dall.), 1788, at 398.

631 St. George Tucker, "Of the Unwritten, or Common Law of England," in *Blackstone's Commentaries*, Vol. 1, p. 432–433. Again, reiterating his point thus: "The judicial power extends likewise to controversies between two or more states; and between a state, and foreign states. These must be proceeded in, and determined according to the law of nations, and not according to the common law." Ibid., p. 421.

632 These Acts were a series of four bills passed in 1798 at the time of the Quasi-War by the Adams administration with the stated aim to protect the federal government against "malicious writing" and enabling it to deport resident aliens in the case of war of if they endangered the country's peace. They led to a sharpening of relations between Federalist and Republicans—Jefferson and Madison arguing that they were not only unconstitutional but also an attempt at stifling dissent at home through constraining the freedom of expression.

exposed the rift between Federalists and Republicans about the status of the common law as federal law. Federalists supported the notion that the common law was part of the law of the United States, but Madison denied this supposition. First, he denied that the principle could be inferred from the Revolutionary era, saying that "[t]he doctrine, on the contrary, is evidently repugnant to the fundamental principle of the Revolution." Nor did he find any support for the contention when examining the Articles of Confederation, concluding that "[t]his instrument does not contain a sentence or a syllable that can be tortured into a countenance of the idea that the parties to it were, with respect to the objects of the common law, to form one community." Finally, as to the 1787 Constitution, Madison delved into an exegesis of the famous "law and equity" clause under article III, sec. 2. To suppose that this clause introduced the common law as federal American law he found preposterous: "Never, perhaps, was so broad a construction applied to a text so clearly unsusceptible of it."[633] In Madison's view, this clause could at best only include civil, and not criminal suits, and therefore does not imply incorporation of the common law. The same applies to the "arising under" clause (also in article III, sec. 2) and the Supremacy clause, both of which, he says, "consist of an enumeration which was evidently meant to be precise and complete. If the common law had been understood to be a law of the United States, it is not possible to assign a satisfactory reason why it was not expressed in the enumeration."[634]

Considering the "doctrine that there is a common law in force in the United States", Jefferson stood with Madison on this issue—which had political ramifications beyond the legal sphere—seeing it as an encroachment upon the Constitution.[635] For the role of Congress and the Judiciary, the non-inclusion of the common law as part of the law of the land would have important consequences. In an ironical note, Madison added that, should the common law have been a part of federal law, then "statutes already passed [by Congress] as may be repugnant thereto would be nullified, particularly the Sedition Act itself, which boasts of being a melioration of the common law; and the whole code, with all its incongruities, barbarisms, and bloody maxims, would be inviolably saddled on the good people of the United States." Another argument Madison raised against incorporation was

633 James Madison, "Report on the Resolutions" (February 7, 1799), in *The Writings of James Madison*, Vol. 6, p. 376.

634 Madison, "Report on the Resolutions" (February 7, 1799), in *The Writings of James Madison*, Vol. 6, p. 378–379.

635 Thomas Jefferson to Charles Pinckney (October 29, 1799), in *The Works of Thomas Jefferson* (New York and London: G.P. Putnam's Sons, 1904–5), Vol. 9, p. 87.

that otherwise it would elevate the common law into a constitutional obligation, thus "confer[ring] on the judicial department a discretion little short of a legislative power."[636] Thus, the committee he wrote the report for had "the utmost confidence in concluding that the common law never was, nor by any fair construction ever can be, deemed a law for the American people as one community."[637]

The problem at this point was that the Constitution appeared to contradict the Judiciary Act, which had been adopted in 1789 to create a federal judiciary. For if we assume that Madison was right in his assertion, it is puzzling why the Judiciary Act had granted lower courts "jurisdiction of crimes (…) under the Law of Nations as part of the common law" as Dickinson inferred from the Act's legislative history.[638] Indeed, it was exactly such jurisdiction that the court resorted to in the famous *Henfield* case, establishing that "the Federal judiciary had jurisdiction of an offense against the Law of Nations and may proceed to punish the offender according to the form of the common law."[639] One modern scholar said that the later abandonment of the common law doctrine in the early 19th century had "lamentable consequences," leading to "shocking violations of the neutrality of the American government."[640] The new construction that was developed entailed drawing jurisdictional authority from the constitutional allocation of powers between the branches, whereby the enforcement of 'perfect rights' would be ensured, while simultaneously recognizing that "the political branches were free to make law in derogation of the law of nations, and that such law would bind courts as the supreme law of the land."[641] What made this question so intractable was once more that it was not merely a legal issue but also a political one. The Democratic-Republicans opposed a broad reading of the jurisdiction for the federal courts on the ground that they believed that judicial defense of America's neutrality policies did not

---

636 Which amounts to a power to review legislation against an exogenous standard, one which the Supreme Court would of course appropriate to itself a few years later in the celebrated case *Marbury v. Madison*.

637 Madison, "Report on the Resolutions" (February 7, 1799), in *The Writings of James Madison*, Vol. 6, p. 381.

638 Edwin Dickinson, "The Law of Nations as Part of the National Law of the United States" *University of Pennsylvania Law Review* 101, no. 6 (April 1953), p. 793.

639 Francis Wharton (ed.), *State Trials of the United States* (Philadelphia: Carey and Hart, 1849), p. 85.

640 J. Whitla Stinson, "The Common Law and the Law of Nations under the Federal Constitution" *California Law Review* 9 (September, 1921), p. 474.

641 Anthony Bellia and Bradford Clark, "The Federal Common Law of Nations" *Columbia Law Review* 109 (January, 2009), p. 58.

serve their political agenda, which was premised on maintaining cordial ties with France. Though the constitutional question involving the Alien and Sedition Acts disappeared with its expiration early into the Jefferson administration, common-law jurisdiction at the federal level was only abandoned in the early 19th century.[642]

Statements of doctrine based on fundamental or common law could thus not resolve the issue about the extent to which the law of nations ought to be applied and enforced as the law of the land in the United States. The only part of the law of nations that seems to have been largely uncontroversial is treaty law. In *Federalist* no. XXII, Alexander Hamilton focused on the notion that treaties should be self-executing under the federal Constitution, writing that "[t]he treaties of the United States, to have any force at all, must be considered as part of the law of the land. Their true import, as far as respects individuals, must, like all other laws, be ascertained by judicial determinations."[643] In the case *Ware v. Hylton*, judge Iredell stressed the ethical dimension of adherence to treaty commitments, saying that "a treaty, when executed pursuant to full power, is valid and obligatory, in point of moral obligation, on all, as well on the legislative, executive, and judicial departments (…) because it is a promise in effect by the whole nation to another nation, and if not in fact complied with, unless there be valid reasons for noncompliance, the public faith is violated."[644] James Madison argued that the authority of treaties under the new Constitution rested on the basis of popular assent resulting from a two-thirds qualified majority approbation in the Senate.[645] Finally, John Jay made the case for treaty compliance very forcefully in the *Federalist Papers*, arguing that internal

642 Edwin Dickinson, "The Law of Nations as Part of the National Law of the United States" *University of Pennsylvania Law Review* 101, no. 6 (April 1953), p. 795. Cases that point in this direction are *United States v. Ravara* (2 U.S. 297 (Dallas), 1793) in which the court asserted jurisdiction to punish crimes only defined under the law of nations, and for which jurisdiction had been established through an Act of Congress, and *United States v. Worrall*, in which common law criminal jurisdiction for offences against the law of nations in federal courts was "said to rest on statute alone." It was the first case in which it was denied that the United States had received the common law, and as a consequence, that criminal jurisdiction could not be founded on that basis. See discussed in Quincy Wright, *The Control of American Foreign Relations* (New York: The Macmillan Company, 1922), p. 197; Anthony Bellia and Bradford Clark, "The Federal Common Law of Nations" *Columbia Law Review* 109 (January, 2009), p. 53.

643 Alexander Hamilton, *Federalist Papers* no. XXII, p. 182.

644 *Ware v. Hylton* 3 U.S. (3 Dall.), 199 (1796), at 272.

645 James Madison to George Nicholas (May 17, 1788), in *The Papers of James Madison* (Chicago: University of Chicago Press, 1967), Vol. 11, p. 46.

squabbles do not provide valid reasons for unilateral abrogation of solemn commitments:

> These gentlemen would do well to reflect that a treaty is only another name for a bargain, and that it would be impossible to find a nation who would make any bargain with us, which should be binding on them ABSOLUTELY, but on us only so long and so far as we may think proper to be bound by it. They who make laws may, without doubt, amend or repeal them; and it will not be disputed that they who make treaties may alter or cancel them; but still let us not forget that treaties are made, not by only one of the contracting parties, but by both; and consequently, that as the consent of both was essential to their formation at first, so must it ever afterwards be to alter or cancel them. The proposed Constitution, therefore, has not in the least extended the obligation of treaties. They are just as binding, and just as far beyond the lawful reach of legislative acts now, as they will be at any future period, or under any form of government.[646]

In *Ware v. Hylton*, Judge Samuel Chase made the point that supremacy could only imply being supreme vis-à-vis state law. With reference to Article VI, he noted that "a treaty cannot be the supreme law of the land, that is, of all the United States, if any Act of a State Legislature can stand in its way."[647] Like Madison, he went on to argue the status of treaties vis-à-vis the federal Constitution in terms of popular consent,[648] saying that since "[t]here can be no limitation on the power of the people of the United States" and since the people had adopted the Constitution, they therewith declared by implication

> that every treaty made by the authority of the United States shall be superior to the constitution and laws of any individual state, and their will alone is to decide. [In addition,] [t]he people of America have been pleased to declare that all treaties made before the establishment of the national Constitution or laws of any of the states contrary to a treaty shall be disregarded.[649]

646 John Jay, *Federalist Papers*, no. LXIV, p. 378.

647 *Ware v. Hylton* 3 U.S. (3 Dall.), 199 (1796), at 236.

648 He did so by distinguishing between three kinds of international law: "The first is universal, or established by the general consent of mankind, and binds all nations. The second is founded on express consent, and is not universal, and only binds those nations that have assented to it. The third is founded on tacit consent, and is only obligatory on those nations which have adopted it." See *Ware v. Hylton* 3 U.S. (3 Dall.), 199, 1796, at 227.

649 *Ware v. Hylton* 3 U.S. (3 Dall.), 199 (1796), at 237.

Hence, said Chase, the treaty of 1783 had been superior to state law, though not to federal law. The conclusion is therefore fully warranted that "[t]he Federal Convention (…) adopted treaties as judicially enforceable laws of the land as a central solution [to the problem of state frustration of treaty obligations]."[650] What is more, given that Chase considered that the 'American people' was fully in charge of the country ever since the adoption of the Declaration of Independence, his statement must also be understood to include the French treaties of alliance of 1778.

The much more complicated question concerned the applicability of the customary law of nations. In the late 18th century, most jurists sharply distinguished between the conventional law of nations (i.e. treaties) and customary law, which comprised the law of nations as a set of unwritten rules as well as the 'usage of nations.' However, no clear distinction was made between principles and usage, and because of the conspicuous omission of explicit references in the Constitution to the law of nations among the categories of law mentioned in Articles III and VI, there has been much controversy about its applicability and status, and opinion is far from uniform. Basing himself on the fundamental law argument, one modern scholar believes that this omission resulted from the fact that "the force of the law of nations stemmed from the conception that it was rooted in natural law."[651] That is to say, once federal courts have exclusive jurisdiction over important categories of the law of nations that directly affect foreign policy, a reference to the law of nations became superfluous because all courts in the United States would be bound by it in any event (by dint of being *necessary law*), whilst the crucial categories were now reserved for interpretation by federal courts only. Another scholar thinks that the reason this distinction between treaties and the law of nations was drawn was because the latter, being unwritten, was "too vague to form rules of conduct,"[652] or because the Framers felt that it "needed congressional definition before it should be treated as supreme law."[653]

650 Martin Flaherty, "History Right? Historical Scholarship, Original Understanding and Treaties as 'Supreme Law of the Land'" 99 *Columbia Law Review,* no. 8 (1999), p. 2152.

651 Stewart Jay, "The Status of the Law of Nations in Early American Law," *Vanderbilt Law Review* 42 (1989), p. 833.

652 For an argument against the inherent vagueness of the natural law concept and its incorporation into American law, see Philip Hamburger, "Natural Rights, Natural Law and American Constitutions" *The Yale Law Journal* 102, no. 4 (1993), pp. 907–960.

653 Michael Ramsey, "The Law of Nations as a Constitutional Obligation," pp. 21–22. Ramsey refers to the argument made by Gouveneur Morris during the Constitutional Convention of 1787.

Yet in spite of the apparent omission, there are some significant statements that suggest that customary international law is part of the law of the land in the United States. The most unequivocal pronouncement to that end was made by Attorney-General Edmund Randolph, who declared in a 1792 opinion that "[t]he law of nations, although not specially adopted by the constitution or any municipal act, is essentially a part of the law of the land."[654] Another statement that supports the view that the customary law of nations comes within the remit of "the laws of the United States" pursuant to Article III, sec. 2, cl. 1 and VI, cl. 2 follows from the *Henfield* case. In this case, the presiding judge, John Jay, recognized that "the laws of the United States" comprise "the law of nations,"[655] in the sense of customary law. Jay reiterated this point in a charge delivered in Virginia, in which he said that "the Constitution, the statutes of Congress, the law of nations, and treaties constitutionally made compose the laws of the United States."[656] In the case *Talbot v. Seeman*, the court explicitly mentioned 'usage' while asserting as a general rule "that the laws of the United States ought not, if it be avoidable, so to be construed as to infract the common principles and usages of nations or the general doctrines of national law."[657] The most ingenious statement in this context comes from Alexander Hamilton, who made a historical argument with reference to the common law to argue in favor of the bindingness of the customary law of nations on the United States:

---

654 Edmund Randolph to Thomas Jefferson (June 26, 1792), in Benjamin Hall (ed.), *Official Opinions of the Attorneys General of the United States* (Washington DC: R. Farnham, 1852), Vol. 1, p. 27.

655 *Henfield's Case*, 11 F. Cas. 1099 (C.C.D. Pa. 1793), at 1101, quoted in Jordan Paust, "In Their Own Words: Affirmations of the Founders, Framers and Early Judiciary Concerning the Binding Nature of the Customary Law of Nations" *U.C. Davis Journal of International Law and Policy* 13, no. 2, pp. 232–33. Paust adds that this view was shared by justices James Wilson and James Iredell, both of whom made charges in this case.

656 John Jay, "Charge to Grand Jury, Richmond, VA" (May 22, 1793), in *The Correspondence and Public Papers of John Jay* (New York: G.P. Putnam's Sons, 1890), Vol. 3, pp. 478–479. See also discussed in Anthony Bellia and Bradford Clark, "The Federal Common Law of Nations" *Columbia Law Review* 109 (January, 2009) and Jordan Paust, "In Their Own Words: Affirmations of the Founders, Framers and Early Judiciary Concerning the Binding Nature of the Customary Law of Nations" *U.C. Davis Journal of International Law and Policy* 13, no. 2, p. 234.

657 5 U.S. (1 Cranch), 1 (1801), at 43. the case itself concerned the capture by the USS Constitution of a vessel belonging to the city of Hamburg that was sailing for France at the time of the Quasi-War. Because there had been no official declaration of war, the application of the laws of war to this case was uncertain, while the ship itself could not be considered an enemy vessel, since Hamburg was a non-belligerent.

> 1. The United States, when a member of the British Empire, were, in this capacity, a party to that law, and not having dissented from it, when they became independent, they are to be considered as having continued a party to it. 2. The common law of England, which was and is in force in each of these States, adopts the law of nations, the positive equally with the natural, as a part of itself. 3. Ever since we have been an independent nation, we have appealed to and acted upon the *modern* law of nations as understood in Europe—various resolutions of Congress during our revolution, the correspondence of executive officers, the decisions of our courts of admiralty, all recognized this standard. 4. Executive and legislative acts, and the proceedings of our courts, under the present government, speak a similar language, [and] refer expressly to the *modern* law of nations, which must necessarily be understood as that prevailing in Europe, and acceded to by this country (…) It is indubitable, that the customary law of European nations is as a part of the common law, and, by adoption, that of the United States.[658]

The above statements taken together clearly suggest that customary international law was and is part of the law of the land. But while article I, sec. 8 enabled Congress to elevate it to the status of supreme law as defined in Article VI, it is not clear whether it actually does. The quotes above from the *Henfield* and *Talbot* cases suggest that it does, and one statement even intimates that it is superior to the Constitution itself: "the law of nations (…) was superior to any act or any law of any nation; it implied the consent of all, and was mutually binding on all, being acquiesced in for the common benefit of all."[659] One 20th-century scholar shares this point of view, saying that "not only are treaties and customary international law of authority superior to national statutes and the Constitution of the United States, but also that national courts in the United States are bound in observing sound principles of law to act upon this fact."[660]

658 Alexander Hamilton, "Camillus no. XX" (1795), in *The Works of Alexander Hamilton*, Vol. 5, pp. 436–437.

659 George Nicholas, "Speech to the Convention of Virginia" in Jonathan Elliot (ed.), *The Debates in the Several State Conventions of the Adoption of the Federal Constitution*, Vol. 3, p. 502.

660 Pitman Potter, "Relative Authority of International Law and National Law in the United States" *American Journal of International Law* 19 no. 2 (1925), p. 326.

But as with the earlier common law discussion, there is also evidence to the contrary. In the case *Chisholm v. Georgia*, for instance, judge Iredell drew the conclusion that

> No part of the Law of Nations can apply to this case, as I apprehend, but that part which is termed "The Conventional Law of Nations;" nor can this any otherwise apply than as furnishing rules of interpretation, since unquestionably the people of the United States had a right to form what kind of Union, and upon what terms they pleased, without reference to any former examples.[661]

The same conclusion follows from *Ware v. Hylton,* in which, as Ramsey said, "the opinions [of justices Iredell, Chase, Cushing, Paterson and Wilson] suggest that the prevailing view did not accept the law of nations as part of supreme law of its own force."[662] St. George Tucker underlined the same point in his analysis of the sources of the Constitution:

> [S]o every such case, whether civil or criminal, and whether it arise under the law of nations, the common law, or law of the state, belongs exclusively, to the *jurisdiction of the states*, respectively. And this, as well from the reason of the thing, as from the express declarations contained in the twelfth and thirteenth articles of the amendments to the constitution.[663]

Hence, there appears to be serious disagreement among early jurists about the applicability and status of the customary law of nations. Bellia and Clark's view that the Supreme Court rejected the assumption of "some members of the founding generation [who] believed that the law of nations applied in American courts" appears to be well-founded, in particular in light of Iredell's stance in *Chisholm*.[664] Paust qualified his position on this matter by adding that "the

661 *Chisholm. v. Georgia*, 2 U.S. (2 Dall.) 419 (1793), at 449. This case concerned a claim by one Alexander Chisholm against the state of Georgia over payments made to that state during the Revolutionary war. Georgia claimed that it did not need to heed a call to appear, it being a "sovereign state." It was the first case with significant impact argued before the Supreme Court.

662 Michael Ramsey, "The Law of Nations as a Constitutional Obligation," pp. 18–19.

663 St. George Tucker, "Of the Unwritten, or Common Law of England" in *Blackstone's Commentaries*, Vol. 1, p. 422.

664 Instead, Bellia and Clark conclude, the Court would come to apply, "certain principles derived from the law of nations as a means of upholding the Constitution's allocation of

meaning of customary international law and treaties has been understood to be dynamic."[665] As a result, Ramsey seems to be incorrect when saying that no case from the early period appears to "unambiguously [give] the law of nations, standing alone, superior effect over state law as a constitutional matter."[666]

All of this is certainly not to argue that each of the principal branches of government did not have a duty to abide by the law of nations; rather the contrary. With respect to the powers of the president, the general tenor was in fact that the president is bound to respect the law of nations—including customary law—but that he has a certain margin of appreciation.[667] A series of cases established beyond a reasonable doubt that the president is bound to to give effect to treaties by virtue of them being supreme federal law,[668] and possibly also to customary law, though perhaps not to the same extent. Thus, in spite of a 1814 decision which had been interpreted to imply that the president can violate international law,[669] an 1822 opinion from the

---

foreign affairs powers to Congress and President." See "The Federal Common Law of Nations" *Columbia Law Review* 109 (January, 2009), p. 7.

665 Jordan Paust, "In Their Own Words: Affirmations of the Founders, Framers and Early Judiciary Concerning the Binding Nature of the Customary Law of Nations" *U.C. Davis Journal of International Law and Policy* 13, no. 2, p. 237.

666 Michael Ramsey, "The Law of Nations as a Constitutional Obligation," p. 19.

667 Based on an extensive analysis of the Washington Administration's law of nations policy, Reinstein concluded that "[m]ajor decision by the administration—validating and interpreting the treaties with France according to principles of strict neutrality, referring disputed legal issues to the Supreme Court, and establishing Rules on Neutrality that were conformable to the treaties and the law of nations—were based on the principle that the Executive was duty-bound to execute the law of nations." See Robert Reinstein, "Executive Power and The Law of Nations in the Washington Administration" *University of Richmond Law Review* 46, no.2 (2012), pp. 420–421.

668 See e.g. *United States v. Robins* 27 F. Cas. 825, (D.S.C. 1799); *United States v. Cooper* 25 F.Cas. 631, 641–642 (C.C.D. Pa. 1800) and *United States v. the Schooner Peggy* 5 U.S. (1 Cranch) 103, 110, 1801.

669 "[t]his usage is a guide which the sovereign follows or abandons at his will. The rule, like other precepts of morality, of humanity, and even of wisdom, is addressed to the judgment of the sovereign, and although it cannot be disregarded by him without obloquy, yet it may be disregarded. The rule is in its nature flexible. It is subject to infinite modification. It is not an immutable rule of law, but depends on political considerations which may continually vary." Joseph Story found it very difficult to agree with Marshall on this point, but conceded that "if Congress should enact (...) a law [confiscating enemy debts], however much I might regret it, I am not aware that foreign nations with whom we have no treaty to the contrary could, on the footing of the rigid law of nations, complain, though they might deem it a violation of the modern policy." See *Brown v. United States* 12 U.S. (8 Cranch) 110, 1814, at 128, 145.

Attorney-General declared that instead the president has a duty to abide not only by "the treaties of the United States, but [also the] general laws of nations which govern the intercourse between the United States and foreign nations; which impose on them (...) the strict observance of a respect for their natural rights and sovereignties (...)."[670]

A key consideration that is often raised in this context is that the Constitution determined that the president see to it "that the Laws be faithfully executed." Plainly speaking, this would imply the existence of a prohibition on violating the law of nations on the part of the executive. Interestingly enough, this position appears to have been shared across party lines as they emerged and existed during the first Washington administration. Alexander Hamilton for instance wrote in his *Pacificus* letters that "the Executive is charged with the execution of all laws, the laws of Nations as well as the Municipal law, by which the former are recognized and adopted."[671] James Madison agreed with Hamilton on this point, saying in his *Helvidius* letters that the executive is "bound to the faithful execution of [all laws], internal and external, by the nature of its trust and the sanction of its oath."[672] The only difference between Hamilton and Madison (and, by extension, Jefferson!) was that while the Constitution seems to suggest that

With respect to the returning of fugitive criminals, Wirt wrote that "even if, by the laws and usage of nations, the obligation existed, and were a perfect obligation, and the proof which is offered of the guilt of the accused also satisfied the requisitions of that law, still the President has no power to make the delivery. The constitution, and the treaties and acts of Congress made under its authority, comprise the whole of the President's powers; neither of these contains any provision on this subject." See William Wirt to James Monroe (November 20, 1821), in Benjamin Hall (ed.), *Official Opinions of the Attorneys General of the United States* (Washington DC: R. Farnham, 1852), Vol. 1, pp. 521–522.

670 William Wirt, "Restoration of a Danish slave" (September 27, 1822), *Official Opinions of the Attorneys-General of the United States*, Vol. 1, p. 570. See also discussed in Jordan Paust, "The President is Bound by International Law" *American Journal of International Law* 81, no. 2 (April 1987), pp. 379–382 and Michael Glennon, *Constitutional Diplomacy* (Princeton, NJ: Princeton University Press, 1990), pp. 232–282.

671 Alexander Hamilton, "Pacificus no. 1" (June 29, 1793), in *The Works of Alexander Hamilton*, Vol. 4, p. 440. Lobel and Paust believe that this statement implies inclusion of customary law as well. See Jules Lobel, "The Limits of Constitutional Power: Conflicts between Foreign Policy and International Law" *Virginia Law Review* 71, no. 7 (October 1985), p. 1116; Jordan Paust, "In Their Own Words: Affirmations of the Founders, Framers and Early Judiciary Concerning the Binding Nature of the Customary Law of Nations" *U.C. Davis Journal of International Law and Policy* 13, no. 2, pp. 243–244.

672 James Madison, "Helvidius no. II" (August-September 1793), in *The Writings of James Madison*, Vol. 6, p. 159.

"Congress' law-of-nations powers (...) bind the President,"[673] Hamilton believed that since the President is charged with the execution of all laws, "[he] must first judge for himself of their meaning."[674] It was only because the Republicans wished to rein in the powers of the executive that Madison *cum suis* disagreed with Hamilton; both were nevertheless convinced of the need for uniform adherence to the law of nations. What is more, there also appeared to be a widely shared understanding that the president's ability to undertake any kind of hostile measures was subjected to Congressional approval. For example, James Iredell declared that "the Constitution of the United States intrusted the Congress alone with the authority of declaring war, or permitting any inferior species of hostility."[675] In the *Henfield* case, James Wilson remarked that only Congress can "lift up the sword of the United States."[676] The most convincing statement arguably comes from George Washington himself, who said that without a fiat from Congress, "no offensive expedition of importance can be undertaken" by the president.[677]

As to the role of the courts and their margin of appreciation, the situation was more complex. Nevertheless, future Chief Justice of the Supreme Court John Jay argued in *Federalist* no. III that an obligation to uniformly apply international law was incumbent on the courts:

---

673 Michael Ramsey, "The Law of Nations as a Constitutional Obligation," p. 12. See also Jay, who noted that responsibilities on interpreting the law of nations was divided between the three branches of government. Constitutionally speaking, the legislative branch is the strongest of the three, having the power to define and even punish offences against the law of nations, which, as was mentioned earlier, includes determining just causes of war. See Jay, "The Status of the Law of Nations in Early American Law," p. 834.

674 Hamilton, "Pacificus no. I" (June 29, 1793), in *The Works of Alexander Hamilton*, Vol. 4, p. 444. On Hamilton's arguments in *Pacificus*, Ramsey remarked that these should not be seen as a result of his "sometimes-idiosyncratic political views" but as being consistent with 18th-century political discourse in line with Montesquieu and Blackstone. See Michael Ramsey, *The Constitution's Text in Foreign Affairs* (Cambridge, MA: Harvard University Press, 2007), p. 85.

675 James Iredell, "A Charge Delivered to the Grand Jury for the District of North Carolina" (June 2, 1794), in Griffith McRee, (ed.), *Life and Correspondence of James Iredell* (New York: D. Appleton and Company, 1858), vol. 2, p. 410.

676 Quoted in Andrew Kent, "Congress's Under-Appreciated Power to Define and Punish Offenses Against the Law of Nations" *Texas Law Review* 85 (2006–07), p. 919.

677 George Washington to William Moultrie (August 28, 1793), in John Fitzpatrick (ed.), *Writings of George Washington, 1741–99*. (Washington DC: Library of Congress, 1931–44), Vol. 33, p. 73.

> Under the national government, treaties and articles of treaties, as well as the laws of nations, will always be expounded in one sense and executed in the same manner. (…) The wisdom of the convention, in committing such questions to the jurisdiction and judgment of courts appointed by and responsible only to one national government, cannot be too much commended.[678]

Hamilton reiterated this point in a later paper, saying that "cases arising upon treaties and the law of nations (…) may be supposed proper for the federal jurisdiction."[679] The Judiciary Act of 1789 further elaborated on the general jurisdiction of the Supreme Court, declaring that, *inter alia*, it shall have "exclusively all such jurisdiction of suits or proceedings against ambassadors, or other public ministers, or their domestics, or domestic servants, as a court of law can have or exercise consistently with the law of nations; and original, but not exclusive jurisdiction of all suits brought by ambassadors, or other public ministers, or in which a consul, or vice consul, shall be a party." Some years later in the case *Chisholm v. Georgia*,[680] Jay repeated his point made in the *Federalist*, suggesting that the applicability of the law of nations extended much wider than just issues concerning diplomatic staff: "the joint [interests] of nations, (…) are regulated by the law of nations and treaties, such cases necessarily belong to national jurisdiction."[681]

There were certainly precedents for having courts administer the law of nations, the most obvious example being prize courts, which, in the words of justice Iredell, became "a court of all the nations in the world, because all persons in every part of the world are concluded by its sentences in cases clearly coming within its jurisdiction."[682] For Hamilton, national security provided another good reason for assigning matters involving international law to the federal judiciary. While arguing that trial juries would lead to "the denial or

678 John Jay, *The Federalist* no. III, p. 95.

679 Alexander Hamilton, *Federalist Papers*, no. LXXX, p. 446.

680 "By taking a place among the nations of the earth, [the United States had] become amenable to the laws of nations, and it was their interest as well as their duty to provide that those laws should be respected and obeyed; in their national character and capacity, the United States were responsible to foreign nations for the conduct of each State relative to the laws of nations and the performance of treaties, and there the inexpediency of referring all such questions to State courts, and particularly to the courts of delinquent States, became apparent." See 2 U.S. (2 Dall.), 419, at 474.

681 *Chisholm v. Georgia*, 2 U.S. (2 Dall.) 419 (1793), at 475.

682 See *Penhallow v. Doane*. 3 U.S. 54 (3 Dall.), 1795, at p. 91. Quoted in Stewart Jay, "The Status of the Law of Nations in Early American Law," p. 822.

perversion of justice by the sentences of courts" and saying that these could easily be perceived as "aggressions against sovereigns" or even "with reason classed among the just causes of war," he argued that "it will follow that the federal judiciary ought to have cognizance of all causes in which the citizens of other countries are concerned."[683] More in general, the need for taking partial responsibility in defending U.S. foreign policy—in particular where it pertains so-called perfect rights, the violation of which allows a country to seek redress by force if necessary[684]—was one reason why the Constitution lodged powers to interpret international law in federal courts.

In general, there appeared to be agreement that ensuring proper enforcement of the law of nations by all branches of government was a necessity for the fledgling republic. The *Federalist Papers*, a series of newspaper articles written over the course of 1787–88 in support of ratification of the Constitution in New York State, are an important early source in this regard, if only because their three authors, Alexander Hamilton, John Jay and James Madison had been among the most prominent delegates present in Philadelphia. In one of the first articles, John Jay made a direct link between the importance of having a single government and responsibility for observance of the law of nations:

> It is of high importance to the peace of America that she observe the laws of nations towards all these powers, and to me it appears evident that this will be more perfectly and punctually done by one national government than it could be either by thirteen separate States or by three or four distinct confederacies.[685]

Enforcement of the law was to be a key element of in America's foreign relations. Therefore, it was only logical, Madison said, that "the law of nations, (...) as far as it is a proper object of municipal legislation, is submitted to the federal government." For good measure, he added that in order to do so properly, government officials "ought not to be altogether ignorant of the law of nations."[686] The opinions of the authors of the *Federalist* were widely shared. Some years later, in his capacity as justice on the Supreme Court, James Wilson also said that peace at home could be served by uniform application of the law among the states: "to ensure domestic tranquillity (...) the law of nations, the rule

683 Alexander Hamilton, *Federalist Papers*, no. LXXX, p. 446.

684 See discussed in Vattel, *The Law of Nations*, Bk. II, Ch. V, p. 297.

685 John Jay, *The Federalist* no. III, p. 95.

686 James Madison, *Federalist Papers*, no. LIII, p. 330.

between contending states, will be enforced among the several states in the same manner as municipal law."[687]

Beyond the legal technicalities regarding the status of the law of nations, the Constitution itself deserves some discussion since it represented a revolutionary departure in international law in many respects with various far-reaching implications for international politics and how Americans viewed opportunities to improve on its architecture. One point that has often been noted is how the transition from the Articles of Confederation to the Constitution led to the creation of a unprecedented kind of polity, being a federal republic on a continental scale. Hendrickson commented on this point that

> [i]f Americans represented a new diplomacy that looked toward a new system of interstate relations, they did so most completely in their hopes for the union. (…) With the construction of their federal union, Americans proposed to take a step beyond the balance of power (…).

As a result, he concluded, the Americans "understood that any continental connections they formed with Europe threatened to undermine the great 'Continental Connexion' they wished to form in America; 'internationalism' was, in this sense, not simply compatible with but a potential auxiliary and abettor of 'isolationism.'"[688]

The role of the Supreme Court in particular appeared to go beyond that of a mere constitutional tribunal. In this regard, James Wilson emphasized some of the international implications of the new federal constitution, viewing the Supreme Court as "in effect an international tribunal for the settlement of disputes between states," making it "an interesting object of study for comparative jurisprudence as an example of an international court."[689] According to Elisabeth Zoller, the transition was only truly completed with the *Marbury v. Madison* decision of 1803, which established the principle of judicial review.[690] It meant that the right to interpret the Constitution was taken away from the

687 *Chisholm. v. Georgia*, 2 U.S. (2 Dall.) 419 (1793), at 465.

688 Hendrickson, *Peace Pact*, p. 176.

689 Randolph C. Adams, "The Legal Theories of James Wilson" *University of Pennsylvania Law Review and American Law Register* 68, no. 4 (June 1920), p. 354. See, for an appraisal of the early court's contribution to interpreting the law of nations, Charles Smith, "Credible Commitments and the Early American Supreme Court" *Law and Society Review* 42, no. 1 (2008), pp. 80–83.

690 Elisabeth Zoller, "Aspects Internationaux du Droit Constitutionnel: Contribution à la Théorie de la Fédération d'États" *Recueil des Cours* 294 (2002), p. 100. For a contemporary interpretation of the Constitution as an international treaty, see Francisco F. Martin, *The*

states which had established it, and put in the hand of judges.[691] Perhaps curiously, this modern view was not shared at the time by one of the Constitution's great interpreters, St. George Tucker. He argued on the basis of the tenth amendment[692] that even under the 1787 Constitution, the United States remained a mere confederation. Drawing on Vattel, he said that the amendment is "nothing more than an express recognition of the law of nations" and then goes on to quote the Neuchâtelois lawyer:

> [S]everal sovereign, and independent states may unite themselves together by a perpetual confederacy, without each in particular ceasing to be a perfect state. They will form together a federal republic: the deliberations in common will offer no violence to the sovereignty of each member, though they may in certain respects put some constraint on the exercise of it, in virtue of voluntary engagements.[693]

At the same time, the Constitution could also be seen as an unequal alliance, again drawing on Vattel,[694] in creating a kind of contract between the federal government and the states whereby the latter "do not contract their sovereign rights into oblivion, but rather *transfer* certain rights to their treaty partner, the federal government."[695] At the domestic level, the shared responsibilities between executive, legislative and judicial branches opened up the prospect for what Edward Corwin famously called "an invitation to struggle for the privilege of directing American foreign policy."[696]

Constitution as Treaty: The International Legal Constructionalist Approach to the U.S. Constitution (Cambridge: Cambridge University Press, 2007).

691 As such, this development had its roots in British constitutional history. Bilder recounts that the right of the Supreme Court to review legislation derived from the fact that the severing of constitutional ties with Britain meant that the Privy Council, whose role it had been to review colonial legislation, had ceased, and that it then fell to the judiciary as a non-political body to take up this role. See Mary Sarah Bilder, "Colonial Constitutionalism and Constitutional Law," *Boston College Law School Faculty Papers* (2008), p. 10.

692 "The powers not delegated to the United States by the constitution, nor prohibited by it to the states, are reserved to the states respectively, or to the people."

693 St. George Tucker, "Of the Unwritten, or Common Law of England," in *Blackstone's Commentaries*, Vol. 1, p. 412. The quote comes from Vattel, *The Law of Nations*, Bk I, ch. 2, para. 10, p. 84.

694 Vattel, *The Law of Nations*, Bk. II, ch. 12, para. 175, pp. 349–352.

695 Tara Helfman, "The Law of Nations in *The Federalist Papers*," p. 122 (emphasis in original).

696 Edward Corwin, *The President: Office and Powers* (4th ed, New York, 1957), 170–171. Quoted in Bradford Perkins, *Cambridge History of American Foreign Relations*, Vol. 1, p. 70.

What this discussion has attested is not only that Americans shared Vattel's notion about the close connection between the domestic and international legal and political orders—and therewith rejected Blackstonian notions about indivisible sovereignty[697]—but also what Wood called "the peculiar American tendency to discuss political issues in constitutional terms—a tendency that had the effect of turning quarrels over policy into contests over basic principles."[698] Another typical thing in the early United States was that judges were often seen as "political magistrates rather than as legal experts separated from politics," a notion which continues to survive in our times.[699] More in general, it can be concluded that among the early American statesmen, there existed a shared reverence for the law of nations—also in the context of the new Constitution. But as we will see in the following chapters, a universally shared reverence for the law of nations and a broad consensus about the need to respect and enforce it at home did not necessarily translate into uniform agreement on its application or enforcement. As with religion, it could lead to a closing of ranks in times of peril, but equally so, give rise to bitter quarrels when other considerations, whether of a political, economic or ideological nature, interfered.

---

697 Alison LaCroix, *The Ideological Origins of American Federalism* (Cambridge, MA: Harvard University Press, 2010), pp. 79–80, 125.

698 Gordon Wood, *Empire of Liberty: A History of the Early Republic, 1789–1815* (New York: Oxford University Press, 2009), p. 185.

699 Wood, *Empire of Liberty*, p. 412.

CHAPTER 5

Law and Foreign Policy in the Federalist Era (1789–1801)

5.1 Towards the Neutrality Proclamation: Hamilton vs. Jefferson

Many historians have framed early American foreign relations by way of contrasting the philosophies of Alexander Hamilton and Thomas Jefferson. While there were a number of other important characters in this respect including John Adams, John Jay, James Madison and even Benjamin Franklin, none of them developed a coherent doctrine that would develop into a mainstream intellectual tradition in foreign relations. While Hamilton and Jefferson served together in the first Washington administration—as secretaries of the Treasury and of State, respectively—they were at the origins of party divisions in the United States, each of them espousing very different visions on how the new nation could best secure its future. Historians have therefore largely subscribed to the idea of distinguishing between Hamiltonian and Jeffersonian traditions,[700] and have contributed to sharpening the differences between them.[701]

The previous chapter showed that most of the early American statesmen and jurists believed that the law of nations had in one way or another been

700 As a short sample, see e.g. David Hendrickson. *Union, Nation or Empire: The American Debate over International Relations, 1789–1941* (Lawrence, KS: University Press of Kansas, 2009), ch. 4; Daniel G. Lang, *Foreign Policy in the Early Republic* (Baton Rouge (LS): Louisiana State University Press, 1985), chs. 4–5; Gordon Wood, *Empire of Liberty: A History of the Early Republic, 1789–1815*. (New York: Oxford University Press, 2009); Albert Bowman, "Jefferson, Hamilton and American Foreign Policy" *Political Science Quarterly*, 71, no. 1 (1956); Robert Kagan, *Dangerous Nation: America's Foreign Policy from its Earliest Days to the Dawn of the 20th Century* (New York: Vintage Press, 2007), pp. 104–112. Varg is exceptional in giving as much credit to Madison as to Jefferson in the struggle with Hamilton. See Paul Varg, *Foreign Policies of the Founding Fathers* (Baltimore, MD: Penguin Books, 1970), pp. 70–94.

701 See e.g. Lawrence Kaplan, *Colonies into Nation: American Diplomacy 1763–1801* (New York: The Macmillan Company, 1972) and Walter Russell Mead, *Special Providence: American Foreign Policy and How It Changed the World* (New York: Alfred A. Knopf, 2001), chs. 4, 6; After a brief review, Kaplan concludes that "[b]ut despite impressive disclaimers, the other statesmen of the period, even when the stamp of their personality is felt, are placed on a Jeffersonian or a Hamiltonian field rather than accorded separate ground of their own." See Kaplan, *Colonies into Nation*, pp. 182–184.

 | DOI 10.1163/9789004305687_007

incorporated into American law. Given the significant differences in political outlooks between Hamilton and Jefferson, one might expect that these differences would also reflect in their views on international law. The purpose here is to investigate whether this is the case and if so, to what extent. Studying Hamilton's and Jefferson's statements and policy advice will help to illustrate the importance which they attached to conducting foreign policy in terms of the law of nations, and how the law held up in the arena of policy-making. Making this subject particularly interesting is not only the fact that foreign policy, in the words of DeConde, "became the outstanding issue between the two national political parties which sprang into existence in [the late 1780s],"[702] but also because by taking a neutral stance, the United States adopted a policy which eminently lend itself to being formulated and defended in terms of the law of nations. The question is then to what extent a policy that was predicated on the basic notion of survival could allow for differentiated interpretations of rights and obligations.

By drawing a general distinction between Hamiltonians and Jeffersonians, one can escape the simple dichotomy between realists and idealists. To begin with, these labels do not do justice to the complexities of the thinking of each of the standard-bearers of these groups, Hamilton and Jefferson. What is more, by drawing such absolute distinctions between them, no room is allowed for the parties to agree on issues. For instance, while both Hamilton and Jefferson dramatically differed over whether the best policy would be to balance against Britain or France, they agreed on the need to use balance-of-power principles to provide for the safety of the country. This chapter will therefore first sketch the main features of Hamilton's and Jefferson's political and legal thinking before studying the diplomatic issues that occupied the first two administrations.

One reason why Alexander Hamilton's political views differed so markedly from those of Thomas Jefferson relates to their personal origins. Unlike Jefferson, Hamilton was neither born in wealth nor into a southern plantation family. Having built up his career in New York City, his sympathies lay with the urban classes, manufacturing industries and the promotion of foreign trade. Philosophically, Hamilton shared the view espoused by Vattel, Pufendorf, Hobbes and others that "[s]elf-preservation is the first duty of a nation."[703] According to Hamilton, securing the country's existence could best be achieved

---

702 Alexandre Deconde, *Entangling Alliance: Politics and Diplomacy under George Washington.* (Durham, NC: Duke University Press, 1958), p. 32.

703 Alexander Hamilton, "Pacificus no. 3" (July 6, 1793), in *The Works of Alexander Hamilton*, Vol. 4, p. 457.

if the United States was to become a powerful nation, for which the promotion of commerce was paramount. Hamilton's trade theory was predicated on the idea that by further developing Anglo-American commerce, a system could be formed "that would emphasize the strengthening of commercial ties within the union rather than the reformation of commercial practices without." As a result, he saw the promotion of economic development as the key to America's future growth as well as security. However, he did not share Jefferson's belief that "the adroit use of trade boycotts and retaliating commercial restrictions would enable the United States to find a substitute for war."[704] This is why in 1789, Hamilton thwarted a proposal by Madison to impose a discriminatory tariff on British goods as a negotiation ploy to obtain better terms of trade in the West Indies. But with scuttling this proposal, the Republicans felt that Hamilton had "perverted and betrayed (...) the framers' original intentions."[705] Hamilton's thinking was however that trying to force free trade on European countries could only lead to war.[706] Although his formal cabinet position in the Washington administrations was that of Treasury secretary, he was able to play such a pivotal role in early foreign policy because he was the principal advisor to the president, a situation which Jefferson greatly resented.[707] He was thus allowed a say on every matter that was discussed by the cabinet, and as a result, managed to balance Jefferson's role in foreign relations against that of his own, if not outweighing it.

On the law of nations, Hamilton by and large subscribed to the general theory as set out by Vattel, whose work he might have found congenial in any event since the Neuchâtelois was as much an Anglophile as Hamilton was. Hamilton's pro-British sentiments may also account for the fact that he regarded the Constitution as having "adopt[ed] the common law of which the law of nations is a part."[708] In his *Camillus* letters, originally written in defense of the Jay Treaty, he expounded his international law philosophy. First, he distinguished the necessary law, which is, he says, "the law of nature applied to nations; or that system of rules for regulating the conduct of nation to nation, which reason deduces from the principles of natural right, as relative to political

704 David Hendrickson, *Union, Nation or Empire: The American Debate over International Relations, 1789–1941* (Lawrence, KS: University Press of Kansas, 2009), p. 43.

705 Onuf and Onuf, *Federal Union, Modern World*, pp. 156–157.

706 Hendrickson, *Union, Nation or Empire*, p. 43.

707 Dumas Malone, *Jefferson and the Rights of Man* (New York: Little, Brown and Co., 1951), p. 452.

708 Quoted from *Rutgers v. Waddington* in Suzanna Sherry, "The Founders' Unwritten Constitution" *The University of Chicago Law Review* 54, no. 4(1987), p. 1137.

societies or states." Secondly, he identified the voluntary law, which he described as "a system of rules resulting from the equality and independence of nations, and which, in the administration of their affairs, and the pursuit of their pretensions, proceeding on the principle of their having no common judge upon earth, attributes equal validity, as to external effects, to the measures or conduct of one as of another, without regard to the intrinsic justice of those measures or that conduct (...)." The third element was treaty law, or pactitious law, as Hamilton called it. While noting that provisions concluded between countries are only valid between the signatories themselves, he added that "yet, when we find a provision universally pervading the treaties between nations, for a length of time, as a kind of formula, it is high evidence of the general law of nations." This point is of course important with respect to the 'free ships, free goods' rule that the United States sought to promote as part of its neutrality policy. The last element was customary law, which he considered to consist of "those rules of conduct, that, in practice, are respected and observed among nations. Its authority depends on usage, implying a tacit consent and agreement. This also is a particular, not a general law, obligatory only on those nations whose acquiescence has appeared, or, from circumstances, may fairly be presumed (...)."[709]

Interestingly, Hamilton's conclusion reflects a rather empirical approach to the application of the law of nations in practice, stressing the primacy of treaty and customary law:

> [t]he [necessary and voluntary law] are discoverable by reason; the [pactitious and customary law] depend on proof, as matters of fact. Hence the opinions of jurists, though weighing, as the sentiments of judicious or learned men, who have made the subject a particular study, are not conclusive, as authorities. In regard to the necessary and voluntary law, especially, they may be freely disregarded, unless they are found to be adopted and sanctioned by the practice of nations. For where REASON is the guide, it cannot properly be renounced for mere OPINION, however respectable. As witnesses of the customary laws, their testimony, the result of careful researches, is more particularly entitled to attention.[710]

---

709 Hamilton, "Camillus no. XX," in *The Works of Alexander Hamilton*, Vol. 5, pp. 421–423. See also discussed in Gerald Stourzh, *Alexander Hamilton and the Idea of Republican Government* (Stanford: Stanford University Press, 1970), pp. 134–135.

710 Hamilton, "Camillus no. XX," in *The Works of Alexander Hamilton*, Vol. 5, p. 423. This opinion was shared years later by Attorney-General Wirt, who wrote that "if, instead of one nation, several nations concur either in the entire non-observance, or in the modified

This approach was also reflected in a later *Camillus* letter: "A pre-established rule of the law of nations can only be changed by their *common consent*. This consent may either be express, by treaties, declarations, etc., adopting and promising the observance of a different rule, or it may be implied by a course of practice or usage. The consent, in either case, must embrace the great community of civilized nations."[711] Hence, while Hamilton claims that the necessary and voluntary laws of nations are discoverable by reason, he still demands sanction and proof for their existence. The impression that Hamilton conveys is that of a lawyer who prefers to adhere narrowly to prevailing legal notions, a position which corresponds neatly with his affection for the British political tradition. Rather than conceiving of the law as a constraint on state power, Hamilton actually wanted to use it as a tool to strengthen the country's vis-à-vis the European powers—in particular by way of the laws of war.[712]

On several matters, Thomas Jefferson was in agreement with Hamilton, such as the importance of the balance of power, commerce, and adherence to the law of nations, albeit that he thought about their utility in a very different way. Jefferson's central objective was never to increase American power *per se*,

observance, of any precept of the law of nations, treating practically, as a matter of discretion, what the writers on that law have treated as a matter of perfect obligation, it would be idle in us to take the measure of our conduct from the precepts of those writers only, in entire disregard of the practice of other nations. We know that the law of nations, as it has been presented by Grotius and the writers who have succeeded him, beautiful as it is in theory, has in many instances been found too perfect to be introduced into practice; and that in many and important particulars it has been made to yield and give way to other rules of action, dictated by the selfishness, the necessities, the pride, and the ambition of nations. Hence, when we are required to give effect to any precept of those writers, it becomes our right and our duty to look to the usage of nations, as furnishing the practical commentary on the precept, beyond which we cannot justly be required to go." See William Wirt to James Monroe (November 20, 1821), in Benjamin Hall (ed.), *Official Opinions of the Attorneys General of the United States* (Washington DC: R. Farnham, 1852), Vol. 1, pp. 511–512.

711 Alexander Hamilton, "Camillus no. XXXI" (1795), in *The Works of Alexander Hamilton*, Vol. 6, p. 100. (emphasis added.). He reiterated this point in the next letter, saying that "No one nation can make a law of nations; no positive regulation of one state, or of a partial nomination of states, can pretend to this character. A law of nations is a law which nature, agreement, or usage, has established between nations." See "Camillus no. XXXII," in ibid., Vol. 6, p. 121.

712 John Fabian Witt, "The Power of War and Peace," draft chapter from *Lincoln's Code: The Laws of War in American History*. Presented at NYU legal history colloquium (February 17, 2010). Witt contends for instance that Hamilton used this reasoning in his *Pacificus* papers to bolster the authority of the executive, and that the 1793 Neutrality Proclamation essentially adopted his philosophy in this respect.

but to secure democracy at home. This is a principal reason why he was satisfied to note that "it is a maxim with us, and I think it a wise one, not to entangle ourselves with the affairs in Europe."[713] Jefferson's perspective on America was certainly closer to that of a 'city on a hill' than Hamilton's. For Jefferson and his followers, "[t]he federal republic was the ultimate, practical embodiment of the dreams of visionary theorists who had long sought to reconstitute the European system for peace and prosperity."[714] However, Jefferson's aversion from entangling the nation did not blind him to the need to conduct realist diplomacy from time to time. Hence, in spite of his affections for France, he believed that both of the two great European nations were "necessary instrument[s] to hold in check the disposition of the other to tyrannize over other nations."[715]

A similar utilitarian approach prevailed as to Jefferson's ideas about commerce. Rather than seeing it as a means to creating wealth, he looked at it as an instrument to promote peaceful intercourse, or when that is not possible, as 'a substitute for war.' A representative reflection of his thinking is contained in a report for Congress in which he described the outlines of a commercial policy—one which he would later pursue as president. Taking a page from Adam Smith, he noted in this report that as a principle, "relieved from all its shackles in all parts of the world, (…) every country [could] be employed in producing that which nature has best fitted it to produce, and each be free to exchange with others mutual surplusses for mutual wants." As a result, "the greatest mass possible would then be produced of those things which contribute to human life and human happiness; the numbers of mankind would be increased, and their condition bettered." One important condition in this regard was to ensure a open seas regime. As Jefferson said: "Were the ocean, which is the common property of all, open to the industry of all, so that every person and vessel should be free to take employment wherever it could be found, the United States would certainly not set the example of appropriating to themselves, exclusively, any portion of the common stock of occupation." But he also made clear that the United States should not shrink from using

713 Jefferson to Edward Carrington (December 21, 1787), in *The Writings of Thomas Jefferson*, Vol. IV, p. 483.

714 Peter Onuf and Nicholas Onuf, *Federal Union, Modern World: The Law of Nations in an Age of Revolutions 1776–1814* (Madison, WI: Madison House, 1992), p. 146.

715 Jefferson to James Monroe (January 8, 1804), in *The Works of Thomas Jefferson*, Vol. 10, pp. 67–68. See also discussed in David Hendrickson, *Union, Nation or Empire: The American Debate over International Relations, 1789–1941* (Lawrence, KS: University Press of Kansas, 2009), pp. 54–56.

coercive means in order to expand and boost international trade: "It is not to the moderation and justice of others we are to trust for fair and equal access to market with our productions, or for our due share in the transportation of them; but to our own means of independence, and the firm will to use them."[716]

This exposition already provides some hints as to Jefferson's views on the law of nations, which he set out in the most comprehensive fashion in his famous *Opinion on the French Treaties*. While he adopts—like Hamilton—a Vattellian mould, he appears to depart from this in some significant respects.[717] Among the principal branches of the law of nations, Jefferson identified "1. The moral law of our nature. 2. The usages of nations. 3. Their special conventions." For the deist Jefferson, the first of these categories has a decidedly divine content, being "the moral law to which man has been subjected by his creator, and of which his feelings or conscience, as it is sometimes called, are the evidence with which his creator has furnished him." Subsequently, the moral duties which follow from this not only inform the duties between individuals within a society, but also those between states. Hence compacts, or treaties, are not mere contracts between states, but have a moral content, resulting in that only if their performance becomes impossible or self-destructive can non-performance be acceptable, for "the law of self-preservation overrules the laws of obligation."[718]

So, while Hamilton's conception of the law of nations is governed by natural law in terms of secularized reason, Jefferson's conception owes more to divine morality. In this sense, he was not exceptional. We already saw that James Wilson's ideas about the origins and the binding character of the law of nations also owe to religion. Even so, most leading members of the founding generation do not appear to have been very religious at all. What is more, religion was not a chief factor either in the early republic's foreign policy. Only in the early 19th century did it gain more importance again.[719]

Still, divine inspiration did play its part in helping Jefferson to undertake diplomatic initiatives to reform the law of nations and to promote peaceful commerce. For instance, when he came to France to succeed Franklin, he did

716 Thomas Jefferson, "Report On the Privileges and Restrictions On the Commerce of the United States In Foreign Countries" (Dec. 16, 1793), in *The Works of Thomas Jefferson*, Vol. 8, p. 117.

717 See also discussed in Daniel G. Lang, *Foreign Policy in the Early Republic* (Baton Rouge (LS): Louisiana State University Press, 1985), pp. 128–129.

718 Jefferson, "Opinion on the French Treaties" (April 28, 1793), in *The Writings of Thomas Jefferson*, Vol. 3, p. 228.

719 See also discussed in Gordon Wood, *Empire of Liberty: A History of the Early Republic, 1789–1815* (New York: Oxford University Press, 2009), pp. 575–578.

so to undertake "nothing less than a diplomatic mission to convert all of Europe to the commercial principles of the American Revolution."[720] Kaplan noted the interrelationship between various elements of Jefferson's perspective: "[t]he links implied in the mutual acceptance of a liberal doctrine of neutral rights and most-favoured nation treatment must include, according to the reasoning of the American minister, the free entry of American products into the French market in exchange for French supplies and manufactures."[721] Sensing that progress had been made since the 1780s, he noted with satisfaction that "the principles of [the law of nations] have been liberalized in latter times by the refinement of manners and morals, (…) evidenced by the declarations, stipulations, and practice of every civilized nation."[722]

Contrasting Hamilton's and Jefferson's approaches to the law of nations, Hendrickson argued that Hamilton "gave greater weight to considerations of customary usage and accepted practice" while Jefferson "was led by his desire for a change in international law to greater reliance on "the natural or necessary law of nations" as discovered by the exercise of dispassionate reason."[723] This only seems to be right insofar as that saying that Hamilton relied more on customary law is not to say that he undervalued natural law or thought that international law was very malleable; rather to the contrary. As to Jefferson, it appears that a divinely-inspired morality may have been a larger influence in his appreciation of international law than dispassionate reason. But, as the evidence will show, even if differences existed between the Founding Fathers in terms of their political or legal views, it appears that up to the 1790s, there existed a strong concordance between American ideals and self-interest.[724]

The first time this consensus came under pressure was in 1790 with the Nootka Sound crisis. At this time, the Washington administration came to consider a possible request by Britain to pass through American territory in order to assert fur trading claims against Spain in the Pacific Northwest. The president sought advice on the issue from his cabinet, as well as the Chief Justice.

---

720 Merrill Peterson, "Thomas Jefferson and Commercial Policy 1783–1793" *William and Mary Quarterly*, vol. 22 (1965), p. 592.

721 Kaplan, *Colonies into Nation*, p. 176. In a letter written in September 1787, Jefferson expressed the hope that the principle of 'free ships, free goods' could be elevated as a rule of the modern law of nations. See Jefferson to Carnes (September 22, 1787), in *The Writings of Thomas Jefferson*, Vol. 6, pp. 318–319.

722 Jefferson to Thomas Pinckney (May 7, 1793), in *The Writings of Thomas Jefferson*, Vol. 9, p. 80.

723 David Hendrickson, *Union, Nation or Empire: The American Debate over International Relations, 1789–1941* (Lawrence, KS: University Press of Kansas, 2009), p. 32.

724 Lint, "Early American Conceptions of International Law," p. 75.

In his extensive analysis, Hamilton considered the writings of Pufendorf and Barbeyrac, but found Grotius and Vattel most congenial, for they argued that in a just war, the party which had 'right' on its side should be granted passage, and that a neutral should stay impartial and grant entry to neither or both sides in cases where the justness of a cause is doubtful. While his main conclusion was that the country should "cultivate [its] neutrality," he added that "there exists in the practice of nations and the dogmas of political writers a certain vague pretension to a right of passage in particular cases and according to circumstances, which is sufficient to afford to the strong a pretext for claiming and exercising it when it suits their interests, and to render it always dangerous to the weak to refuse, and sometimes not less so to grant it." He added that neither Spain nor France would have a reason to complain, because while a state has a right under international law to permit passage, it "is not bound to expose itself to a war, merely to shelter a neighbor from the approaches of its enemy."[725] The opinion of the Chief Justice, John Jay, went in the same direction, holding that while the ideal policy would be to deny passage of foreign troops across American territory at all times, the best option under the present circumstances would be "to consent to such a passage" because threatening with a refusal might lead to humiliation or war should the requesting party continue to insist on free passage.[726]

The Secretary of State, Thomas Jefferson, was not prepared to surrender American neutrality so easily to the British, even if in his letter to the president, he conveyed that the only danger he saw was indeed war with Great Britain.[727] However, not being in a pusillanimous mood, he suggested that "if Louisiana and the Floridas be added to the British empire, (…) in my opinion, we ought to make ourselves parties in the *general war* expected to take place, should this be the only means of preventing the calamity." (emphasis in original) However, it was not Jefferson's goal to steer towards this course, his preference being "for preserving neutrality as long, and entering in war as late, as possible." Thus, his advice was to steer "a middle course, [being] to avoid giving

725 Alexander Hamilton, "Cabinet paper: Answer to Questions Proposed by the President of the United States to the Secretary of the Treasury" (September 15, 1790), in *The Works of Alexander Hamilton*, Vol. 4, p. 321.

726 John Jay, "Opinion of the Chief Justice" (August 28, 1790), in Barbara Oberg and Jefferson Looney (eds.), *The Papers of Thomas Jefferson Digital Edition* (Charlottesville: University of Virginia Press, Rotunda, 2008), Vol. 17, p. 136.

727 Albert Bowman, "Jefferson, Hamilton and American Foreign Policy" *Political Science Quarterly* 71, no. 1 (March 1956), p. 21.

any answer."[728] Bowman even said that Hamilton's opinion in this case "foreshadowed the repeated surrenders of the Federalist administration to British requirements," concluding that "[t]he tough-minded champion of American interests was Jefferson; the apparition of British power unnerved Hamilton."[729] A rather different reading of events is made by Harper, who acknowledged that Hamilton's and Jefferson's policies—stressing neutrality above all—ostensibly did not differ, but credited the former with "ground[ing his approach] in the realities of the situation, that of a rising and vulnerable country," while Jefferson's objective was in fact to help further the creation of an alliance with France and Spain.[730] Yet ultimately, the call from the British never came, and the crisis blew over. Nevertheless, it helped to expose the conceptual differences that existed in the Washington administration: while the cabinet was united in its overall goals, little agreement existed over the means and approaches to achieve these.

The next major disagreement between Hamilton and Jefferson came in 1792, when France declared itself a republic, and the question arose whether the United States would continue to be beholden in its obligations towards the new overseas republic, and whether the new government should be recognized at all. Hamilton instinctively veered towards non-recognition, and suggested that the United States need not continue servicing its debt towards France.[731] Jefferson pre-empted the discussions by writing to Gouverneur Morris, the American minister in France, that changes of government should not make a difference in terms of recognition:

> It accords with our principles to acknolege any government to be rightful which is formed by the will of the nation substantially declared. The late government was of this kind, & was accordingly acknoleged by all the branches of ours. So any alteration of it which shall be made by the will of the nation substantially declared, will doubtless be acknoleged in like manner.[732]

728 Thomas Jefferson, "Opinion on Course of United States Towards Great Britain and Spain" (August 28, 1790), in *The Works of Thomas Jefferson*, Vol. 6, p. 143.

729 Albert Bowman, "Jefferson, Hamilton and American Foreign Policy" *Political Science Quarterly* 71, no. 1 (March 1956), pp. 21–22.

730 John L. Harper, *American Machiavelli: Alexander Hamilton and the Origins of U.S. Foreign Policy* (Cambridge: Cambridge University Press, 2004), p. 87.

731 Lint, "Early American Conceptions of International Law," p. 87.

732 Jefferson to Gouverneur Morris (November 7, 1792), in *The Works of Thomas Jefferson*, Vol. 7, p. 175. In a letter to Pinckey, the American minister in London, Jefferson made essentially the same point: "We certainly cannot deny to other nations that principle

After consultation with the president in early 1793, Jefferson went ahead in writing to the minister that the American government would recognize the new French government, and would resume honoring its debt payments:

> Since that we learn that a Convention is assembled, invested with full powers by the nation to transact it's affairs. Tho' we know that from the public papers only, instead of waiting for a formal annunciation of it, we hasten to act upon it by authorizing you, if the fact be true, to consider the suspension of paiment, (…) as now taken off, and to proceed as if it had never been imposed; considering the Convention, or the government they shall have established as the lawful representatives of the Nation and authorized to act for them.[733]

With these letters, Jefferson had established America's doctrine of recognition, which was, as Goebel said, "his own invention [and] far removed (…) from the accepted canons of international law."[734] This appraisal is somewhat surprising when one considers that Vattel himself had deemed that "foreign powers take for their rule the circumstance of actual possession" as the yardstick for determining recognition.[735]

But where Jefferson and the government ultimately adopted a practical approach where France was concerned, a question about recognition elsewhere posed real problems in terms of reconciling principles and interests. This concerned the recent revolution in Saint-Domingue, later to become Haiti, which started in 1791. The revolution in this French possession was directly inspired by the revolution that had engulfed France itself, and by liberal Enlightenment thought espoused by the Abbé Raynal and Denis Diderot.[736]

---

whereon our government is founded, that every nation has a right to govern itself internally under what forms it pleases, and to change these forms at its own will; and externally to transact business with other nations through whatever organ it chooses, whether that be a King, Convention, Assembly, Committee, President, or whatever it be: The only thing essential is, the will of the nation." See Jefferson to Thomas Pinckney (December 30, 1792), in *The Writings of Thomas Jefferson*, Vol. 9, pp. 6–8.

733 Jefferson to Morris (December 30, 1792), in *The Works of Thomas Jefferson*, Vol. 7, p. 199.

734 Jules Goebel, *The Recognition Policy of the United States* (New York: Longman, Green & Co, 1915), p. 98.

735 Emer de Vattel, *The Law of Nations*, Bk. IV, ch. 5, para. 68, p. 688. See also discussed in Robert Reinstein, "Slavery, Executive Power and International Law: The Haitian Revolution and American Constitutionalism" *American Journal of Legal History,* (forthcoming), p. 67.

736 The key text being Raynal's 1770 study *Histoire Philosophique des Deux Indes*, a good deal of which was authored by Diderot.

Being the first slave revolt, it created a huge dilemma for a nation whereby legal principles were ultimately trumped by political and economic interests. During the Washington and Adams administrations, the government was largely supportive of the slave rebellion, mostly because it would weaken France and its ambitions on the American continent, and because St. Domingue was a key trade partner for the young republic.[737] In the 1790s, Hickey notes, "some five hundred ships were employed in this trade, and St. Domingue stood second only to Great Britain in the foreign commerce of the United States."[738]

Throughout the 1790s, the government, Federalists and Republicans all continued to equivocate on the question of recognizing the independence of Haiti, the result being that formal recognition remained in abeyance. In 1798, however, the outbreak of the Quasi-War led to a decision to block all trade with French colonies including St. Domingue. But upon the insistence of Toussaint l'Ouverture, the rebel leader, an exception was negotiated, and Adams reopened trade with the island from August 1799 onwards.[739] Jefferson and his future Secretary of the Treasury, Albert Gallatin, opposed the granting of this exception, which constituted one more step to recognizing Haitian independence. This was because independence could make it a prey for Great Britain, or worse, that the island could be used to harm American commerce with the Caribbean.[740] As a result, this recognition question would not be resolved until Jefferson had become president.

Meanwhile, issues concerning recognition continued to arise in relation to revolutionary France. When in early 1793, France's previous minister was recalled and Edmond-Charles Genêt was sent to the United States to succeed him, president Washington submitted a number of questions to his cabinet asking whether the new minister should be received at all and on what terms, and whether the treaties with France ought to be suspended or not. Since the United States had already *de facto* recognized the new French government, Jefferson found the

737 Donald Hickey, "America's Response to the Slave Revolt in Haiti 1791–1806" *Journal of the Early Republic* 2, No. 4 (Winter, 1982), pp. 361–362, 365. However, Adams disagreed with this policy, thinking "[w]ill it not involve us in a more inveterate and durable hostility with France, Spain, and Holland, and subject us more to the policy of Britain than will be consistent with our interest or honor?" John Adams to Thomas Pickering (July 17, 1799), in *The Works of John Adams,* Vol. 8, p. 634.

738 Hickey, "America's Response to the Slave Revolt in Haiti 1791–1806", p. 363.

739 See discussed in Hickey, "America's Response to the Slave Revolt in Haiti 1791–1806", pp. 366–367.

740 Hickey, "America's Response to the Slave Revolt in Haiti 1791–1806", p. 368.

questions tendentious and suspected Hamilton's hand behind them.[741] A cabinet meeting on the questions was held on April 18, 1793. Despite protestations from Hamilton's side, it was unanimously agreed that Genêt should be received; however, he pleaded for a qualification to be added with respect to the French treaties, arguing on the basis of Vattel that the treaties could be considered voidable.[742] What gave this matter such immediacy was the fact that France had declared war on Britain, and that this could very likely drag the United States into the conflict due to its treaty commitments. The question as such was not immediately resolved, and papers were to be written by Hamilton, Randolph and Jefferson to be considered in a subsequent meeting.[743]

In his paper, Hamilton argued, with reference to Burlamaqui, Barbeyrac and Pufendorf, that the war undertaken by France is an offensive war and that in accordance with the stipulations of the treaty of alliance, a *casus foederis* cannot be said to exist.[744] As to the treaties themselves, Hamilton argued for "temporarily and provisionally" suspending the treaties based on the fact that they were concluded with the French monarch in a personal capacity, while admitting that a change in government *per se* is not a sufficient reason for abrogating treaties. Yet, this could be accepted when the treaty pertained to the nature of governments themselves. In support, he cited Grotius, who said that abrogating a treaty is possible when its intent was "peculiar to the form of government, as when free states enter into an alliance for the defence of their liberties."[745] Vattel was quoted next, saying that "when [a] change [in government] renders the alliance useless, dangerous, or *disagreeable*, it may be renounced."[746]

---

741 Jefferson, "The Anas I," in *The Works of Thomas Jefferson*, Vol. 1, p. 267.

742 Jefferson, "The Anas I," p. 268. Jefferson notes that Hamilton was to point this out to Randolph, but could not since he had no copy of Vattel with him! See for Hamilton's cabinet paper (April, 1793), in *The Works of Alexander Hamilton*, Vol. 4, pp. 369–396.

743 In *The Anas*, Jefferson notes that Randolph had written and submitted a statement, but no record of this is available in the authoritative *Opinions of the Attorneys-General*.

744 The young John Quincy Adams agreed with Hamilton's reasoning, and took it even one notch further: "it is a general principle of the laws of nations, that the rights and obligations of treaties survive the internal revolutions of government, and therefore that the republic of France may be entitled to the benefits of engagements contracted with the former Monarch, (…) the first Constituent Assembly [took exception to this] opinion that they thought the nation absolved from all such treaties previously made, as might be injurious to their interests." See John Quincy Adams, "Marcellus no. III (May 11, 1793), in *The Writings of John Quincy Adams*, Vol. 1, pp. 142–143.

745 Hugo Grotius, *The Rights of War and Peace*, Bk. II, ch. 16, para. 16, p. 865.

746 Emer de Vattel, *The Law of Nations*, Bk. II, ch. 12, para. 197, p. 365 (emphasis in original).

And having consulted "the practice of nations" as well, Hamilton concluded that the United States would be justified in suspending the operation of the treaties, or eventually to abrogate them. In the fashion of Bynkershoek, he reminded his colleagues that "an admission of the operation of the treaties has been considered as equivalent to taking part with France, [i.e.] to pass from a state of neutrality to that of being an ally."[747]

In response to Hamilton's challenge, Jefferson wrote a highly significant memorandum, in which he rebutted the claims of the New Yorker point-by-point. As to the first argument, that the treaties would bind the United States to a "perfect despotism," he said that France was equally so in 1778, when the treaties were concluded. And with reference to his recognition policy, he

> consider[s] the people who constitute a society or nation as the source of all authority in that nation; [and] that all the acts done by these agents under the authority of the nation, are the acts of the nation, are obligatory to them and ensure to their use, and can in no wise be annulled or affected by any change in the form of the government, or of the persons administering it, consequently the treaties between the United States and France, (...) though both of them have since changed their forms of government, the treaties are not annulled by these changes.[748]

Next, Jefferson addressed the potential dangers inherent in articles 17 and 22 of the commercial treaty, which regulate privateers and prizes, concluding that neither of these could pose serious problems, while the rights extended to the French in the latter article could even be refused for the sake of upholding neutrality. In examining reasons for abrogating treaties, he reviewed the positions of Grotius,[749] Pufendorf,[750] Wolff[751] and Vattel. While concluding that the first three agree that "treaties remain obligatory notwithstanding any change in the form of government, except in the single case where the preservation of

747 Hamilton, "Cabinet paper" (April, 1793), in *The Works of Alexander Hamilton*, Vol. 4, p. 391.

748 Thomas Jefferson, "Opinion on the French Treaties" (April 28, 1793), in *The Writings of Thomas Jefferson*, Vol. 3, pp. 227–228.

749 Grotius, *The Rights of War and Peace*, Bk. II, ch. 16, para. 16, p. 865.

750 Samuel von Pufendorf, *De Jure Naturae et Gentium Libri Octo* (*On the Laws of Nature and Nations*, Oxford: Clarendon Press, 1934), Bk. VIII, ch. 9, para. 6.

751 Christian Wolff, *Institutiones Iuris Naturae et Gentium* (Venezia: Nicolaum Pezzana, [1750] 1761), para. 1146.

that form was the object of the treaty," he acknowledged the problem with Vattel. But after having studied other passages in Vattel, and having identified several instances where Vattel expresses his "respect (…) for the sanctity of treaties,"[752] he found Hamilton's reliance on this particular passage unwarranted, saying that:

> We should hardly have expected that, rejecting all the rest of his book, this scrap would have been culled and made the hook whereon to hang such a chain of immoral consequences. Had the passage accidentally met our eye, we should have imagined it had fallen from the author's pen under some momentary view, not sufficiently developed to found a conjecture what he meant, and we may certainly affirm that a fragment like this cannot weigh against the authority of all other writers; against the uniform and systematic doctrine of the very work from which it is torn; against the moral feelings and the reason of all honest men. If the terms of the fragment are not misunderstood, they are in full contradiction to all the written and unwritten evidences of morality.[753]

752 For instance, see Bk. II, ch. 12, para. 158: "lezion cannot render a treaty invalid. It is his duty, who enters into engagements, to weigh well all things before he concludes. He may do with his property what he pleases, he may relinquish his rights, renounce his advantages, as he judges proper: the acceptant is not obliged to inform himself of his motives nor to weigh their just value. If we could free ourselves from a compact because we find ourselves injured by it, there would be nothing firm in the contracts of nations. (…) The happiness & peace of nations require manifestly that their treaties should not depend on a means of nullity so vague & so *danger*ous."

Bk. II, ch. 12, para. 163: "It is demonstrated in natural law that he who promises another confers on him a perfect right to require the thing promised, & that, consequently, not to observe a perfect promise, is to violate the right of another; it is as manifest injustice as to plunder any one of their right. (…) the reproach of perfidy is a bitter affront among sovereigns: now he who does not observe a treaty is assuredly perfidious, since he violates his faith."

Bk. II, ch. 15, para. 219: "Who will doubt that treaties are of the things sacred among nations? They decide matters the most important. (…) But treaties are but vain words if nations do not consider them as respectable engagements, as rules, inviolable for sovereigns, & sacred through the whole earth."

Bk. II, ch. 15, para. 220: "The faith of treaties, that firm & sincere will, that invariable constancy in fulfilling engagements, of *which* a declaration is made in a treaty, is there holy & sacred, among nations, whose safety & repose it ensures; & if nations will not be wanting to themselves, they will load with infamy whoever violates his faith." (all passages are as quoted by Jefferson).

753 Jefferson, "Opinion on the French Treaties" (April 28, 1793), in *The Writings of Thomas Jefferson*, Vol. 3, p. 241.

To counter the argument, Jefferson argued that a change of government as had occurred in France could not justify the United States renouncing its treaty of alliance, unless (1) "the danger which absolves us must be great, inevitable and imminent,"[754] or (2) if "the alliances [were] contracted with a view to preserve the present government." Since neither is the case in this instance, he concluded that the United States was beholden to honor its treaty commitments. As a general principle, Jefferson declared that only "[w]hen performance, for instance, becomes *impossible*, [is] non-performance [of contracts] not immoral. So if performance becomes *self-destructive* to the party, the law of self-preservation overrules the laws of obligation to others."[755] Hence, Jefferson dismissed the view of Vattel, arguing that

> it is true, that nations are to be judges for themselves, since no one nation has a right to sit in judgment over another. But the tribunal of our consciences remains, & that also of the opinion of the world. These will revise the sentence we pass in our own case, & as we respect these, we *must* see that in judging ourselves we have honestly done the part of impartial & vigorous judges.[756]

And, by rejecting this claim, he also rejected the position of Hamilton. In a letter to Madison, Jefferson duly exclaimed: "Would you suppose it possible that it would have been seriously proposed to declare our treaties with France void on the authority of an ill understood scrap in Vattel (…)?"[757] He thus concluded that "not renouncing the treaties now is so far from being a breach of neutrality, that the doing it would be the breach, by giving just cause of war to France."[758] This battle was won by Jefferson, and the treaties remained in place.[759]

---

754 One is here reminded of the famous *Caroline* doctrine with respect to the right of self-defense in international law.

755 This first condition is codified in modern international law as the principle of *rebus sic stantibus*, under article 62 of the Vienna Convention on the Law of Treaties.

756 Jefferson, "Opinion on French Treaties" (April 28, 1793), in *The Works of Thomas Jefferson*, Vol. 7, p. 286.

757 Jefferson to Madison (April 28, 1793), in *The Works of Thomas Jefferson*, Vol. 7, p. 301.

758 Jefferson, "Opinion on French Treaties" (April 28, 1793), in *The Works of Thomas Jefferson*, Vol. 7, p. 301.

759 Kaplan noted here that "In the perspective of later American diplomatic history, Jefferson's stand on the recognition of foreign powers had become identified with American respect for the sanctity of treaties, the acceptance as binding of an obligation made to another country irrespective of the government in power as long as the latter fulfils its responsibilities

Having decided that the alliance treaties with France would stay in place, the cabinet had to decide on whether or not it had to honor its commitments as an ally. As we have seen, Hamilton argued that there was no *casus foederis*, the war being waged by France being a war of aggression, and was strongly in favor of declaring America to be neutral in the European conflict. John Quincy Adams, at the time a Boston-based lawyer, admitted that the first rule as a neutral was that "an impartial and unequivocal neutrality between the contending parties is prescribed to us as a duty, unless we are bound by some existing contract or stipulation, to make a common cause with one of them."[760] But making this 'common cause' was not warranted as a result of the aggression having been initiated by France. What is more, he added, if the French are themselves responsible for having provoked military conflict, it is not even necessary "to fatigue the public with the pedantry of quotations from the writers upon natural and political Law, but it may be laid down as an universal principle, that no stipulation contained in a treaty, can ever oblige one nation to adopt or support the folly or injustice of another."[761] As before with the Nootka sound crisis, the president decided to seek counsel from the Supreme Court, and found Jay ready to write a first draft of a proclamation that would stake out America's neutrality.[762] This was remarkable because a few months later he indicated to the president that the court could not entertain legal questions on how to enforce

towards the United States." He adds that if this position was inaugurated in 1793, "it was neither by forethought or by express intention." See *Colonies into Nation*, p. 221.

760 John Quincy Adams, "Marcellus no. II (May 3, 1793), in *The Writings of John Quincy Adams*, Vol. 1, p. 139. One author wrote on this point that in the late 18th century, "[t]he principle that the government of a neutral State should not only remain impartial, but also refrain from even impartial participation in the conflict was so reasonable and expedient from every point of view, that nations were bound to accept it as a canon of international law." See Charles C. Hyde, *International Law, Chiefly as Interpreted and Applied by the United States* (Boston: Little, Brown, 1945), Vol. 3, p. 2225.

761 John Quincy Adams, "Marcellus no. III (May 11, 1793), in *The Writings of John Quincy Adams*, Vol. 1, pp. 144–145.

762 Jay, "Draft of Proclamation of Neutrality" (April 11, 1793), in Henry Johnston (ed.), *The Correspondence and Public Papers of John Jay* (New York: G.P. Putnam's Sons, 1890), Vol. 3, pp. 474–477. See also Gordon Wood, *Empire of Liberty: A History of the Early Republic, 1789–1815* (New York: Oxford University Press, 2009), p. 414; Walter Stahr, *John Jay, Founding Father* (New York: Hambledon and Continuum, 2006), pp. 301–302 and Stewart Jay, "The Status of the Law of Nations in Early American Law" *Vanderbilt Law Review* 42,p. 840. However, Nys notes that while its writing has generally been attributed to Jay, it is more likely that it was written by Randolph. See his *Les États-Unis et le Droit des Gens*, p. 82.

neutrality since this would violate the separation of powers.[763] In the event, France actually chose not to call on the United States to fulfil its obligations under the 1778 treaty, since it deemed the American navy incapable to be of any use.[764] Instead, it was thought on the French side that "[a] neutral America fulfilling the promises of the commercial treaty of 1778 would be of much more use than a belligerent America whose ships would be subject to British seizure and whose armies would probably require French subvention and rescue."[765]

For Jefferson, the only way to oppose the enunciation of a neutrality declaration was on constitutional grounds, arguing that given that Congress had the power power to declare war, it also had the power to do the obverse, i.e. to declare neutrality.[766] In response to Jefferson's claims about the alleged unconstitutionality of a proclamation, Hamilton wrote a number of newspaper articles in its defense—which also highlighted the interconnectedness between constitutional and international law. He agreed with Jefferson that it is the prerogative of Congress to declare war, but added that the executive should be tasked with the maintenance of peace, emanating from the fact that it is the president's duty to "take care that the laws be faithfully executed."[767] In reconciling the demands of the French treaties of alliance and a neutrality proclamation, Hamilton emphasized the role of the president as the one "who must first judge for himself of their meaning."[768] One more reason why Hamilton disliked the French revolutionary government is because he felt that the declarations it

763 "Chief Justice Jay and Associate Justice to President Washington" (August 8, 1793), in Henry Johnston (ed.), *The Correspondence and Public Papers of John Jay* (New York: G.P. Putnam's Sons, 1890), Vol. 3, pp. 488–489. For the questions submitted, see Jefferson, "To the Chief Justice and Judges of the Supreme Court of the United States" (July 18, 1793), in *The Works of Thomas Jefferson*, Vol. 7, pp. 451–452.

764 Samuel F. Bemis, "Washington's Farewell Address: A Foreign Policy of Independence." *American Historical Review* 39, no. 2 (1934), p. 250.

765 Kaplan, *Colonies into Nation*, p. 225.

766 Jefferson to Madison (June 23, 1793) in Albert E. Bergh (ed.), *The Writings of Thomas Jefferson.* (Washington, DC: Taylor & Maury, 1907), Vol. 9, p. 138. Madison shared Jefferson's concerns. See Bradford Perkins, *The Creation of a Republican Empire*, p. 88. See also discussed in Robert Tucker and David Hendrickson, *Empire of Liberty, the Statecraft of Thomas Jefferson* (New York: Oxford University Press, 1990), p. 70 and Ernest Nys, *Les États-Unis et le Droit des Gens*, p. 82. Nys notes that in spite of Jefferson's opposition, he signed the proclamation nonetheless.

767 Alexander Hamilton, "Pacificus No. 1" (June 23, 1793), in *The Works of Alexander Hamilton*, Vol. 4, p. 444. In this context, he reiterated that "our treaties, and the laws of nations, form a part of the law of the land."

768 Samuel F. Bemis, *The Jay Treaty* (New Haven, CT, 1962), p. 193.

had issued at the end of 1792, and which called upon people to arise against their governments, were "little short of a declaration of War against every government of Europe and as a violent attack upon *the freedom of opinion of all mankind*."[769] It has been said that such discussions "appear out of place in the writings of a man patently more concerned with international power than with international forms,"[770] but it does demonstrate—and it is in that respect not the only example—that debates about international legal questions could find their way into popular writings and their consequences be understood by concerned citizens.

In spite of Jefferson's objection, a proclamation was issued, and, so Rosen concluded, with its emphasis on international law "to restrain Americans and American power to restrain foreigners, [it] clearly reflected Hamilton's position."[771] In the end, while Jefferson remained sympathetic to the French cause and was unwilling to break off treaty relations with France, he also did not want to embroil the country in war as a result, and therefore supported the new policy.[772] The only thing Jefferson was able to achieve is that the word 'neutrality' itself did not feature in the pronouncement:

> Whereas it appears that a state of war exists between Austria, Prussia, Sardinia, Great Britain, and the United Netherlands, of the one part, and France on the other; and the duty and interest of the United States require, that they should with sincerity and good faith adopt and pursue a conduct friendly and impartial toward the belligerant Powers; I have therefore thought fit by these presents to declare the disposition of the United States to observe the conduct aforesaid towards those Powers respectfully; (...) And I do hereby also make known, that whatsoever of the citizens of the United States shall render himself liable to punishment or forfeiture under the law of nations, by committing, aiding, or abetting hostilities against any of the said Powers, or by carrying to any of

769 Alexander Hamilton, "Pacificus No. 2" (July 3, 1793), in *The Works of Alexander Hamilton*, Vol. 4, p. 454 (emphasis in original).

770 Stephen Rosen, "Alexander Hamilton and the Domestic Uses of International Law," *Diplomatic History* 5, no. 3 (1981), p. 192.

771 Rosen, "Alexander Hamilton and the Domestic Uses of International Law," *Diplomatic History* 5, no. 3 (1981), p. 199.

772 Gordon Wood, *Empire of Liberty: A History of the Early Republic, 1789–1815* (New York: Oxford University Press, 2009), pp. 182–183. In fact, as Varg noted, the president actually supported Jefferson's notion of "fair neutrality" that would "keep [the United States] out of the calamities of a war." See Jefferson to Madison (April 28, 1793), in *The Works of Thomas Jefferson*, Vol. 7, p. 302 and Varg, *Foreign Policies of the Founding Fathers*, p. 84.

> them those articles which are deemed contraband by the modern usage of nations, will not receive the protection of the United States, against such punishment or forfeiture; (...).[773]

As such, the Proclamation had precedents in previous treaties of the United States. For instance, provisions that prohibited individuals who find themselves on the territory of a neutral state from engaging in activities that could jeopardise a state's neutrality had been adopted in various treaties before 1793, e.g. with France in 1778, with the Netherlands in 1782 and with Sweden and Prussia in 1783 and 1785.[774] In addition, in diplomatic practice, there were ample precedents for providing non-military assistance, called 'benevolent neutrality', whereby one nation would be favored over another without participating in military activities.[775] Timothy Pickering's later statement that the Proclamation was "founded on the law of nations" is therefore certainly not unwarranted.[776]

Among historians, the Proclamation has received very different receptions. Samuel Bemis said for example that "[t]he proclamation of neutrality was a tangible expression of a sane American policy not of isolation but of diplomatic independence. Washington" he added, "refused all new foreign alliances."[777] Another approving voice was Charles Hyneman, who concluded that "the exigencies of the political, economic and geographic situation of the United States (...) did much to crystallize the principal features of that very policy [of neutrality] into requirements of international

773 "Proclamation of Neutrality"(April 22, 1793), in *American State Papers: Foreign Relations*, Vol. 1, p. 140.

774 Charles C. Hyde, *International Law, Chiefly as Interpreted and Applied by the United States* (Boston: Little, Brown, 1945), Vol. 3, p. 2225.

775 Michael Ramsey, *The Constitution's Text in Foreign Affairs* (Cambridge, MA: Harvard University Press, 2007), p. 80.

776 Timothy Pickering to Charles C. Pinckney, John Marshall and Elbridge Gerry (July 15, 1797), in *Instructions to the Envoys Extraordinary and Ministers Plenipotentiary from the United States of America to the French Republic*, (...) (Philadelphia: W. Ross, 1798), p. 4. Still, Fenwick writes that such proclamations are "purely domestic regulations and form no part of the body of international law." Charles Fenwick, *The Neutrality Laws of the United States* (Washington DC: Carnegie Endowment for International Peace, 1913), p. 11. John Jay shared Pickering's assessment, saying that the Proclamation is "exactly consistent with and declaratory of the conduct enjoined by the law of nations." See John Jay, "Charge to Grand Jury, Richmond, Va" (May 22, 1793), in Francis Wharton (ed.), *State Trials of the United States* (Philadelphia: Carey and Hart, 1849), p. 49–52.

777 Bemis, "Washington's Farewell Address: A Foreign Policy of Independence," p. 260.

law."[778] A dissenting voice among the chorus is Albert Bowman, who argued that it was "really irrelevant to the national interest at that time. The real issue was not neutrality, but whether the United States could maintain freedom of action—diplomatic independence. Rather than asserting that independence, the much-admired proclamation resolved the issue by surrendering it."[779]

If Bemis and Hyneman were correct on paper, then Bowman was correct in reality. For soon after the Proclamation had been issued, the French National Convention adopted a new decree which declared that enemy goods found on any kind of ship, and destined for an enemy port, may be brought into French ports by their vessels. In other words, France was denying the Americans their asserted right as neutrals to carry British goods to Great Britain.[780] When James Monroe became the new minister to France in June 1794, he was instructed by Randolph to do his utmost to push France to revoke its decrees affecting American shipping.[781] As a sympathiser with the French Revolution, Monroe sought a sympathetic hearing:

> Britain may dispute the law of nations, however clear its doctrine even with respect to contraband; but with France it is in both respects regulated by treaty. Besides we are allies, and what is more interesting, the friends of France. (…) Will she say that the injuries of Britain furnish a justificatory example for her to render us like injuries? Will our ally contend with that nation in rivalship, which shall harrass our commerce

778 Charles Hyneman, "Neutrality During the European Wars of 1792–1815: America's Understanding of Her Obligations." *American Journal of International Law* 24, no. 2 (April 1930), p. 285. However, prior to that, he said that "the conduct of the United States in 1793 is to be explained as arising out of belief on the part of the President and his cabinet that the future independence of the young American nation depended on a strong assertion of its sovereignty, rather than arising out of belief that the United States owed particular duties at international law." see ibid., p. 284. In his general survey on the law of neutrality, Stephen Neff wrote that the American policy of self-restraint was "a shining example of acceptance by neutral countries of their responsibilities." Stephen Neff, *The Rights and Duties of Neutrals: A General History* (Manchester: Manchester University Press, 2000), p. 76.

779 Albert Bowman, "Jefferson, Hamilton and American Foreign Policy" *Political Science Quarterly* 71, no. 1 (March 1956), p. 22.

780 Decree of May 9, 1793. See discussed in Samuel Bemis, "Washington's Farewell Address: A Foreign Policy of Independence" *American Historical Review* 39, Vol. 2 (January, 1934), p. 252.

781 See Edmund Randolph to James Madison (July 30, 1794), in *American State Papers: Foreign Relations*, Vol. 1, pp. 669–670.

> most and do us the greatest detriment? This is surely not a relation for the two Republics to bear towards each other. Other sentiments will I hope inspire their common councils; sentiments more congenial with their mutual interests and consonant to the dispositions of the citizens of both countries.[782]

For a while, Monroe's exertions were to no avail. The decrees were blunted in January 1795, but that was only a few months after the Jay Treaty had been signed, which would put the United States on a more serious collision course with France.

But even if the United States did not become directly involved in the war between France and Britain, a challenge to its newly declared neutrality had appeared on the horizon when the new French minister Edmond-Charles "Citizen" Genêt, arrived on American soil in Charleston, South Carolina, on April 8, 1793. An abrasive thirty year-old who had already been declared *persona non grata* in St.Petersburg, Genêt was greeted with much enthusiasm by the locals. His presence in the United States would put the Jeffersonian faction on the defensive. Initially however, believing that the United States would be interested in uniting with its overseas republican counterpart, Genêt proposed a pact between the United States and France according to which a political and economic framework would be established between the two countries on the basis of freedom and brotherhood,[783] an offer which the administration swiftly rebuffed, not wanting to risk getting drawn into the war.[784] At the same time, Genêt had also begun with equipping privateer ships, the first of which was christened *Citizen Genêt* and sailed from Charleston already on April 18. Genêt justified this action with reference to article 22 of the Treaty of Amity and Commerce, which forbade entry of British prizes into U.S. ports or the servicing of English privateers.[785] The British minister to the United States, George Hammond, a thirty year-old former secretary to David Hartley at the time of

782 James Monroe, "Letter to the Committee of Public Safety" (September 3, 1794), in *The Writings of James Monroe*, Vol. 2, pp. 42–43.

783 Genêt to Jefferson (May 23, 1793), in *American State Papers: Foreign Relations*, Vol. 1, p. 147.

784 Nys, *Les États-Unis et le Droit des Gens*, p. 80.

785 "It shall not be lawful for any foreign Privateers, not belonging to Subjects of the most Christian King nor Citizens of the said United States, who have Commissions from any other Prince or State in enmity with either Nation to fit their Ships in the Ports of either the one or the other of the aforesaid Parties, to sell what they have taken or in any other manner whatsoever to exchange their Ships, Merchandizes or any other lading; neither shall they be allowed even to purchase victuals except such as shall be necessary for their going to the next Port of that Prince or State from which they have Commissions."

the 1783 peace negotiations, immediately lodged a complaint, in particular after a British vessel, the *William*, had been captured on May 3rd, and spoke of "breaches of neutrality (…) and direct contraventions of the [Neutrality] proclamation."[786] He added that setting up prize courts on American soil is "not warranted by the usage of nations or (…) existing treaties."[787] Not surprisingly, Hamilton shared Hammond's views, finding Genêt's reasoning spurious:

> It is a plain dictate of reason and an established principle of the law of nations that a neutral state (…) cannot make itself, or suffer itself to be made, with its own consent, permission, or connivance, an instrument of the hostility of one party against the other, and as a consequence of these general principles cannot allow one party to prepare within its territories the means of annoying the other, or to carry on from thence against the other, with means prepared there, military expeditions of any sort by land or water. To allow such practices is manifestly to associate with one party against the other. The state which does it, ceases thereby to be a neutral state, becomes an enemy, and may be justly treated as such.[788]

Hence, Hamilton squarely denied France the implied right in article 22 of the Treaty of Commerce for French privateers to be fitted out in U.S. ports. The Secretary of State could not but accept Hamilton's argument, and agree that Genêt's actions were in violation of the 1778 treaties. In a letter to Jefferson, Genêt denied the charges made by Hammond. According to the French envoy the 1778 treaty "authorizes exclusively all the vessels of war, French or American, armed by the two states, or by individuals, to conduct freely, wherever they please, the prizes they shall have made of their enemies, without being subjected to either Admiralty or any other duties." As to the charge that Genêt assisted in arming privateers, he believed that these "cannot be matter of offence in the citizens of the United States."[789]

786 George Hammond to Jefferson (May 8, 1793), in *The Papers of Thomas Jefferson*, Vol. 2, pp. 686–687, quoted in William Castro, "Foreign Affairs Crises and the Constitution's Case for Controversy Limitation: Notes from the Founding Era" *The American Journal for Legal History* 46, no. 3 (July, 2004), p. 245.

787 Castro, "Foreign Affairs Crises and the Constitution's Case for Controversy Limitation: Notes from the Founding Era," p. 246.

788 Alexander Hamilton, "No Jacobin No. 4" (?September 1793), in *The Works of Alexander Hamilton*, Vol. 5, pp. 40–41. In support, he mentions Vattel, *The Law of Nations*, Bk. III, Ch. 7, para. 104, pp. 523–524; Bynkershoek, *Quaestionum Juris Publici Libri Duo*, Bk. I, ch. 4.

789 Edmond Genêt to Jefferson (May 27, 1793), in *American State Papers: Foreign Relations*, Vol. 1, pp. 149–150.

Jefferson answered Genêt that not only is it "the *right* of every nation to prohibit acts of sovereignty from being exercised by any other within its limits," but even more so it is "the *duty* of a neutral nation to prohibit such as would injure one of the warring powers," adding that in accordance with the law of nations—as part of the law of the land—the government would ask for reparations for offences committed as a result of illegal privateering.[790] Genêt however persisted in his position in a number of letters addressed to Jefferson.[791] The latter then pointed out to Genêt that his actions could have serious consequences for America's relations with Britain, since they were obviously in violation of the Treaty of Commerce of 1778, in particular article 17 about warships or privateers bringing prizes into each other's ports: "the entry of an armed vessel into a port, is one act; the equipping a vessel in that port, arming it, manning it, is a different one, and not engaged by any article of the treaty." For good measure, he added that notwithstanding treaty obligations, the administration's opinions are also "dictated by that law and usage; and this had been very maturely inquired into before it was adopted as a principle of conduct."[792] In support, he cited a passage from Vattel, namely that

> Tant qu'un peuple neutre veut jouir surement de cet état, il doit montrer en toutes choses une exacte impartialité entre ceux qui se font la guerre. Car s'il favorise l'un au préjudice de l'autre, il ne pourra pas se plaindre, quand celui-ci le traitera comme adhérent & associé de son ennemi. Sa neutralité seroit une neutralité frauduleuse, dont personne ne veut être la dupe.—Voyons donc en quoi consiste cette impartialité qu'un peuple neutre doit garder.[793]

In justifying the prohibition to raise armies on American soil, he cited once more Vattel, in addition to Wolff.[794] In summarizing his position, he concluded that

---

790 Jefferson to Genêt (June 5, 1793), in *The Works of Thomas Jefferson*, Vol. 7, p. 363. A position which Hamilton obviously agreed with, see letter to Richard Harrison (June 13–15), in *The Papers of Alexander Hamilton*, Vol. 14, p. 539.

791 See letters dated June 14 and June 15, 1793, in *American State Papers: Foreign Relations*, Vol. 1, pp. 152–154, 158.

792 Jefferson to Genêt (June 17, 1793), in *The Writings of Thomas Jefferson*, Vol. 9, p. 134.

793 See Vattel, Bk. 3, para. 104 (as cited by Jefferson), or *The Law of Nations*, Bk. 3, ch. 7, p. 523.

794 See Vattel, *The Law of Nations*, Bk. 3, ch. 2, p. 478–479; Wolff, *Institutiones Juris Naturae et Gentium* (Venezia: Nicolaum Pezzana, 1761), para. 1174, p. 485. In French, it was rendered by Jefferson as "Puisque le droit de lever des soldats est un droit de majesté, qui ne peut être violé par une nation etrangere, il n'est pas permis de lever des soldats sur le territorie

> [b]y our treaties with several of the belligerent powers, which are a part of the laws of our land, we have established a state of peace with them. But without appealing to treaties, we are at peace with them all by the law of nature. For by nature's law, man is at peace with man, till some aggression is committed, which, by the same law, authorizes one to destroy another as his enemy.[795]

In the face of these appeals to authority, Genêt remained unperturbed. In his reply, he reiterated that the United States were beholden to perform their obligations under the 1778 treaty. First of all, he appealed to Jefferson's republican sentiments, and implored him "not [to] lower ourselves to the level of ancient politics by diplomatic subtleties." He famously added that it was not acceptable to him to "bring forward aphorisms of Vattel, to justify or excuse infractions committed on positive treaties."[796] Moreover, he suggested that by taking the stance the administration took, it pre-empted the judgment of Congress, while he was also convinced that the people of the United States would favor his opinion over that of the administration. Based on article 22 of the said treaty, which prohibited the fitting out of privateers by foreigners in either American or French ports, Genêt inferred that it is "incontestable" that the French *did* have such rights in the United States.[797]

In a letter to Gouverneur Morris, Jefferson denied Genêt's inference: "Is this an *express* permission to France to do it? Does the negative to the enemies of France, & silence as to France herself, imply an affirmative to France? Certainly not. (…) And if the parties had meant an affirmative stipulation, they would have provided for it expressly; they would never have left so important a point to be inferred from mere silence or implications."[798] In the same letter, Jefferson

d'autrui, sans le consentement du maître du territorie." See letter to Genêt (June 17, 1793), in *The Writings of Thomas Jefferson*, Vol. 9, p. 135.

795 Jefferson to Genet (June 17, 1793), in *The Writings of Thomas Jefferson*, Vol. 9, p. 135.

796 Elsewhere in his correspondence, Genêt called the works of Grotius and Vattel "worm-eaten volumes on the law of nations" whose contents, he thanked God, have long been forgotten. See Genêt to Jefferson (October 27, 1793), quoted in Henry Wheaton, "An Anniversary Discourse delivered before the New-York Historical Society" (December 20, 1820), p. 314.

797 Genêt to Jefferson (June 22, 1793), in *American State Papers: Foreign Relations*, Vol. 1, pp. 155–156.

798 Jefferson to Gouverneur Morris (August 16, 1793), in *The Writings of Thomas Jefferson*, Vol. IX, p. 187. As Lint noted, the question ultimately revolved around the matter when a treaty could be interpreted broadly or narrowly. In this respect, no party could impose its interpretation at the expense of the other; the meaning of provisions as established when they

restated his unequivocal support of the government's neutrality policy, defining this in very strict terms:

> Examining this question under the law of nations, (…) we have produced proofs from the most enlightened and approved writers on the subject that a Neutral nation must, in all things relating to the war, observe an exact impartiality towards the parties; that favors to one to the prejudice of the other, would import a fraudulent neutrality, of which no nation would be the dupe; that no succor should be given to either, unless stipulated by treaty, in men, arms, or anything else directly serving for war (…).[799]

What Jefferson found most irksome was the fact that Genêt attempted to speak directly to Congress on this issue. Jefferson told him firmly that the Executive can be his only interlocutor; Congress having no standing on these matters.[800] Quite clearly, whatever credit Genêt may have had with Jefferson had by now entirely dissipated. In order to undercut Genêt and remove any ambiguities in America's neutrality stance, the cabinet issued a series of rules to settle the privateering issue.[801] Among these were (1) that "[t]he original arming and equipping of vessels in the ports of the United States by any of the belligerent parties, for military service, offensive or defensive, is deemed unlawful"; (2) "Equipments in the ports of the United States by any of the parties at war with France, of vessels fitted for merchandise and war, (…) are deemed lawful" and

---

were created should normally prevail. See Gregg Lint, "Early American Conceptions of International Law and their Influence on Foreign Policy: 1776–1803" (unpublished manuscript, Michigan State University, 1975), pp. 163–165.

Genêt's disdain for Vattel and other authors of the law of nations, as well as his continuous attempts to explain the law in favor of French interests in the face of contrary evidence made Jefferson exclaim that "[Genêt's] ignorance of everything written on the subject is astonishing. I think he has never read a book of any sort in that branch of science." See Jefferson to Madison (August 3, 1793), in *The Works of Thomas Jefferson*, Vol. 7, p 464.

799 Jefferson to Morris (August 16, 1793), in *The Works of Thomas Jefferson*, Vol. 7, p. 484. At the same time, Hyneman noted, the administration still decided that America's treaty obligations should prevail over its neutrality stipulations; a position which received tacit consent even from the British. See Charles Hyneman, "Neutrality During the European Wars of 1792–1815: America's Understanding of Her Obligations." *American Journal of International Law* 24, no. 2 (April 1930), p. 286.

800 See e.g. Jefferson to Genêt (December 31, 1793), in *The Works of Thomas Jefferson*, Vol. 8, p. 135.

801 This was chiefly a result of instructions drafted by Hamilton to U.S. customs authorities. See discussed in Charles Fenwick, *The Neutrality Laws of the United States* (Washington DC: Carnegie Endowment for International Peace, 1913), pp. 22–23.

(3) "Equipments of every kind in the ports of the United States, of privateers of the powers at war with France, are deemed unlawful."[802]

For Genêt, even this set of rules did not make any difference, and his actions only inflicted further embarrassment on Jefferson. Most painful for him became the episode concerning the *Little Democrat*, a vessel which was fitted out for privateering by order of Genêt in the port of Philadelphia. When the governor of Pennsylvania prohibited the ship from going out to sea, Genêt not only ignored this warning by sailing the ship out of the Delaware bay and making a capture, but added insult to injury by levelling criticism at Washington and his neutrality policy.[803] When Genêt also engaged in setting up prize courts on American soil,[804] and raised an army to stage an attack on New Orleans and Florida,[805] the only option left to Jefferson was to join the cabinet in asking for the recall of Genêt.[806]

The Genêt affair had led to a number of cases before the American courts, which showed much willingness to support the administration's neutrality policy. But before the passing of the Proclamation itself and subsequent formal legislation, the courts had faced some serious jurisdictional problems. One instance was in 1792, when Spain and France complained about transgressions of the law and demanded satisfaction from the American authorities. Outlining his opinion, Jefferson expressed doubt about the ability of the courts to deal

---

802 "Rules governing Belligerents" (August 3, 1793), in *The Works of Thomas Jefferson*, Vol. 7, pp. 460–461. Indeed, these rules reflect the opinion of the Attorney-General, Edmund Randolph, who had written to Washington shortly after the Neutrality Proclamation had been adopted, that the French treaty of 1778 was made "many years ago without relation to the present war, and it is therefore no breach of neutrality to fulfil it (…)" Randolph to Washington (May 6, 1793), quoted in Robert Reinstein, "Executive Power and The Law of Nations in the Washington Administration" *University of Richmond Law Review* 46, no. 2 (2012), p. 433, fn. 286.

803 Kaplan, *Colonies into Nation*, pp. 226–228.

804 In fact, a whole series of prize courts were set up under the authority of various French consuls present in American ports. See William Castro, "Foreign Affairs Crises and the Constitution's Case for Controversy Limitation: Notes from the Founding Era" *The American Journal for Legal History* 46, no. 3 (July, 2004), p. 243.

805 Tucker and Hendrickson, *Empire of Liberty*, p. 54. Hyneman noted however that Jefferson actually supported Genêt's plans to invade Spanish territories, and even helped put him "in touch with persons who would help him advance his cause." See Hyneman, "Neutrality During the European Wars of 1792–1815: America's Understanding of Her Obligations." *American Journal of International Law* 24, no. 2 (April 1930), p. 289.

806 Jefferson, "Cabinet opinions on Recall of Genet" (August 23, 1793), in *The Works of Thomas Jefferson*, Vol. 8, pp. 5–6. See also Kaplan, *Colonies into Nation*, pp. 228–229; Varg, *Foreign Policies of the Founding Fathers*, pp. 86–87.

with international matters. Also, the Judiciary Act appeared not to provide a sufficient basis to ensure prosecutions under international law by federal courts.[807] In a response, Edmund Randolph, the attorney-general, asserted that the Constitution and the Judiciary Act taken together provided an adequate basis for prosecution, saying that "[t]he federal judiciary has also cognizance of offences against the law of nations, because that law is attached to the U.S. from the nature of the subject, without an express adoption of it, and because offences, cognizable under the authority of the U.S. are clearly subjected by the judicial law to the circuit court."[808]

The most prominent instance in which violations of the Neutrality Proclamation were addressed was *Henfield's case*, which became the most celebrated court case to arise out of the Genêt affair.[809] It concerned an American national who acted under French instructions as a privateer on their behalf. According to James Wilson, Henfield was punishable under the law of nations, "a law that was in existence long before Gideon Henfield existed." Henfield's conduct, so Wilson argued, could lead "to *Reprisals certainly*: and if so; *probably* to War."[810] Randolph argued this point rather with reference to the Constitution, saying that because treaties are "the Supreme law of the land," he was indictable "at the Common Law, because his conduct comes within the description of disturbing the Peace of the United States."[811] Indeed, in accordance with treaty law, the federal government had a right, if not an obligation, to prosecute Henfield under the law of nations. In his charge to the court, Chief Justice John Jay said as much when he stated that "[t]he respect which this very country owes to itself imposes a duty on its government to cause all its laws to be respected and obeyed, and that not only by its proper citizens, but that also by those strangers who may visit and occasionally reside within its territories."

---

807 Jefferson, "Opinion on Fugitive Slaves" (December 3, 1792), in *The Works of Thomas Jefferson*, Vol. 7, pp. 188–191.

808 Randolph, "Opinion on Offenses against the Law of Nations." (December 5, 1792) in Barbara Oberg and Jefferson Looney (eds.), *The Papers of Thomas Jefferson Digital Edition* (Charlottesville: University of Virginia Press, Rotunda, 2008), Vol. 24, pp. 702–703.

809 One earlier case in this context was *Findlay v. The William* (9 F. Cas. 57 (D. Pa. 1793), no. 4790).

810 See "Henfield's Case" in *The Collected Works of James Wilson*, Vol. 1, p. 368; William Castro, "Foreign Affairs Crises and the Constitution's Case for Controversy Limitation: Notes from the Founding Era" *The American Journal for Legal History* 46, no. 3 (July, 2004), p. 256 (emphasis in original).

811 Edmund Randolph, "Opinion on the Case of Gideon Henfield" (May 30, 1793), in Barbara Oberg and Jefferson Looney (eds.), *The Papers of Thomas Jefferson Digital Edition* (Charlottesville: University of Virginia Press, Rotunda, 2008), Vol. 26, pp. 145–146.

In a comment clearly aimed at Genêt, he added that "[h]ence, it follows that the subjects of belligerent powers are bound, while in this country, to respect the neutrality of it, and are punishable in common with our own citizens for violations of it, within the limits and jurisdiction of the United States." More specifically, "[t]he right of levying soldiers is a sovereign right belonging only to the nation. No foreign power can lawfully exercise it without permission (...) on this head the law of nations is explicit."[812] To the dismay of the administration, the jury actually acquitted Henfield, the reason being that the latter claimed to have become a French citizen, and that he was therefore not subject to American neutrality regulations.[813] As a result, the federal government resolved to urge Congress to pass a law that would make violations of neutrality a penal offence. This became the Neutrality Act of June 5, 1794, which addressed citizens from *all* nations.[814]

In comparison with other cases that concerned neutrality issues, the *Henfield* case is unique in that it explicitly referred to the treaties and the law of nations as a basis for prosecution, rather than domestic statutes. In a later case, an attorney declared that in fact, "the prosecution against Henfield was not expressly on the treaty, but on the law of nations, which is a part of the common law of the United States."[815] Incidentally, Peter Stephen Duponceau, a counsel on behalf of Henfield, found that judge Wilson had "rather weakened than strengthened the ground of prosecution in placing the law of nations on the same footing with the municipal or local law." Duponceau's conception was altogether different:

> The law of nations, being the common law of the civilised world, may be said, indeed, to be a part of the law of every civilised nation; but it stands

---

812 Francis Wharton (ed.), "Trial of Gideon Henfield, in the Circuit Court of the United States for the Penn-sylvania District" (May 22, 1793), in *State Trials of the United States* (Philadelphia: Carey and Hart, 1849), pp. 55, 56.

813 William Castro, "Foreign Affairs Crises and the Constitution's Case for Controversy Limitation: Notes from the Founding Era," p. 260. Another reason Henfield brought forth was that he was unaware of the "unlawfulness of his undertaking," an argument that both Randolph and Jefferson eventually accepted. See ibid., p. 262.

814 Quincy Wright, *The Enforcement of International Law Through Municipal Law in the United States* (Urbana, IL: University of Illinois, 1916), pp. 115–116. Earlier that year, Washington had issued a second neutrality proclamation, which made more explicit that enlistment of citizens within the United States is "contrary to the laws of nations." Quoted in Charles Fenwick, *The Neutrality Laws of the United States* (Washington DC: Carnegie Endowment for International Peace, 1913), p. 172.

815 *United States v. Worrall*, 2 U.S. 384 (F.Cas.) 2 Dall. 384, at 392.

> on other and higher grounds than municipal customs, statutes, edicts, or ordinances. It is binding on every people and on every government. It is to be carried into effect at all times under the penalty of being thrown out of the pale of civilisation, or involving the country into a war. Every branch of the national administration (...) is bound to administer it. (...) [T]his universal common law can never cease to be the rule of executive and judicial proceedings until mankind shall return to the savage state.[816]

Consistent with Duponceau's criticism, subsequent cases concerning neutrality laws invariably led to a strict application of the law of nations, in particular with respect to the outfitting of privateers, prohibiting the establishment of prize courts, and circumscription of diplomatic privileges.[817]

What these early court cases reflected was that the privateering issue in combination with America's attempt to steer a neutral course between France and Great Britain compelled the United States to take a conservative position

816 See Peter Stephen Duponceau, *A Dissertation on the Nature and Extent of the Jurisdiction of the Courts of the United States.* (Philadelphia: Abraham Small, 1825), pp. 3–4 (emphasis in original).

817 Typical examples include, e.g., *United States v. Ravar*a 2 U.S. 297 (Dall.), 1793, and *United States v. Guinet, et.al.*, 2 U.S. 321 (Dall.) 1795. See also discussed in Albert Washburn, "The American View of Neutrality" *Virginia Law Review* 2, no. 3 (December 1914), p. 166. In the case *Glass v. Sloop Betsey* 3 U.S. (3 Dall.), 6, 1794, the court declared that since "no foreign Power can, of right, institute or erect any court of judicature, of any kind, within the jurisdiction of the United States but only such as may be warranted by, and be in pursuit of, treaties, it is therefore decreed and adjudged that the admiralty jurisdiction, which has been exercised in the United States by the consuls of France, no being so warranted, is not of right." See ibid, at 16.

In fact, the issue of prize courts on American soil had already been addressed in a circular to French consuls on September 7, 1793: "Finding by the protests of several of the consuls of France, (...) that they claim, and are exercising, within the United States, a general admiralty jurisdiction, and in particular, assume to try the validity of prizes, and to give sentence thereon, as judges of admiralty; and moreover, that they are undertaking to give commissions within the United States, and to enlist, or encourage the enlistment of men, natives or inhabitants of these States, to commit hostilities on nations with whom the United States are at peace, in direct opposition to the laws of the land: I have it in charge, from the President of the United States, to give notice to all the consuls and vice consuls of France, in the United States, as I hereby do to you, that if any of them shall commit any of the acts before mentioned, or assume any jurisdiction not expressly given by the convention between France and the United States, the exequatur of the consul so transgressing will be immediately revoked, and his person be submitted to such prosecutions and punishments as the laws may prescribe for the case." See "Circular to the French consuls" (September 7, 1793), in *The Works of Thomas Jefferson*, Vol. 8 p. 31.

on the law of nations, having to retreat from some of the innovations it had tried to push since the Revolution. Ironically, given the problems with Genêt, the French government had actually offered in 1792 to open negotiations with various countries to bring an end to the practice of privateering. Initially, the French proposal was received positively by Thomas Jefferson, who deemed it "worthy of the nation from which it comes" and therefore declared to be "ready to enter into negotiation."[818] However, because of the outbreak of war between France and Britain, nothing came of the proposal.

As a consequence of the war, the United States also had to gradually abandon its 'free ships, free goods' position. This was clearly reflected in some letters written by Hamilton that addressed the capture of French goods seized from American ships. Drawing support from Vattel and Bynkershoek, he acknowledged that "the goods of an enemy in the ships of a friend (that is, of a neutral power) are lawful prizes, and that the goods of a friend in the ships of an enemy (those called contraband excepted) are not lawful prizes." Hamilton also admitted that the United States had supported the principle of the League of Armed Neutrality that 'free ships shall make free goods,' noting that the United States never 'acceded' to the League, and moreover, that the United Kingdom never accepted the new principle. He therefore concluded dryly that "[a]n established rule of the law of nations can only be altered by agreements between all the civilized powers, or a new usage generally adopted and sanctioned by time."[819] As a result, vis-à-vis the United Kingdom, the United States is only bound by the existing law of nations.[820]

With respect to the seizures of French prizes sold in the United States, Hamilton was equally unyielding. While France complained that the United

---

818 Jefferson, to the French Minister, Jean-Baptiste Ternant (Oct. 16, 1792), in *The Works of Thomas Jefferson,* Vol. 7, pp. 164–165.

819 Alexander Hamilton, "No Jacobin No. 3" (?September 1793), in *The Works of Alexander Hamilton,* Vol. 5, pp. 36, 37. The references can be found in Vattel, *The Law of Nations,* Bk. III, Ch. 7, paras. 115–116, pp. 532–533; Bynkershoek, *Quaestionum Juris Publici Libri Duo,* Bk. I, chs. 13, 14.

820 Hamilton revisited this issue in a series of remarks on the treaties in 1795, in which he noted that "some of the powers which combined to introduce [the free ships make free goods principle], now support in arms a contrary principle; and all the neutral powers—the United States included—have expressly or virtually relinquished the ground in the whole course of the present war." See "Remarks On the Treaty of Amity, Commerce, and Navigation, Made Between the United States and Great Britain" (July 9, 1795), in *The Works of Alexander Hamilton,* Vol. 5, p. 167.

States therewith violated article 17 of the Treaty of Commerce,[821] Hamilton said that, first, the goods concerned were captured within its territorial waters, and secondly, that as a neutral power, America had a "right of redress, against the power making [the seizure], for the purpose of effecting a restitution of the person or thing captured." Against the opinion of various writers on international law, Hamilton maintained that in these circumstances, the United States did not need to negotiate over restitution, but was entitled to seize the goods outright.[822]

Hamilton's letters reflected the fact that in 1793, the government had altered its position on the 'free ships' rule—which had been a central aim of America's policy on international law since the days of the Revolution. Jefferson too quietly acquiesced in the new state of affairs. For instance, in a letter to Genêt, he wrote that he could not see how French goods captured on board American ships could be recovered, since the British had acted on that principle of "the general law of nations, [according to which] the goods of a friend found in the vessel of an enemy are free, and the goods of an enemy found in the vessel of a friend are lawful prize." He therewith acknowledged that while other countries had attempted to introduce different principles, these "tak[e] effect between such nations only as have so agreed to control it [by treaty]."[823] In other words, the administration accepted that 'free ships make free goods' could not be considered part of the general law of nations, if only because the most important maritime power of the day, Great Britain, continued to vehemently oppose its general acceptance. While the issue divided opinion among the American statesmen of the day—Madison, for one, strongly deplored this departure from a key principle of international law which the young country had sought to promote—the United States appeared to have little choice for the time being.[824] Jefferson's exasperation was aptly captured in one of his many letters to Genêt, in which he confided that while "we are endeavouring to advance [towards the

821 "It shall be lawful for the Ships of War of either Party & Privateers freely to carry whithersoever they please the Ships and Goods taken from their Enemies, without being obliged to pay any Duty to the Officers of the Admiralty or any other Judges; nor shall such Prizes be arrested or seized, when they come to and enter the Ports of either Party; nor shall the Searchers or other Officers of those Places search the same or make examination concerning the lawfulness of such Prizes, but they may hoist Sail at any time and depart and carry their Prizes to the Places express'd in their Commissions, which the Commanders of such Ships of War shall be obliged to shew (…)."

822 Alexander Hamilton, "No Jacobin No. 2" (?August, 1793), in *The Works of Alexander Hamilton*, Vol. 5, pp. 28–30.

823 Jefferson to Genêt (July 24, 1793), in *The Writings of Thomas Jefferson*, Vol. 9, p. 170.

824 See James Madison, "letter to—" (August 23, 1795), in *The Writings of James Madison*, Vol. 6, pp. 238–257.

principle of 'free ships make free goods,'] it depends on the will of other nations, as well as our own, we can only obtain it when they shall be ready to concur." For now, however, he had to admit that British practice was consistent with the general law of nations, and in spite of various nations attempting to introduce a new principle "much less embarrassing to commerce," he confessed to be "at a loss on what principle to reclaim it."[825]

Meanwhile, the Neutrality Proclamation—while an obvious move away from the onerous obligations issuing from the French treaties—did not do much to soothe British sentiment towards the United States. Because of the unequal power relations between France and Great Britain, American neutrality was bound to favor the British, since they were in the position to dictate their terms to the United States with France being able to do anything about this. Britain chose however to exploit this situation by forcing the Americans to comply with their self-imposed strictures by means of adopting more exacting Orders in Council on June 8, 1793. The first aspect of these orders concerned neutral commerce, and specifically targeted American trade by effectively restoring the Rule of 1756.[826] Henceforth, British naval vessels would hold neutral ships containing cargo originating from French colonies, or which held cargo destined for these colonies. Subsequently, British admiralty courts would decide on the status of the seized cargo.[827] In effect, this amounted to blocking French ports to neutral ships. In a letter to Jefferson explaining the new policy, Hammond contended that "with respect to the rule that has been adopted relative to ports blockaded, it is confirmable to the general law and practice of all nations (…)."[828] And in fact, both Vattel and Pufendorf gave some credence to the idea that the Rule of 1756 could have standing in international law, since neutrals were not supposed to be able to enrich themselves in wartime by taking over trade which previously belonged to a belligerent.[829] However, rather than insisting on a rule in international law that was only accepted by Britain itself, its real motive was to acquire the trade for itself. One reason why it felt it could afford the imposition of this principle is because, as Gould argued,

825 Jefferson to Genêt (July 24, 1793), in *American State Papers*: *Foreign Relations*, Vol. 1, pp. 166–167.

826 Lint considers that the Rule of 1756 constituted a one-sided rupturing by Great Britain of the 1674 Anglo-Dutch treaty. See Lint, "Early American Conceptions of International Law," p. 25.

827 Ernest Nys, *Les États-Unis et le Droit des Gens*, p. 91.

828 George Hammond to Jefferson, (September 12, 1793), in *American State Papers*, p. 240.

829 See Vattel, *The Law of Nations*, Bk. III, ch. 7, para.113, p. 531 and Samuel von Pufendorf, *De Jure Naturae et Gentium Libri Octo* (*On the Laws of Nature and Nations*, Oxford: Clarendon Press, 1934), Bk. VIII, ch. 6, para. 1.

Britain considered the outer Atlantic as a 'zone of war' where "the legal interpretation embraced by the strong trumped that favored by the weak."[830]

Still, the Washington administration did not accept the British position without protest. While the general principles of the law of nations could not be contested, Jefferson stated that Britain could not interfere with neutral trade: "when two nations go to war, those who choose to live in peace retain their natural right to pursue their agriculture, manufactures, and other ordinary vocations; (...) the war among others shall be, for them, as if it did not exist." Thus, he said about the reinstated Rule of 1756 that it was "so manifestly contrary to the law of nations, that nothing more would seem necessary, than to observe that it is so."[831] Madison also registered his disapproval, noting that "I observe that our vessels are frequently and insolently seized and searched for French goods. Is not this complained of by our own people as a breach of the modern law of nations; and whilst British goods are protected by the neutrality of our bottoms, will not remonstrances come from France on the subject?"[832]

One respect in which Jefferson defended America's neutral position was by pointing out that "[t]he character of our coast (...) would entitle us in reason to as broad a margin of protected navigation as any nation whatever." He then stated that doctrine prescribes that "[t]he greatest distance to which any respectable assent among nations has been at any time given, has been the extent of the human sight, estimated at upwards of 20 miles, and the smallest distance I believe, claimed by any nation whatever is the utmost range of a cannon ball, usually stated at one sea-league."[833] According to Jefferson, the

830 Eliga Gould, "Zones of Law, Zones of Violence: The Legal Geography of the British Atlantic, circa 1772" *William and Mary Quarterly* (3rd series) 60, no. 3 (July, 2003), pp. 487–488. Elsewhere, he notes that in the Mediterranean, this led to a perversion whereby Britain, by signing treaties with the Barbary States in order to protect its own trade interests "implicitly condoned activities that, according to the law of nations, constituted piracy." See ibid., p. 491.

831 Jefferson to Thomas Pinckney (September 7, 1793), in *The Writings of Thomas Jefferson*, Vol. 9, p. 221.

832 Madison to Jefferson (June 29, 1793), in *Letters and Other Writings of James Madison* (Philadelphia: J.B. Lippincott, 1865), Vol. 1, p. 585. James Monroe expressed to Randolph how he felt "extremely embarrassed" about asking the French to respect the 1778 Treaties posed in light of British depredations of American ships. See his letter dated November 7, 1794, in *The Writings of James Monroe*, Vol. 2, pp. 98–108.

833 This is the famous rule outlined by Cornelius van Bynkershoek in his *De Dominio Maris*: "I should think (...) that the possession of a maritime belt ought to be regarded as extending just as far as it can be held in subjection to the mainland. (...) [o]n the whole it seems a better rule that the control of the land (over the sea) extends as far as cannon will carry." See quoted in Dickinson, *The Law of Nations*, p. 346.

president had given instructions to claim "the distance of one sea-league or three geographical miles from the sea shore."[834] Two years later, this rule was transformed into policy, in which it was declared that "[a]s it is contrary to the law of nations that any of the belligerent Powers should commit hostility on the waters which are subject to the exclusive jurisdiction of the United States, so ought not the ships of war, belonging to any belligerent Power, to take a station in those waters in order to carry on hostile expeditions from thence."[835]

Another major issue at this time was contraband, on the definition of which the Americans and British sharply disagreed. In the same letter in which Hammond defended the new Order in Council, he said with reference to contraband that in his estimation, "by the law of nations, as laid down by the most modern writers, it is expressly stated, that all provisions are to be considered as contraband, and as such, liable to confiscation, in the case where the depriving of an enemy of these supplies, is one of the means to be employed for reducing him to reasonable terms of peace."[836] While historian Paul Varg called this a "dubious assertion,"[837] Vattel actually provides support for Hammond's interpretation, including among contraband items "arms, ammunition, timber for ship-building, every kind of naval stores, horses,—and even provisions, in certain junctures, when we have hopes of reducing the enemy by famine."[838] Apart from doctrinal opinion, London also pushed its position through a series of treaties with Russia, Spain, Prussia and Austria, in which it managed to have a definition of contraband accepted that went beyond mere military equipment to include corn, grain and other kinds of provisions and also committed the contracting parties to seize such goods from neutral vessels. Once more, Vattel was explicitly relied upon for justification of Britain's policy when Lord Grenville, Britain's foreign minister, informed Jefferson of his country's policy.[839]

For Jefferson, however, the doctrinal and practical evidence adduced by the British foreign minister and ambassador were not sufficient to convince him of the justness of their position. In a defiant mood, and implicitly responding to

834 Jefferson to Hammond (November 8, 1793), in *The Works of Thomas Jefferson*, Vol. 8, p. 63.

835 Edmund Randolph, "Circular to the Governors of the several States" (April 16, 1795), in *American State Papers: Foreign Relations*, Vol. 1, p. 608.

836 George Hammond to Jefferson, (September 12, 1793), in *American State Papers*, p. 240.

837 Paul Varg, *Foreign Policies of the Founding Fathers* (Baltimore, MD: Penguin Books, 1970), p. 96.

838 Vattel, *The Law of Nations*, Bk III, ch. 7, para. 112, p. 530.

839 William Grenville to Thomas Jefferson" (September 12, 1793), in *Instructions to the British Ministers to the United States, 1791–1812* (Washington DC: Government Printing Office, 1941), p. 240. The passage concerned is almost verbatim taken from the letter of Hammond to Jefferson (September 12, 1793).

Vattel, he wrote that Britain may "feel the desire of starving an enemy nation; but she can have no right of doing it at our loss, nor of making us the instrument of it."[840] Jeffersonian—if not American—sentiment in that regard was very well reflected early in the 19th century by William Duane, who wrote that "[t]he utmost that the law of necessity (…) allows to a belligerent, is to delay or interrupt a supply of contraband, it can give no right to rob a neutral; and the contraband, if stopped, should be paid for. Necessity can never exist contrary to justice." Consequently, he believed that "the laws of nature, instead of justifying, absolutely forbid any interruption of neutral commerce."[841] Still, for the moment, the United States found itself in a position in which the only realistic option was to accept Britain's reasoning on the issue, and Hamilton in fact conceded that there was some justification in Britain's actions under international law.[842] However, when Britain issued a second Order in Council in November, not even Hamilton could come up with a satisfactory defense: it attempted to strangle all neutral trade with the French West Indies by having the British navy capture all ships transporting goods to and from the islands. The measure went even beyond the Rule of 1756, since it prohibited shipping from ports which had been open to American vessels before the outbreak of war.[843]

What the foregoing survey of the critical year of 1793 has tried to demonstrate among other things is that when beliefs meet practice, it is not easy to bracket practitioners and their ideas: Jefferson, being pro-French, rebuffed Citizen Genêt, while Hamilton rejected Britain's expansive definition of the Rule of 1756 under the second Order in Council in 1793. As a consequence, early American foreign policy has often confounded historians, since many of the Founding Fathers have been so difficult to pigeonhole. For example, Albert Bowman wrote that to assume that Hamilton represented a realist and Jefferson an idealist position is in fact to reverse their outlooks since Hamilton's singular focus on British commerce "blinded him to the importance to the United States of a balance of European interests in America," which Jefferson always

840 Jefferson to Thomas Pinckney (September 7, 1793), in *The Writings of Thomas Jefferson*, Vol. 9, p. 224.

841 William Duane, *The Law of Nations, Investigated in a Popular Manner* (Philadelphia, William Duane, 1809), pp. 33–34. See also Lauren Benton, *A Search for Sovereignty: Law and Geography in European Empires, 1400–1900* (New York: Cambridge University Press, 2010), p. 111.

842 George Hammond to William Grenville (May 17, 1793), referred to in Samuel Bemis, "The United States and the Abortive Armed Neutrality of 1794" *The American Historical Review* 24, no. 1 (October 1918), p. 29.

843 Kaplan, *Colonies into Nation*, pp. 230–231.

kept in view.[844] Walter Russell Mead also reconsidered the old dichotomies. While saying that Hamiltonians may have thought like Continental realists, he believed that their thinking in terms of the national interest was not oriented on balance of power, but on commerce, which they saw as "a cause for peace."[845] Jeffersonians however feared the 'imperial temptation' which they thought inherent in Hamiltonian approaches. This was just one reason why Jefferson was never enamoured of an unqualified commercial alliance with Britain. In terms of strategic thinking, Jefferson proved to be more of a realist than Hamilton, wishing instead, as Mead said, to "balance any aspiring power on the continent of Europe," whether it was Britain as a sea power or France as a land power.[846] As president, Jefferson would in fact consider both alternatives, and was prepared to conclude balancing alliances with either, the objective being "to lure Britain and France into a bidding war for American support."[847]

But the similarities between Hamiltonians and Jeffersonians are just as important as the differences. For instance, while they disagreed about the purposes of commerce, both considered it an important element for enhancing America's well-being, and believed that "[i]n times of general European war (…) American shipping would always be a vital factor in the balance of power."[848] The need to countenance the balance of power, to defend America's neutrality policy and to promote freedom of the seas were all areas which Hamiltonians and Jeffersonians could agree upon. Finally, we have noted that despite the differences of opinion on certain legal issues, there also existed a consensus about the fact that the law of nations is part of the law of the land, and that it was in the interest of the United States to do its utmost to ensure compliance with it at home.[849] As a result, Hendrickson concluded that a

844 Albert Bowman, "Jefferson, Hamilton and American Foreign Policy" *Political Science Quarterly* 71, no. 1 (March 1956), p. 20.

845 Walter Russell Mead, *Special Providence: American Foreign Policy and How It Changed the World* (London: Routledge, 2002), p. 103.

846 Mead, ibid., p. 198.

847 Mead, ibid., p. 199.

848 Reginald Horsman, *The Diplomacy of the New Republic, 1776–1815* (Arlington Heights, Ill.: Harlan Davidson, 1985), p. 70.

849 Although it should be added that Grey noted a divergence of opinion whereby on the one hand "the legalist and elitist conception of fundamental law would more often be identified with the conservative forces in American society--those who favored a strong central government, a strong executive and judiciary (…)." On the other hand, "the purely ethical and egalitarian conception was more associated with those who favored state autonomy

"commitment to the "constitutional tradition in diplomacy" in a Grotian mould could be considered as the characteristic world-view of American diplomatists in the eighteenth and nineteenth centuries, [who] attached vital significance to the law of nations in various spheres, especially the law of neutrality."[850] Politically speaking, the broad consensus that existed regarding the greater principles of the law of nations and the legalistic way in which foreign policy was conducted contributed to obscuring party-political differences for as far as the results of American diplomacy up to 1793 are concerned. Therefore, Hendrickson's statement that "we are all realists, we are all idealists" looks to be justified when applied to the period between the revolution and 1793, writing further that "practical idealism" was the 'leitmotif' of American politics, equally shared by Adams and Hamilton as well as Jefferson and Franklin.[851] The guiding principles of the law had proved to comport well with the republic's founding ideology itself. However, due to the Jay Treaty, this strenuously-wrought consensus would meet its most serious challenge yet.

5.2 Balancing Neutral Rights and Treaty Obligations

The years between the adoption of the Neutrality Proclamation and the ascent of Thomas Jefferson would show that being neutral does not equate to being friends with everyone, but rather, that one is regarded with hostility by all. This is not to say that under Jefferson, America's position as a neutral was assured; it is to say that at least, the United States was freed from having to balance between France and the United Kingdom. But before the country entered the 19th century, it had to manage steering the ship of state safely between Scylla and Charybdis in the shape of Revolutionary France and the mightiest naval power on the planet, Britain.

(…)." See Thomas Grey, "Origins of the Unwritten Constitution: Fundamental Law in American Revolutionary Thought" *Stanford Law Review* 30 (1978), p. 892.

850 David Hendrickson, *Union, Nation or Empire: The American Debate over International Relations., 1789–1941* (Lawrence, Ks: University Press of Kansas, 2009), p. 9. The phrase "constitutional tradition in diplomacy" can be traced back to an essay by Martin Wight, published in Martin Wight and Herbert Butterfield, *Diplomatic Investigations: Essays in the Theory of International Politics.* (London: Allen & Unwin, 1966). The idea of Grotian internationalism goes back to Hedley Bull, most prominently his *The Anarchical Society* (New York: Columbia University Press, 1977).

851 David Hendrickson, *Peace Pact: The Lost World of the American Founding* (Lawrence, KS: University of Kansas Press, 2003), p. 169.

As we saw in the previous section, tensions between the United States and Britain reached a peak in late 1793 and early 1794, in particular as a result of the November Orders in Council. The situation was such that a majority of Americans actually favored war with Britain.[852] Madison and Jefferson made a new push for imposing a shipping embargo against London and on March 26, 1794, Congress adopted a law which prohibited British vessels from leaving American ports. By next month, the shipping ban was extended to all foreign vessels, and was thus equally injurious on Britain and France.[853] Hamilton wanted to avoid a clash with Britain at all costs, and hoped that the conclusion of a commercial treaty could help to assuage matters. However, when the British minister, George Hammond, had arrived in the United States, he carried no instructions to begin negotiations for a commercial treaty. Even so, a commercial treaty would not nearly have solved all outstanding matters between the two countries. The British continued to occupy fortifications in the north-west, and continued to assail American shipping rights. However, by mid-1794, the earlier June Order had been repealed, while the order from November had been softened in January of 1794. In hindsight, even Britain considered the Orders untenable under international law.[854]

At the same time, an opportunity emerged for the United States to join another league of armed neutrality, which was being finalized between Denmark and Sweden. But unlike the one from 1780, Russia and Prussia did not intend to join this new league, since the last thing these countries wished was to antagonize Britain while clouds were gathering over Paris. When the league was formalized in March of 1794, president Washington declined to join it. He did not want to sacrifice an opportunity to possibly conclude a treaty with Britain in exchange for membership in an ineffectual and probably inconsequential league. In reality, it was Hamilton who wanted to ensure that the government kept its hands free to negotiate an agreement with the British. In explaining the decision to Hammond, Hamilton wrote that the government wished "to avoid entangling itself with European connexions, which could only tend to involve this Country in disputes, wherein it might have no possible interest, and commit it in a common cause with allies, from whom in the

852 Samuel Bemis, "The United States and the Abortive Armed Neutrality of 1794" *The American Historical Review* 24, no. 1 (October 1918), p. 35.

853 See discussed in Paul Varg, *Foreign Policies of the Founding Fathers* (Baltimore, MD: Penguin Books, 1970), pp. 99–102.

854 Samuel Bemis, "The United States and the Abortive Armed Neutrality of 1794" *The American Historical Review* 24, no. 1 (October 1918), p. 42.

moment of danger, it could derive no succour."[855] In a fit of hyperbole, Bemis said about this episode that Hamilton's successful opposition to involving the United States in a European compact constitutes "the first definitive acceptance by the government of the United States of the principle of abstention from foreign entanglements."[856] For this feat, Bemis even called Hamilton "the author of one-half of the Monroe Doctrine, just as nearly thirty years later John Quincy Adams was the author of the other half."[857]

The stark reality was however that at the time, Hamilton was in the process of preparing a mission behind the scenes to negotiate an agreement with Britain that would bring both countries back from the brink of war. With sentiment against Britain raging as high as it did, no other time in the history of the early republic was arguably less propitious for agreeing to a treaty with Britain, but at no time were the stakes for a peaceful solution any higher. The odds for getting a treaty to resolve the most vexatious issues were however not very strong. To increase the odds, Hamilton decided to entrust John Jay, the sitting Chief Justice, with this most delicate mission. Among the most versatile of the Founding Fathers, Jay had served in more government positions than anyone else in the early republic. But in spite of his wealth of experience, Jay, a staunch Federalist, was also among the most distrusted people with Jeffersonians. They feared that he would sell out the United States—as he was alleged to have done in 1785–1786 when negotiating access to the Mississippi with Spain.

In terms of Jay's views on the law of nations, it could be expected that, in spite of his Federalist credentials, he would still stand up to Britain in defending his country's neutral rights. He attached great importance to the law of nations as such, including in relation to the Constitution, and he was supportive of punishing transgressions of the country's neutrality laws. As an example, he said in a charge in Virginia in 1790 that it was incumbent upon the nation to observe a "[s]trict impartiality [which] is our duty in all cases where prior treaties do not stipulate for favours, and it is no less our interest than our duty to act accordingly. A just war is an evil, but it is not the greatest; oppression and disgrace are greater."[858] More specifically, Jay was equally adamant in prosecuting American citizens violating the law as foreigners, given that "the

855 Hamilton to Grenville (Aug. 3, 1794), quoted in Deconde, *Entangling Alliance*, p. 107.

856 Samuel Bemis, "The United States and the Abortive Armed Neutrality of 1794" *The American Historical Review* 24, no. 1 (October 1918), p. 46.

857 Samuel Bemis, "The United States and the Abortive Armed Neutrality of 1794" in ibid., p. 47.

858 John Jay, "Charge to Grand Jury, Richmond, VA" (May 22, 1793), in *The Correspondence and Public Papers of John Jay*, Vol. 3, p. 482.

belligerent powers owe duties to us as well as we to them." Indeed, whoever is found engaging in acts of hostility against the United States should be considered "guilty of high misdemeanour."[859] What is more, in spite of Jay's antipathy towards France, he felt compelled to honor America's treaty obligations towards the revolutionary republic. In a speech in 1790 he had said as much couched in a more general context:

> You will recollect that the laws of nations make part of the laws of this and of every other civilized nation. (...) To this head also belong those rules or laws which by agreement become established between particular nations, and of this kind are treaties, conventions, and the like compacts; as in private life a fair and legal contract between two men cannot be annulled nor altered by either without the consent of the other, so neither can treaties between nations. States and legislatures may repeal their regulating statutes, but they cannot repeal their bargains. Hence it is that treaties fairly made and concluded are perfectly obligatory, and ought to be punctually observed. We are now a nation, and it equally becomes us to perform our duties as to assert our rights.[860]

Jay also subscribed to a divine view on the origins of the law of nations. Saying that "it is much to be wished that [the law of nations] may be more generally studied and understood, "he added that the answer to the question who created it was "he [i.e. God] from whose will proceed all moral obligations, and which will is made known to us by reason or by revelation."[861] In his piety and

---

859 John Jay, "Charge to Grand Jury, Richmond, VA" (May 22, 1793), in *The Correspondence and Public Papers of John Jay*, Vol. 3, pp. 483.

860 John Jay, "The charges of Chief Justice Jay to the Grand Juries on the Eastern circuit at the circuit Courts held in the Districts of New York on the 4th, of Connecticut on the 22d days of April, of Massachusetts on the 4th, and of New Hampshire on the 20th day of May, 1790." in Henry Johnston (ed.), *The Correspondence and Public Papers of John Jay* (New York: G.P. Putnam's Sons, 1890), Vol. 3, pp. 393–394.

861 In explaining the moral bindingness of international law, Jay made an interesting comparison between families and nations: "Suppose twenty families should be cast on an island and after dividing it between them conclude to remain unconnected with each other by any kind of government, would it thence follow that there are no laws to direct their conduct towards one another? Certainly not. Would not the laws of reason and morality direct them to behave to each other with respect, with justice, with benevolence, with good faith—would not those laws direct them to abstain from violence, to abstain from interfering in their respective domestic government and arrangements, to abstain from causing quarrels and dissensions in each other's families? If they made treaties,

deference for international law—in particular with its implicit emphasis on natural law—he fitted in the same mould as Hamilton and Wilson. And given his respect for the sanctity of treaties, it was no problem for him to accept that in his negotiations with the British, the only non-negotiable points would be that no commitments were entered into that would violate the obligations under the 1778 treaties with France, and that American ships would have direct access to the British West Indies.[862]

Jay's agenda for the negotiations was quite full. Among the items he had to discuss were (1) to settle grievances deriving from the 1783 peace treaty; (2) to gain British recognition of America's neutral rights; (3) to obtain compensation for impressment practices and (4) to obtain—if possible—a commercial treaty. In his official instructions as drafted by Secretary of State Edmund Randolph, Jay was told to mention "with due stress, the general irritation of the United States at the vexations, spoliations, captures etc." Another issue Randolph pointed at was that British agents stop "stirring up (…) the different tribes of Indians against [the United States]."[863] In listing the items for the treaty, Randolph asked Jay to seek to obtain, among other things, access to the West Indies, and acceptance of the 'free ships, free goods' principle. As to contraband articles, Jay was to try and obtain "[p]roper security for the safety of neutral commerce (…) [b]y declaring provisions never to be contraband, except in the strongest possible case, as the blockade of a port; or, if attainable by abolishing contraband altogether." Such a provision, noted Randolph, would be "of infinite advantage to obtain [for the United States]."[864] But, if such a

---

would they not be bound to observe them? Or if by consent expressed or implied they gave occasion to usages mutually convenient, would not those usages grow into conventional laws ? The answer is obvious. (…) In like manner the nations throughout the world are like so many great families placed by Providence on the earth, who having divided it between them, remain perfectly distinct from and independent of each other. Between them there is no judge but the great Judge of all. (…); in a word, one has no right to interfere in the affairs of another, but all are bound to behave to each other with respect, with justice, with benevolence, and with good faith." See John Jay, "Charge to Grand Jury, Richmond, VA" (May 22, 1793), in *The Correspondence and Public Papers of John Jay*, Vol. 3, pp. 481–482.

862 Kaplan, *Colonies into Nation*, p. 238; Bradford Perkins, *Cambridge History of American Foreign Relations*, Vol. 1, p. 97.

863 This is a reference to a speech by the governor-general of Canada, Lord Dorchester, who gave a rousing speech inciting Indians to rise up in the northern and western parts of the United States, in effect stirring a rebellion.

864 Edmund Randolph, "Instructions to mr. Jay" (May 6, 1794), in *American State Papers: Foreign Relations*, Vol. 1, p. 472.

definition of contraband was not attainable, a definition of blockades in accordance with that of the armed neutrality should be sought. Most startling perhaps, Randolph wrote that if there would be no danger of compromising a possible agreement with Britain, Jay should approach Nordic ministers to inquire "upon the probability of an alliance with their nations to support the principles [of neutral rights]."[865]

But because Randolph was a Virginian—and not a highly respected one in the cabinet at that—Jay was much more inclined to taking instructions from Alexander Hamilton, with whom he would frequently correspond. Indeed, Hamilton's objectives as to Jay's mission were much less ambitious than Randolph's—being significantly more inclined towards British views on the law of nations. In a cabinet paper that Hamilton wrote in advance of the Jay mission, he suggested that the latter raise the question about the Rule of 1756, the extended application of which under the most recent Orders in Council had almost led to warfare between Britain and the United States.[866] In particular, Hamilton noted that while Britain held that "a neutral nation ought not to be permitted to carry on, in time of war, a commerce with a nation at war, which it could not carry on with that nation in time of peace [i.e. the Rule of 1756]," it would be 'unwise' for her to continue to insist on this, since so much of Britain's imports are shipped from the United States.[867] In his last days as Secretary of State, Jefferson had been more straightforward, insisting that Britain accept the 'free ships, free goods' rule,[868] and believing that, in Varg's words,

865 Edmund Randolph, "Instructions to mr. Jay" (May 6, 1794), in *American State Papers: Foreign Relations*, Vol. 1, p. 473–474. See also discussed in Alexandre Deconde, *Entangling Alliance*, p. 106.

866 A.L. Burt "Neutral Rights," in Patrick White (ed.), *The Critical Years: American Foreign Policy 1793–1823* (New York: John Wiley & Sons, 1970), p. 61.

867 Hamilton to Jay (May 6, 1794), in *The Works of Alexander Hamilton*, Vol. 5, p. 125.

868 Paul Varg, *Foreign Policies of the Founding Fathers*, p. 107. In one of his last notes as Secretary of State, Jefferson laid out in great detail that his support for the 'free ships, free goods' principle is not merely based on theoretical grounds, but also on custom arising from treaty law. He starts out by saying that "[i]t cannot be denied that according to the general law of nations, the goods of an enemy are lawful prize in the bottom of a friend, and the goods of a friend privileged in the bottom of an enemy; or in other words, that *the goods follow the owner.*" Next he proffers examples that demonstrate that "[t]he inconvenience of this principle in subjecting neutral vessels to vexatious searches at sea, has for more than a century rendered it usual for nations to substitute a *conventional* principle *that the goods shall follow the bottom,* instead of the *natural* one before mentioned." Indeed, he claims that the principle was even agreed between France and Britain after the American War of Independence. The reason for Jefferson to insist on the old rule during the Genêt affair was because Genêt demanded that the United States arm their vessels to

"American interests would have benefited tremendously by a universal acceptance of [America's] interpretation of neutral rights."[869]

Approaching the issue in a tactical fashion, Hamilton thought it possible to achieve a trade-off between settling issues emanating from the 1783 peace treaty and to mitigate the fallout from the November Order in Council, one item in this grand bargain being a commercial treaty: "[t]he object of indemnification for the depredations committed on our trade, in consequence of the instructions of the 6th of November, is very near the hearts and feelings of the people of this country," Hamilton felt that if "solid arrangements with regard to the points unexecuted of the treaty of peace [could be obtained], the question of indemnification may be managed with less rigor, and may be still more laxly dealt with, if a truly beneficial treaty of commerce, embracing privileges in the West India Islands, can be established."[870]

Another central issue was contraband. Here in particular, Hamilton hoped to convince Britain to accept to live by the rule as settled in doctrine: "The desirable rule is that which theoretical writers lay down as the rule of the law of nations—to wit: that none but articles by general usage deemed contraband shall be liable to confiscation, and that the carrying of such articles shall not infect other parts of a cargo, nor even a vessel carrying them, where there are no appearances of a design to conceal."[871] A connected issue is that concerning blockades, on which Hamilton also insisted on acceptance of the rule as it stands in international law: "The idea of a place blockaded or besieged by construction, which is not actually so, ought to be excluded (…)."[872] Interestingly, the instructions say nothing about the impressment question—the British practice of arresting alleged British citizens serving on American ships—which had been a sensitive issue since the Revolution, and would become even more charged during the Jefferson and Madison administrations.

---

protect French goods from British depredations, while French ships kept American goods seized from British bottoms, and that at that time "we had no right to make war for the enforcement of it." Now, however, Jefferson wishes that the United States "should endeavor to extend [the new principle] to England, Spain, and other powers." (emphasis in original) See Jefferson, "Opinion on Neutral Trade" (December 20, 1793), in *The Works of Thomas Jefferson*, Vol. 8, p. 123.

869 Paul Varg, *Foreign Policies of the Founding Fathers*, p. 112.

870 Hamilton to Jay (May 6, 1794), in *The Works of Alexander Hamilton*, Vol. 5, p. 309.

871 Hamilton, "Points to be Considered in the Instructions to Mr. Jay, Envoy Extraordinary to Great Britain" (April 23, 1794), in *The Works of Alexander Hamilton*, Vol. 5, p. 301.

872 Hamilton, "Points to be Considered in the Instructions to Mr. Jay, Envoy Extraordinary to Great Britain" (April 23, 1794), in ibid., p. 301.

When Jay arrived in London, he was received very cordially by his British counterparts, and in order not to burden the negotiations, the debates in Congress on Madison's navigation system were suspended. At the outset, Jay sensed that Britain, which was already embroiled in full-fledged war with France, was not seeking to make the United States another enemy. The negotiations were successful, and a treaty was signed on November 19, 1794. One result was that the British agreed to vacate fortresses along the American border, which was secured in article II of the treaty. Other issues that were resolved included the establishment of an arbitration commission to delineate the northern boundaries of the Mississippi river (article IV) as well as further commissions to discuss and settle war debts and arrange compensation for damages incurred during the Revolutionary war (arts. VI–VIII).[873] But in spite of these results, the British had managed to sign another treaty with the United States—the 1783 treaty being the first—that avoided many of the key issues. Kaplan listed the shortcomings as follows:

> [N]ot only had [the treaty] nothing to say [about British depredations on sea], but [it] also appeared to accept the British definitions of neutral rights and freedom of the seas. British interpretations of international law were written into the treaty. Nor did Jay secure the commercial treaty Hamilton had wanted or the privileges such a treaty would have accorded American commerce (...). Conspicuous by its silence in the treaty was the flaming issue of impressment (...). Westerners were upset over Jay's failure to gain a British commitment against interference in Indian affairs in the Northwest, while southerners were angry over his failure to provide compensation for loss of slave property carried away by the British army during the war.[874]

As to the reasons why the British ceded so little ground vis-à-vis the United States, the same author concluded that "Jay's inability to make the most of his possibilities in London must be blamed in large measure upon the limits of the British willingness to concede (...) but their rigidity owed much to Hamilton's

873 The arbitration commissions that were created pursuant to the treaty inaugurated a revival in international arbitration as a means for the peaceful settlement of disputes according to some observers. See e.g. Cornelis van Vollenhoven, *The Three Stages in the Evolution of the Law of Nations*, p. 42; Wilhelm Grewe, *The Epochs of International Law* (Berlin/New York: Walter de Gruyter, 2000), pp. 365–366 and Arthur Nussbaum, *A Concise History of the Law of Nations* (New York: Macmillan Press, 1954), p. 128.

874 Kaplan, *Colonies into Nation*, pp. 241–242.

interposition in the negotiations."[875] Thus, if the ire on the part of Jeffersonians about the treaty was so fierce, it was because, as Bemis had noted, that the treaty might as well have been called "Hamilton's Treaty."[876]

So, while peace with Britain was restored and trade resumed, dissatisfaction with the outcome was widespread, principally because the treaty contained no affirmation of neutral rights and remained silent on the impressment issue, while trade with the West Indies was opened up only partially. What is more, the Republicans saw the treaty as Federalist defeatism and cowardice, since it surrendered the U.S. right to impose commercial and discriminatory duties or sanctions for a period of ten years.[877] Perhaps even worse, the Jay treaty "forfeit[ed America's] standing as a neutral power" and "discredited the Jeffersonian conception of treaties as instruments of a liberal foreign policy that would unshackle commerce and promote peace."[878] Despite the fact that, according to the letter of the treaty, it did not affect existing treaty obligations, they also believed that it effectively "reduced the alliance [with France] to nullity."[879]

According to Stahr, the "one great lapse" in the treaty was article XII, which inadvertently (at least from Jay's point of view) prohibited "the carrying any Melasses, Sugar, Coffee, Cocoa or Cotton in American vessels, either from His Majesty's Islands or from the United States, to any part of the World, except the United States" from the West Indies, where in fact, only the *British* West Indies were intended.[880] Even Hamilton found this article "an exceptionable one."[881]

875 Kaplan, *Colonies into Nation*, p. 239. Elsewhere, Kaplan said that "[n]o critic faulted [Jay's] sincerity in advancing American power in international affairs. He sought as hard as any radical to press on Europe the American interpretation of neutral rights through treaties and when blocked gave impetus to the idea of mixed national commissions to resolve differences with other parties." See ibid., p. 157.

876 Kaplan, *Colonies into Nation*, p. 239, quoting from Samuel Bemis, *Jay's Treaty: A Study in Commerce and Diplomacy* (New Haven, 1962), p. 373.

877 Gordon Wood, *Empire of Liberty: A History of the Early Republic, 1789–1815* (New York: Oxford University Press, 2009), p. 197; Peter Onuf and Nicholas Onuf, *Federal Union, Modern World: The Law of Nations in an Age of Revolutions 1776–1814* (Madison, WI: Madison House, 1992), p. 160. See also Madison, "The Jay Treaty: Speech in the 4th Congress" (April 6, 1796), in *The Writings of James Madison*, Vol. 6, pp. 263–296; Albert Gallatin, "Execution of British Treaty" (April 26, 1796), in Annals of Congress (House of Representatives), 4th Congress, 1st Session, p. 1190.

878 Peter Onuf and Nicholas Onuf, *Federal Union, Modern World*, p. 160.

879 Paul Varg, *Foreign Policies of the Founding Fathers*, p. 120.

880 Walter Stahr, *John Jay, Founding Father* (New York: Hambledon and Continuum, 2006), p. 325.

881 Alexander Hamilton, "Remarks On the Treaty of Amity, Commerce, and Navigation, Made Between the United States and Great Britain" (July 9, 1795), in *The Works of Alexander Hamilton*, Vol. 5, p. 162.

The most serious issues lay elsewhere, however. First of all, although Jay had managed to have the British by implication revoke the extension of the November Order in Council, he had not insisted on acceptance of the 'free ships, free goods' principle, and instead had the old rule reaffirmed: "in all cases where vessels shall be captured or detained on just suspicion of having on board enemy's property, or of carrying to the enemy any of the articles which are contraband of war, (…) any property of an enemy (…) shall be made prize, and the vessel shall be at liberty to proceed with the remainder without any impediment." In his *Remarks on the Treaty*, Hamilton defended the provision by appealing to current international law. Encouraging Americans to live by the rules of international law, he merely asked them to obey "the reality of external powers":[882]

> It is impossible to deny that the principle recognized is conformable with the laws of nations. It is the uniform doctrine of writers, and was the uniform and universally allowed practice of nations before the armed neutrality brought it into controversy. A combination like this, formed in the midst of a war of temporary duration, and on special motives of policy, not acceded to by all the powers of Europe, not having acquired the sanction of time, is clearly not sufficient to alter a rule in the law of nations. This might be done by common consent, or by long and general usage. Neither is the case here. On the contrary, some of the powers which combined to introduce the innovation, now support in arms a contrary principle; and all the neutral powers—the United States included—have expressly or virtually relinquished the ground in the whole course of the present war. None, that I know of, has seriously contended for it, even in argument.

"Besides," Hamilton concluded, "that one or a few nations cannot justly make and attempt to enforce a new principle, it is folly in a young and weak country like ours to take a ground which cannot clearly be maintained on precedent and principle."[883]

Madison was of quite a different opinion. He believed that with admitting the British view that free ships shall not make free goods, "the progress towards a compleat & formal establishment of a principle in the law of nations so

882 Stephen Rosen, "Alexander Hamilton and the Domestic Uses of International Law," *Diplomatic History* 5, no. 3 (1981), p. 196.

883 Hamilton, "Remarks On the Treaty of Amity, Commerce, and Navigation, Made Between the United States and Great Britain," (July 9, 1795), in *The Works of Alexander Hamilton*, Vol. 5, pp. 167–168.

favorable to the general interest and security of Commerce, receive[d] all the check the U.S. could give to it."[884] Worse, he said, "every principle of liberality, every consideration of interest has been sacrificed to the arbitrary maxims which govern the policy of [Great Britain]. Nay a new principle has been created (...) against the fundamental rights of nations & duties of humanity, for the purpose of aiding the horrible scheme of starving a whole people out of their liberties."[885] What astonished Albert Gallatin most about Jay's surrendering the 'free ships, free goods' principle is that England itself had consented to it in a treaty it had signed with France as recent as 1788. By admitting the British principle, not only had the United States relinquished what should have been a "sine qua non," but it had also recognized "the principle the most fatal to the liberty of commerce, and to the security of our navigation."[886] A modern observer even concluded that "[a] concept of neutral rights that had been argued since 1776 had been ignored, and the absolute necessity of a tight commercial tie to Great Britain had been conceded."[887]

On the same issue, Madison also highlighted the inequality between protection provided to British goods on American ships against its enemies, while enemy goods on American ships remained liable to seizure by the British. More subtly perhaps, Madison also suggested that the most-favored-nation provision in the Jay Treaty (article XV) actually inhibited the United States from being able to conclude trade agreements with other countrie. Under the provision, the United States could only receive privileges from third parties if these third parties agreed also to extend these privileges to the United Kingdom—with Britain having to pay nothing in return.[888]

---

884 Madison to—(draft, August 23, 1795), in *The Writings of James Madison*, Vol. 6, p. 249. See also "The Jay Treaty: Speech in the 4th Congress" (April 6, 1796), in *The Writings of James Madison*, Vol. 6, p. 285.

885 Madison to—(draft, August 23, 1795), in *The Writings of James Madison*, Vol. 6, p. 243. Speaking in the House of representatives, Madison reiterated this point, saying that "[t]here was an evident distinction between silently acquiescing in [the British doctrine], and giving it the support of a formal and positive stipulation. The former was all that could be required, and the latter was more than ought to have been unnecessarily yielded." See "The Jay Treaty: Speech in the 4th Congress" (April 6, 1796), in *The Writings of James Madison*, Vol. 6, p. 285.

886 Albert Gallatin, "Execution of British Treaty" (April 26, 1796), in *Annals of Congress* (House of Representatives), 4th Congress, 1st Session, p. 1190.

887 Reginald Horsman, *The Diplomacy of the New Republic, 1776–1815* (Arlington Heights, ILL.: Harlan Davidson, 1985), p. 64.

888 Madison to—(draft, August 23, 1795), in *The Writings of James Madison*, Vol. 6, pp. 254–255.

If the relinquishment of the 'free ships, free goods' principle was bad enough, the concessions Jay made to the British on the issue of contraband were considered even more iniquitous. Article XVIII of the treaty contained a list of contraband goods that went beyond what the law of nations would prescribe, and included items which the United States had hitherto not recognized as constituting contraband. Moreover, it contained a clause that permitted more items to be added to the list at a later point:

> And whereas the difficulty of agreeing on the precise cases in which alone provisions and other articles not generally contraband may be regarded as such, (…) [i]t is further agreed that whenever any such articles so becoming contraband, according to the existing laws of nations, shall for that reason be seized, the same shall not be confiscated, but the owners thereof shall be speedily and completely indemnified (…)

Madison criticized this provision, saying that the United States "had given way to the particular views of the other party."[889] In particular, he decried the ambiguity of the sub-clause "according to the existing Laws of Nations," which suggested "that one of the cases might be that which had been assumed and put in force by Great Britain in relation to the United States."[890] His fellow party-member Gallatin inferred that the second and third clauses read together created the possibility that articles which are not generally considered contraband could nonetheless be considered as such and in effect admit "a principle unknown to the Laws of Nations, infringing our neutrality, destructive of our trade, and liable to every misconstruction."[891]

Hamilton was not feeling concerned however. In his estimation, the definition of contraband adopted "made no change for the worse in our prior situation, but in some particulars made our ground better." Given the difficulties of the negotiations, it was to be commended that "[n]o clear right is abandoned, no material interest of the nation injured."[892] In discussing the details of the provision, he contended that given the circumstances, "in *doubtful* cases, the inconveniences to the neutral party being obviated or

889 Madison, "The Jay Treaty: Speech in the 4th Congress" (April 6, 1796), in *The Writings of James Madison*, Vol. 6, p. 285.

890 Madison, "The Jay Treaty: Speech in the 4th Congress" (April 6, 1796), in ibid., p. 286.

891 Albert Gallatin, "Execution of British Treaty" (April 26, 1796), in *Annals of Congress* (House of Representatives), 4th Congress, 1st Session, p. 1197.

892 Hamilton, "Camillus no. XXXII," in *The Works of Alexander Hamilton*, Vol. 6, p. 115.

lessened by compensation, there may be the less cause or temptation to controversy and rupture, the affair may be more susceptible of negotiation and accommodation." What is more, because the determination whether a good is deemed contraband should be made in accordance with the "existing law of nations," this makes each party "as free as the other to decide whether the laws of nations do, in the given case, pronounce them contraband or not, and neither is obliged to be governed by the opinion of the other." Reassuringly, Hamilton concluded that "[i]f one party, on a false pretext of being authorized by the laws of nations, makes a seizure, the other is at full liberty to contest it, to appeal to those laws, and, if it thinks fit, to oppose, even to reprisals and war."[893]

But despite Hamilton's attempts at squaring the circle, the contraband stipulation had in fact helped to modify the administration's policy, and had now come in line with the British position—one which the United States had opposed on multiple occasions before.[894] Indeed, the British actually tried soon after to exploit the ambiguities in the treaty's article XVIII. In a discussion with John Quincy Adams, Lord Grenville argued that in accordance with the Jay Treaty, provisions could be declared contraband, and that these could be seized without the need to pay indemnities.[895] In reply, Adams said that the treaty did not in fact imply "an admission of the legality of this order," adding that "[p]rovisions are among the most valuable articles of our export trade. They are indeed more valuable, proportionally speaking, to us than to any other commercial nation; a restraint therefore upon the freedom of this trade by external power has a more extensive operation upon our interests than upon those of any others, and it has the appearance of being specially pointed against us."[896] In a discussion later that month, Grenville tried to convince Adams that the principle that the United Kingdom sought to establish with the Orders in Council of November 6, 1793 would be in the long-term interest of the United States if that country should get involved in a war. Adams responded however with disarming logic that "the Americans chose rather to admit the Law of Nations as *it is,* than to aim at the settlement of principles which might be favorable to their particular interest; and further that they did not wish to

893 Hamilton, "Camillus no. XXXII," in *The Works of Alexander Hamilton*, Vol. 6, p. 119–120.

894 Lint, "Early American Conceptions of International Law," p. 135.

895 John Quincy Adams to Thomas Pickering (December 5, 1795), in *The Writings of John Quincy Adams*, Vol. 1, p. 438. The relevant discussion in Vattel can be found in Bk. III, ch. 7, para. 112–114, pp. 529–532.

896 Adams to Pickering, in *The Writings of John Quincy Adams*, Vol. 1, p. 438, 439–440.

suppose a state of war between themselves and any other nation, as it was their desire to remain at peace with all the world."[897]

Predictably, France was dismayed when it learned about the treaty between the United States and Britain. French foreign minister Charles-François de la Croix declared that

> this act, concluded in the midst of hostilities, [constitutes] a breach of the friendship which unites the United States and this republic and (...) an abandonment of the tacit engagement which subsisted between the two nations upon this point since their treaty of commerce of 1778.

As a consequence, the minister added, the Directory "thinks itself founded, in regarding the stipulations of the treaty of 1778, which concern the neutrality of the flag, as altered and suspended in their most essential parts, by this act (...)."[898] Further annoying the French, Secretary of State Pickering had the temerity to suggest that the French were bound by the 'free ships, free goods' rule, while acknowledging that Britain was free to do as it pleased. President Washington remained unrepentant, and squarely asserted America's right to conclude treaties with whomever: "if we are to be told by a foreign Power (if our engagements with it are not infracted) what we *shall do*, and what we shall *not do*, we have Independence yet to seek, and have contended hitherto for very little."[899]

France was particularly annoyed about article XXIV of the treaty, which prohibited foreign privateers from operating out of American ports. Alexander Hamilton, as always, defended article XXIV, noting in a matter-of-fact way "that Congress in the commencement and through the greater part of our revolution war, authorized our ships of war and privateers to capture enemy property on board neutral ships, and our admiralty courts uniformly restored neutral property found on board enemy ships." Hence, said Hamilton, the Americans themselves conformed to the prevailing law of nations, not seeking to change this through practice.[900] However, trying to reassure the French, Hamilton also

897 John Quincy Adams to John Adams (December 29, 1795), in *The Writings of John Quincy Adams*, Vol. 1, p. 474 (emphasis in original).

898 French Foreign minister De La Croix to the U.S. minister, Monroe (July 7, 1796), in *American State Papers: Foreign Relations*, Vol. 1, p. 739.

899 George Washington to Hamilton (May 8, 1796), in John Fitzpatrick (ed.), *The Writings of George Washington*, (Washington DC: U.S. Government Printing Office, 1931–1944), Vol. 35, p. 40 (emphasis in original).

900 Alexander Hamilton, "Camillus no. XXX" (1795), in *The Works of Alexander Hamilton*, Vol. 6, pp. 96–97.

stressed that the American government pledged not to act in contravention of existing understandings with other nations, underlining that article XXV provides that "[n]othing in this treaty contained shall, however, be construed or operate contrary to former and existing public treaties with other sovereigns or States."[901]

In fact, up to 1795, what France had regarded as a right under the treaty of 1778 the Americans had only deemed a privilege at best, but one which they consistently denied the French.[902] This did not stop the new French representative, Pierre-Auguste Adet, from continuing to complain about arrests of French privateers and confiscation of their prizes. In reply, Hamilton contended that not only were these ships captured in the territorial waters of the United States, they were mostly owned by Americans as well.[903] For good measure, he repeated on the same occasion that the United States had not abandoned modern international law by not adhering to the 'free ships, free goods' doctrine. Based on France's own maritime laws, Hamilton argued, France had no right to complain.[904] Eventually, as a concession, France was granted the right to bring British prizes into American harbors, though it did not have the right to sell them there.[905] The uncertainty created by the American administration about French rights in light of the Jay Treaty made that, as Kaplan said, "it was understandable if Frenchmen such as Genêt could even have concluded that [article XXII of the French Treaty] granted those rights implicitly to the allies which it explicitly denied to the enemies."[906]

Another issue that was quickly brought to the attention of American diplomats was the contraband provision of the Jay Treaty. As the American minister, James Monroe, reported from Paris: "the attention of many has been drawn with some degree of solicitude to the contents of the second paragraph of the

901 Alexander Hamilton, "Camillus no. XXXV" (1796), in *The Works of Alexander Hamilton*, Vol. 6, p. 150. The respective articles of the Jay Treaty are 24 and 25.

902 See Lint, "Early American Conceptions of International Law," pp. 169–171.

903 Alexander Hamilton, "Americanus: the Answer from the Minerva" (December 6, 1796), in *The Works of Alexander Hamilton*, Vol. 6, pp. 215–229.

904 Alexander Hamilton, "Americanus: the Answer from the Minerva" (December 6, 1796), in *The Works of Alexander Hamilton*, Vol. 6, pp. 223–224. As Hamilton says: "By the marine laws of France, Reg. Dec. 1744, Art. 5, it is directed, that "if there are found on board of neutral vessels, of whatever nation they may be, merchandises or effects belonging to the enemies of his Majesty, they shall be good prize, even though they are not of the growth or manufacture of the enemy's country, but the vessels shall be released."" Ibid.

905 Timothy Pickering to French minister Adet (November 15, 1796), in *American State Papers: Foreign Relations*, Vol. 1, pp. 655–656.

906 Kaplan, *Colonies into Nation*, pp. 247–248.

18th article, (…) as that article leaves the law of nations unsettled, and provides payment for seizures in cases of contraband, and of course for those which are not contraband, whereby the complaints of our citizens are prevented, and the British construction by implication countenanced,—this Republic has a right to complain of it."[907] In the face of increasing bellicosity on the part of France towards the United States, Monroe became correspondingly more defensive. In early 1796, he was convinced that the French had no justifiable right to complain, saying that "although we have not ameliorated the law of nations in that respect, yet certainly we have not changed it for the worse; and which alone could give you just cause of complaint."[908] In the same letter, Monroe also denied the claim that the United States had abandoned the principles of the Armed Neutrality.[909] In a follow-up letter, Monroe entered into a brief discussion about when the law of nations could be deemed to have changed. De la Croix had argued that the permission granted by France by dint of the 1778 treaty for American ships to carry enemy goods had now become a universal principle. Monroe however argued that any changes in the law would only be valid "among nations who have formed treaties to that effect (…) but further the doctrine could not be carried." While citing from Vattel and Bynkershoek to support his contention, Monroe wrote that

907 James Monroe to Edmund Randolph (August 17, 1795), in *The Writings of James Monroe*, Vol. 2, p. 341.

908 James Monroe, "Letter to the Minister of Foreign Affairs" (March 15, 1796), in *The Writings of James Monroe*, Vol. 2, p. 480. Hamilton later added the argument that France had acquiesced in its own treaties with an expansion of the definition, and that this represents the modern law of nations. See Alexander Hamilton, "Americanus: the Answer from the Minerva" (December 6, 1796), in *The Works of Alexander Hamilton*, Vol. 6, pp. 224–225. Hamilton cites here from the Franco-Danish treaty of August 23, 1724.

909 James Monroe, "Letter to the Minister of Foreign Affairs" (March 15 & 20, 1796), in *The Writings of James Monroe*, Vol. 2, p. 479. Monroe wrote that "These principles [of the League of Armed Neutrality] are extremely dear to us; because they are just in themselves, and in many respects very important to our welfare: We insert them in every treaty we make with those powers who are willing to adopt them; and our hope is, that they will soon become universal. But even in the war of which you speak, and when the combination against England was most formidable, all the maritime powers being arranged against her, you well know that she never acceded to them. How compel her then, upon the present occasion, when that combination was not only broken, but many of the powers, then parties to it and against England, were now enlisted on her side, in support of her principles? You must be sensible, that under these circumstances, it was impossible for us to obtain from that power the recognition of those principles; and that, of course, we are not culpable for having failed to accomplish that object." See ibid.

> [i]t cannot be said, for instance, that the assent of a particular number of nations to a rule which ought to operate between themselves only, is to become a rule for other nations who have never assented to it; or, in other words, that a part of the civilized nations would have a right to dictate a law to another part: Such a doctrine would substitute force to right, and might be productive, in other cases, and especially in the hands of governments less friendly to liberty than yours and ours are, of consequences the most fatal to society: It is therefore in my judgment not a sound doctrine.[910]

But notwithstanding Monroe's defense of the Jay treaty and Hamilton's soothing language towards France, Republicans were and remained extraordinarily critical of the treaty, up to accusing the Federalists—and Jay in particular—to have committed what amounts to treason. For instance, Thomas Jefferson denounced the treaty in violent language, calling it "an infamous act, which is nothing more than a treaty of alliance between England and the Anglomen of this country against the legislature and the people of the United States."[911] Indeed, across the country, effigies of Jay were burnt publicly, and when Hamilton attempted to defend the Treaty in the streets of New York, he was stoned by the crowd.[912] Republicans were so agitated that most of them rejected ratification of the treaty out of hand, preferring war with Britain over what was considered outright surrender.[913] But the chances that Britain would actually have declared war on the United States had it refused to ratify the treaty were remote, and Republicans knew this, even if they did not say so publicly.[914] In light of the furor that had erupted, president Washington had

910 In support, he cites both Bynkershoek and Vattel. See James Monroe to De La Croix (July 14, 1796), in *The Writings of James Monroe* (New York: G.P. Putnam's Sons, 1900), Vol. 3, pp. 29–30. For a further elucidation, see Monroe's 1797 "A View of the Conduct of the Executive, in the Foreign Affairs of the United States (…)," in *The Writings of James Monroe* (New York: G.P. Putnam's Sons, 1900), Vol. 3, p. 383ff.

911 Thomas Jefferson to Edward Rutledge (30 November 1795), in *The Works of Thomas Jefferson*, Vol. 8, p. 200.

912 Albert Bowman, "Jefferson, Hamilton and American Foreign Policy" *Political Science Quarterly* 71, no. 1 (March 1956), p. 37.

913 Although Gallatin actually called for postponing its ratification until further clarifications had been procured from the British. See Albert Gallatin, "Execution of British Treaty" (April 26, 1796), in *Annals of Congress* (House of Representatives), 4th Congress, 1st Session, pp. 1197–1198.

914 Robert Tucker and David Hendrickson, *Empire of Liberty, the Statecraft of Thomas Jefferson* (New York: Oxford University Press, 1990), p. 69.

decided to keep the terms of the treaty a secret for as long as possible. But not long after its arrival in Philadelphia on March 7, 1795, details of the terms were divulged through the Republican press. For Washington, this was only more reason to push for a speedy ratification.[915] The treaty passed the Senate with a 20–10 vote on June 24. In the wake of this turbulent episode, many Republicans now abandoned the idea that "the world could be made safe for neutrals through treaties," becoming more inward-looking and wary of ties to any country.[916]

The Jay Treaty was not the only major treaty concluded during the Washington administration. If this treaty's main objective was to address Britain's maritime pretensions and to secure American rights, it was largely unsuccessful. But in terms of America's territorial pretensions, it was a victory, one that was complemented and completed by another major agreement, Pinckney's Treaty with Spain. The chief negotiator, Thomas Pinckney, was given the task to translate a series of ambitious territorial aims into a favorable treaty. When Pinckney arrived in Spain, he found that the Spanish wanted at first an alliance and a guarantee of all Spanish possessions in the new world, but the Federalist government was not willing to acquiesce to such terms: neither willing to commit to non-commercial entanglements nor to renounce claims to territory it hoped to acquire in the decades to come. However, while Jay found himself in a weak negotiating position, the very fact that he was about to conclude an Anglo-American pact made that Pinckney found himself in a strong position vis-a-vis the Spanish, who feared that a combined effort might soon move against Spanish possession in the Americas. As a result, the Spanish went to great lengths to placate the United States, agreeing to many of its demands. Consequently, the eventual treaty of San Lorenzo that was concluded in October 1795 ascertained not just America's boundaries with the Floridas and along the entire length of the Mississippi, but also secured that "the navigation of the said River in its whole breadth from its source to the Ocean shall be free only to his Subjects, and the Citizens of the United States."[917]

---

915 Which was recommended by Randolph, while Hamilton had by this time already left the cabinet. See Randolph to Washington (July 12, 1795), in Worthington C. Ford, "Edmund Randolph on the British Treaty" *American Historical Review* 12, no. 3 (April 1907), p. 595.

916 Onuf and Onuf, *Federal Union, Modern World*, p. 163. Indeed, most scholarly opinion is in agreement with Republican sentiments. See Albert Bowman, "Jefferson, Hamilton and American Foreign Policy" *Political Science Quarterly* 71, no. 1 (March 1956), p. 39; Deconde, *Entangling Alliance*, p. 109; but see also Robert Tucker and David Hendrickson, *Empire of Liberty, the Statecraft of Thomas Jefferson*, p. 72.

917 Art. IV, Treaty of Friendship, Limits, and Navigation Between Spain and The United States. The complete reversal of the Spanish position on this issue is highlighted by the fact that

Moreover, Pinckney succeeded in having Spain accept American interpretations of neutral rights along the lines of the League of Armed Neutrality.[918] The eventual clause stipulating these principles also contained a favorable reference to contraband, and even included a prohibition on impressment:

> It shall be lawful for all and singular the Subjects of his Catholic Mayesty, and the Citizens People, and inhabitants of the said United States to sail with their Ships with all manner of liberty and security, no distinction being made who are the proprietors of the merchandises laden thereon from any Port to the Places of those who now are or hereafter shall be at enmity with his Catholic Majesty or the United States. (…) [A]nd it is hereby stipulated that Free Ships shall also give freedom to goods, and that every thing shall be deemed free and exempt which shall be found on board the Ships belonging to the Subjects of either of the contracting Parties although the whole lading or any part thereof should appertain to the Enemies of either; contraband goods being always excepted. It is also agreed that the same liberty be extended to persons who are on board a free Ship, so that, although they be Enemies to either Party they shall not be made Prisoners or taken out of that free Ship unless they are Soldiers and in actual service of the Enemies.[919]

As a whole, the treaty was arguably the most successful one concluded up to the Louisiana Purchase. Taken together, the Jay and Pinckney treaties were able, in the words of Wood, "to secure the territorial integrity of the United States in a way the diplomacy of the Confederation had been unable to do."[920]

The relative successes of the treaties with Britain and Spain could however not disguise that whatever additional security and privileges were obtained,

---

barely a year earlier, Casa Yrujo, Spanish minister to the United States, had still vehemently protested the Jay Treaty's provision on the Mississippi, which stipulated that the river would be freely navigable for both British and American ships.

918 Pinckney stressed the significance of the League's principles saying they were "founded upon reason, and supported by the sentiments of the most enlightened writers [and which are] further established by the express approbation of the commercial nations of Europe, of whom there is scarcely one who has not adopted these principles in their late treaties (…)." See Thomas Pinckney to the Prince of Peace (September 20, 1795), in *American State Papers: Foreign Relations*, Vol. 1, p. 539.

919 Art. XV, Treaty of Friendship, Limits, and Navigation Between Spain and The United States.

920 Gordon Wood, *Empire of Liberty: A History of the Early Republic, 1789–1815* (New York: Oxford University Press, 2009), pp. 131–132.

were inevitably purchased at the price of further antagonizing France. In a way, the problem lay with the fact that the United States had tried to remain neutral in the midst of an epochal struggle that did not permit for taking a middle position. In his famous *Farewell Address*, George Washington still advised his successors to "steer clear of permanent alliances with any portion of the foreign world."[921] He knew of course that this would not be easy, if only because domestically, there were powerful forces that opposed such a policy:

> It remains to be seen whether our country will stand upon independent ground, or be directed in its political concerns by any other nation. A little time will show who are its true friends, or, what is synonymous, who are true Americans; those who are stimulating a foreign nation to unfriendly acts, repugnant to our rights and dignity, and advocating all its measures, or those whose only aim has been to maintain a strict neutrality, to keep the United States out of the vortex of European politics, and to preserve them in peace.[922]

History would bear out that ultimately, the gravest threat to American neutrality and prosperity lay not at home, but abroad. Geopolitically, by the end of the 18th century, it was already a fiction to assume that the United States could isolate itself from the rest of the world, if only because of its commercial ties and—equally important—the fact that the great powers all had territorial possessions on the North-American continent. What is more, the years following the adoption of the Neutrality Proclamation proved that declaring neutrality was not sufficient to placate the British, albeit more than sufficient to anger the French. The solution that was resorted to—concluding a treaty with Britain to balance the treaty with the French—only helped to aggravate the situation.

921 George Washington, "Farewell Address" (September 19, 1796), in John Fitzpatrick (ed.), *The Writings of George Washington* (Washington DC: U.S. Government Printing Office, 1931–1944), Vol. 35, p. 234. Although he added two important caveats, namely 1) that the country should "not be understood as capable of patronizing infidelity to existing engagements" and 2) that "we may safely trust to temporary alliances for extraordinary emergencies." Since the Farewell Address was to a great extent authored by Hamilton (who, incidentally, persuaded the president to abandon a first draft written by Madison), it is the second occasion on which Hamilton expresses a opinion favoring non-engagement in European affairs. For a further discussion of the drafting history, see Felix Gilbert, *To The Farewell Address* (Princeton, NJ: Princeton University Press, 1961), pp. 115–136.

922 George Washington to Thomas Pinckney (28 May, 1797), in Worthington C. Ford (ed.), *The Writings of George Washington* (New York: G.P. Putnam's Sons, 1892), Vol. 13, pp. 389–390.

It would lead to an undeclared war with France at the end of the 18th century and, after a protracted struggle, a declared war with Britain.

When it had become clear that president Washington decided not to seek a third term (which, in itself, was a revolutionary constitutional innovation), France seized its opportunity in trying to get Jefferson elected the next president. Its representative in Philadelphia, Pierre-Auguste Adet, said that, should Adams be elected, he would suspend his functions as French envoy to the United States.[923] To heap further pressure on the Federalists, the French government issued a decree on July 2, 1796, which entailed that France would henceforth treat neutral vessels in the same manner as they were treated by the English.[924] Secretary of State Pickering criticized this French move, saying that "[t]his decree makes no distinction between neutral Powers who can claim only the rights secured to them by the law of nations, and others, between whom and the French republic treaties have imposed special obligations." France, he concluded, should respect its obligations under the 1778 treaty. What is more, he added

> [t]he captures made by the British, of American vessels having French property on board, are warranted by the law of nations. The force and operation of this law was contemplated by France and the United States when they formed their treaty of commerce; and their special stipulation on this point [declaring that free ships make free goods] was meant as an exception to an (sic) universal rule. Neither our weakness nor our strength have any choice, when the question concerns the observance of a known rule of the law of nations.

This is why in his view, France would only have a right to complain should the United States "by a *perfidious condescension*, [have] permitted the English to violate a right which it ought, *for its own honor and interest*, to defend (…)." Yet, given America's inability to challenge the British on this point, it had to 'suffer what it must', Pickering said implicitly.[925]

French attempts at influencing the election were ineffective, for John Adams was chosen as the new president. But rather than faithfully toeing a pro-Federalist line, Adams sought to follow a strict neutral policy, consistent with his philosophy

923 Kaplan, *Colonies into Nation*, p. 250.

924 Quoted in Samuel F. Bemis, "Washington's Farewell Address: A Foreign Policy of Independence." *American Historical Review* 39, no. 2 (1934), p. 264. A further decree was adopted on March 2, 1797.

925 Thomas Pickering to the French minister, Adet (November 1, 1796), in *American State Papers: Foreign Relations*, Vol. 1, p. 578 (emphasis in original).

going back to his drafting of the Model Treaty. The new president believed he could have it both ways, and honor American commitments deriving from the 1778 and 1794 treaties, as well as the Neutrality Proclamation, all at the same time. But just as the United States managed to alienate both France and Britain, Adams alienated both of the main political factions in the country, and actually contributed to deepening existing political rifts, making the president belong to what has been called "a party of one."[926] Thus, Adams' foreign policy showed that reliance on the law of nations could only spell disaster when this meant having to honor contradictory obligations.

In the first years of his presidency, Adams avidly tried to retain true impartiality in a peaceful fashion.[927] For a little while, he even toyed with the idea to revive the Armed Neutrality against Britain, but had dismissed that idea by 1798, when revolutionary France appeared to become an even graver danger to free shipping.[928] Early in his administration, it became quite clear that holding a neutral line was untenable in the face of the cataclysmic war that was unfolding in Europe. Indeed, throughout the 1790s, relations between France and the United States continued to be shaped by the fact that the former needed the latter's neutral trade in order to ensure the delivery of produce from the French colonies. France was seeking to apply the same rules towards neutral shipping that existed between the United States in Britain, notwithstanding the relevant provisions of the 1778 treaties.

Hamilton helped to increase frustration on the French side by reiterating the points earlier made by Pickering,[929] namely that while Britain had not violated America's neutral rights under international law, France was treaty-bound to respect the 'free ships, free goods' principle:

> from the exercise of that right by Great Britain, when not forbidden by any treaty, [it] can certainly derive no justification for the imitation of the

926 See James Grant, *John Adams: Party of One* (New York: Farrar, Strauss and Giroux, 2005).

927 One example was the concern he showed in restraining clandestine privateering. See Adams, "Speech to Both Houses of Congress" (May 16, 1797), in *The Works of John Adams*, Vol. 9, p. 116. In response to his plea, Congress adopted an Act on June 14 which made offences committed "without the limits" of the United States also punishable. See discussed in Charles Fenwick, *The Neutrality Laws of the United States* (Washington DC: Carnegie Endowment for International Peace, 1913), p. 30.

928 Samuel F. Bemis, *John Quincy Adams and the Foundations of American Foreign Policy* (New York: Alfred A. Knopf, 1949), p. 92.

929 Which, Bemis said, were inspired and informed by Hamilton. See Bemis, "Washington's Farewell Address: A Foreign Policy of Independence." *American Historical Review* 39, no. 2 (1934), p. 265.

> practice, in opposition to the precise and peremptory stipulations of her treaties. (…) To make its unequal operation in an existing war an excuse for disregarding the rule, is therefore a subterfuge for a breach of faith, which hardly seeks to save appearances. France, as she once was, would have blushed to use it. It is one, among many instances, of the attempts of revolutionary France to dogmatize mankind out of its reason, as if she expected to work a change in the faculties as well as in the habits and opinions of men.[930]

Taking another stab at France's insistence that the 'free ships, free goods' principle has become universal, he reiterated that "the stipulation of two powers to observe between themselves a particular rule in their respective wars (…) can, on no known or reasonable principle of interpretation, be construed to intend that they will insist upon that rule with all other nations."[931]

A good example of American vacillating on the issue came when the commercial treaties with Prussia were up for renewal. In negotiating the new treaties, John Quincy Adams, American minister to Prussia, was instructed by Secretary Pickering to let the reference to 'free ships make free goods' lapse, because while it was still among "the earnest wishes of the United States that the principle that *free ships should make free goods,* should become universal," the reality was

> that the abandonment of that principle was suggested by the measures of the belligerent powers during the present war, in which we have found that neither its obligation by the pretended modern law of nations, nor the solemn stipulations of treaties, secured its observation. On the contrary it has been made the sport of events. Under such circumstances it appeared to the President desirable to avoid renewing an obligation which would probably be enforced when our interest should require its dissolution, and be continued when we could derive some advantage from its observance.[932]

---

930 Hamilton, "Americus: The Warning no. v" (March 13, 1797), in *The Works of Alexander Hamilton,* Vol. 6, pp. 250–251.

931 Hamilton, "Titus Manlius: The Stand no. v" (April 16, 1798), in *The Works of Alexander Hamilton,* Vol. 6, pp. 295–296.

932 Timothy Pickering to John Quincy Adams ("The Writings of Instructions," July 17, 1797), in *The Writings of John Quincy Adams,* Vol. 2, p. 189.

Adams, however, disagreed with the idea to abandon the notion of 'free ships, free goods.'[933] He felt that it would hurt American interests in the long run, saying that "France is still attached to the principles of the armed neutrality, and yet more attached to the idea of compelling Great Britain to assent to them." It was therefore generally true, he felt, that

> every naval state is interested in the maintenance of liberal maxims in maritime affairs against the domineering policy of Britain. Every instance, therefore, in which these principles are abandoned by neutral powers which favor the rights of neutrality, is to be regretted as furnishing argument, or at least example, to support the British doctrines.[934]

Ironically, the Prussians pushed the Americans on this point, and wished to see a reference to the principle also inserted in the new treaty. In the end, the parties proposed "after the return of a general peace, to agree, either separately between themselves or jointly with other Powers alike interested, to concert with the great maritime Powers of Europe such arrangements and such permanent principles

933 See discussed in Gregg Lint, "Early American Conceptions of International Law and their Influence on Foreign Policy: 1776–1803" (unpublished manuscript, Michigan State University, 1975), pp. 146–148

934 John Quincy Adams to Timothy Pickering (October 31, 1797), in *The Writings of John Quincy Adams*, Vol. 2, p. 219. In a letter written to Secretary Pickering just before hostilities were initiated between France and the United States, John Quincy Adams intimated that while the two republics were now at the brink of war, the true spoiler was Great Britain, which continued to refuse to accept the new "liberal principle" of maritime commerce: "In truth I am fully convinced that there is only one power in Europe averse to the general establishment of the principle favorable to neutrality, a power which does not even disguise the pretension of domineering upon the ocean, and whose naval force is almost equal to that of all the world besides. It must be admitted that so long as she rejects the liberal principle, every agreement of other nations between themselves admitting it, excepting contingently as above stated, must if it have any operation, operate altogether in her favor and to her advantage. For while it gives her the benefit of a safe and protected neutral conveyance of her goods, it refuses the same to her enemy." See John Quincy Adams to Thomas Pickering (May 17, 1798), in *The Writings of John Quincy Adams*, Vol. 2, pp. 287–288. He further expanded on this issue in another letter to Pickering (May, 25, 1798), in ibid., pp. 289–290.

Ironically, Chitty noted that in 1798, the British government had relaxed its interpretation of the Rule of 1756, at least allowing neutral vessels "to carry on a direct commerce between the colony of the enemy and their own country (...)." See Joseph Chitty, *A Practical Treatise on the Law of Nations, Relative to the Legal Effect of War on the Commerce of Belligerents and Neutrals* (Boston: Bradford and Reid, 1812), p. 169.

as may serve to consolidate the liberty and the safety of the neutral navigation and commerce in future wars."[935]

Meanwhile, between the United States and France, the only way forward now was that tensions would escalate, and from 1797 on, the United States resorted on multiple occasions to taking retaliatory measures against belligerent nations. Fortunately for the United States, for as long as such measures were seen as being retaliatory in nature, the countries at war did not regard these measures as compromising America's neutrality stance.[936] However, it was clear to most—not least also to president Adams—that ultimately, the situation was untenable. Just before hostilities with France commenced, he delivered a gloomy report to Congress in which he noted that

> whether the war in Europe is or is not to continue, I hold it most certain that perfect tranquillity and order will not soon be obtained. The state of society has so long been disturbed, the sense of moral and religious obligations so much weakened, public faith and national honor have been so impaired, respect to treaties has been so diminished, and the law of nations has lost so much of its force, while pride, ambition, avarice, and violence, have been so long unrestrained, there remains no reasonable ground on which to raise an expectation, that a commerce, without protection or defence, will not be plundered.[937]

To try and resolve the crisis, Adams sent a commission of three to France in 1797 to negotiate a solution with the new foreign minister, Talleyrand, consisting of Charles Cotesworth Pinckney, Elbridge Gerry and John Marshall. However, the long-standing French complaints were too much to handle for the commissioners. The mission thus became a failure and by the summer of 1798, conflict had become unavoidable. The *de facto* trigger was provided by the XYZ affair, which involved an attempt by three French negotiators to offer further peace negotiations in exchange for a series of payments, loans and

935 Article XII, Treaty of Amity and Commerce (Prussia-United States, July 11, 1799), in Jonathan Elliot (ed.), *The American Diplomatic Code Embracing a Collection of Treaties and Conventions between the United States and Foreign Powers: From 1778 to 1834* (Washington DC: J. Elliot, 1834), Vol. 1, p. 364.

936 Charles Hyneman, "Neutrality During the European Wars of 1792–1815: America's Understanding of Her Obligations." *American Journal of International Law* 24, no. 2 (April 1930), p. 287.

937 John Adams, "Speech to both Houses of Congress" (November 23, 1797), in *The Works of John Adams*, Vol. 9, p. 122.

even a bribe to Talleyrand.[938] In response, the American government decided to break off relations with France, and formally renounced the 1778 treaties.[939] At the same time, the United States effectively established "an undeclared quasi-alliance" with Britain, whereby the Royal Navy came to provide protection to American battle and merchant ships—amounting to a military alliance in all but name.[940]

The undeclared war with France was the first military engagement with a great power since the Revolutionary war, and its ambiguous nature prompted a number of issues in regard to the law of nations. One of these was in relation to the Alien Enemies Act—one of the notorious Alien and Sedition Acts—according to which aliens could be subject to removal from American territory if they were found to have offended against the law of nations, as defined by Congress.[941] On the subject of the nature of the war itself, there existed some confusion on how to categorise the conflict—the determination of which was important in terms of rights and obligations of states and individuals. The problem stemmed partially from the fact that the conflict was not preceded by an official declaration, although it should be said that already by the end of the 18th century, formal declarations of war were scarcely issued anymore.[942] Connected with this was the question whether the war was a perfect or imperfect war. This was a distinction that went back to Grotius and which was later also further developed by Burlamaqui and Vattel. In Burlamaqui's concise description, the distinction is that

> [a] perfect war, is that which entirely interrupts the tranquillity of the state, and lays a foundation for all possible acts of hostility. An imperfect war, on the contrary, is that which does not intirely interrupt the peace,

938 Kaplan, *Colonies into Nation*, p. 274. At the time of the affair, the French government was even making plans for eventually undertaking a conquest of America. Talleyrand showed little respect for the United States, saying that the country "merited no more consideration than Genoa or Geneva." See ibid., p. 268. Elsewhere, Kaplan concluded that "[f]ormal war with France did not follow the XYZ crisis, but everything short of a declaration did." See ibid., p. 277.

939 See "An Act to Declare the Treaties Heretofore Concluded with France, no Longer Obligatory on the United States" (July 7, 1798), *United States Statutes at Large*, 1 Stat. 578, available at <http://press-pubs.uchicago.edu/founders/documents/a2_2_2-3s23.html>.

940 Robert Kagan, *Dangerous Nation*, pp. 120–121.

941 See "An Act Respecting Alien Enemies" (July 6, 1798), United States Statutes at Large, 1 *United States Congress Public Acts of the Fifth Congress*, second session, Ch. LXVI, p. 577.

942 Charles Lofgren, "War-Making under the Constitution: The Original Understanding" *Yale Law Journal* 81, no. 4 (1972), p. 680, 691.

> but only in certain particulars, the public tranquillity being in other respects undisturbed.[943]

The issue was explicitly addressed by the Supreme Court in the case *Bas v. Tingy*, in which justice Chase further expounded on the laws of war, saying that "[i]f a general war is declared [by Congress], its extent and operations are only restricted and regulated by the *jus belli*, forming a part of the law of nations but if a partial war is waged [i.e., an imperfect war], its extent and operation depend on our municipal laws."[944] Apart from specifying that the applicable laws corresponded to the nature of a conflict, the court also reaffirmed the central position of Congress. Albert Gallatin had argued in favor of the same principle: "By virtue of [the war power], Congress could [act], provided it be according to the laws of nations and to treaties."[945] In the case *Talbot v. Seeman*, the reach of the law of nations was further extended. While judge Marshall admitted that "[t]he whole powers of war [were] vested in Congress," he declared that in the case of partial hostilities too, "the laws of war (…) must be noticed."[946] The idea behind Marshall's assertion was to "enlarge the sphere of neutral commerce" and it was a good example of making foreign policy from the bench.[947] That the war had to be regarded as a full-scale conflict was argued by the Attorney-General in 1798, who said that "it is my opinion that there exists not only an *actual* maritime war between France and the United States,

943 Jean-Jacques Burlamaqui, *The Principles of Natural and Politic Law* [1747] (Indianapolis: Liberty Fund, 2006), Vol. II, Part IV, ch. 3, p. 475. Speaking about imperfect wars, Burlamaqui said that these are generally called reprisals. Vattel develops the same point, but does not explicitly equate reprisals with imperfect wars. See *The Law of Nations*, Bk. Ii, ch. 18, pp. 460–467.

944 *Bas v. Tingy*, 4 U.S. (4 Dall.) 37 (1800), at 43. This case concerned the payment due to a recaptor of an American ship that had originally been captured by the French during the Quasi-War. The issue was whether the recaptor was entitled to receiving 1/8 or 1/2 of the ship's value, based on different pieces of legislation passed by Congress.

945 Statement of representative Albert Gallatin in Congress (1798), quoted in Jordan Paust, "In Their Own Words: Affirmations of the Founders, Framers and Early Judiciary Concerning the Binding Nature of the Customary Law of Nations" *U.C. Davis Journal of International Law and Policy* 13, no. 2, p. 220.

946 *Talbot v. Seeman*, 5 U.S. 1 (Cranch), at 28. See also discussed in George G. Wilson, "International Law and the Constitution" *Boston University Law Review* 13, no. 3 (1933), pp. 482–483.

947 Quoted from *The Nereide*, in John Fabian Witt, *Lincoln's Code: The Laws of War in American History* (New York: The Free Press, 2012), p. 58. Marshall's approach in general is discussed on pp. 55–59.

but a maritime war *authorized* by both nations."[948] Apart from many other consequences, the episode demonstrated that on many issues, the United States resorted to framing questions of war and peace in terms of the law of nations, whether to ascertain rights or obligations, or simply to provide clarity on otherwise confusing questions.

At the end of the war, the two sides agreed on a new treaty to replace the treaties of 1778. In exchange for agreeing to declare the Act of Congress of 1798 —which had annulled the 1778 Treaties—as never to have been enacted, the American negotiators managed to get an agreement in which it was implicitly understood that "the vessels of [France and Britain] received equal treatment, neither nation enjoying all of the privileges which its treaty specified."[949] Yet, the treaty, known as the Convention of 1800 or the Treaty of Mortefontaine, reflected in many respect the liberal attributes that were also present in the 1778 commercial treaty.[950] For instance, it contained provisions stating that trade between the two nations shall be free and subject to most favored nation principles (article VI and XI), and that "free ships shall give a freedom to goods" (article XIV).[951] At the same time, both the contraband and blockade stipulations were formulated in such a manner as not to constitute undue restrictions on neutral trade. By admitting the liberal inklings of the treaty, Napoleon had even tried to make the Americans appear as accepting the principles of a League of Armed Neutrality that he attempted to revive.[952]

Still, while the Americans reconfirmed their attachment to neutral rights, they also strained themselves to ensure that the treaty was compatible with their obligations under the Jay Treaty, reflecting some "British views on international law."[953] As an example, it was agreed that goods belonging to the other party found on enemy ships—whether contraband or not—could be confiscated (article XV). Trescot concluded on this point that the Convention

---

948 Charles Lee to the Secretary of State (August 21, 1798), in Benjamin Hall (ed.), *Official Opinions of the Attorneys General of the United States* (Washington DC: R. Farnham, 1852), Vol. 1, p. 84 (emphasis in original).

949 Charles Hyneman, "Neutrality During the European Wars of 1792–1815: America's Understanding of Her Obligations." *American Journal of International Law* 24, no. 2 (April 1930), p. 293.

950 Lint, "Early American Conceptions of International Law," p. 202.

951 This same article contained an interesting clause with respect to impressment, noting that "the same liberty be extended to persons, who are on board a free ship, with this effect, that altho' they be enemies to either party, they are not to be taken out of that free ship, unless they are soldiers and in actual service of the enemy."

952 Kaplan, *Colonies into Nation*, p. 301.

953 Kaplan, ibid., p. 298.

was "the necessary complement to the treaty with England. They were both the efforts of a nation too weak to hold its own in the face of stronger and unscrupulous powers. (…)" More in general, he added that "[n]eutrality is scarcely ever a brilliant policy. It is always difficult, sometimes dangerous, and often demands hard sacrifices from national pride. But in the case of the United States, their interests clearly required it (…)."[954] Kaplan drew a largely similar conclusion, noting that

> [the treaty] dramatized American recognition that political alliances of any kind with Europe imposed intolerable burdens upon the young republic. The unhappy experiences with the French alliance confirmed the wisdom of John Adams in the plan of 1776, of Thomas Paine in *Common Sense*, and of Benjamin Franklin in his periodic reminders about the perils of a European connection.[955]

The American spirit as to fighting for neutral rights was aptly reflected in the 1798 letter of the American commissioners to Talleyrand. Having noted that "no nation is more deeply interested in its establishment, (…) the wish to establish [the] principle [of free ships, free goods] is essentially different from a determination that it is already established." In light of the decade and a half that was to follow, it is remarkable that the letter notes that no matter the zeal for this principle on the American side, "she never conceived the idea of obtaining that consent by force." On a sobering note, the commissioners concluded that "neither their policy nor their interests permit them to arm, in order to compel a surrender of the rights of others."[956]

Nevertheless, on the eve of Thomas Jefferson's inauguration, the United States had finally managed to wrest itself out from under the yoke of the European great powers, having acquired more freedom of action than it had enjoyed ever before. At the same time, "Anglo-American thinking about law and order in the society of nations was moving towards convergence [in sharing the belief that] the diplomatic system of Europe [as based on Vattel's

954 William Trescot, *The Diplomatic History of the Administrations of Washington and Adams, 1789–1801* (Boston: Little, Brown and Co, 1857), p. 223.

955 Kaplan, *Colonies into Nation*, p. 297.

956 Charles C. Pinckney, John Marshall and Elbridge Gerry "To the Minister of Foreign Affairs of the French Republic" (January 27, 1798), in *Instructions to the Envoys Extraordinary and Ministers Plenipotentiary from the United States of America to the French Republic, (…)* (Philadelphia: W. Ross, 1798), p. 55.

conception of the law of nations] was defunct."[957] Nevertheless, in the area of maritime rights, the United States would continue to push its neutralist position; the United Kingdom being the nation's principal antagonist. Initially, under Jefferson, the United States would try to persuade its former overlord through economic means. When these proved ineffectual, Madison did not shrink from entering into a military conflict to vindicate what he and many others regarded as the country's rights under international law. But the result was that while the Convention of 1800 had closed the chapter on alliance politics, the country's new-found independence in foreign policy did not equate to actual independence being indefeasible. American insistence on its perceived or real rights—depending on your point of view—made that it had to live through a dozen more treacherous years, which at times endangered independence itself.

---

957 Onuf and Onuf, *Federal Union, Modern World*, p. 174.

CHAPTER 6

Law and Foreign Policy under Thomas Jefferson

6.1 The Mississippi and Beyond: The Law of Nations and Territorial Expansion

The election of Thomas Jefferson to the highest office in the country has sometimes been called the "Revolution of 1800." In a way, it not only augured a new era in domestic politics, but also marks a turning point in how the United States would come to use the law of nations in its foreign policy. The first two decades of the 19th century came to witness a different nation; one that had slowly divested itself of its defensive stance, and which began to assert itself both on sea as well as on land. Still, the United States continued to play to its strengths, and early on, these lay rather on land than at sea. As a result, while the country largely continued to adhere to prevailing international law at sea—even if it continued to promote its own neutrality principles—on land the country was moving in another direction. Most certainly, such developments can be seen as a reflection of domestic security imperatives, but one can also detect a more flexible manner of interpreting international law within the American constitutional context.

For Americans, territorial expansion was not simply a question of power politics. On the contrary: a policy of expansionism was mainly justified on the basis of an aversion to balance-of-power politics. It served Americans both from an ideological and a strategic point of view—in fact, these concerns went hand in hand. Preventing the establishment of a balance of power on the North American continent was not only supposed to save it from the perennial wars that had plagued the European continent, but also from the attendant "evils incident to the system",[958] such as the raising of standing armies, limitations on individual freedom and economic prosperity. For Jeffersonians, expansion served an ulterior and ideological purpose: one, as a means of guaranteeing America's national security (by upending or thwarting the creation of a balance on the North-American continent) and two, as a way to further consolidating the federal republic.

From the point of view of the law of nations, Americans were well aware that ever since the days of Vitoria and Grotius, there had been a vibrant current

958 Quoted from Allan B. Magruder, *Political, Commercial and Moral Reflections*, p. 42, in Peter Onuf and Nicholas Onuf, *Federal Union, Modern World: The Law of Nations in an Age of Revolutions 1776–1814* (Madison, WI: Madison House, 1992), p. 151.

 DOI 10.1163/9789004305687_008

in international legal doctrine that criticized or condemned territorial acquisition by other than peaceful means.[959] In the 18th century, the right of conquest as such was denied altogether by authors like Montesquieu and later Kant.[960] Sensing the duty to live up to the demands of a more humane kind of international law, early American statesmen professed to only pursue territorial expansion by way of international agreement. For instance, in an report for American envoys to Madrid, Jefferson wrote that "[i]t is an established principle, that conquest gives only an inchoate right, which does not become perfect till confirmed by the treaty of peace, and by a renunciation or abandonment of a former proprietor."[961] On the eve of the Louisiana Purchase, Albert Gallatin, then Treasury Secretary under Jefferson, voiced a similar sentiment, saying that "the existence of the United States as a nation presupposes the power enjoyed by every nation of extending their territory by treaties (…)."[962]

However, this ideal came to clash very violently with another notion, being a widely shared belief that the United States was entitled to rule the entire North American continent. This belief became particularly strong from the early 19th century onwards. As Kagan noted, the United States at that time had a very expansionist approach in foreign policy, openly professing that "the nations of Europe [needed to recognize] that the United States and North America were identical."[963] Traders were interested in expanding markets; the

959 See e.g. Matthew McMahon, *Conquest and Modern International Law: The Legal Limitations on the Acquisition of Territory by Conquest* (Kraut Reprint, 1975); Sharon Korman, *The Right of Conquest: The Acquisition of Territory by Force in International Law and Practice* (New York: Oxford University Press, 1996) and Lindsay G. Robertson, *Conquest by Law: How the Discovery of America Dispossessed Indigenous Peoples of their Lands* (New York: Oxford University Press, 2005).

960 Nys notes that Montesquieu had changed the text on this point between the 1721 and 1754 editions of his *Lettres Persanes.* In the first edition, he wrote that "Le droit de la conquête n'est pas un droit. Une société ne peut être fondée que sur la volonté des associés; si elle est détruite par la conquête, le peuple redevient libre: il n'y a plus de nouvelle société, et si le vainqueur en veut former, c'est une tyrannie." In the later edition, it was modified to "La conquête ne donne point un droit par elle-même: lorsque le peuple subsiste, elle est un gage de la paix et de la réparation du tort; et, si le peuple est détruit ou dispersé, elle est le monument d'une tyrannie." Nys, *Les États-Unis et le Droit des Gens*, p. 95. For Kant, see his 1795 essay *Perpetual Peace* (various editions).

961 Jefferson to William Carmichael and William Short (March 18, 1792), in *American State Papers: Foreign Relations*, Vol. I, p. 252.

962 Albert Gallatin to Thomas Jefferson (January 18, 1803), in *The Writings of Albert Gallatin*, Vol. 1, p. 113.

963 Robert Kagan, *Dangerous Nation: America's Foreign Policy from its Earliest Days to the Dawn of the 20th Century* (New York: Vintage Books 2007), pp. 138–140

Indian menace had to be contained and secure borders were sought for the country as a whole.[964] Taken together, the ideological and strategic imperatives led at first to painful compromises, but eventually required outright violations of the law, also when seen from the perspective of American constitutional law.

The expansionist streak in American political thinking had been evident from the very days of the Revolution. Earlier, we noted Franklin's vistas on a country that would encompass the entire continent. In pursuit of this idea, the Continental army had actually undertaken two invasions of Quebec—even when simultaneously, Congress was negotiating with the province, trying to convince it to join the new country to their south. Both of these initiatives remained fruitless.[965] One of the reasons for wishing to see Quebec included in the new union was in order to protect the northern border, which, as a result of the failed efforts, remained insecure well into the 19th century. At the same time, a separate state of Quebec allowed the British to capitalize on much of the fur trade and other produce taking place in the northern regions of New England and New York state, and in turn led Vermont to consider seceding from the United States on a few occasions.[966] Hence, British control of the northern border regions not only posed a strategic problem, but also impacted American economic interests. As a result, one could conclude that up to 1815, as historian Reginald Stuart noted, "territorial expansion was primarily opportunistic and defensive."[967]

However, true continental expansion was not to proceed vertically but horizontally, implying a westward move. An often overlooked detail here is that, upon independence, the western border of the newly independent country did not run across the Appalachians, but was in fact marked by the Mississippi river. In other words, by 1783, the United States had already managed to more than double its original size as a result of the cession by the United Kingdom of all the lands between the 1763 Proclamation line and the Mississippi river, all the way up to its presumed source, which made up about 70% of the country's territory henceforth—all of this without the need for a formal purchase.

964 Reginald Stuart, *United States Expansionism and British North America, 1775–1871* (Chapel Hill and London: The University of North Carolina Press, 1988), pp. 5–6.

965 Walter Nugent, *Habits of Empire: A History of American Expansion* (New York: Alfred A. Knopf, 2008), p. 16, 23.

966 Reginald Stuart, *United States Expansionism and British North America, 1775–1871* (Chapel Hill and London: The University of North Carolina Press, 1988), pp. 28–53, *passim.*

967 Reginald Stuart, *United States Expansionism and British North America, 1775–1871*, p. 5.

Nugent concluded that it was all a matter of luck—both in terms of timing and the nature of the interlocutors on both sides.[968] In any event, as a starting point for westward expansion, "the 1783 boundaries were an absolutely essential platform."[969]

While we saw above that after independence, the Spanish refused to grant the Americans any right to navigation of the river, and even asked them to renounce such rights in exchange for a trade agreement (which never materialized), from the American side various voices kept insisting on their rights to make use of the river—often with reference to the law of nations. For instance, in the context of a 1783 case, James Wilson argued—with reference to Grotius, Vattel and Rutherforth—that the United States had a right to use the entire Mississippi for navigation in peacetime, pursuant to article eight of the recent peace treaty which explicitly declared that "[t]he navigation of the Mississippi, from its source to the ocean, shall forever remain free and open to the subjects of Great Britain and the citizens of the United States."[970] In the *Federalist Papers*, the Mississippi issue had also been highlighted as a key to the economic development of the western states: "Spain thinks it convenient to shut the Mississippi against us on the one side, and Britain excludes us from the Saint Lawrence on the other; nor will either of them permit the other waters which are between them and us to become the means of mutual intercourse and traffic."[971]

That such a situation was untenable in the long run came up on several occasions during the various ratification debates in 1787–88, most prominently in Virginia. There, the anti-Federalist William Grayson asserted that ceding the Mississippi by treaty "would deprive us of a right to which, by the law of nations, we are inalienably and indefeasibly entitled", adding that "[n]ations who inhabit on the sources of rivers have a right to navigate them, and go down, as well as the waters themselves."[972] A few days earlier, James Madison had made the same point in even more strenuous terms: "Neither the old Confederation nor the New Constitution involves a right to give up the navigation of the Mississippi. It is

---

968 Walter Nugent, *Habits of Empire: A History of American Expansion* (New York: Alfred A. Knopf, 2008), pp. 39–40.

969 Walter Nugent, *Habits of Empire*, p. 5.

970 The *San Antonio* (Debadie v. Russell), 95, Recs. Ct. App., 1783. Henry Bourguignon, "Incorporation of the Law of Nations during the American Revolution—The Case of the San Antonio" *American Journal of International Law* 71 (1977), p. 290.

971 John Jay, *The Federalist Papers,* no. IV, p. 98.

972 William Grayson "Speech in the Convention of Virginia" June 18, 1788, in *Elliot's Debates*, Vol.3, p. 506.

repugnant to the law of nations."[973] The most forceful statement came however from Virginia governor Randolph, who said that the Constitution could not be a basis for relinquishing rights to the Mississippi, since there existed "a prohibition naturally resulting from the nature of things, it being contradictory and repugnant to reason, and the law of nature and nations."[974]

Consolidation of the union and to paving the way for future expansion were already among the key objectives of the Washington administration for reaching an understanding with the British and improve mutual relations. According to Kaplan, the administration's thinking was that "[a]n accommodation with Britain could be the shortest path to the opening of the Mississippi and to the guarantee of the loyalty of the west."[975] The Mississippi question was also a consideration in the negotiations that led to the treaty of 1794 with Britain. Hamilton emphasized this point in his instructions to Jay, writing that "[t]he navigation of the Mississippi is to us an object of immense consequence. Besides other considerations connected with it, if the Government of the United States can procure and secure the enjoyment of it to our Western country, it will be an infinitely strong link of union between that country and the Atlantic States."[976]

Thomas Jefferson himself had laid out his early views in a cabinet paper written in the run-up to the negotiations with Spain, which would result in the 1795 treaty. In a lengthy report, he laid out the case for freedom of navigation on the Mississippi, with reference to treaty stipulations and the law of nations. Noting that "[o]ur right to navigate [the Mississippi] from it's source to where our Southern boundary strikes it, is not questioned," he claimed that the 1763 treaty of Paris established "a right to all to navigate the whole length of the river in common."[977] While he conceded that during

973 James Madison, "June 13, Mississippi Negotiations", (June 13, 1788), in *The Works of James Madison*, Vol. 5, p. 181.

974 Edmund Randolph, "Speech in the Convention of Virginia", June 13, 1788, in *Elliot's Debates*, Vol. 3, p. 362.

975 Kaplan, *Colonies into Nation*, p. 193.

976 Hamilton to Jay (May 6, 1794), in *The Works of Alexander Hamilton*, Vol. 5, pp. 127–128. Hamilton added that "[i]f anything could be done with Great Britain to increase our chances for the speedy enjoyment of this right, it would be, in my judgment, a very valuable ingredient in any arrangement you could make. Nor is Great Britain without a great interest in the question, if the arrangement shall give to her a participation in that navigation, and a treaty of commerce shall admit her advantageously into this large field of commercial adventure." Ibid.

977 Jefferson, "Report on Negotiation with Spain" (March 18, 1792), in *The Works of Thomas Jefferson*, Vol. 6, pp. 422–423.

the War of Independence, the Spanish had taken possession of several posts in the Floridas (i.e., at the mouth of the Mississippi), this "could not be considered as a conquest *of the river.*" (emphasis in original). As a result, the freedom of navigation on the river, "was confirmed to them by the only power who could pretend claims against them [i.e. Great Britain] founded on the state of war, [since] that common right [has not] been transferred to Spain by either conquest or cession."[978]

Next, Jefferson expatiated on the law of nations. Before discussing treatment of the subject of riparian rights by the authorities of international law, Jefferson made a remarkable and sentimental appeal to the law "as we feel it written in the heart of man," posing the rhetorical question: "what sentiment is written in deeper characters, than that the Ocean is free to all men, & the Rivers to all their inhabitants? Is there a man, savage or civilized, unbiassed by habit, who does not feel & attest this truth?" Pleading on the basis of natural law, Jefferson argued that

> in all tracts of country united under the same political society, we find this natural right universally acknoleged & protected by laying the navigable rivers open to all their inhabitants. When their rivers enter the limits of another society, if the right of the upper inhabitants to descend the stream is in any case obstructed, it is an act of force by a stronger society against a weaker, condemned by the judgment of mankind. The late case of Antwerp and the Scheld was a striking proof of a general union of sentiment on this point: as it is believed that Amsterdam had scarcely an advocate out of Holland, and even there its pretensions were advocated on the ground of treaties, & not of natural right.

The very expanse of land in the west of the United States in itself justified use of the Mississippi by the United States in Jefferson's opinion. As to the law of nations itself, he found that in those areas where Spain had exclusive rights to the river, at least "an innocent passage along it is a natural right in those inhabiting it's borders above" [i.e., the United States].[979] He then went on to say that the United States had a right to navigate the river on the basis of "a principle that the right to a thing gives a right to the means without which it could not be used, that is to say, that the means follow their end." This right is "founded

978 See Jefferson, "Report on Negotiation with Spain" (March 18, 1792), in *The Works of Thomas Jefferson*, Vol. 6, pp. 423–425.

979 See Jefferson, "Report on Negotiation with Spain" (March 18, 1792), in ibid., Vol. 6, p. 425. The authorities cited by Jefferson include Grotius, Pufendorf, Wolff and Vattel.

in natural reasons, is evidenced by the common sense of mankind, and declared by the writers before quoted." What is more, he argued that "[t]he Roman law, which, like other municipal laws, placed the navigation of their rivers on the footing of nature, as to their own citizens, by declaring them public declared also that the right to the use of the shores was incident to that of the water."[980] And since no provision to the contrary was to be found in the treaty of Paris, this right had to be supposed to exist implicitly.

Having arrived at this conclusion, Jefferson suggested that a commission be dispatched to negotiate access to the Mississippi, insisting "that no phrase should be admitted in the treaty, which would express or imply that we take the navigation of the Missisipi (sic) as a *grant* from Spain." After all, "she cannot in reason ask a compensation for yielding what we have a right to, that is to say, the navigation of the river, & the conveniences incident to it of natural right."[981] It would only be in 1795 that Spain agreed to opening negotiations with the United States,

---

980 Jefferson here continues by saying that "[t]his incidental right extends even beyond the shores when circumstances render it necessary to the exercise of the principal right", supported by arguments from Justinian's *Institutes*: "Riparum quoque usus publicus est, ut volunt jura gentium sicut et ipsius fluminis usus publicus est. Itaque et navigium ad ripas appellere et funes de arboribus ibi natis religare, et navis onera in his locis reponere, liberum cuique est: sicuti nec per flumen ipsum navigare quisquam prohibetur." In translation: "Again, the public use of the banks of a river, as of the river itself, is part of the law of nations; consequently every one is entitled to bring his vessel to the bank, and fasten cables to the trees growing there, and use it as a resting-place for the cargo, as freely as he may navigate the river itself." See *The Institutes of Justinian,* tr. by John B. Moyle (Oxford: Clarendon Press, 1906), Bk. II, tit. 1, para 4, p. 37.

981 But, he added "however disagreeable it would be to subscribe to such a sentiment, yet were the conclusion of a treaty to hang on that single objection, it would be expedient to waive it, & to meet, at a future day, the consequences of any resumption they may pretend to make, rather than at present those of a separation without coming to any agreement." See Jefferson, "Report on Negotiation with Spain" (March 18, 1792), in *The Works of Thomas Jefferson*, Vol. 6, p. 436.

Interestingly, about a year later, Attorney-General Edmund Randolph would argue exactly the opposite (i.e. the Spanish position) when discussing the seizure of a French ship, the *Grange*, by a British vessel in the estuary of the Delaware in 1793 in violation of America's neutrality policy, laying down as a ground rule that while the high seas belong to mankind, rivers could be "appropriated because (…) were they open to all the world, they would provide the inlets of perpetual disturbance and discord." See Randolph, "Seizure in Neutral Waters" (May 14, 1793), in Benjamin Hall (ed.), *Official Opinions of the Attorneys General of the United States* (Washington DC: R. Farnham, 1852), Vol. 1, pp. 34–35. In support, Randolph cites several instances from Grotius, Pufendorf, Vattel and Rutherforth, all of which suggest that a country that is in control of both banks of a river can claim full possession.

and chiefly as a result of American-British rapprochement. The treaty affirmed in explicit terms that Spain "has likewise agreed that the navigation of the said River in its whole breadth from its source to the Ocean shall be free only to his Subjects, and the Citizens of the United States (...)."[982]

Obtaining navigational rights was only the beginning of the story. The continental designs that were framed in the decades before made that the Louisiana territory should be next on the list of American acquisitions. The Spanish were well aware of this, and in the years following the acquisition of the territory in 1762, began to create a "network of alliances [on the basis of] written treaties with the representatives of local Indian nations" in an attempt to stave off British and French designs west of the Mississippi—while discontinuing to make claims on the basis of papal bulls or rights deriving from conquest.[983] Only after the start of the French Revolution did the French government begin to show an interest in recovering the area. Sensing the need for American support, the French representative to the United States, Comte de Moustier, wrote a memorandum in 1789 in which he argued that French reacquisition of the territory could help strengthen relations with America if France would open the Mississippi for American commerce with France benefiting from increased trade at the same time.[984] A further impetus arrived when inhabitants of New Orleans expressed grievances to the *Convention* in Paris in 1793 over the cession of their city to Spain. The first consul, Napoleon Bonaparte, became interested in recovering Louisiana once more, believing that this would create a useful buffer between Spanish and American possessions on the North-American continent. For the Spanish, a retrocession would relieve the country of a high administrative burden that the governing of the territory brought with it.[985] In the end, while France had briefly considered to capture the Louisiana area, it actually obtained it by way of a secret treaty just as it concluded the Treaty of Mortefontaine with the United States.

Once the terms of the Treaty of San Ildefonso, which was concluded on October 1st, 1800, and which returned Louisiana into French hands, became known in the United States, outrage ensued in Congress.[986] Federalists called

---

982 *Treaty of Friendship, Limits, and Navigation* (Spain and the United States, San Lorenzo el Real, October 27, 1795), art. IV.

983 Eliga Gould, "Entangled Histories, Entangled Worlds: The English-Speaking Atlantic as a Spanish Periphery" *The American Historical Review* 112, no. 3 (2007), p. 777.

984 DeConde, *Entangling Alliance*, p. 26.

985 Nys, *Les États-Unis et le Droit des Gens*, p. 115.

986 The terms of the treaty were confirmed in a further secret treaty, signed at Aranjuez on March 21, 1801.

for a war of conquest in order to pre-empt French occupation, fearing that it could otherwise lead to exporting the French revolution to American soil. But Federalists were not the only faction to feel concerned. Jefferson too, writing to the American minister to France, expressed great anxiety about the consequences of the new Franco-Spanish treaty. Showing himself attached to France by temperament, he nevertheless suggested that the United States might need to join up with Britain to forestall new French imperial designs on the North American continent:

> [W]e have ever looked to [France] as our *natural friend,* as one with which we never could have an occasion of difference. Her growth therefore we viewed as our own, her misfortunes ours. There is on the globe one single spot, the possessor of which is our natural and habitual enemy. It is New Orleans, through which the produce of three-eighths of our territory must pass to market (…) France placing herself in that door assumes to us the attitude of defiance. (…) The day that France takes possession of N. Orleans fixes the sentence which is to restrain her forever within her low water mark. It seals the union of two nations who in conjunction can maintain exclusive possession of the ocean. From that moment we must marry ourselves to the British fleet and nation.[987]

The emotive language Jefferson used was most likely meant to demonstrate to the French government that the United States was sincerely concerned about the developments regarding Louisiana. Historian Lawrence Kaplan found these words, "characteristic of the ex-revolutionary of every era, who, finding his love betrayed, will seek any means to destroy the former object of his affections."[988] Jefferson found himself in a cul-de-sac, and employed *realpolitik* in order to secure his objectives. In fact, he "was never serious about an Anglo-American military alliance (…)."[989] In October 1802, the Americans suffered a further blow when Spain closed New Orleans to American shipping, thus suspending the right of Americans to freely navigate the Mississippi in accordance

---

987 Jefferson to Robert Livingston (April 18, 1802), in *The Works of Thomas Jefferson,* Vol. 9, pp. 364–65. The letter was to be brought to the attention of Versailles by Pierre Samuel Du Pont De Nemours, a long-time friend of Jefferson. See Lawrence Kaplan, "The Louisiana Purchase 1803", in Patrick White (ed.), *The Critical Years: American Foreign Policy 1793–1823* (New York: John Wiley & Sons, 1970), pp. 47–48.

988 Kaplan, "The Louisiana Purchase 1803", p. 49.

989 Gordon Wood, *Empire of Liberty: A History of the Early Republic, 1789–1815,* (New York: Oxford University Press, 2009), p. 368.

with the Pinckney Treaty of 1795—a move behind which the hand of the French was suspected.[990] But the order came directly from the Spanish king, Charles IV. "Legally, [the Spanish] were on solid grounds. Militarily and politically, facing both France and the United States, they were hopelessly quixotic."[991] As it was, the blockade was lifted soon however.

This event served only as one more reminder for the United States to continue to press for the acquisition of the transfluvial territory at the earliest available moment. Initially, the government only intended to buy New Orleans and a strip of land along the Mississippi so as to ensure access to sea—which would have precluded the Spanish henceforth from blocking American ships from the Mississippi. At the time of the Spanish blockade, James Monroe was already on his way to Paris to meet the resident minister, Livingston, in order to negotiate a treaty to that end with France. However, when the envoys finally met with Napoleon, he stunned them by declaring that he was prepared to sell the Americans the entire colony of Louisiana. Jumping at this opportunity and without consultation, they agreed to the proposal. A formal treaty was concluded on April 30, 1803, and ratifications were exchanged on October 21 of the same year. Legally speaking, the Spanish minister in Washington, Casa Yrujo, argued that the sale by Napoleon was invalid and "a manifest violation of the most solemn engagements entered into by France" because it violated the earlier treaty of San Ildefonso with Spain.[992] But shortly after, in early 1804, the Spanish king dropped his objections, in the hope that good relations with the United States would help him in holding on to the Floridas and Texas.

The story of the quest for territorial acquisition is not just a chronicle of great power interaction. It also concerns the position of the original inhabitants. That their status in terms of legal rights and obligations was thought to be different as opposed to those belonging to the "civilized" European peoples and their offspring had been emphasized from the very moment the North-American continent became subject to colonization. As a rule, natives were not considered to enjoy any inherent or natural rights under the law of nations. For instance, the Royal Proclamation of 1763 did not confer any rights on

990 Lawrence Kaplan, "The Louisiana Purchase 1803", in Patrick White (ed.), *The Critical Years: American Foreign Policy 1793–1823* (New York: John Wiley & Sons, 1970), p. 48. The reason why Spain could take this decision as late as 1802 is because the formal transfer of the territory pursuant to the San Ildefonso treaty had not materialized yet.

991 Walter Nugent, *Habits of Empire: A History of American Expansion* (New York: Alfred A. Knopf, 2008), p. 61.

992 See *Annals of Congress* (1803–1804), 8th Congress, Vol. 2, p. 570, quoted in Walter Nugent, *Habits of Empire: A History of American Expansion* (New York: Alfred A. Knopf, 2008), pp. 67–68.

natives who lived in what was previously French territory, and stipulated that all lands belonging to natives could only be bought by the British government.[993] And following the Revolutionary war, whatever sovereign rights were recognized before to the Iroquois confederation were assumed to have expired as a result of the fact that the confederation had been split during the war.[994] These were just some of the means with which the rights of the natives were either abused or nullified.

American historiography usually maintains that land acquisitions occurred not on the basis of rights deriving from discovery or conquest, but on the basis of treaty agreements. This approach was reflected in the 1787 Northwest Ordinance, which proclaimed that "[t]he utmost good faith shall always be observed towards the Indians; their lands and property shall never be taken from them without their consent; and, in their property, rights, and liberty, they shall never be invaded or disturbed, unless in just and lawful wars authorized by Congress; but laws founded in justice and humanity, shall from time to time be made for preventing wrongs being done to them, and for preserving peace and friendship with them."[995] In the 1790s, Thomas Jefferson was still convinced that the American approach towards land owned by the natives was different enough from that exercised by the Europeans that he even considered it a cornerstone of a distinct American tradition of international law: "We consider it as established by the usage of different nations into a kind of Jus gentium for America, that a white nation settling down and declaring that such and such are their limits, makes an invasion of those limits by any other white nation an act of war, but gives no right of soil against the native possessors."[996] It is likely however that this policy was more the result of weakness than moral rectitude, since in the late 18th century, the young country simply "lacked the political resources to carry out expansion."[997] In spite of the record up to that moment, John Quincy Adams argued in an 1814 letter that at

993 See Green and Dickason, *The Law of Nations and the New World*, pp. 99–101; Paul Frymer, "Building an American Empire: Territorial Expansion in the Antebellum Era," U.C. *Irvine Law Review* 1, no 3 (2011), p. 931.

994 Hermes, "The Law of Native Americans, to 1815", p. 54.

995 Article 3, *Ordinance for the Government of the Territory of the United States Northwest of the Ohio River*, 1787.

996 "Notes of a Conversation with Mr. Hammond" (June 7, 1792), in *The Works of Thomas Jefferson*, Vol. 1, p. 225. See also discussed in Ian Hunter, "Vattel in Revolutionary America: From the Rules of War to the Rule of Law," in Lisa Ford and Tim Rowse, *Between Indigenous and Settler Governance* (New York, Routledge Press, 2013), pp. 16–18.

997 Paul Frymer, "Building an American Empire: Territorial Expansion in the Antebellum Era," U.C. *Irvine Law Review*, Vol. 1, no 3 (2011), p. 930.

least the United States demonstrated a kinder disposition towards the Indians than the English had when they had colonized the continent. In support, he alluded to "a celebrated writer, to whose authority British jurists have taken particular satisfaction in appealing" and who, after having stated

> in the most explicit manner the legitimacy of colonial settlements in America, to the exclusion of all rights of uncivilized Indian tribes, has taken occasion to praise the moderation of the first settlers of New England, and of the founder of Pennsylvania, in having purchased of the Indians the lands they resolved to cultivate, notwithstanding their being furnished with a charter from their sovereign.[998]

Subsequently, Adams described America's policy vis-à-vis the Indian tribes dwelling in North-America:

> It is this example which the United States, since they became by their independence the sovereigns of the territory, have adopted and organized into a political system. Under that system the Indians residing within the United States are so far independent that they live under their own customs and not under the laws of the United States; that their rights upon the lands where they inhabit or hunt, are secured to them by boundaries defined in amicable treaties between the United States and themselves, and that whenever those boundaries are varied it is also by amicable treaties, by which they receive from the United States ample compensation for every right they have to the lands ceded by them. They are so far dependent as not to have the right to dispose of their lands to any private persons, nor to any power other than the United States, and to be under their protection alone, and not under that of any other power.[999]

As we saw above, however, such a simple reading obscures the fact that in practice, treaties only transpired as a result of a process that often involved settler

998 The author is, of course, Vattel: "We cannot help praising the moderation of the English puritans who first settled in New England; who, notwithstanding their being furnished with a charter from their sovereign, purchased of the Indians the land of which they intended to take possession." The reference can be found in *The Law of Nations*, Bk. I, ch. 19, para. 209, p. 216.

999 John Quincy Adams, "Answer to the British Commissioners" (September 9, 1814), in *The Writings of John Quincy Adams*, Vol. 5, pp. 127–28. See also discussed in Eliga Gould, *Among the Powers of the Earth: The American Revolution and the Making of a New World Empire.* (Cambridge, MA: Harvard University Press, 2013), pp. 42–43.

incursions, skirmishes or outright fighting, followed by the conclusion of a treaty which itself was often extorted from chiefs whose authority often remained unclear. Such treaties would invariably cede to the United States all kinds of extractive rights in perpetuity, and ultimately led to "[t]he land [being] subsequently (...) absorbed in every way, including legal and political, becoming official U.S. territory."[1000] However, experience would demonstrate that, rather than introducing and applying a new doctrine towards native peoples different from that of previous European conquerors, "[t]he United States on becoming independent maintained as international law what had been maintained by European states colonizing America."[1001]

A strong argument can be made that already by the time of Jefferson's presidency, the United States had begun to behave as any European great power, pursuing their national self-interest in a ruthless fashion. In a way, it confirmed what Alexander Hamilton had pointed out in the *Federalist Papers*, namely that republics were no less belligerent than monarchies.[1002] Historians Tucker and Hendrickson ironically noted that "[w]hat Montesquieu and Frederick the Great said of the diplomacy of the *ancien régime* might also be said of Jefferson's. In both cases, "the fundamental rule of governments" was "the principle of extending their territories.""[1003] Certainly, American westward expansion was watched with apprehension in Europe. François Guizot, the French statesman and historian, openly wondered why Britain's, Russia's and France's power should be checked, while the growth of American power remained unchecked.[1004]

For Jefferson, however, expansion was not to be pursued merely for its own sake. Its ulterior purpose was to preserve the "Republican character of the Union."[1005] At the same time, his foreign policy was also good balance-of-power politics.[1006] More specifically, "[t]he acquisition of Louisiana freed

1000 Walter Nugent, *Habits of Empire: A History of American Expansion* (New York: Alfred A. Knopf, 2008), p. 45.

1001 George G. Wilson, "International Law and the Constitution" *Boston University Law Review* 13 (1933), p. 254.

1002 Alexander Hamilton, *Federalist* no. VI, in *The Works of Alexander Hamilton*, Vol. 11, p. 38ff.

1003 Robert Tucker and David Hendrickson, *Empire of Liberty: The Statecraft of Thomas Jefferson* (New York, Oxford University Press, 1990), p. 17.

1004 Henry Blumenthal, *France and the United States, Their Diplomatic Relations, 1789–1914* (Chapel Hill: The University of North Carolina Press, 1970), p. 40.

1005 Robert Tucker and David Hendrickson, *Empire of Liberty: The Statecraft of Thomas Jefferson* (New York, Oxford University Press, 1990), p. 162.

1006 Albert Bowman, "Jefferson, Hamilton and American Foreign Policy" *Political Science Quarterly* 71, no. 1 (March 1956), p. 25.

American statesmen from a fear which had been constantly recurring" namely to enter into alliances in order to protect and preserve essential interests, whether strategic or economic.[1007] In essence, it constituted another step towards the elimination of balance-of-power politics in North America, one that neatly fitted Jefferson's key foreign policy objective as set out in his first inaugural address in which he called for "peace, commerce and honest friendship with all nations, entangling alliances with none."[1008]

Yet, although Louisiana fell into America's lap without the need for a shot to be fired, it should not be assumed that Jefferson would have declined to use force had it been necessary—even if this would have been in contravention of the law of nations, or required concluding an alliance with Britain. The very purchase of Louisiana itself became a contentious legal question, the issue being whether it was lawful at all under the Constitution. Jefferson himself even acknowledged having doubts on this matter, but proceeded nonetheless for the simple reason that the interest of the state trumped legal considerations.[1009] In response, the New England Federalists drafted a project in 1803 and 1804 for the North-Eastern states to secede from the union, claiming that the unconstitutional acquisition had created "a new confederacy." Hamilton strongly opposed this idea however, seeing more merit in extending the advantages that the union had brought forth. The subsequent question regarding the quest for acquiring the Floridas would come to demonstrate however that in matters of territorial expansion international law was regarded as important, but only secondary in consideration.

6.2 Freedom of the Seas and Maritime Commerce

In the realm of maritime affairs, the United States also demonstrated an inclination to refuse to adhere to prevailing norms of international law at the time of Jefferson's presidency, but rather in the opposite direction compared with its expansionist policies. On this front, the administration did not necessarily ignore international law for the sake of a narrowly-defined national interest,

1007 Dexter Perkins, *A History of the Monroe Doctrine* (Boston: Little, Brown and Co., 1955), p. 20.

1008 Thomas Jefferson, "Inaugural Address" (March 4, 1801), in *The Writings of Thomas Jefferson*, Vol. 9, p. 197.

1009 See David Hendrickson, *Union, Nation or Empire: The American Debate over International Relations, 1789–1941* (Lawrence, KS: University Press of Kansas, 2009), pp. 50–51 and Robert Tucker and David Hendrickson, *Empire of Liberty: The Statecraft of Thomas Jefferson* (New York, Oxford University Press, 1990), pp. 117–118.

but pushed international legal norms that had been a cornerstone of foreign policy since independence and "very much a part of the American Revolution."[1010]

The Jeffersonian approach dated back to the late 1780s and early 1790s, when James Madison had developed proposals with the aim of isolating Britain on the maritime front through tariff measures. For instance, as a counterpoise to the Orders in Council of 1783 and subsequent British policies, Madison introduced a bill in 1789 with the aim of levying higher duties on goods coming from countries with which the United States did not have a formal treaty of commerce. While this plan was introduced as a means to generate more income for the country, it was effectively targeted at British commerce, which made up almost 90% of all imports at the time. By granting preferential treatment to treaty partners, the United States would also uphold the most-favored nations clauses the agreements contained. Hamilton feared that this measure could lead to serious shortages if French commerce could not replace that of the British—which was a realistic concern, even apart from the fact that it would further antagonize the British.[1011]

Even if Madison's proposals were eventually defeated in the Senate,[1012] Jefferson was quite enamoured of them, seeing an opportunity to wrest America away from Britain's commercial preponderance. He believed that "[t]his Act [of 1789] is perfectly innocent as to other nations, is strictly just as to the English, cannot be parried by them, and if adopted by other nations would inevitably defeat their navigation act and reduce their power on the sea within safer limits. It is indeed extremely to be desired that other nations would adopt it."[1013] Being framed in the enlightened and equitable language of the law of nations, Jefferson saw in it "a peacetime equivalent of the League of Armed Neutrals in conformity with the spirit of the Plan of 1776."[1014]

In early 1794, Madison again tried to have legislation passed for the promotion of American commerce, this time by way of treaties. This time his approach was more aggressive, and called for concluding reciprocal treaties with countries the United States had had no ties with up to then (excepting Britain),

---

1010 Gordon Wood, *Empire of Liberty: A History of the Early Republic, 1789–1815* (New York: Oxford University Press, 2009), p. 189.

1011 Kaplan, *Colonies into Nation*, pp. 194–196; Varg, *Foreign Policies of the Founding Fathers*, pp. 73–78.

1012 Paul Varg, *Foreign Policies of the Founding Fathers*, p. 77.

1013 Jefferson to the U.S. Minister in Portugal, David Humphreys (March 15, 1791), in *The Works of Thomas Jefferson*, Vol. 6, p. 219.

1014 Kaplan, *Colonies into Nation*, p. 205.

while threatening retaliatory measures "against [countries] that had already showed [their] hostility towards the United States by refusing to vacate American territory" and which rejected reciprocal agreements.[1015] The move came in response to British seizures of American ships, which had followed the notorious Orders in Council of November 1793. The debate in Congress clearly exposed the different approaches of Republicans and Federalists. Whereas the former wished to fight Britain with commercial measures, the latter proposed to shore up American defense, and called for an expansion of the navy. Madison thought he understood the ulterior motives of the Federalists, writing to Jefferson that "you understand the game behind the curtain too well not to perceive the old trick of turning every contingency into a resource for accumulating force in the government."[1016] In more general terms, the Republican strategy reflected the conviction that tying all nations together through commerce would help to advance republican values and the demise of monarchy worldwide.[1017] This principled stance was also carried over into the Republican's legal thinking. Both Jefferson and Madison shared a belief in the obligatory character of the law of nations and refused to repudiate the writings of the 18th-century writers on the subject. Rather, their objective was "to further the tentative efforts to reform that law, particularly in securing a wide berth for the rights of neutrals."[1018] In this respect, it is fascinating if not curious to note that while the advancement of neutral rights was much more in the interests of maritime traders based in the northeast—most of them Federalists—the defense of these rights was primarily something that Republicans pushed for, who even endured the opprobrium of the Federalist party in this pursuit.[1019]

The central issue in the early 19th century continued to be the question whether free ships made free goods and the extent to which the Rule of 1756 could be considered a lawful abridgement of that principle. While it was as much a political as an economic question, it was primarily discussed in the language of the law of nations. On the American side, the reasons for this were manifold. Making the analogy between domestic and international

1015 Gordon Wood, *Empire of Liberty: A History of the Early Republic, 1789–1815* (New York: Oxford University Press, 2009), p. 193.

1016 Madison to Jefferson (March 14, 1794), quoted in Varg, *Foreign Policies of the Founding Fathers*, p. 102.

1017 Gordon Wood, *Empire of Liberty: A History of the Early Republic, 1789–1815* p. 630.

1018 Robert Tucker and David Hendrickson, *Empire of Liberty, the Statecraft of Thomas Jefferson* (New York: Oxford University Press, 1990), p. 48.

1019 Gordon Wood, *Empire of Liberty: A History of the Early Republic, 1789–1815* pp. 624–25.

order, the law of nations served in some ways as "a constitution for international society, bringing order and justice to the world just as the American constitutions had to the United States." Another reason was that, as we saw above, in the eyes of American statesmen, natural law and the law of nations—being its derivative—enjoyed *a priori* legitimacy.[1020] There was perhaps also a more pedestrian reason, being that, as Montague said, "in the early years of its diplomacy, [the United States] had little experience and no precedents of its own as a guide through the tangle of debts and immunities, commercial restrictions, seizures, impressments, blockades, and the rights of privateers in the ports of neutral nations."[1021] There were thus critical advantages to be gained from relying on the great authors of the law of nations for counsel. While the British often answered in deeds to American demands, English authors were happy to oblige in supplying legal justifications for their country's behaviour.

An early example and important reference point in this debate was an influential pamphlet by Charles Jenkinson, Lord Hawkesbury, first published in 1757 and reprinted on many occasions thereafter into the early 19th century. With reference to Grotius, Bynkershoek and the *Consolato del Mare*, Jenkinson argued that Britain had a definite right to seize enemy goods on neutral ships. Based on a survey of treaty rights, principles and practices, he concluded that the introduction of the Rule of 1756 was thoroughly justified, saying that "it manifestly appears, that by a general stipulation in favour of trade with the enemy of another power, negociators never intended to imply a right to carry freely the effects of that enemy; but that to establish such a right, it is necessary to have it expressly mentioned."[1022] Another example in this vein was novelist and legal historian Robert Ward's 1801 *Treatise on the Relative Rights and Duties of Belligerent and Neutral Powers in Maritime Affairs*. In it, he concluded that "the enquiries of my own mind have produced satisfactions that the neutral right is on the side of the Belligerent; and that the neutral claim, where allowed, is a matter of the purest convention." Hence, he contended there was no such thing as that free ships make free goods as a general principle of law. To be sure, he added that the claim that principles contained in various treaties therewith

1020 Gregg Lint, "Early American Conceptions of International Law and their Influence on Foreign Policy: 1776–1803" (unpublished manuscript, Michigan State University, 1975), p. 31.

1021 Andrew Montague, "John Marshall", in Samuel F. Bemis (ed.), *The American Secretaries of States and their Diplomacy* (New York: Albert A. Knopf, 1927), Vol. II, p. 260.

1022 Charles Jenkinson, "A Discourse on the Conduct of the Government of Great-Britain in Respect to Neutral Nations", *in A Collection of All the Treaties of Peace, Alliance, and Commerce, Between Great-Britain and Other Powers* (London: J. Debrett, 1785), p. xxiii.

create law for other states "is really too absurd to demand one moment's attention."[1023]

At around the same time, British prize courts produced a series of judgements that pronounced on the validity of the Rule of 1756, mainly as a result of the fact that in order to circumvent it, a practice of re-export trade had evolved, which allowed colonial powers like Spain and France to trade with their colonies by shipping their cargo through American ports, making it technically "neutral trade."[1024] In the *Immanuel* case,[1025] prize court judge Sir William Scott, Lord Stowell, settled this doctrine of continuous voyage, declaring "the illegality of the direct trade between the colony and the parent state of the enemy [by neutrals]."[1026] However, only a year later, in the *Polly* case,[1027] Scott relaxed the rule as established in *Immanuel*, saying that "it is not my business to say what is universally a test of *bona fide* importation",[1028] and holding that, as Perkins summarized the point, "the captor must provide proof of fraudulent intent."[1029] In proportion to the magnitude of the issue, this apparent climbdown from a strict interpretation of the Rule of 1756 led to a "widespread feeling of benevolence toward England."[1030] What was more, a decision by the Advocate General of England in 1801 to admit re-exportation and the principle of broken voyage all but settled the matter.[1031] As a result, the United States enjoyed a few years of very profitable trade relations from re-exportation as well as shipping produce from the West Indies to Europe, including Britain, with which trade took place almost unfettered, since the French navy was

---

1023 Robert Plumer Ward, *Treatise on the Relative Rights and Duties of Belligerent and Neutral Powers in Maritime Affairs* (London: J. Butterworth, 1801), p. 172.

1024 See discussed in Stephen Neff, *The Rights and Duties of Neutrals: A General History* (Manchester: Manchester University Press, 2000), pp. 66–68, 78–79.

1025 2 C. Robinson 187 (1799). In a case dating from the same year, *The Maria*, judge Scott reaffirmed the principle that a prize court is a court of all the world, saying that "the law itself has no locality. (…) If, therefore, I mistake the law in this matter, I mistake that which I consider, and which I mean should be considered, as the universal law upon the question (…)." See *The Maria* (1 Rob. rep. 340, 350), quoted in Edwin Dickinson, *A Selection of Cases and Other Readings on The Law of Nations, Chiefly as Interpreted and Applied by British and American Courts* (New York: McGraw Hill, 1929), p. 40.

1026 Joseph Chitty, *A Practical Treatise on the Law of Nations, Relative to the Legal Effect of War on the Commerce of Belligerents and Neutrals* (Boston: Bradford and Reid, 1812), p. 169.

1027 2 C. Robinson 362 (1800).

1028 2 C. Robinson 362 (1800), at 369.

1029 Bradford Perkins, "Sir William Scott and the *Essex*" *William and Mary Quarterly* 13, no. 2 (April 1956), p. 172.

1030 Kaplan, *Colonies into Nation*, p. 284.

1031 Lint, "Early American Conceptions of International Law", p. 151.

incapable to hamper American shipping.[1032] Yet, the resumption of war between Britain and France in 1805 led the British to overturn their more liberal stance. That same year, the Admiralty Court declared in the celebrated *Essex* case that goods could no longer be neutralized by re-exporting them through American ports.[1033] Because of his alleged involvement in the case, Sir William Scott's reputation in the United States now plummeted—undeservedly so, according to Perkins, who found that Scott in fact demonstrated a 'judicial awareness' of the rights of neutrals.[1034]

Nonetheless, Congress was not in the least prepared to compromise on a vital principle. It held that American ships had always had a right to transport produce from the West Indies to Europe, and that this trade was legitimized, also by dint of the fact that British courts had earlier accepted the "broken voyage" principle.[1035] The rekindled war only helped to further underline the importance of the subject, something that was clearly reflected in the writings of the early 19th century. On both sides, pamphleteers became more combative, a good example on the British side being James Stephen's pungently titled 1805 tract *War in Disguise*. His basic claim was that neutral trade harmed the British in their war against Napoleonic France. Simply put, "the flag of the United States was, for the most part, used to protect the property of the French planter."[1036] Spewing his wrath, Stephen wished to expose the insidiousness of American merchant shipping practices:

> If neutral merchants will violate the obligations of truth and justice, in order to profit unduly by the war, the societies to which they belong, will soon feel the poisonous effects, in the deterioration of private morals; for habits of fraud and perjury, will not terminate with the neutralizing employments that produced them.[1037]

Various of the pamphlet's suggestions found their way into the Orders in Council of 1807. Its provocative language elicited a spirited response on the

---

1032 Reginald Horsman, *The Diplomacy of the New Republic, 1776–1815* (Arlington Heights, Ill.: Harlan Davidson, 1985), p. 95.

1033 Samuel Bemis, *A Diplomatic History of the United States*, pp. 140–141.

1034 Perkins, "Sir William Scott and the *Essex*", p. 173.

1035 See also discussed in A.L. Burt "Neutral Rights", in Patrick White (ed.), *The Critical Years: American Foreign Policy 1793–1823* (New York: John Wiley & Sons, 1970), pp. 61–62.

1036 James Stephen, *War in Disguise, or the Frauds of the Neutral Flags* (London: J. Hatchard, Piccadilly, 1805), p. 20.

1037 James Stephen, *War in Disguise*, p. 92.

American side by Gouverneur Morris, writing that "in the zeal of argument, [it] overleaps the bound of reason." Essentially, Morris' point was that a rule that was crafted under specific circumstances and which no nation ever assented to cannot be deemed a part of international law.[1038] Whilst trying to find support in the private language of judge Scott, he concluded that Britain had no right to restrict neutral shipping rights if a belligerent decided under domestic law to relax shipping monopolies on their colonies, allowing neutrals to engage in carrying goods to the metropolis.[1039]

Another representative—and perhaps much more typical—example of how Americans defended neutral rights comes from a short survey on the law of nations written by William Duane, a newspaper publisher from Philadelphia. His writing was typical because of the emphasis he put on the binding force of the natural law of nations, which had become a veritable American trait. As a result, he could write that

> it matters not, how many have written, or what writers have said, unless they assumed as the basis of their reasoning, the moral laws of nature and the principles of universal justice. If therefore, every writer upon the laws of nations had advocated the right of belligerents to seize an enemy's property in neutral ships, that right would neither be established nor justified.[1040]

In particular, he focused on the earlier claims made by Jenkinson justifying the Rule of 1756. Having investigated a long list of authorities, including Grotius, Vattel and Bynkershoek—several of which Jenkinson and other British authors had invoked to defend the British position—Duane concluded that "[t]he authority of these writers (...) cannot sustain the British doctrine."[1041] Most characteristic of Duane's approach is that he framed the rights of neutrals not in terms of American self-interest, but as serving the greater good of mankind: "The influence of neutrals must promote rather than abridge, the interests of states, and the cause of humanity (...) for when the prospects of maritime

1038 Gouverneur Morris, *An Answer to War in Disguise, or, Remarks Upon the New Doctrine of England, Concerning Neutral Trade* (New York: Hopkins and Seymour, 1806), p. 6, 10–11.

1039 Gouverneur Morris, *An Answer to War in Disguise, or, Remarks Upon the New Doctrine of England, Concerning Neutral Trade*, p. 23.

1040 William Duane, *The Law of Nations, Investigated in a Popular Manner* (Philadelphia, William Duane, 1809), pp. 20–21.

1041 William Duane, *The Law of Nations, Investigated in a Popular Manner*, p. 22.

plunder are frustrated and obscured by an acknowledgement of our neutral rights, the principal cause of maritime wars will be removed."[1042]

Duane's views were entirely consistent with those of Jefferson himself. Indeed, in a letter written early into his first term, Jefferson suggested that in his view, the rule that 'free ships shall make free goods' was now part of the general law of nations, since "this (…) principle has by every maritime nation of Europe been established, to a greater or less degree, in it's treaties with other nations; insomuch, that all of them have, more or less frequently, assented to it, as a rule of action in particular cases."[1043] While it never becomes clear whether this assumption also included Britain, he implicitly suggested that it did when saying that

> [n]o nation ever pretended a right to govern by their laws the ship of another nation navigating the ocean. By what law then can it enter that ship while in peaceable & orderly use of the common element [i.e. the high seas]? We recognize no natural precept for submission to such a right; & perceive no distinction between the movable & immovable jurisdiction of a friend, which would authorize the entering the one & not the other, to seize the property of an enemy.[1044]

Jefferson regretted that it had been necessary in the 1790s to deny the general application of the 'free ships, free goods' rule, and that it had to be denied to France when it was claimed by Genêt. On the matter of contraband, he took an absolutist position, saying that "[e]ither everything which may aid or comfort an enemy [is contraband], or nothing. Either all commerce which would accommodate him is unlawful, or none is. (…) No line between them can be drawn. Either all intercourse must cease between neutrals & belligerents, or all be permitted." In his opinion, he added, "the practice of seizing what is called contraband of war, is an abusive practice, not founded in natural right."[1045]

Yet, while he went to great lengths to profess his support for a more liberal system of international law—and in particular the free ships doctrine—by

1042 William Duane, *The Law of Nations, Investigated in a Popular Manner* p. 30. Possibly, Duane quotes here from Barbeyrac, though this is not entirely clear in the textual framing.

1043 Thomas Jefferson to Robert Livingston (September 9, 1801), in *The Writings of Thomas Jefferson*, Vol. 10, p. 278.

1044 Jefferson to Livingston (September 9, 1801), in ibid., Vol. 10, pp. 279–80.

1045 Jefferson to Livingston (September 9, 1801), in ibid., Vol. 10, p. 280.

saying that "the nations of Europe have originally set out in error", he also said that in practice, the United States will not engage in war to help establish it, notwithstanding its sincere friendliness towards it.[1046] Jefferson's caution with regard to directly challenging Britain went so far that he even declined to take up Napoleon's proposal in 1800 in Mortefontaine to agree to "a treaty that would uphold the liberal interpretation of neutral rights so that the small naval powers of Northern Europe would have the necessary model for joining the League of Armed Neutrality against British sea power."[1047] As an interesting aside, Witt noted on this issue that as a matter of fact, "American diplomats put relatively little effort into demanding that European states [adopt the 'free ships, free goods' rule]." The reason was because the prevailing British rule was "extraordinarily easy to evade."[1048]

But while Jefferson had become very reluctant to practice what he preached, Federalist minds were becoming outright despondent. In a letter to John Marshall, John Adams wrote that he had little faith left in seeing the doctrine of 'free ships, free goods' ever prevailing:

> once really established and honestly observed, it would put an end forever to all maritime war, and render all military navies useless. However desirable this may be to humanity, how much soever philosophy may approve it and Christianity desire it, I am clearly convinced it will never take place. The dominant power on the ocean will forever trample on it. (…) We must treat the subject with great attention, and, if all other nations will agree to it, we will. But while one holds out, we shall be the dupes, if we agree to it.[1049]

1046 Jefferson to Livingston (September 9, 1801), in ibid., Vol. 10, p. 283.

1047 Lawrence Kaplan, "Jefferson's Foreign Policy and Napoleon's Idéologues" *William and Mary Quarterly* 19 (3rd. series, July, 1962), p. 349; Alfred Vagts, "The United States and the Balance of Power" *The Journal of Politics* 3, no. 4 (November 1941), p. 410.

1048 John Fabian Witt, "The Power of War and Peace," draft chapter from *Lincoln's Code: The Laws of War in American History*. Presented at NYU legal history colloquium (February 17, 2010), p. 13. See also Stephen Neff, *The Rights and Duties of Neutrals: A General History* (Manchester: Manchester University Press, 2000), p. 79.

1049 John Adams to John Marshall (October 3, 1800), in *The Works of John Adams*, Vol. 9, pp. 86–87. Interestingly, Marshall expressed similar sentiments in a letter some years before to Talleyrand, writing that "[h]owever humanity may deplore the application of the principle [that belligerents have a right to seize enemy goods on neutral ships], there is perhaps no one to which man has more universally assented, or to which jurists have more uniformly agreed. (…) It yields by common consent to the superior right of a neutral to protect, by virtue of its sovereignty, the goods of either belligerent power, found within

John Quincy Adams, who during the administration of his father had still pleaded for inserting a positive reference to the free ships doctrine in the new treaty with Prussia, conceded that only the British interpretation could be countenanced. Writing in unequivocal language, he said that

> the government of the United States have long since declared their opinion, that by the law of nations, independent of the stipulations of treaties, an enemy's cargo cannot be protected by a neutral bottom; and though always anxious to establish the contrary by voluntary agreement, they have ever disavowed all pretence of a right to force its adoption upon other powers, and by the positive engagement of a treaty [the Jay Treaty] are bound to acquiesce in the practice of the rule as it originally stood.[1050]

Adams had even become outright hostile where the principles of the second League of Armed Neutrality were concerned, declaring that "[t]he fundamental principles of this league seem unjust (…). It assumes a right of legislation upon the sea. It is an enactment by the nations, of laws upon objects of common concern to all, with a declaration, that if other nations will not consent to them peaceably, they shall be forced upon them at the mouth of the cannon. It is impossible to assume the supremacy of the seas more plainly and arrogantly than this."[1051]

There was one instance however where the territorial and maritime approaches to the law of nations dramatically clashed and led to utter indecisiveness. This was the situation concerning the independence of Haiti, where slavery issue took center stage. This inconclusive approach was illustrated by the fact that when Jefferson had become president, he had overturned Federalist policy by opposing independence for what was officially still considered a French colony,[1052] but he also sought to avoid

its jurisdiction." Charles C. Pinckney, John Marshall and Elbridge Gerry "To the Minister of Foreign Affairs of the French Republic" (January 27, 1798), in *Instructions to the Envoys Extraordinary and Ministers Plenipotentiary from the United States of America to the French Republic,* (…) (Philadelphia: W. Ross, 1798), p. 53.

1050 John Quincy Adams to John Marshall (February 21, 1801), in *The Writings of John Quincy Adams*, Vol. 2, p. 503.

1051 Adams to Marshall (February 21, 1801), in *The Writings of John Quincy Adams*, Vol. 2, p. 503.

1052 Donald Hickey, "America's Response to the Slave Revolt in Haiti 1791–1806" *Journal of the Early Republic* 2, No. 4 (Winter, 1982), p. 368. However, Tim Matthewson argued the opposite, namely that Jefferson in fact encouraged independence, although he agrees with Hickey that the president sought to keep a distance from the rebel leadership. See Tim

jeopardizing American trade with the island, if only because most of its produce was exported to Southern states. Officially, Jefferson's policy was to steer a neutralist course, the idea being that given that the situation surrounding the island was still unresolved, recognition of an independent state could have been considered a *casus belli* by the French (as French recognition of the United States effectively was back in 1778). However, because Jefferson "formally acknowledged continued French sovereignty over the island," he did in fact take sides.[1053]

When in 1804 Haiti had declared its independence and American commercial vessels carried both arms and contraband goods its ports, both British and French agents lodged protests with the American government, declaring that these deliveries were in contravention of the law of nations. James Madison, Secretary of State, acknowledged these claims, noting that "the United States are bound by the law of Nations to nothing further than to leave their offending Citizens to the consequences of an illicit trade."[1054] However, in this instance, the Americans would only pay lip-service to this notion. For when in 1805, Talleyrand announced that all vessels bound for the newly independent republic would be regarded as lawful prize, a bill was introduced in Congress the year after that called upon American merchants to respect the provisions of the Convention of 1800 and international law. But in the end, the resulting Clearance Act turned out only to "satisfy the French and serve notice on American merchants that they traded with Haiti at their own risk."[1055] In other words, in reality, the Act was not in the least meant to affect trade between Haiti and the United States.

That American policies towards Haiti worked entirely at cross-purposes is best illustrated by the fact that on the one hand, the contraband trade with Haiti amounted to military support to the rebelling slave republic, while on the other, Southerners were profoundly concerned about the impact the rebellion would have on slaves in the United States, for it provided inspiration for a domestic uprising. What is more, after 1805, the new republic offered citizenship

---

Matthewson, "Jefferson and the Nonrecognition of Haiti," *Proceedings of the American Philosophical Society* 140, no 1 (1996), p. 22.

1053 Robert Reinstein, "Slavery, Executive Power and International Law: The Haitian Revolution and American Constitutionalism" *American Journal of Legal History,* (forthcoming), p. 71.

1054 Madison to Livingstone (March 31, 1804), in *The Writings of James Madison* (New York: G.P. Putnam's Sons, 1900). Vol. 7, p. 135.

1055 Donald Hickey, "America's Response to the Slave Revolt in Haiti 1791–1806" *Journal of the Early Republic* 2, No. 4 (Winter, 1982), pp. 374–76.

to any black person who would arrive on their shores.[1056] Hence, the conflict between commercial, social, moral and legal imperatives could not be greater, and helped to sow many doubts in American minds about the feasibility and desirability of a moral approach to enforcing the law of nations, let alone to reform it for the better.

Shifting opinions on the desirability and efficacy of enforcing and promoting international law within the United States were also reflected by the Supreme Court in some early 19th-century rulings. In the 1800 case *Bas v. Tingy*, the Court made a move in privileging federal statute law over the law of nations by declaring that "a suspension of the law of nations [on the right of captures] can only be authorized by an act of the government", albeit that justice Chase warned that this would amount to "an act of hostility."[1057] A more cautious approach was developed four years later in *Murray v. the Charming Betsey*, in which Justice Marshall stressed in particular the need for neutral rights to be adhered to:

> An act of Congress ought never be construed to violate the law of nations if any other possible construction remains, and consequently can never be construed to violate neutral rights or to affect neutral commerce further than is warranted by the law of nations as understood in this country.[1058]

1056 Tim Matthewson, "Jefferson and the Nonrecognition of Haiti," *Proceedings of the American Philosophical Society* 140, no 1 (1996), p. 22, 26. Jefferson, contemplating the possibility of a domestic uprising in the wake of the Gabriel Prosser slave revolt in Richmond in 1800, even considered to move all slaves to islands in the West Indies, the best choice being St. Domingue, because there "nature seems to have formed these islands to become the receptacle of the blacks transplanted into this hemisphere." Jefferson to Monroe (Nov. 22, 1801), in *The Writings of Thomas Jefferson*, Vol. 9, p. 317. Peter Onuf concluded in this regard that "while Jefferson acknowledged the original injustice against them, neither people could appeal to the law -under the constitution of Virginia or under the law of nations- for redress." Peter Onuf, ""To Declare Them a Free and Independant People": Race, Slavery, and National Identity in Jefferson's Thought," *Journal of the Early Republic* 18, No. 1 (Spring, 1998), pp. 37–38.

1057 *Bas v. Tingy*, 4 U.S. 4 (Dall.) 37, at 44. See also discussed in Anthony Bellia and Bradford Clark, "The Federal Common Law of Nations" *Columbia Law Review* 109 (January, 2009), p. 64.

1058 See 6 U.S. (2 Cranch), 64, at 118. This case concerned a claim by an American captor of the schooner *Charming Betsey* against its owner, arguing that he was entitled to sell it in the United States, since he captured it from the French and had violated a law against commerce between France and the United States. The ship's owner, Jared Shattuck, claimed however that he was Danish, not American.

This dictum became known as the *Charming Betsey* rule, and according to one scholar, gave impetus to further "incorporat[ing] international law into the interstices of American law."[1059] With the decision, the Court "applauded a France that had returned to the flock of international law-respecting states"[1060] now that its early revolutionary zeal from the days of Citizen Genêt had subsided. However, the statement could also be read as circumscribing the extent of the application of the law of nations in the United States. Ernest Nys concluded that this is evidence that while the administration was more reformist in its approach, the Court was more conservative.[1061]

But in spite of its more reformist spirit, the Jefferson administration in its first term essentially capitulated to British naval power, finding itself unable to challenge the hegemon in pushing its conception of natural rights, even if rhetorically, Jefferson continued to be wedded to his reformist ideas. His non-committal stance earned him an admonition from an otherwise sympathetic chronicler of his two terms, Henry Adams, who criticized the president for taking a too narrow position on violations of the law of nations in general. Saying that "the so-called rule of 1756 was neither more nor less than a rule of force", he wondered

> when was international law itself anything more than a law of force? The moment a nation found itself unable to show some kind of physical defence for its protection, this wisdom of Grotius and Bynkershoek could not prevent it from being plundered; and how could president Jefferson complain merely because American ships were forbidden by England to

1059 Frederick Leiner, "The *Charming Betsey* and the Marshall Court" *The American Journal of Legal History* 45, no. 1 (Jan. 2001), p. 1.

1060 Frederick Leiner, "The *Charming Betsey* and the Marshall Court" ibid., p. 18.

1061 "On a pu dire que la cour suprême, appliquait des règles viellies et obsolètes, oubliant les changements que le progrès avait introduits dans les relations internationales; on a pu soutenir que (…) le pouvoir exécutif s'est montré animé de l'esprit de réforme, tandis que le pouvoir judiciaire s'est complu dans le conservatisme." See Ernest Nys, *Les États-Unis et le Droit des Gens*, p. 76–77. In the case *Rose v. Himely*, the Supreme Court declared that it could not pronounce itself on the question of recognition in relation to Haiti, given that this is a question "addressed to sovereigns, not to courts." The result was, as Reinstein notes, that "[b]y treating the issue as a non-justiciable political question, the Supreme Court in effect gave presidents authority to remove recognition decisions from the restraints of the law of nations and to convert them to matters of executive discretion." See Robert Reinstein, "Slavery, Executive Power and International Law: The Haitian Revolution and American Constitutionalism" *American Journal of Legal History*, (forthcoming), p. 96, 97.

> carry French sugars to France, when he looked without protest while England and France committed much greater outrages on every other country within their reach?[1062]

If Jefferson was hesitant or felt powerless to complain or even challenge violations of international law committed by the great European powers, he had no such qualms about confronting piracy in the Mediterranean—a scourge which had serious effects on American trade in the region. These pirates emanated from the so-called Barbary states, the semi-autonomous provinces of the Ottoman Empire of Algiers, Tunis and Tripoli, as well as the independent kingdom of Morocco. Already in 1784, as a minister to France, Jefferson had proposed to create an "international league for the permanent policing of the Mediterranean" with the U.S. in the lead role, along the lines of the first Armed Neutrality as created by Catherine II. Ultimately, Britain did not support the plan, nor did Congress provide any funding.[1063] What is more, there also arose suspicion some years later that Britain conveniently ignored the Barbary pirates as a result of a treaty that Portugal had signed with Algeria in 1793. It was feared that with peace reigning, the Algerians would now be able to take their ships into the Atlantic, and attack American ships. Since Portugal was allied to Britain at the time, the latter was suspected to have had a hand in these developments.[1064] One of the responses from the American side was the adoption of a Naval Act one year later, which was the starting point for the creation of a veritable American navy. However, the United States was not in a position at that time to take on the Barbary states militarily, and despite the fact that pirates were regarded as outlaws, as "enemies of mankind" without any rights under international law, saw itself compelled to conclude treaties with the Maghreb principalities. Agreements were signed with Algiers 1795, Tripoli 1796-97[1065] and Tunis 1797, under which it promised to pay monetary

1062 Henry Adams, *History of the United States of America during the Administrations of Thomas Jefferson* (New York: Library of America, 1986), p. 525.

1063 Robert Kagan, *Dangerous Nation*, p. 98. See also Frederick Marks, "Power, Pride and Purse: Diplomatic Origins of the Constitution", Diplomatic History 11, no. 4 (1987) p. 306.

1064 Kaplan, *Colonies into Nation*, p. 234.

1065 It is article XI of the 1796 treaty with Tripoli which contained the remarkable passage about the religious nature of the United States: "As the government of the United States of America is not in any sense founded on the Christian Religion,-as it has in itself no character of enmity against the laws, religion or tranquility of Musselmen,-and as the said States never have entered into any war or act of hostility against any Mehomitan nation, it is declared by the parties that no pretext arising from religious opinions shall ever produce an interruption of the harmony existing between the two countries."

tribute, something which hitherto it had categorically refused to do. Hence, in terms of its purposes, "actual policy in the Mediterranean [came to follow] traditional European lines."[1066]

In the early 1800s, the situation was different, at least in Jefferson's estimation, who now felt powerful enough to confront the problem head-on. International law considerations constituted no inhibition for him in that regard, saying that "although nations have treated with the piratical States, they have not, in malice, ever been considered as entitled to all the favors of the laws of nations."[1067] Between 1801 and 1805, the U.S. navy engaged in several naval expeditions throughout the Mediterranean, besieging numerous cities but failing to stage a coup d'etat in Tripoli.[1068] In the process, the United States established an extensive network of posts around the Mediterranean.[1069] These naval operations fitted the generally accepted notion among both political parties in the United States that "the promotion and protection of American commerce overseas would require naval power with a global reach."[1070] Still, the deployment of the navy in the Mediterranean could not conceal the fact that engaging it against the European powers was still well beyond reach. These engagements during Jefferson's first administration were not the end of the story. Only after new wars had been fought in 1815 and 1816 could definitive peace treaties be concluded that ended the Barbary practices of extorting tributes and ransoms: with Algeria in 1816 and with Tunis in 1824.[1071]

During the second Jefferson administration, relations with Britain further deteriorated. Indeed, while between 1795 and 1804, British policy towards naval commerce had been "comparatively tolerant,"[1072] new exigencies as a result of the continuing war against Napoleon made that London tightened the screws on American shipping rights. One of these was that from 1805 on—and partly as a result of the *Essex* ruling—the Rule of 1756 was suddenly being applied

---

1066 Reginald Horsman, *The Diplomacy of the New Republic, 1776–1815* (Arlington Heights, Ill.: Harlan Davidson, 1985), p. 84.

1067 Jefferson to Madison (August 25, 1803), in *The Writings of Thomas Jefferson*, Vol. 10, p. 413.

1068 Robert Kagan, *Dangerous Nation*, pp. 99–100.

1069 See described in e.g. Paul Varg, *Foreign Policies of the Founding Fathers*, pp. 148–150, and Kagan, *Dangerous Nation*, pp. 97–101.

1070 Kagan, *Dangerous Nation*, p. 62.

1071 Gordon Wood, *Empire of Liberty: A History of the Early Republic, 1789–1815*, p. 697.

1072 Bradford Perkins, "Sir William Scott and the *Essex*" *William and Mary Quarterly* 13, no. 2 (April 1956), p. 169.

more strictly,[1073] with Britain now forcing neutral ships to call into British ports if they wished to trade between enemy states and their colonies. For Madison, such a principle was largely nonsensical since "the effect of her doctrine and her practice is not to deprive her enemy of their colonial trade but merely to lessen the value of it in proportion to the charges incident to the circuitous course into which it is forced."[1074] What is more, Madison also added that the contested principle was not consistently respected by Britain itself:

> It is well known to be her invariable practice in time of war, by relaxations in her navigation laws, to admit neutrals to trade in channels forbidden to them in times of peace; and particularly to open her Colonial trade both to Neutral vessels and supplies, to which it is shut in times of peace; and that one at least of her objects, in these relaxations is to give to her trade an immunity from capture, to which in her own lands it would be subjected by the war.[1075]

Hence, by frustrating neutral trade, Britain deprived itself of a means of safe passage of produce from its own colonies to the metropolis, since it gave its enemies an excuse to harass neutral ships in search for British goods.

Another major issue that resurfaced at this time was impressment, the conscripting of British subjects who serve on board American ships. This had been an issue since the 1790s, and possibly attracted more attention under Jefferson due to the fact that the protection of individual life and

---

1073 Madison's surprise at this change in British policy is reflected in a letter from 1806 in which he wrote that "the British order of Council bearing date 24th June 1803, and subjecting to capture vessels on a return voyage, which had carried contraband in the outward voyage, was never promulgated, nor was it known that such a rule was to be enforced until the summer of 1805." See Madison to James Monroe and William Pinkney (May 17, 1806), in *The Writings of James Madison*, Vol. 7, pp. 386–87.

1074 Madison to Monroe (April 12, 1805), in *The Writings of James Madison*, Vol. 7 p. 106.

1075 Madison to Monroe (April 12, 1805), in ibid., Vol. 7 p. 178. In a letter to the British Foreign Secretary, Monroe restated extensively the American position with regard to the Rule of 1756, and their reinforcement through Orders in Council. He noted that the U.K. held "that neutral powers ought not to complain of this restraint because they stand under it, on the same ground, with respect to that commerce, which they held in time of peace. But this fact, if true, gives no support to the pretention. The claim involves a question of right, not of interest. If the neutral powers have a right in war to such commerce with the colonies of the enemies of Great Britain, as the parent states respectively allow, they ought not to be deprived of it by her, nor can its just claims be satisfied by any compromise of the kind alluded to." See James Monroe to Lord Mulgrave (September 23, 1805), in *The Writings of James Monroe*, Vol. 4, p. 322.

liberty had been a key tenet of the Jefferson-authored Declaration of Independence.[1076] Historically, although the doctrine of impressment (angary) had an old pedigree—it was already mentioned in the *Corpus Juris Civilis*—its basis and modalities have always remained questionable under international law.[1077] Concretely, the fact was that in the early 19th century "almost half the American merchant marine was made up of British subjects and deserters of the British navy." Indeed, as Witt says, "American reliance on thousands of former British seamen to keep its small fleet afloat was an open secret."[1078] However, the obvious problem with impressment was that in practice it was very difficult to distinguish between nationals and non-nationals, especially when it concerned differentiating between Americans and British. But as was customary in the United States, this topic was also approached from a theoretical if not moralistic angle. A good example in case comes from John Adams, who wrote a letter in which he vehemently denied that there was an established right to impress nationals on neutral ships, asking his reader:

> And in what principle or law is this founded? Is there any law of God to support it? Is there any law of nature to justify it? Is there any law of England to authorize it? Certainly not. The laws of England have no binding force on board American ships, more than the laws of China or Japan. The laws of the United States alone, of which the law of nations is a part, have dominion over our merchant ships. In what law, then, is it grounded? In the law of nations? It is a counterfeit foisted into that law, by this arbitrary, fraudulent proclamation, for the first time.[1079]

But despite the moral outcries from the American side, it appears that there was credible evidence that the British were in fact in the right on the matter.

Initially, Britain and the United States attempted to arrive at a negotiated solution to resolve these maritime issues, something which Jefferson had already contemplated doing since 1804. On the matter of 'free ships, free goods', the United States was prepared to compromise, as the instructions to the principal negotiators, James Monroe and William Pinkney, attest. For instance, they would accept an abridged version of the Rule of

1076 Kagan, *Dangerous Nation*, p. 143.

1077 Arthur Nussbaum, *A Concise History of the Law of Nations*, p. 134.

1078 Witt, *Lincoln's Code: The Laws of War in American History*, p. 62.

1079 John Adams, "The Inadmissible Principles of the King of England's Proclamation of October 16, 1807, Considered." in *The Works of John Adams*, Vol. 9, p. 315.

1756 if the British did not agree to a full concession on this point, because "too much ought not to be risked by an inflexible pursuit of abstract right."[1080] In addition, Madison proposed that a most-favored nation clause would not only extend to commerce, but also to "points which relate to the rights and duties of belligerents and neutrals." To this end, he suggested that

> [such] an arrangement (...) would secure to Great Britain the same rights in relation to the admission of her armed vessels in our ports and to the exclusion of her enemies privateers and of their prizes, which are now enjoyed by Holland, Spain and other most favored nations; whilst it would place the rights of the United States as neutrals on the same footing with Russia or the most favored nation in respect to search, Convoys, blockades and contraband.[1081]

Jefferson's basic strategy was aimed at getting concessions on neutral rights for American ships in exchange for lifting the Non-Importation act of 1806, an act passed by Congress to pressure Britain in abandoning its impressment policy. However, the negotiations turned out to be disappointing for the American side. Apart from the lifting of a British prohibition on the re-exportation trade, they insisted on an article that essentially enshrined a limited British interpretation on the seizing of vessels that excluded the Rule of 1756.[1082] On the issue of impressment, Jefferson and his cabinet decided that any treaty concluded should include a satisfactory solution to this issue, to be stipulated explicitly in the agreement.[1083] But since the British remained unyielding on this point, and because of insufficient concessions on the British part as to guaranteeing

1080 Madison to James Monroe and William Pinkney (May 17, 1806), in *The Writings of James Madison*, Vol. 7, p. 380.

1081 Madison to Monroe and Pinkney (May 17, 1806), in ibid., p. 389.

1082 See article 8 of the draft treaty: "It is agreed, that in all Cases where vessels shall be captured or detained on just suspicion of having on board Enemy's property or of carrying to the Enemy any of the Articles which are Contraband of War, *or for other lawful cause*, the said Vessel shall be brought to the nearest or most convenient Port; And if any Property of an Enemy should be found on board such Vessel, that part only, which belongs to the Enemy, or is otherwise confiscable, shall be made Prize and the Vessel, unless by Law subject to condemnation, shall be at liberty to proceed with the remainder of the Cargo, without any impediment." (emphasis added).

1083 Madison to Monroe and Pinkney (February 3, 1807 and May 20, 1807), in *The Writings of James Madison*, Vol. 7, p. 421.

neutral rights, the administration declined to submit the draft treaty for approval by the Senate.[1084]

Soon after the rejection of the treaty, the impressment issue burst onto the public scene with the infamous *Chesapeake* affair in June of 1807. It concerned an American vessel, the USS *Chesapeake,* which was attacked and shot at by a British navy vessel just outside territorial waters off the coast of Norfolk, Virginia, resulting in the death of three American seamen. The British vessel's objective was to inspect the American ship in search for deserters to be impressed. Four men were indeed taken off board, one of whom was hanged. The incident galvanized American public opinion in unanimously condemning British naval practices.

The initial response from the administration was to give Britain time to apologize for acts committed by the ships flying the British flag, although it could equally well have been that time was used in order to let warlike sentiments grow so as to put extra pressure on the British.[1085] As it was, the British government, already embroiled in conflict with France, was in a conciliatory mood, and while it denied that it had claimed the right to impress neutral vessels in the first place, it recalled the commander who had ordered the action.[1086] Nevertheless, Jefferson sent the ship *Revenge* to England to demand satisfaction for injuries suffered. The ship also carried a letter for the American representative in London, James Monroe, instructing him to negotiate "the entire abolition of impressment from vessels under the flag of the United States." However, with such a demand, the Americans overplayed their hand and made no progress on the issue whatsoever.[1087] What had aggravated the issue was that in the years before the *Chesapeake* affair, Britain had extended its impressment activities to within the territorial waters of the United States. To the Secretary of State, James Madison, it was clear that there was no legal basis for such practices. In a letter to Monroe, he wrote that the English "must produce then such an exception in the law of nations in favor of the right she contends

1084 Paul Varg, *Foreign Policies of the Founding Fathers,* p. 185; Bradford Perkins, *Cambridge History of American Foreign Relations*, Vol. 1, p. 124. That the treaty was very promising indeed and could have led to Anglo-American entente is argued in Donald Hickey, "The Monroe-Pinkney Treaty of 1806: A Reappraisal" *William and Mary Quarterly,* 3rd ser, Vol. 4, no. 1 (1987), pp. 65–88.

1085 Bradford Perkins, *Prologue to War: England and the United States 1805–1812* (Berkeley and Los Angeles: University of California Press, 1961), p. 146. In fact, Witt noted, in terms of the law of nations, the British were most likely in the right. See John Fabian Witt, *Lincoln's Code: The Laws of War in American History* (New York: The Free Press, 2012), pp. 62–63.

1086 Gordon Wood, *Empire of Liberty*, p. 648.

1087 Bradford Perkins, *Cambridge History of American Foreign Relations*, Vol. 1, p. 126.

for." But, he added, "in what written and received authority will she find it? In what usage except her own will it be found?" Obviously, in none, Madison thought. In particular, Madison examined British practice, but concluded that "[w]hether (...) we consult the law of nations, the tenor of treaties, or the dictates of reason and justice, no warrant, no pretext can be found for the British practice of making impressments from American vessels on the high seas."[1088] Yet while war fever was getting higher in the fall of 1807, Treasury Secretary Gallatin urged caution to Jefferson, since the country was in his opinion not prepared to bear the costs of war.

With the escalation of the war in Europe, the opportunities for American merchant shipping dramatically diminished. First, Napoleon decreed in November 1806 that all trade with Britain was forthwith prohibited through the imposition of the Continental System. In response, Britain issued a series of Orders in Council which, by November 1807, forbade all trade with France except when licensed by the British—the practical consequence being that all American merchandise would first have to pass through an English port before it could be shipped onwards to the continent.[1089] The measure also affected American shipping in that it included a prohibition on all trade taking place between ports under the control of France. In effect, this decision amounted to "an extension of the Rule of 1756."[1090] British Foreign Secretary George Canning was willing enough to admit that "he had no defence to offer for the Orders in Council [of November 1807] as between England and America", but that they had to be regarded as "an extension of that law."[1091]

But the extension of the Rule of 1756 did not constitute the only inhibition on neutral trade. Once the Continental System was put in place, American merchants had to be careful not to moor in blockaded ports, to which they had no access under international law. The rule was that neutral ships could not be confiscated if they sailed into a blockaded port by accident. But, so the Supreme Court ruled, if the captain knew the port to be blockaded, American ships were obliged to "conduct [themselves] during the voyage as an American" on penalty of forfeiting their neutral status if they repeatedly attempted to enter a

1088 Madison to Monroe (January 5, 1804), in *The Writings of James Madison*, Vol. 7, p. 95.

1089 This policy was earlier suggested by James Stephen in his 1806 pamphlet *War in Disguise*. See Stephen Neff, *The Rights and Duties of Neutrals: A General History* (Manchester: Manchester University Press, 2000), pp. 79–80.

1090 See discussed in A.L. Burt "Neutral Rights", in Patrick White (ed.), *The Critical Years: American Foreign Policy 1793–1823* (New York: John Wiley & Sons, 1970), pp. 63–64.

1091 Henry Adams, *History of the United States of America during the Administrations of James Madison* (New York: Library of America, 1986), pp. 45–46.

known blockaded port.[1092] In a way, blockades were much more harmful to American interests because belligerent states could simply declare a blockade and then seize whatever goods it could find on neutral ships, including goods not belonging to the enemy state whose port was blockaded. Of course, such a principle met with opposition from the American side. Madison, for one, found that "[t]he British doctrine of blockades exemplified by practice, is different from that of all other nations, as well as from the reason and nature of that operation of War."[1093] William Duane was more specific, writing that as a general rule "no town or port is to be considered blockaded, that is not so well guarded by a belligerent force, both by land, and sea, as to render an attempt, on the part of a neutral to enter, dangerous."[1094] What is more, "neutrals may trade to belligerent ports, not blockaded, in any articles but those directly used for warlike operations."[1095]

The most comprehensive reflections on America's plight at this juncture came from James Madison in his 1806 *Examination of the British Doctrine*. Considered to be "an expert on international law, the history of treaties and the rulings of British courts",[1096] Madison laid out a detailed argument with reference to many international law authors essentially to conclude that if the rule of law in international affairs is going to prevail, its had to be based on law concluded in peacetime, not in wartime. The essay breathed Madison's strong disposition against war, a position which he had stuck to consistently over the years.[1097] This sentiment was also clearly expressed in his assumptions. As a first rule, he set out that "the trade between a neutral and belligerent nation is

1092 This was in accordance with the Jay treaty with Great Britain, art. XVIII, and decided in the case *Fitzsimmons v. Newport Insurance Company* 8 U.S. (4 Cranch) 185, 1808.

1093 Madison to Monroe and Pinkney (February 3, 1807), in *The Writings of James Madison*, Vol. 7, p. 435.

1094 William Duane, *The Law of Nations, Investigated in a Popular Manner* (Philadelphia, William Duane, 1809), p. 15.

1095 Duane, *The Law of Nations, Investigated in a Popular Manner,* p. 15. Madison shared Duane's assessment on this point, finding that only port cities that were "actually besieged" could be subjected to blockades. See "An Examination of the British Doctrine, Which Subjects to Capture a Neutral Trade, Not Open In Time of Peace" (1806) in Gaillard Hunt (ed.), *The Writings of James Madison*, Vol. 7, p. 205.

1096 Varg, *Foreign Policies of the Founding Fathers*, p. 179. Another author praised Madison's "ability as a scholar [and] his fund of information as a student of international law and international relations." See Charles Hill, "James Madison", in Samuel F. Bemis (ed.), *The American Secretaries of States and their Diplomacy* (New York: Albert A. Knopf, 1927), Vol. III, p. 107.

1097 See e.g. Madison, "Universal Peace" (*National Gazette*, February 2, 1792), in Gaillard Hunt (ed.), *The Writings of James Madison*, Vol. 6, pp. 88–91.

as free as if the latter were at peace with all nations, and the cases in which it is not as free being exceptions to the general rule, the exceptions, according to a received maxim of interpretation, are to be taken strictly, against those claiming the benefit of the exceptions, and favorably for those claiming the benefit of the general rule." Secondly, he noted that "the necessity [of such exceptions] ought to be evident and urgent. In proportion as the necessity may be doubtful, and still more, in proportion as the sacrifice of neutral interests would exceed the advantage to the belligerent, the exception fails." The third point was more of a philosophical nature, and linked international law to the preservation of peace: "The progress of the law of nations, under the influence of science and humanity, is mitigating the evils of war, and diminishing the motives to it, by favoring the rights of those remaining at peace, rather than of those who enter into war. Not only are the laws of war tempered between the parties at war, but much also in relation to those at peace."[1098]

In the first part of the essay, Madison considered the writings of the principal authors on the law of nations as well as ancient codes such as the *Consolato del Mare*. Having considered Grotius on the law of the sea,[1099] Madison concluded that he "has taken express notice of the several questions of contraband, of blockades, and of the carriage of enemy's property, which formed all his exceptions to the freedom of neutral commerce." However, while Madison finds that "his ideas are much less precise and satisfactory than those which are to be found in succeeding authorities", Grotius provided in his view no evidence that supported the British position. After an inconclusive discussion on Pufendorf, he proceeded to discuss Bynkershoek, finding that "he lays it down as a general rule, that the trade of neutrals with the nations at war, provided it be impartial, is as if there were no war; but that certain articles, as instruments of war, form an exception to this general rule." In addition, Madison took note of Bynkershoek's restrictive definition of contraband which he understood as "things which in *their actual state* are *adapted to war;* without considering whether apart from war, they may also be of use; there being few instruments of war, which may not be used for other purpose." Having further looked into Bynkershoek's comments on sieges, blockades and enemy goods on neutral vessels, Madison concluded "that the whole weight of his authority is opposed to the principle advanced by Great Britain." Studying Vattel, whom Madison considered the most important authority for his purposes, he found "that [his]

1098 James Madison, "An Examination of the British Doctrine, Which Subjects to Capture a Neutral Trade, Not Open In Time of Peace" (1806) in Gaillard Hunt (ed.), *The Writings of James Madison*, Vol. 7, p. 207.

1099 Madison studied *The Rights of War and Peace*, Bk. III, Ch. 1, sec. 5 and Bk. III, Ch. 6, sec. 6.

authority (…) coincides perfectly with the preceding authorities" and that the author has "left less room for mistaking or perverting his meaning" in this part of his treatise than in any other part. Finally, Madison considered Martens, though his conclusions are no different from those he drew from Vattel.[1100]

The second part of the essay looked more in particular at British pronouncements as well as British practice since the 1600s. Following a very lengthy excursion through many sources, Madison concluded that Britain itself had not been consistent in its practices in wartime, and that it had equally engaged in relaxing its shipping acts "for the purposes of substituting neutral vessels and mariners in place of those which she finds it expedient to employ in the operations of war." Ironically, he found support for this position in decisions rendered by Sir William Scott. Madison's conclusion is therefore that the Rule of 1756 was unjustified, and that if Robert Ward—whom he was arguing against on this particular point—wanted to be consistent, he had to "either relinquish his argument, or condemn the practice of his own government."[1101]

For a more general solution to the issue of incessantly arguing over the law in wartime, Madison was looking to treaties concluded in peacetime as a sounder and in the long run more reliable basis for the law of nations. His argument started from the premise that treaties "*constitut*[*e*] a law of themselves." The main problem, in his view, was that

> The law of nations, as derived from mere usage or practice during (…) periods [of war], is evidence for (…) the interest (…), which weighty individuals, or perhaps bodies of individuals have, in widening the field of predatory wealth.

In Madison's view, interaction between nations based on treaty relations promised a different kind of world, given that treaties "consist[ed] of those rules of conduct which reason deduces, as consonant to justice and common good, from the nature of the society existing among independent nations (…)." The vista that he imagined was that "the spirit of treaties [being], with few, if any exceptions, at all times more just, more rational, and more benevolent, than the spirit of the law derived from practice only; (…) all enlightened friends

1100 James Madison, "An Examination of the British Doctrine, Which Subjects to Capture a Neutral Trade, Not Open In Time of Peace" (1806) in Gaillard Hunt (ed.), *The Writings of James Madison*, Vol. 7, pp. 230–231 (all quotations have been rendered as cited by Madison; emphasis in original).

1101 James Madison, "Treaties" (1806) in Gaillard Hunt (ed.), *The Writings of James Madison*, Vol. 7, p. 365.

to the happiness of nations ought to favor the influence of treaties on the great code by which their intercourse is to be regulated."[1102] His broader point was, in the words of Varg, that countries that were strong today should realize that someday they will be weak, and like to draw the benefits from a more equitable system of international law.[1103]

But Madison's innovative thinking on the law of nations was far removed from the realities of the day. The 1807 Orders in Council, which had been a response to Napoleon's 1806 decree, had been followed in turn by an even more severe French measure, the Milan decree, which declared that all neutral ships that cooperated in the British licensing scheme would be deemed to have surrendered their neutral character.[1104] The result was that British and French measures had effectively "outlaw[ed] all American trade with their two empires."[1105] According to one historian, this not only "challenged American national dignity, [but] even independence" since America was not free in deciding now with whom it wished to trade.[1106] The situation became even more pernicious once the Continental System had been put in place in its full extent. Neutral powers, including the United States, now found themselves caught between two evils. The question was, said Burt, "[w]ould they cooperate with Napoleon in upholding it, or with Britain in undermining it?"[1107] Madison noted the obvious in this regard when he pointed out that Britain was at liberty to decide whether or not to comply with legal strictures at sea:

> As long as the British navy has so complete an ascendency on the high seas, its commanders have not only an interest in violating the rights of neutrals within the limits of neutral patience, especially of those whose commerce and mariners are unguarded by fleets: they feel moreover the strongest temptation, as is well known from the occasional language of some of them, to covet the full range for spoliation opened by a state of War.[1108]

1102 James Madison, "Treaties" (1806) in Gaillard Hunt (ed.), *The Writings of James Madison*, Vol. 7, pp. 239–240.

1103 Varg, *Foreign Policies of the Founding Fathers*, p. 180

1104 Stephen Neff, *The Rights and Duties of Neutrals: A General History* (Manchester: Manchester University Press, 2000), pp. 82–83.

1105 Bradford Perkins, *Cambridge History of American Foreign Relations*, Vol. 1, pp. 118–119.

1106 Ibid., p. 121.

1107 Burt, "Neutral Rights", in Patrick White (ed.), *The Critical Years: American Foreign Policy 1793–1823*, p. 65.

1108 Madison to Monroe and Pinkney (February 3, 1807), in *The Writings of James Madison*, Vol. 7, p. 398.

Still, for Jeffersonians the moral position of neutrals in wartime remained crystal clear: they have a right to continue their business as if there were no war, as Duane underlined in his survey. Echoing the sentiments of Benjamin Franklin on the rights of humanity, he wrote that

> by the natural laws of nations, and the principles of universal good and justice, a neutral has a right to pursue its own welfare, by conveying the citizens and property of belligerents from the colonies to the mother country, or from port to port, when such conduct does not violate the laws of humanity by directly promoting the destruction of men. And, that, as the laws of nature are paramount to all others, no customs or conventions contrary to their dictates, are binding nor should be respected by free states.[1109]

The quote also conveyed the belief that neutrals could play a pivotal role in wartime, and that American commerce could make a difference in the context of the European conflagration. In that spirit, Congress responded to the imbroglio by adopting an Embargo Act on December 18, 1807, which called for American ships to obtain special permission to dock in foreign ports. The main purpose of the Act was to prohibit foreign vessels from carrying American exports to Britain. Still, British ships could continue to carry their goods into America. The simultaneously revived Non-Importation Act, which had been drafted in 1806, led to a prohibition on the importation of only some categories of British goods, the reason being that "the federal government was so dependent on customs duties on its imports that cutting off all imports would have bankrupted it."[1110] A second, and even more "draconian" Embargo act was passed in January 1809, but only survived until March, when Madison took over the presidency and the act was repealed following enormous pressure from various corners in Congress, including Republicans.[1111] In its place, a Non-Intercourse act was adopted, which prohibited direct trade with both England and France.

In the end, the belief that a neutral United States could be a "decisive factor in the outcome of the European war"[1112] was clearly overblown. While Republicans

---

1109 William Duane, *The Law of Nations, Investigated in a Popular Manner* (Philadelphia, William Duane, 1809), p. 18.

1110 Gordon Wood, *Empire of Liberty: A History of the Early Republic, 1789–1815*, p. 650.

1111 Gordon Wood, *Empire of Liberty*, pp. 657–58

1112 Henry Blumenthal, *France and the United States, Their Diplomatic Relations, 1789–1914* (Chapel Hill: The University of North Carolina Press, 1970), p. 20.

had hoped that, in the words of Wood, "[t]his experiment might (...) bring about a commercial world that Americans had dreamed about ever since the model treaty of 1776,"[1113] the Embargo could not make any marked difference on how the European powers conducted their wartime activities. What is more, historians by and large agree that the Embargo had proved a failure because it was inordinately difficult to enforce.[1114] It also led to many contradictions. The first was that while Jefferson thought that "commerce was [the] best weapon for [America's] defense",[1115] the fact was that without a navy, it was impossible to credibly uphold the Embargo, let alone to challenge Britain's maritime hegemony. And even if at times Jefferson had shown that he understood this reality, he nevertheless backed away from seeking military confrontation at sea in support of the Embargo. Secondly, the Embargo's stranglehold on American shipping turned out in effect to be more deleterious to American rather than British commercial interests. Lord Castlereagh, the British Secretary of War and future Foreign Secretary, highlighted the bitter irony when he said in early 1808 that "I look upon the embargo as operating at present more forcibly in our favour than any measure of hostility we could call forth were war actually declared."[1116] Moreover, the British also criticized neutral powers like the United States for having "confused "the indulgences and relaxations" which Britain "may, from time to time, have granted" with pretended rights,"[1117] claiming that these pretended rights encroached upon British maritime rights. Perhaps cynically, American insistence on its neutral rights was regarded by the British as another way to supporting the French revolutionary cause. But irrespective of whether the Embargo would have worked in Britain's favor or not, the British would most likely not have relented in any event since it was believed that "victory over Napoleon and their greatness as a nation depended upon

1113 Gordon Wood, *Empire of Liberty: A History of the Early Republic, 1789–1815* (New York: Oxford University Press, 2009), pp. 652.

1114 See e.g. Bradford Perkins, *Cambridge History of American Foreign Relations*, Vol. 1, p. 130; Samuel Bemis, *A Diplomatic History of the United States*, p. 150; Paul Varg, *Foreign Policies of the Founding Fathers,* chs. x, xi, *passim*; Robert Tucker and David Hendrickson, *Empire of Liberty: The Statecraft of Thomas Jefferson* (New York: Oxford University Press, 1992), p. 222. However, Wiltse contended that "had the government been strong enough to secure [the Embargo's] more rigid enforcement, [it] might have prevented the War of 1812." See Charles Wiltse, "Thomas Jefferson on the Law of Nations", p. 80.

1115 Louis M. Sears, "Thomas Jefferson and the Law of Nations" *The American Political Science Review* 13, no. 3 (August 1919), pp. 398–399.

1116 Quoted in Horsman, *The Diplomacy of the New Republic, 1776–1815*, p. 109.

1117 [Two gentlemen at Halifax], "The Present Claims and Complaints of America", letter I, quoted in Onuf and Onuf, *Federal Union, Modern World*, p. 195.

vigorous assertion of their maritime rights."[1118] At the same time, the fact that with the Embargo Acts, the United States had *de facto* become part of Napoleon's Continental System[1119] did not give American ships any credit in French eyes, for in 1808 Napoleon further tightened French policy by seizing all American ships docked in French ports, arguing that these ships must actually be British given the self-imposed American embargo.[1120]

Within the American context, the puzzling consequence was that Jefferson's policies resulted in "[the] agricultural section of the country making immense sacrifices on behalf of commerce, which the commercial interest of the country (the eastern states) found unconstitutional, officious, tyrannical, and hostile to commerce."[1121] In other words, while the defense of neutral rights was supposed to serve commercial interests and were thus intimately linked, Jefferson actually "turned with a vengeance on the sordid motives of commercial men."[1122] The most painful point was possibly that rather than shoring up America's standing as a neutral power, the Embargo had actually damaged it.[1123] Thus, in spite of positive evaluations of the Embargo as "Jefferson's great experiment in pacifism" and a "test on a magnificent scale of a theory of international law",[1124] the fact that the United States had not only allowed its avowed principles to be compromised with impunity but had also engaged in the selfsame tactics as the British and the French made that its long-term reputation as a neutral power was now damaged beyond immediate repair.

What is more, the fundamental issues between the United States and Britain remained far from resolved. What is interesting here is that while arguing conflicting positions in legal terms is usually seen as a way to solve conflicts peacefully, between American and British authors, such arguments only helped to further fan the flames between the two sides. In general, the debates in the early 19th century revolved around "sharp disagreements over the content of the laws of war" which, as Witt noted, "produced radically divergent views on

---

1118 Horsman, *The Diplomacy of the New Republic, 1776–1815*, p. 107.

1119 Lawrence Kaplan, "Jefferson's Foreign Policy and Napoleon's Idéologues" *William and Mary Quarterly* 19 (3rd. series, July, 1962), p. 357.

1120 Bradford Perkins, *Cambridge History of American Foreign Relations*, Vol. 1, p. 129.

1121 David Hendrickson, *Union, Nation or Empire: The American Debate over International Relations, 1789–1941* (Lawrence, KS: University Press of Kansas, 2009), pp. 44–45.

1122 Robert Tucker and David Hendrickson, *Empire of Liberty: The Statecraft of Thomas Jefferson* (New York: Oxford University Press, 1992), p. 179.

1123 Henry Blumenthal, *France and the United States, Their Diplomatic Relations, 1789–1914* (Chapel Hill: The University of North Carolina Press, 1970), p. 21.

1124 Louis M. Sears, "Thomas Jefferson and the Law of Nations" *The American Political Science Review* 13, no. 3 (August 1919), pp. 398–399, 379.

the retaliation rights of the nations that claimed to be aggrieved."[1125] The result of this exchange of legal barbs was, in the words of British pamphleteer William Cobbett, an exacerbation of the conflict between Britain and the United States. "[T]he greatest curse of all," he said, were the "volumes innumerable [that have been] written on the subject," adding that what makes the issue even more serious was that most of these tracts were written by lawyers.[1126] In that regard, it did not help that Thomas Jefferson saw political conflicts mostly through an ideological-legalistic prism. Tucker and Hendrickson noted on this point that it was Jefferson's "deepest tendency (…) to convert questions of interest into matters of right and wrong, which then assumed a kind of independent character and became inseparably annexed to the honor and independence of the country."[1127] Thus, even if in practice Jefferson turned out to be more a realist than an idealist,[1128] this was only a matter of submitting to temporary inconveniences. The ultimate goal of Jeffersonian foreign policy continued to be premised on "reject[ing] existing realities and [seeking] to implement an ideal."[1129]

1125 John Fabian Witt, "The Power of War and Peace," draft chapter from *Lincoln's Code: The Laws of War in American History*. Presented at NYU legal history colloquium (February 17, 2010), p. 18. See also Robin Fabel, "The Laws of War in the 1812 Conflict" *Journal of American Studies* 14, no. 2 (1980), *passim*.

1126 William Cobbett, "Cobbett's Weekly Political Register" (January 13, 1810), in *Cobbett's Political Register*, Vol. XVII, p. 43.

1127 Robert Tucker and David Hendrickson, *Empire of Liberty: The Statecraft of Thomas Jefferson* (New York: Oxford University Press, 1992), p. 179.

1128 Louis M. Sears, "Thomas Jefferson and the Law of Nations" *The American Political Science Review* 13, no. 3 (August 1919), p. 383.

1129 Paul Varg, *Foreign Policies of the Founding Fathers*, p. 146.

CHAPTER 7

From the War of 1812 to the Monroe Doctrine

7.1 The War of 1812: Fighting Over the Law of Nations

When James Madison assumed the presidency in 1809, American foreign policy reverted to a more prudential course. Compared to Jefferson, Madison's ideological outlook on international affairs and the law of nations was much more sober. For one, Madison had toned down expansive definitions of neutral rights,[1130] making impressment a negligible issue after 1807. Philosophically speaking, Madison was neither satisfied by a law of nations grounded in balance-of-power principles nor one based on natural law. Neither could supply a justification for "a resort to arms" in his view.[1131] As we saw in the previous chapter, Madison sought a new basis for international law based on the perceived virtues of treaty law as a law of peace.[1132] In complementary fashion, Madison's foreign policy was guided by a "search for an alternative to war with Britain,"[1133] which had been looming for about a decade. However, Madison's aversion to military conflict and the repeal of the Embargo did not prove to be sufficient to avoid renewed strife between Washington and London.

While in Congress, a realization had set in that the restrictions imposed on exports had become unsustainable even in the short run due to serious domestic protest from merchants, the ardor for asserting neutral rights was still very much present. Thus, a new approach was adopted when in the House of Representatives, a bill was enacted in May 1810 to replace the burdensome Non-Intercourse Act. With this new piece of legislation, which came to be known as Macon's Bill no. 2, the export restrictions of the Non-Intercourse Act were repealed to open up trade with all countries, potentially including France and the United Kingdom. However, in regard to these two belligerents, the United States pledged to maintain non-intercourse measures against one power if the other was to lift its restrictions on American commerce.[1134]

1130 Peter Onuf and Nicholas Onuf, *Federal Union, Modern World* (Madison, WI: Madison House, 1993), p. 212.

1131 Onuf and Onuf, *Federal Union, Modern World,* p. 208.

1132 Onuf and Onuf, *Federal Union, Modern World*, p. 202.

1133 Bradford Perkins, *Cambridge History of American Foreign Relations*, Vol. 1, p. 87.

1134 Reginald Horsman, *The Diplomacy of the New Republic, 1776–1815* (Arlington Heights, Ill.: Harlan Davidson, 1985), p. 113; Paul Schroeder, *The Transformation of European Politics 1763–1848* (Oxford: Clarendon Press, 1994), pp. 437–438.

 | DOI 10.1163/9789004305687_009

Shortly thereafter, Napoleon decided to exploit this opportunity to stoke further tensions and possibly war between the United States and Britain by offering to revoke all restrictions against American ships provided that Britain would abolish its decrees aimed at the United States.[1135] With this objective in mind, president Madison tried throughout 1811 to persuade Britain to repeal its legislation in this regard, but without success. Consequently, Madison saw no other option but to prohibit British trade from reaching American shores.

War only became all but inevitable when in early 1812, a hawkish Congress was elected into office. Many general accounts of the era have it that the war was fought to avenge America's national honor.[1136] While this is true, the actual reasons behind it were continuing British infringements on American rights—at least in the perception of the Republican party. It needs to be added however that the French had disrespected American rights arguably just as much since Napoleon had come to power, and that Americans had regularly "evaded their own laws and bent the international rules in their favour."[1137] At one level, it could be said that a realist reading of the causes of the outbreak of the War of 1812 is correct; that is, that in contrast to the 1790s, employing the "tactics of the weak" were no longer considered acceptable for a rising power such as the United States.[1138] At the same time, however, while one could concede that the Republic was stronger in 1812 than it was in the 1790s, it was far from being on a par with Great Britain—and certainly not at sea. Also, it is difficult to argue that Congress voted for the war for economic or other strategic interests.[1139] If this were the case, then the Federalists should have been the cheerleaders, since their freedom to trade was at stake. But in fact, it were the Republicans who voted in favor of war, not carrying a single Federalist vote. So just as in the days of Jefferson, the Republicans stood up to fight over a principle that was ostensibly only in the interest of northeastern Federalist

1135 Perkins, *Cambridge History of American Foreign Relations*, Vol. 1, p. 131.

1136 Perkins, ibid., Vol. 1, p. 140; George Herring, *From Colony to Superpower:* U.S. *Foreign Relations since 1776* (New York: Oxford University Press, 2008), pp. 126–127; Kagan, *Dangerous Nation* (New York: Vintage Books, 2008) pp. 144–145; Gordon Wood, *Empire of Liberty: A History of the Early Republic 1789–1815* (New York: Oxford University Press, 2009), p. 659.

1137 Paul Schroeder, *The Transformation of European Politics 1763–1848*, p. 439.

1138 Kagan, *Dangerous Nation*, p. 145.

1139 In the literature, there has been a debate on whether territorial expansion into Canada was an actual reason for war, or whether it was just a means for putting Britain under pressure to concede at sea. See discussed in, e.g. Walter Nugent, *Habits of Empire: A History of American Expansion* (New York: Alfred Knopf, 2008), pp. 324–325. Most historians now seem to reject the claim that annexing Canada was a war objective.

merchants—who declined to support the war. As a result, it can be argued that for the Americans, the war was fought in the end to uphold rights to neutral commerce; it was a war fought over principles of the law of nations.[1140]

This also partly explains why it took several years for war to actually break out. It could as well have happened already in 1807 following the *Chesapeake* affair. But the "American faith in the law of nations" created a need to find a sufficient array of legal arguments to abet a *jus ad bellum* before exercising it.[1141] In terms of the legal justifications, the war had already been fought for several years prior to the military conflict. William Duane's work served in that respect almost as a legal equivalent of Paine's *Common Sense* with its strident and uncompromising language. For instance, he made short shrift of European claims to adhere to international law:

> This creation of arbitrary and jealous power has no foundation in reason or justice (…) it is at variance both with the sovereignty of every free state and the natural law of nations; it is barbarism restored. Yet, (…) this is a material part of that system, which at this day subjects all commercial states to evils that ought only to be felt by those engaged in wanton and wicked wars.[1142]

In Madisonian fashion, Duane added that if it were accepted that valid rights could be created in wartime, then "*the rights of belligerents are paramount to the rights of neutrals;* or in other words, the rights of robbers and murderers, [would be] superior to the rights of the peaceful and the virtuous."[1143]

British views were however equally self-righteous. A typical unrepentant tract in this vein was Joseph Chitty's 1812 *Treatise on the Law of Nations*.[1144] At the very outset of his book, he declared that "[n]o principle is more clearly established than that when war takes place between two nations, all

1140 Even Gordon Wood, who otherwise does not devote any attention to matters of international law in his standard work on the period acknowledges that the British Orders-in-Council and the impressment issue were a "major cause" of the outbreak of war. Wood, *Empire of Liberty*, p. 660.

1141 Reginald Stuart, *War and American Thought from the Revolution to the Monroe Doctrine* (Kent, OH: Kent State University Press, 1982), pp. 110–111.

1142 Duane, *The Law of Nations, Investigated in a Popular Manner*, p. 13.

1143 Duane, *The Law of Nations, Investigated in a Popular Manner*, p. 14 (emphasis in original).

1144 This is the same Chitty who also edited an English-language edition of Vattel's *Law of Nations* (1833).

commercial intercourse between them must cease."[1145] He wanted to be very clear in his repudiation of various neutral rights as claimed by the United States. For instance, while he granted the right of neutrals to continue their "accustomed trade," he denied that they had the right to carry a trade in wartime that was not available in peacetime,[1146] thus reaffirming the maligned Rule of 1756. Moreover, in spite of the earlier *Polly* ruling (1800), the *Essex* decision demonstrated to Chitty that the continuous voyage doctrine is unlawful.[1147] If this were not enough, he also continued to deny that the principle of 'free ships, free goods' is part of the law of nations,[1148] and condoned impressment on the high seas.[1149] Cobbett's acerbic comment quoted in the previous chapter was therefore fully warranted. Rather than helping to bring about a solution to the outstanding issues between the United States and Great Britain, legal treatises invariably only helped to further heighten the tension between the two nations.

In an address to Congress right before the vote on a declaration of war on June 1, 1812, Madison deliberately drew a sharp distinction between American and British motivations. With ample references to alleged violations of neutral rights, he carefully built up his case against Great Britain. One of the major issues he highlighted was of course the impressment question, one in which, Madison noted, "British jurisdiction is thus extended to neutral vessels in a situation where no laws can operate but the law of nations and the laws of the country to which the vessels belong." Another injury which Madison remonstrated against was the imposition of "pretended blockades." Most incisively, he noted that what rendered these "mock blockades (…) [which lacked] the presence of an adequate force" most insupportable was the fact that official British policy prescribed that blockades were only considered to be in place when "ports [are] actually invested and previous warning given to vessels bound to them not to enter." Having summed up American grievances, it was clear for Madison that British depredations with respect to American shipping were not grounded in a logic of war. Instead, he said, "[i]t has become, indeed,

1145 See Joseph Chitty, *A Practical Treatise on the Law of Nations, Relative to the Legal Effect of War on the Commerce of Belligerents and Neutrals* (Boston: Bradford and Reid, 1812), p. 1.

1146 Chitty, *A Practical Treatise on the Law of Nations*, pp. 159–165, with reference to the *Immanuel* case (2 C. Robinson 186, 1799), adjudged by Sir William Scott.

1147 Chitty, *A Practical Treatise on the Law of Nations*, pp. 181–182.

1148 Ibid., p. 118.

1149 Ibid., pp. 33, 37, 47.

sufficiently certain that the commerce of the United States is to be sacrificed, not as interfering with the belligerent rights of Great Britain; not as supplying the wants of her enemies, which she herself supplies; but as interfering with the monopoly which she covets for her own commerce and navigation." Madison, apparently believing that there was no inevitable need for commercial rivals to go to war, sadly observed that "[w]e behold, in fine, on the side of Great Britain, a state of war against the United States, and on the side of the United States a state of peace toward Great Britain."[1150]

The War of 1812 has also been called the "Second War for Independence," and there are indeed various parallels to be drawn between the two wars. To start with, Madison's very speech to Congress appears to have taken a cue from Jefferson's Declaration of Independence in the way it builds up its case against Britain, using predominantly legal language. In that way, both documents set the tone for conflicts which, from the American point of view, were conflicts over rights, and more specifically, one could argue, over the law of nations. John Quincy Adams made the point in so many words in a letter to Madison:

> It has been so uniformly and invariably the policy of the United States to keep themselves aloof from all the political combinations of Europe, that the British government seems to have taken it for granted that their controversies with us might always be managed upon principles not applicable to their intercourse with other powers, and that what they might be compelled to submit to as law of nations with the rest of Europe, they might break through with impunity in their relations with America. They (…) have alleged that it was a dispute involving principles of internal administration, as if the United States were a mere appendage to the British dominions.[1151]

The main reason why Americans would fight over rights was that in their view, rights were not merely instrumental, but carried moral connotations—which made a difference of opinion a non-negotiable issue.[1152] This was certainly also

1150 James Madison, "To the Senate and House of Representatives of the United States" (June 1, 1812), in *The Writings of James Madison*, Vol. 8, pp. 193–199.

1151 John Quincy Adams to James Madison (July 14, 1813), in *The Writings of John Quincy Adams*, Vol. 4, p. 494.

1152 According to Ziegler, the question of 'free ships, free goods' was "debated with more zeal and more vigor than any other in the late eighteenth and early nineteenth century [because] neutral nations, driven by their eager desire for greater material wealth, sought to extend their legal rights at the expense of belligerents (…)." Benjamin Ziegler, *The International Law of John Marshall* (Chapel Hill: The University of North Carolina Press, 1939), p. 239.

the case for James Madison. According to Onuf and Onuf, the key problem thus became that "Madison's conception of the modern law of nations presupposed what Britain did not believe—that the United States could function as one of many law-making sovereigns in world society. Only war could settle the point."[1153]

One of the often-mentioned ironies about the war was that within days of the adoption of the war resolution, the British government took the pragmatic decision to revoke the very Orders in Council that had been vexing American-British relations for so long and which were a prime cause for the war. The slow means of communication made it however impossible to stop the war in its tracks. And while the Americans had hoped that it would be a short affair, it lasted for two long years with considerable losses on the American side, including the burning of the new capital.[1154] The justness of the war was never in doubt, however. John Jay, for one, entertained the opinion that "[t]he law of all the nations prescribed the conduct which they were to observe towards each other, and allowed war to be waged by an innocent against an offending nation, when rendered just and necessary by unprovoked, atrocious, and unredressed injuries."[1155] At the same time, Madison emphasized again the fact that the United States was fighting the good war, on behalf of improving the law of nations so as to make it favor peaceful interaction:

> The Law of Nations has been made by the powerful nations; and these having been warlike in their dispositions and institutions, the law has been moulded to suit belligerent rather than peaceable nations. With the faculties for war, it is to be hoped, our country will continue friendly to peace, and exert the influence belonging to it, in promoting a system favorable to Nations cherishing peace and justice, rather than to those devoted to ambition and conquest.[1156]

1153 Peter Onuf and Nicholas Onuf, *Federal Union, Modern World* (Madison, WI: Madison House, 1993), p. 147.

1154 In fact, the British defended the burning of the capital under the laws of war by, *inter alia*, claiming that "the city had not been capitulated but abandoned" as well as that it was an act of retribution and/or retaliation following earlier American actions, being an assassination attempt at a British general and the destruction of York, a provincial capital in Canada. See quoted and discussed in Robin Fabel, "The Laws of War in the 1812 Conflict" *Journal of American Studies* 14, no. 2 (1980), pp. 210–211.

1155 John Jay to John Murray (April 15, 1818), in William Jay (ed.), *The Life of John Jay* (New York: J & J. Harper, 1833), p. 394. See discussed in Stuart, *War and American Thought from the Revolution to the Monroe Doctrine*, p. 156.

1156 Madison to C.J. Ingersoll (July 28, 1814), in *The Writings of James Madison*, Vol. 8, p. 286.

When the war was over and negotiations at Ghent for a peace treaty had been concluded, it became clear however that the United States had achieved few if any of its war objectives. Neither the impressment issue nor America's interpretation of neutral rights,[1157] which had been advanced as reasons for war, were mentioned in the peace treaty. Historian Gordon Wood claims that the fact that the Treaty of Ghent never even mentioned these issues "did not matter." In fact, he says,

> [a]lthough the treaty seemed to have settled none of the issues that had caused the War of 1812, it actually had settled everything. (…) It was not merely the fact that the end of the European war rendered the issue of neutral rights moot; more important was the fact that the results of the war vindicated what those issues had come to symbolize—the nation's independence and sovereignty.[1158]

This is true at least insofar as that the country felt that it had proved to itself that it was actually prepared to take up arms against the world's most powerful country in assertion of its claimed rights. The chief negotiators, John Quincy Adams, Henry Clay and Albert Gallatin did not suffer personally from the disappointing outcome, but the question about justifications for the war remained.[1159] At the same time, and in spite of the various real and alleged violations of the laws of war over the course of the conflict, one observer concluded that at least "the War of 1812 was fought on both sides with cognizance of a common code of rules essentially corresponding to Vattel's."[1160]

In the years following the 1814 Treaty, various attempts were undertaken to finally settle the searing points of contention between the United States and Britain, which included beyond the impressment and trade issues also slavery, boundaries and fisheries rights. When negotiating a new treaty, Albert Gallatin and Richard Rush proposed in 1818 to the British that in exchange for prohibiting

1157 Still, by the end of the war, Madison contended that practice and doctrine had altered in such way as to warrant the claim that "[w]ere the question [regarding free ships, free goods] to be regarded as unsettled, and open to fair discussion, I am persuaded, that the weight of authority furnished by reason, public good, treaties, and the luminaries of public law, preponderates in favor of [this] principle." See Madison to C.J. Ingersoll (July 28, 1814), in *The Writings of James Madison*, Vol. 8, pp. 283–284.

1158 Gordon Wood, *Empire of Liberty: A History of the Early Republic, 1789–1815*, p. 697.

1159 Paul Varg, *Foreign Policies of the Founding Fathers*, p. 300.

1160 Robin Fabel, "The Laws of War in the 1812 Conflict" *Journal of American Studies* 14, no. 2 (1980), p. 217. See, for a more detailed discussion on the outcomes of the negotiations in Ghent, ibid., pp. 214–216.

"native born British subjects" from serving on American ships, Britain would give up its practice of impressment.[1161] The British foreign secretary, Lord Castlereagh, was not prepared to go that far, and made a more limited counter-proposal: he would agree to abolishing the practice of impressment, but with two conditions attached: (1) it will be a limited treaty in time (i.e. 8–12 years), with a period for abrogation of a few months' notice, and (2) British officers would have the right to board a ship for inspection, but the decision to transfer someone into British hands would be in the hands of the American authorities. The first point was not an issue for the United States delegation, but the second was vehemently objected to. Shortly thereafter, Castlereagh in fact conceded the second point, which opened the way for a treaty to be concluded that would put a definitive end to impressment.

This was not the only issue the Americans wished to see resolved, however. Another concerned free trade. On this point, the American negotiators pushed for a fuller treaty on commerce and navigation, based on reciprocal relations between the United States and British colonies in North America (including in the West Indies). Castlereagh was however not prepared to go beyond a renewal of the Commercial Convention of 1815, which was much more limited in scope.[1162]

A final issue that was raised and which was left unresolved at Ghent pertained the return of slaves who had fled into British territory. It had been mentioned briefly in article one of the 1814 treaty, but had never been acted upon due to differences in interpretation. When the question was taken up again in 1818, the negotiators agreed to disagree and to submit the matter to arbitration. Russian Czar Alexander I was subsequently asked to arbitrate the dispute. In the course of the proceedings, the American representative Henry Middleton—a slave owner from South Carolina—claimed that attempts at emancipating slaves by the enemy constituted a violation of the law of nations. Indeed, the institution of slavery as such—even if seriously contested in the United States itself—had been defended by the negotiators at Ghent, who demanded a return of slaves arguing they constitute private property. In 1820, the Czar ruled that the American interpretation of the treaty was the correct one.[1163] Meanwhile, a comprehensive treaty that dealt with all major issues

---

1161 Samuel F. Bemis, "The Convention of 1818," in Patrick White (ed.), *The Critical Years: American Foreign Policy 1793–1823* (New York: John Wiley & Sons, 1970), pp. 130–131.

1162 Bemis, "The Convention of 1818," p. 131.

1163 John Fabian Witt, "The Power of War and Peace," draft chapter from *Lincoln's Code: The Laws of War in American History*. Presented at NYU legal history colloquium (February 17, 2010), p. 26.

eluded both sides due to a perceived technical loophole.[1164] The result was that the treaty that was eventually signed only dealt with four issues: fisheries, boundary demarcations, navigation rights and trade.

The disappointing outcome of the War of 1812 and the subsequent failed attempts at redressing the remaining thorny legal questions did not dent American confidence in ability of the law of nations as a means for promoting American aims. One arena in which this was clearly reflected was the Supreme Court, whose legal philosophy had scarcely changed since the late 18th century. A typical example includes the *Venus* case, in which Chief Justice John Marshall declared that the law of nations was "founded on the great and immutable principles of equity and natural justice."[1165] In *Thirty Hogsheads of Sugar v. Boyle*, Marshall further expounded on the Court's philosophical position while commenting on the influence of foreign pronouncements on the law:

> the law of nations is the great source from which we derive those rules respecting belligerent and neutral rights which are recognized by all civilized and commercial states throughout Europe and America. (…) [A]s these principles will be differently understood by different nations under different circumstances, we consider them as being in some degree fixed and rendered stable by a series of judicial decisions. The decisions of the courts of every country, so far as they are founded upon a law common to every country, will be received not as authority, but with respect.[1166]

1164 Bemis, "The Convention of 1818," p. 141. The issue was that the second article stipulated that each party would "draw up and deliver to the other within eighteen months following 'signature' a list of all the naturalized seamen known to be in its maritime service at that date. (…) The American negotiators explained in great detail that it would be impracticable and impossible to get up a definitive list because of the previous deficiencies of their Federal and state registration laws. (…) Constitutional doubts over *ex post facto* legislation (…) impelled them to insist that the list itself go into effect only at ratification of the treaty rather than from its signature." According to the British, this would create unacceptable loopholes, allowing "hordes of British seamen to naturalize themselves before the treaty went into effect."

1165 12 U.S. (8 Cranch), 253, 1814, at 297. This case concerned a ship captured by Americans, where the owner was American but resided in Britain, and whereby the capture took place after the declaration of war of the United States against Britain with the owner being unaware of the state of war. The Court decided that the captured goods were subject to seizure nonetheless.

1166 13 U.S. (9 Cranch), 191, 1815, at 198. In this case, the Supreme Court considered whether goods shipped from an island, Santa Cruz, that later became British, should be considered enemy goods, liable to capture. Since the goods were shipped after the island was captured by the British, they were considered such.

The longest-serving Chief Justice on the Supreme Court, a student of George Wythe in Williamsburg and a great admirer of George Washington (about whom he wrote a five-volume biography), Marshall has been difficult to categorize as a legal thinker.[1167] The statements above suggested a natural-law approach, and indeed, it has been said that for him, the law of nations and nature continued to be "closely allied concepts."[1168] The same point appeared in the *Nereide* case.[1169] Quincy Wright, one of the most distinguished scholars in the field, said that even if Marshall believed that "the courts apply national law alone," he was also influenced by notions of higher law in his understanding of the incorporation of international law into the law of the United States.[1170] As an envoy to France in the XYZ affair in 1798, Marshall wrote to France's Foreign Minister in a letter that "the law of nations (…) forms (…) a rule of action by which the sovereignties of the civilized world consent to be governed."[1171] Hence, if anything, Marshall's legal philosophy can well be called eclectic.

1167 Benjamin Ziegler, *The International Law of John Marshall* (Chapel Hill: The University of North Carolina Press, 1939), p. 9. See also discussed in Richard Brisbin, "John Marshall and the Nature of Law in the Early Republic" *The Virginia Magazine for History and Biography* 98, no. 1 (1990), pp. 59–62.

1168 G. Edward White, "The Marshall Court and International Law: The Piracy Cases" *American Journal of International Law* 83, no. 4 (October 1989), pp. 728–729. With reference to prize law, Marshall said that America's former attachment to Britain ought not to be left out of consideration: "The United States having at one time formed a component part of the British Empire, their prize law was our prize law. When we separated, it continued to be our prize law so far as it was adapted to our circumstances and was not varied by the power which was capable of changing it." See *Thirty Hogsheads of Sugar v. Boyle,* 13 U.S. (9 Cranch), 191, 1815, at 198.

1169 Anthony Bellia and Bradford Clark, "The Federal Common Law of Nations" *Columbia Law Review* 109 (January, 2009), pp. 73–74. The *Nereide* case concerned a claim for restitution of Spanish goods belonging to a merchant in Buenos Aires from a British ship that was seized by an American privateer during the War of 1812. In the decision, the court ruled against the government -and applied Vattel's- dictum on the issue, namely, that it is the nationality of the person to whom the goods belong that prevails, and not the nationality of the ship on which the goods are carried. See also Vattel, *The Law of Nations,* Bk III, Ch. 5, p. 510.

1170 Quincy Wright, *The Enforcement of International Law Through Municipal Law in the United States* (Urbana, IL: University of Illinois, 1916), p. 225.

1171 Charles C. Pinckney, John Marshall and Elbridge Gerry, "To the Minister of Foreign Affairs of the French Republic" (January 27, 1798), in *American State Papers: Foreign Relations,* Vol. 2, p. 171.

Still, the Court's natural law tendencies did not imply that the principles of the law of nations always carried the day versus domestic imperatives. As a general rule, as White noted, "the Justices [of the Marshall court] believed [that] natural law might yield to the positive enactments of sovereign nations."[1172] But at the same time, Marshall and his colleagues were also careful not to overstretch the authority they claimed. A pattern in this respect was already shaped before the War of 1812. In the case *Rose v. Himely*[1173] Marshall discussed the influence of foreign court rulings in other jurisdictions. Stating that "the law of nations is the law of all tribunals in the society of nations, and is supposed to be equally understood by all,"[1174] he found that sentences of courts abroad could only be ignored if they overstepped their own jurisdiction (which thus included the law of nations as a rule). Another prominent case in this genre was *Schooner Exchange vs. M'Faddon et.al.*[1175] While this ruling has clear political overtones,[1176] the result was that Marshall chose to interpret the law very strictly in terms of constitutional law, saying that "[t]he jurisdiction of the nation within its own territory is necessarily exclusive and absolute. It is susceptible of no limitation not imposed by itself." Hence, the rights of foreign sovereigns had to be "traced up to the consent of the nation itself," the consequence being that executive or legislative decisions could overrule the law of nations.[1177] In a subsequent case one year later, *Williams v. Armroyd*, the Supreme Court conceded that even if a foreign court decision "is avowedly made under a decree subversive of the law of nations, [it] will not help the

1172 G. Edward White, "The Marshall Court and International Law: The Piracy Cases" *American Journal of International Law* 83, no. 4 (October 1989), p. 729.

1173 *Rose v. Himely* 8 U.S. (4 Cranch), 241, 1808.

1174 *Rose v. Himely* 8 U.S. (4 Cranch), 241, 1808, at 277.

1175 11 U.S. 116 (7 Cranch), 3 L.Ed. 287, 1812.

1176 The case concerned a ship, the schooner *Exchange*, owned by two Americans, which was seized on December 30, 1810 by the French authorities and refitted as a public vessel called the *Balaou*. Once the ship moored again in an American port, they filed a claim demanding restitution of their property, holding that the French seizure had been illegal. Because of French involvement in the War of 1812 in support of the Americans, the Supreme Court was not easily disposed to rule in favor of the alleged former American owners. The court ruled that the Constitution did not provide for jurisdiction in cases such as this where consent of the foreign sovereign is required in order to submit to "ordinary judicial tribunals." Indeed, unless there is an express declaration to the contrary, it could not be presumed that a foreign military vessel would submit itself to the ordinary jurisdiction of a foreign country when entering the port of a friendly nation—especially not when as the result of distress, as was the case here. Marshall therefore decided that the *Exchange* was exempted from American jurisdiction. See 11 U.S. (7 Cranch), at 146.

1177 11 U.S. (7 Cranch), at 136, 144.

appellant's case, in a court which cannot revise, correct, or even examine that sentence."[1178]

Apart from conflicts between municipal law and the law of nations, the courts also had to deal with conflicts between the natural and positive law of nations. This came most conspicuously and controversially to the fore in regard to the slave trade. It had become prohibited in the United States in 1808 (though not domestically between states!) and was put on an equal footing with piracy through an Act of Congress in 1820, making it a punishable crime no matter where it was committed. The first case to reach a court only arrived in 1821. In concerned a French vessel, the *Jeune Eugenie*, which had been seized by an American ship off the coast of Africa, being suspected to engage in the slave trade. The question that the sitting judge, Joseph Story, had to adjudicate was whether the schooner could be condemned on the basis of being in violation of American legislation and the law of nations, or whether it had to be released either because the slave trade had to be deemed permissible under international law or simply because it was subject to French municipal regulations. For someone like Story, the question proved to be a monumental dilemma—the echoes of which went back to Roman times, when Ulpianus found that while slavery was contrary to natural law, it did exist under the law of nations.[1179] Slavery had been known for centuries as a category of international law in the Christian world, and was by and large adopted by the English and introduced by them in the American colonies.[1180]

Addressing the issue from the point of customary law, Story noted "that [slavery] has existed in all ages of the world, and has been tolerated by some, encouraged by others, and sanctioned by most, of the enlightened and civilized nations of the earth in former ages, admits of no reasonable question. (…) Sitting, therefore, in an American court of judicature, I am not permitted to deny, that under some circumstances it may have a lawful existence; and that the practice may be justified by the condition, or wants, of society, or may form a part of the domestic policy of a nation. It would be unbecoming in me here to assert, that the state of slavery cannot have a legitimate

1178 11 U.S. (7 Cranch), at 433. The syllabus summarized the decision as such: "A sentence of a foreign tribunal condemning neutral property under an edict unjust in itself, contrary to the law of nations, and in violation of neutral rights, and which has been so declared by the legislative and executive departments of the government of the United States, changes the property of the thing condemned."

1179 See Charles Mullett, *Fundamental Law and the American Revolution*, p. 17.

1180 Christopher Tomlins, *Freedom Bound: Law, Labor, and Civic Identity in Colonizing English America, 1580–1865* (Cambridge: Cambridge University Press, 2010), pp. 423–424.

existence, or that it stands condemned by the unequivocal testimony of the law of nations."[1181]

Having conceded this point, Story went on to say that "[it] carries us but a very short distance towards the decision of this cause," following which he makes a very impassioned argument condemning the slave trade and appealing to one's consciousnesses:

> It is not, as the learned counsel for the government have justly stated, on account of the simple fact, that the traffic necessarily involves the enslavement of human beings, that it stands reprehended by the present sense of nations; but that it necessarily carries with it a breach of all the moral duties, of all the maxims of justice, mercy and humanity, and of the admitted rights, which independent Christian nations now hold sacred in their intercourse with each other. What is the fact as to the ordinary, nay necessary course, of this trade? It begins in corruption, and plunder, and kidnapping. It creates and stimulates unholy wars for the purpose of making captives. It desolates whole villages and provinces for the purpose of seizing the young, the feeble, the defenceless, and the innocent. It breaks down all the ties of parent, and children, and family, and country. It shuts up all sympathy for human suffering and sorrows. It manacles the inoffensive females and the starving infants. It forces the brave to untimely death in defence of their humble homes and firesides, or drives them to despair and self-immolation. It stirs up the worst passions of the human soul, darkening the spirit of revenge, sharpening the greediness of avarice, brutalizing the selfish, envenoming the cruel, famishing the weak, and crushing to death the broken-hearted. This is but the beginning of the evils. Before the unhappy captives arrive at the destined market, where the traffic ends, one quarter part at least, in the ordinary course of events perish in cold blood under the inhuman, or thoughtless treatment of their oppressors.

In summary, Story said, "[t]here is," as one of the greatest of modern statesmen has declared, "something of horror in it, that surpasses all the bounds of imagination."[1182] As a consequence, he firmly rejected appeals to custom to establish a legal basis for the existence of the slave trade:

1181 *Report on the Case of the Jeune Eugenie, Determined in the Circuit Court of the United States, for the First Circuit, at Boston, December 1821* (Boston: Wells and Lilly, 1822), pp. 68–69.

1182 *Report on the Case of the Jeune Eugenie,* pp. 69–70. Story quotes here from a speech by William Pitt the Younger on the slave trade, 1792.

> We are not to be told, that war is lawful, and slavery lawful, and plunder lawful, and the taking away of life is lawful, and the selling of human beings is lawful. Assuming that they are so under circumstances, it establishes nothing. It does not advance one jot to the support of the proposition, that a traffic, that involves them all, that is unnecessary, unjust, and inhuman, is countenanced by the eternal law of nature, on which rests the law of nations.

Having thus rejected any resort to custom or even treaty law, he then proceeded to frame the issue in natural-law terms. The undeniable key point was, according to Story, that the slave trade

> is founded in a violation of some of the first principles, which ought to govern nations. It is repugnant to the great principles of Christian duty, the dictates of natural religion, the obligations of good faith and morality, and the eternal maxims of social justice. When any trade can be truly said to have these ingredients, it is impossible, that it can be consistent with any system of law, that purports to rest on the authority of reason or revelation. And it is sufficient to stamp any trade as interdicted by public law, when it can be justly affirmed, that it is repugnant to the general principles of justice and humanity.[1183]

Story's ruling was very clear. While he humbly acknowledged the fact that American courts cannot pretend to speak for courts everywhere,[1184] he found that "the slave trade is a trade prohibited by universal law and by the law of France, and that, therefore, the claim of the asserted French owners must be rejected."[1185]

1183 *Report on the Case of the Jeune Eugenie*, pp. 73–74.

1184 Having said that "[i]t appears to me, (...) that in an American court of judicature, I am bound to consider the trade an offence against the universal law of society," he added that "[n]o one has a right to sit in judgment generally upon the actions of another; at least to the extent of compelling its adherence to all the principles of justice and humanity in its domestic concerns. (...) No nation has ever yet pretended to be the *custos morum* of the whole world; and though abstractedly a particular regulation may violate the law of nations, it may sometimes, in the case of nations, be a wrong without a remedy." *Report on the Case of the Jeune Eugenie*, pp. 75–77.

1185 *Report on the Case of the Jeune Eugenie*, p. 91.

In Story's case, natural law prevailed over positive law. However, in the first case on the slave trade before the Supreme Court, judge Marshall had ruled in the opposite direction. With apparent regret, he concluded in the *Antelope* case that

> the Christian and civilized nations of the world, with whom we have most intercourse, have all been engaged in [the slave trade]. However abhorrent this traffic may be to a mind whose original feelings are not blunted by familiarity with the practice, it has been sanctioned in modern times by the laws of all nations who possess distant colonies, each of whom has engaged in it as a common commercial business which no other could rightfully interrupt. It has claimed all the sanction which could be derived from long usage, and general acquiescence. That trade could not be considered as contrary to the law of nations which was authorized and protected by the laws of all commercial nations; the right to carry on which was claimed by each, and allowed by each.[1186]

What is more, rather than judging the lawfulness of a slave-trading vessel on the basis of the law of nations, Marshall took municipal law as the basis for his considerations,[1187] adding the caveat that "[i]n the United States, different opinions have been entertained in the different circuits and districts."[1188] Without further discussing these American precedents, Marshall went straight into discussing the merits under the law of nations. "That [the slave

1186 23 U.S. (10 Wheat.) 66, 1825, at 114–115. This case concerned a claim by the Portuguese and Spanish governments to restore to them slaves captured from their ships by an American-controlled vessel. Under the law of nations and under American law, such slaves were entitled to freedom, the slave trade having been prohibited.

1187 At this point, he also refers to a case adjudicated by Sir William Scott, saying he held that "[t]he act of trading in slaves, however detestable, was not, he said, "the act of freebooters, enemies of the human race, renouncing every country, and ravaging every country, in its coasts and vessels, indiscriminately." It was not piracy. He also said that this trade could not be pronounced contrary to the law of nations. "A court, in the administration of law, cannot attribute criminality to an act where the law imputes none. It must look to the legal standard of morality; and, upon a question of this nature, that standard must be found in the law of nations, as fixed and evidenced by general, and ancient, and admitted practice, by treaties, and by the general tenor of the laws and ordinances, and the formal transactions of civilized states; and, looking to those authorities, he found a difficulty in maintaining that the transaction was legally criminal."" 23 U.S. (10 Wheat.) 66, 1825, at 118–119.

1188 23 U.S. (10 Wheat.) 66, 1825, at 120.

trade] is contrary to the law of nature" Marshall said, "will scarcely be denied. But, he added, "as the world has agreed that it is a legitimate result of force, the state of things which is thus produced by general consent, cannot be pronounced unlawful." He supports his argument with a revealing insight into his legal reasoning—showing himself to be eminently positivist in his approach:

> Whatever might be the answer of a moralist to this question, a jurist must search for its legal solution in those principles of action which are sanctioned by the usages, the national acts, and the general assent of that portion of the world of which he considers himself as a part, and to whose law the appeal is made. If we resort to this standard as the test of international law, the question, as has already been observed, is decided in favor of the legality of the trade. Both Europe and America embarked in it; and for nearly two centuries it was carried on without opposition, and without censure. A jurist could not say that a practice thus supported was illegal, and that those engaged in it might be punished, either personally, or by deprivation of property.[1189]

Given that the slave trade was not illegal under international law, Marshall also dismissed the claim that equated it with piracy, implicitly including the American statute of 1820 that defined it as such. Being left with municipal law, he said that "[since] the courts of no country execute the penal laws of another (...) [i]t follows, that a foreign vessel engaged in the African slave trade, captured on the high seas in time of peace, by an American cruiser, and brought in for adjudication, would be restored."[1190] A closer subsequent investigation of the particular facts led to a judgement in favor of the claimant. Of course, the larger issue of slavery would continue to hover over American law and politics for another four decades. But in spite of its discouraging outcome, the *Antelope* case also contained elements that indicate a definite awareness of the harrowing nature of the slave trade, promising a future in which the law of nations and morality could be brought into agreement. Monroe hinted at this future when he said that "[the slave trade] is an abominable practice, against which

1189 23 U.S. (10 Wheat.) 66, 1825, at 121–122.

1190 23 U.S. (10 Wheat.) 66, 1825, at 123. Elsewhere, Marshall added that "[n]o principle of general law is more universally acknowledged than the perfect equality of nations. Russia and Geneva have equal rights. It results from this equality, that no one can rightfully impose a rule on another. (...) As no nation can prescribe a rule for others, none can make a law of nations (...)." ibid., pp. 121–122.

nations are now combining, & it may be presumed that the combination will soon become universal."[1191]

On the key tenet of America's foreign policy—neutrality—the Supreme Court made no significant concessions. The only point at which the Court could not explicitly affirm the American position was on the 'free ships, free goods' doctrine, which was one of the key issues in *The Nereide*. In the case, Marshall noted that while the armed neutrality had been a valiant—but failed—attempt at "a great revolution in the law of nations," the American record up to 1815 turned out to be a mixed bag:

> [I]n the various treaties which have been formed, some contain no article on the subject, and consequently leave the ancient rule in full force. Some stipulate that the character of the cargo shall depend upon the flag, some that the neutral flag shall protect the goods of an enemy, some that the goods of a neutral in the vessel of a friend shall be prize of war, and some that the goods of an enemy in a neutral bottom shall be safe, and that friendly goods in the bottom of an enemy shall also be safe.[1192]

In the case of *The Hazard*, the same question came before the Supreme Court, but it declined to discuss the matter, simply affirming an earlier decision by the Circuit Court in Georgia.[1193]

On matters of prize law, the Court defended America's neutrality ever more strongly. One example is *Hudson v. Guestier*, in which Justice Marshall observed that "the practice of condemning prizes of war while lying in neutral ports has prevailed in England and has been adopted in France." While he considered this deplorable, and believed that "[t]he objections to this practice may perhaps be sufficient to induce nations to change it by common consent," the reality was that "until they change it, the practice must be submitted to, and the sentence of condemnation passed under such circumstances will bind the property unless the Legislature of the country in which the captured vessel may be claimed or the law of nations, shall otherwise direct."[1194] However,

1191 Monroe to Daniel Bennett (September 17, 1821), in *The Writings of James Monroe*, Vol. 6, p. 196. To encourage this process, the House of Representatives had passed a resolution in February 23rd, 1823 to the end of requesting the president to strive, by way of concluding treaties, for "the effectual abolition of the African slave trade, and its ultimate denunciation as piracy under the law of nations, by the consent of the civilized world." Monroe to the United States Senate (May 21, 1824), in *The Writings of James Monroe*, Vol. 7, p. 24.

1192 13 U.S. (9 Cranch), at 421.

1193 13 U.S. 205 (Cranch), 1815.

1194 8 U.S. (4 Cranch) 293, 1808, at 295.

when the Napoleonic wars had ended, the Court's approach became more strident again in terms of defending the country's neutral prerogatives. For instance, in the case *Alerta v. Moran*, the court used unequivocal language, affirming that whenever captures are made within the territorial waters of a neutral, its prize courts have sole jurisdiction over such captures. In addition, it reaffirmed with reference to the 1794 Neutrality laws that under American law, "the illegality of equipping a foreign vessel of war within the territory of the United States (…) is clearly recognized."[1195]

At the same time, there was also a continuing recognition that upholding neutrality meant making violations against the law of nations punishable under municipal laws. In 1805, Treasury Secretary Albert Gallatin said as much in conjunction with illegal trade concerning the rebelling French colony of St. Domingue. As a principle, he believed that neutral countries "are not obliged to enforce the law of nations by positive statutes against their own subjects or citizens. (…) Nor are nations bound to pass laws prohibiting to their subjects or citizens commerce, such as that with the colonies of another nation, which is illicit only by reason of the particular statutes of other nations." In reality, however, "it [had to] be allowed that there are circumstances under which the conduct of illicit traders might go such length, especially if they shall use force, as would render it necessary for the purpose of preserving national peace that the country to which they belong should, by prohibitory or restrictive statutes, prevent the acts of violence which endanger that peace."[1196]

In order to address and mitigate jurisdictional issues, president Madison decided in 1816 to reinforce America's neutrality laws. He noted that "[i]t is found that the existing laws have not the efficacy necessary to prevent violations of the obligations of the United States as a nation as peace toward belligerent parties and other unlawful acts on the high seas by armed vessels equipped within the waters of the United States."[1197] It being the "era of good feelings," Congress gladly obliged, passing new neutrality legislation on March 3, 1817, and on April 20, 1818, which, taken together, provided a comprehensive set of laws that was to guide the conduct of American foreign relations for many decades, if Henry Adams's words are to be believed:

1195 13 U.S. (9 Cranch), at 365.

1196 Albert Gallatin to S. Mitchell (January 3, 1805), in *The Writings of Albert Gallatin*, Vol. 1, pp. 220–221.

1197 James Madison "Special Message to Congress" (December 26, 1816), in John B. Moore and Francis Wharton (eds.), *A Digest of International Law* (…) (Washington DC: Government Printing Office, 1906), Vol. 1, p. 172.

> Nearly fifty years were to pass before the people of the United States learned to realize the full importance of [these Acts], which laid the foundation for all the subsequent measures taken by the United States and Great Britain for preserving neutrality in their relations with warring countries.[1198]

Adams was not the only one to have praised America's neutrality policy in the first decades of its existence. During a parliamentary debate in April of 1823, the British Foreign Secretary, George Canning, said that "[i]f I wished for a guide in a system of Neutrality, I should take that laid down by America in the days of the presidency of Washington and the secretaryship of Jefferson."[1199] A 20th century legal scholar concluded that America's neutrality policy "was inspired by a high conception of neutrality and won the praise of foreign statesmen and writers."[1200] Therewith, neutrality had become firmly established as a key tenet of American foreign policy—a stance to which the country had become ideologically wedded, and which was by now solidly anchored in the law of nations.

7.2 To the Monroe Doctrine

While the country's neutrality policy was an expression of its revolutionary tendencies, its westward continental strategy was motivated by more conservative inclinations. To put the distinction more sharply: whereas America's objective in terms of the law of nations at sea was to differentiate itself from Europe, with respect to the continent it was rather the opposite, developing a discourse which bound the country together with Europe while excluding others, beginning with the North American natives. This discourse centered around the ideas of civilization in conjunction with Christianity, which were from the beginning closely entwined with the law of nations. A typical example of the operation of this discriminatory concept appeared in a dissenting opinion by judge Marshall in the 1814 *Venus* case, in which he stated that the law of nations is a rule that is "admitted by all such as are civilized."[1201]

1198 Henry Adams, *History of the United States of America during the Administrations of James Madison* (New York: Library of America, 1986), p. 1282.

1199 *Hansard's Parliamentary Debates*, Vol. VIII, p. 1056. Quoted in Charles Hyneman, "Neutrality during the European Wars of 1792–1815, p. 308.

1200 Arthur Nussbaum, *A Concise History of the Law of Nations*, p. 134.

1201 See *The Venus*. 12 U.S. (8 Cranch), 253, 297, 1814. Quoted in Dickinson, *The Law of Nations*, p. 13, fn. 8.

Among the biggest champions of this civilizational cum Christian basis for the law of nations was John Quincy Adams, who became well-known in the first half of the 19th century for his staunchly nationalist views. The peace negotiations in Ghent provided an early occasion on which Adams enunciated such ideas, in particular with reference to the natives. Deploring the use natives as middlemen doing the martial bidding of the British to fight against the Americans, he proposed to include an article prohibiting a mode of warfare which either country should deign to practice:

> [T]he employment of savages, whose known rule of warfare is the indiscriminate torture and butchery of women, children, and prisoners, is itself a departure from the principles of humanity observed between all civilized and Christian nations even in war. [Great Britain herself employs them only in her wars against the United States and] the United States have constantly protested and still protest against it as an unjustifiable aggravation of the barbarities and horrors of war.

As examples of inadmissible modes of warfare, he noted "the massacre of wounded prisoners in cold blood, and the refusal of the rites of burial to the dead, under the eyes of British officers, who could only plead their inability to control those savage auxiliaries, have been repeated and are notorious to the world." Still, Adams would not be the kind of proud American nationalist had he not gone on to draw a distinction between British and American practice, essentially demonstrating to London that America is more faithful to Christian and civilizational principles than the presumed cradle of modern civilization itself:

> The United States have with extreme reluctance been compelled to resort on their part to the same mode of warfare thus practiced against them. The United States might at all times have employed the same kind of force against Great Britain, and to a greater extent than it was in her power to employ it against them; but from their reluctance to resort to means so abhorrent to the natural feelings of humanity, they abstained from the use of them, until compelled to the alternative of employing themselves Indians who would otherwise have been drawn into the ranks of their enemies. (...)[1202]

1202 John Quincy Adams, "Answer to the British Commissioners" (September 9, 1814), in *The Writings of John Quincy Adams*, Vol. 5, pp. 125–126.

Although a prominent example, Adams was of course not the only one to express such views. Another representative and significant statement comes from the Attorney-General, William Wirt, who submitted the following consideration in response to a question whether the Cherokees could levy a federal tax on people with whom they engaged in trade.

> If the Cherokee nation is to be considered as an independent sovereign nation, and this question is to be answered by an appeal to the natural law of nations, there can be no doubt of their right to pass what laws they please, and to enforce whatsoever laws they may choose to pass within the limits of their proper sovereignty. But it appears to me that it would be fallacious to view the subject in this light. The history and condition of those people, the relations which we have borne and still bear towards them, and the treaties which subsist between them and the United States, will not permit us to regard the question as one between equal sovereigns, to be decided by the laws of nature as applied to nations. Whatsoever philosophy or philanthropy might, in the abstract, dictate upon this subject, we are constrained to look at things as they are, and to decide this question upon narrower grounds. Still, however, it is not to be decided by our arbitrary pleasure. The time has passed away in which it would be tolerated to treat these people as we please, because we are Christians and they are heathens.[1203]

So, Adams' and Wirt's statements provide solid evidence that the natives—even if they could be considered to be constituted of "independent sovereign nations"—could continue to be denied rights (and duties) under the law of nations because they lacked civilizational or Christian traits, even if attitudes towards them were gradually changing.

But the natives were not the only ones who were considered beyond the realm of civilization. The same applied to most if not all other countries beyond the self-proclaimed North Atlantic civilization. In this respect, Adams specifically defined a concept of a "Christian law of nations." In his understanding, this entailed "not one code of laws, binding alike upon all the nations on earth, but a system of rules, varying according to the character and condition of the parties concerned, [whereby the necessary law] can be enforced only between

1203 William Wirt to the Secretary of War (April 2, 1824), in Benjamin Hall (ed.), *Official Opinions of the Attorneys-General of the United States* (Washington DC: R. Farnham, 1852), Vol. 1, p. 645.

nations who recognize the principle that a state is a state of peace."[1204] To put the point beyond any doubt, Adams said that this law as it applies between Christian nations "is the law recognized by the constitution and laws of the United States, as obligatory upon them in their intercourse with the European states and colonies."[1205] What is however interesting about Adams' discourse is that he did not just draw a distinction between civilized and non-civilized nations, but went on to claim that there existed many more kinds of international law: "We have a separate and different Law of Nations for the regulation of our intercourse with the Indian tribes of our own Continent; another law of nations between us and the woolly-headed natives of Africa—another with the Barbary Powers and the Sultan of the Ottoman Empire—a law of nations with the inhabitants of the Isles of the Sea (...) and, lastly, a law of nations with the flowery land, the Celestial Empire, the Mantchou Tartar dynasty of Despotism (...)."[1206] A lone but interesting dissenting voice in this regard came from William Duane, whose progressive disposition and scepticism towards religion as a motivating factor make him a veritable torch-bearer of Enlightenment ideas into the 19th century:

> If the maxims of Christianity were practised by its preachers or professors, the moral law would supercede the necessity of a law of nations; but unfortunately the greatest violators of national and social order, are those who employ the name, of "religion and order," as a mask to cover outrages upon all mankind.[1207]

Duane's solitary protests had little effect on American thinking and practice, however; most certainly not when it came to territorial expansion. In that respect, the United States pursued its goals with at times preciously little regard for that selfsame law of nations which it guarded so dearly in its maritime affairs.

1204 John Quincy Adams, "Lecture on the War with China" (Massachusetts Historical Society), *Niles' National Register* (January 22, 1842), p. 326. It goes without saying that the reference to a "state of peace" serves to exclude non-Christian states as well as "savage nations," like American natives etc.

1205 John Quincy Adams, "Lecture on the War with China" (Massachusetts Historical Society), *Niles' National Register* (January 22, 1842), p. 326.

1206 John Quincy Adams, "Lecture on the War with China", p. 326.

1207 William Duane, *The Law of Nations, Investigated in a Popular Manner* (Philadelphia, William Duane, 1809), p. 3.

The story of the acquisition of the Floridas is a good illustration of how the United States was struggling with its commitment to the law of nations and eventually chose to bend or circumvent the law for ulterior purposes. The Floridas, made up of two separate areas called East and West Florida, had been Spanish property before 1763, when it fell in British hands. The colonies, which stretched from the Mississippi to the Atlantic coast, were returned to Spain in 1783 at the end of the Revolutionary war. The United States had eyed the Floridas since the early days of the Republic, and became more intent on acquiring it when the Spanish permitted it to be used as a base for attacks by native tribes. Already in 1800, Rufus King, Minister to the Court of St. James, had declared that the U.S. "should be unwilling to see [Florida and Louisiana] transferred except to ourselves," a statement that presaged the Monroe doctrine some 23 years later.[1208] In 1804, Jefferson sent James Monroe to Madrid to join Charles Pinckney in an effort to negotiate a treaty to obtain the Floridas. Spain was however not to open to this. In 1808, Jefferson sensed another opportunity at acquiring the Floridas after Napoleon had invaded Spain the year before, thinking rather unrealistically that Napoleon would be happy to obtain America's neutral trade with the Spanish colonies in the Americas in exchange for lifting some of his trade decrees and perhaps also to cede the Floridas to the United States in the process.[1209] It was another example where Jefferson overestimated the geopolitical importance of the United States.

Only in 1810 was a first serious move made when on October 27, Madison unilaterally annexed West Florida up to the Pearl River, claiming that this territory had always been part of the United States by virtue of the Louisiana Purchase.[1210] The immediate occasion was a rebellion that had been under way in the area since June. This questionable seizure was followed by the adoption of a secret resolution at Madison's request, stating that "the United States (…) cannot, without serious inquietude, see any part of [Florida] pass into the hands of any foreign power," adding that the administration would have the authority to use force if necessary to take whatever part of the Floridas if approved by whatever power was in charge of the territory (i.e. the Spanish

1208 Bradford Perkins, *Cambridge History of American Foreign Relations*, Vol. 1, p. 114. As such, Perkins added, "the United States claimed an option on the hemisphere, exercisable when and where it wished." Ibid.

1209 Gordon Wood, *Empire of Liberty: A History of the Early Republic, 1789–1815* (New York: Oxford University Press, 2009), p. 654.

1210 Walter Nugent, *Habits of Empire: A History of American Expansion* (New York: Alfred A. Knopf, 2008), p. 107.

themselves or even local insurgents), or if the area was in danger of being captured by a foreign power.[1211] Another concrete operation saw American forces undertaking a foray into East Florida in early 1812, marching on St. Augustine. However, after the battle for control had descended into chaos in the first months of 1813, American troops were withdrawn.

The end of the Napoleonic wars in Europe created fresh opportunities for the United States to increase pressure on Spain to cede Florida. Now that it had become stronger militarily speaking, its proclivity to use force was also stronger. Tellingly, John Calhoun thought that Americans ought to "rejoice at the acquisition of those national qualities necessary to meet the vicissitudes of war."[1212] Military action followed in 1818, when general Andrew Jackson invaded Florida on the pretext of pursuing fleeing Seminoles, and seized the fortification of St. Marks in the process. This move sparked a vivid debate back in Washington, because while Monroe and Jackson agreed on the right to self-defense as well as the right to undertake reprisals,[1213] the president was "alarmed" when he heard reports about Jackson having taken the Spanish army post. He informed Jackson that under international law, he could pursue an enemy, but that taking a Spanish position amounted to an act of war.[1214] A Spanish historian concluded that Jackson had "violated all international laws and without declaring war on Spain, attacked Spanish forts that (...) could not resist."[1215] Despite the expansive notion of self-defense that the

1211 Bradford Perkins, *Cambridge History of American Foreign Relations*, Vol. 1, p. 152; Walter Nugent, *Habits of Empire: A History of American Expansion*, p. 110.

1212 Reginald Stuart, *War and American Thought* (Kent, Oh: Kent State Univ. Press, 1982), p. 136.

1213 Stuart, *War and American Thought from the Revolution to the Monroe Doctrine*, p. 156.

1214 As Monroe wrote: "The United States stand justified in ordering their troops into Florida in pursuit of their enemy. They have this right by the law of nations, if the Seminoles were inhabitants of another country and had entered Florida to elude pursuit. Being inhabitants of Florida with a sovereignty over that part of the territory, and a right to the soil, our right to give such an order is the most complete and unquestionable. It is not an act of hostility to Spain. It is the less so, because her government is bound by treaty to restrain, by force of arms if necessary, the Indians there from committing hostilities against the United States. But an order by the government to attack a Spanish post would assume another character. It would authorize war, to which, by the principles of our Constitution, the Executive is incompetent." See James Monroe to Andrew Jackson (July 19, 1818), in *The Writings of James Monroe*, Vol. 6, pp. 55–56, and discussed in Stuart, *War and American Thought from the Revolution to the Monroe Doctrine*, p. 173.

1215 Jerónimo Becker, *Historia de los relaciones exteriores de España durante el siglo* XIX (1924), Vol. 1, pp. 460–461, quoted in Walter Nugent, *Habits of Empire: A History of American Expansion* (New York: Alfred A. Knopf, 2008), p. 123.

administration had appropriated, they remained careful not to transgress principal norms of the law of nations.

The debate that took place in the Senate remained unresolved as to whether Jackson's actions had overstepped the line. Speaking for a slim majority, Thomas Nelson of Virginia held that "Jackson had violated the laws of the United States, of nations, and of humanity." The speaker for the minority, Richard Johnson, found that Jackson's acts had been justified based on the ground that the Spanish, in whose territory the Seminoles resided, had been unable to control the Indians. Reprisals were therefore an appropriate response.[1216] The debate did not end there, however. It gestated into a larger discussion about how America should wage war, which saw two sides emerge, one defending the more traditional "limited-war mentality" and the other the "American war myth."[1217] The opinion of the latter side was very pithily captured by Congressman John Rhea from Tennessee:

> General Jackson was authorized by the supreme law of nature and nations, the law of self-defence, corresponding with the great national maxim, namely, the safety of the people (…) to enter the Spanish territory of Florida in pursuit of, and to destroy, hostile, murdering savages, not bound by any obligation, who were without the practice of any moral principle reciprocally obligatory on nations.[1218]

In response, Massachusetts Congressman Thomas Fuller refuted the claim that "savage" methods of warfare should beget a corresponding answer. The object was to "conquer the enemy and compel him to do justice." Apparently, he noted, "the usages of savage nations (…) seem to have led to the erroneous opinion that indiscriminate slaughter is the unmodified state of war, by right. But the rightful laws of war are immutable; they are the same between the most ferocious as between the most humane nations." Therefore, he concluded,

> [i]n all cases the evils of war must be limited to a reasonable probability of effecting the purpose for which war was commenced. (…) The lawfulness of war itself, in the nature of self-defence, for redress of injuries,

1216 Stuart, *War and American Thought from the Revolution to the Monroe Doctrine*, p. 175.

1217 Ibid.

1218 *Debates and Proceedings in the Congress of the United States* (15th Congress, 2nd session, Nov. 16, 1818 to March 3, 1819), p. 867, quoted in Stuart, *War and American Thought from the Revolution to the Monroe Doctrine*, p. 176.

> cannot well be doubted; but that its desolation and carnage ought not to be strictly limited to the attainment of the objects, is a doctrine which would legalize wanton cruelty and useless bloodshed.[1219]

But in spite of the protests, the executive remained unmoved and supported the operations undertaken by Jackson—which included a military occupation.[1220] Expressing the point of view of the cabinet, Secretary of State John Quincy Adams wrote on this occasion that

> the President will neither inflict punishment, nor pass a censure upon General Jackson, for that conduct, the motives for which were founded in the purest patriotism; (…) and the vindication of which is written in every page of the law of nations, as well as in the first law of nature—self-defense. He thinks it, on the contrary, due to the justice which the United States have a right to claim from Spain [that] a suitable punishment [be] inflicted upon [the local Spanish commanders], for having, in defiance and violation of the engagements of Spain with the United States, aided and assisted these hordes of savages in those very hostilities against the United States which it was their official duty to restrain.[1221]

Historian Reginald Stuart concluded that while the debate did not end at this point, it had become clear that "[t]he emerging war myth would prevail over the traditions of the limited-war mentality which the Revolutionary generation had cherished and sought to propagate."[1222]

1219 *Debates and Proceedings in the Congress of the United States* (15th Congress, 2nd session, Nov. 16, 1818 to March 3, 1819), p. 999.

1220 Nys, *Les États-Unis et le Droit des Gens*, p. 96.

1221 John Quincy Adams to George W. Erving (November 28, 1818), in Worthington C. Ford (ed.), *The Writings of John Quincy Adams* (New York: The Macmillan Company, 1916), Vol. 6, pp. 486–487. Several years later, Albert Gallatin supplied a further justification, holding that by not preventing Britain from landing troops in Florida harbors under Spanish control and subsequently to permit the British to attack the United States from those footholds made an American invasion of Florida "the unavoidable consequence of the inability of Spain to fulfil those duties which, as possessing a territory adjacent to the United States, she was by the law of nations and by express treaty stipulations bound to perform." See Albert Gallatin to Baron Pasquier (June 24, 1823), *The Writings of Albert Gallatin*, Vol. 2, p. 188.

1222 Ibid., pp. 486–487. See also Stuart, *War and American Thought from the Revolution to the Monroe Doctrine*, p. 177.

After general Jackson's 1818 raid, Spanish negotiator Luis de Onís was forced into negotiating a cession of Florida, for both Madison and Congress threatened otherwise to take over the entire territory unilaterally.[1223] As a result, a treaty was agreed in 1819 between Adams and Onís that not only handed Florida to the United States, but drew the boundary of the United States across the continent to the Pacific Ocean, giving further rise to vistas of continental empire. During the negotiations, Adams managed to greatly upset his Spanish interlocutor Onís by having the audacity to ask Spain to pay damages to the United States for not having "restrained" the Indians in the area, even if the United States was clearly guilty of having committed acts of aggression and of having violated international law with the invasion of East Florida led by general Jackson.[1224]

The episode provides a good illustration on how American attitudes towards the law of nations on land had shifted in a matter of a few decades. The revolutionary generation had sought to abjure doctrines of conquest as expounded by the Spanish and the British. For instance, in 1790, Jefferson wrote that "[t]here are but two means of acquiring the native title. First, war; for even war may, sometimes, give a just title. Second, contracts or treaty."[1225] In the first decades of the 19th century, this cautious position had gradually been abandoned in favor of a more forceful doctrine which admitted that rights could accrue from conquest. In the Supreme Court, the first instance in which this doctrine was alluded to came in 1810, when it declared in a case concerning land seizure in the state of Georgia that "the nature of the Indian title, which is certainly to be respected by all courts until it be legitimately extinguished, is not such as to be absolutely repugnant to a seisin in fee on the part of the State."[1226] The clearest example is the case *Johnson v. M'Intosh*,[1227] in which judge Marshall held that rights obtained through discovery—and indirectly, through conquest—could validly be held against natives:

> The United States, then, has unequivocally acceded to that great and broad rule by which its civilized inhabitants now hold this country. They hold and assert in themselves the title by which it was acquired. They

1223 Bradford Perkins, *Cambridge History of American Foreign Relations*, Vol. 1, pp. 153–154.

1224 Walter Nugent, *Habits of Empire: A History of American Expansion* (New York: Alfred A. Knopf, 2008), p. 126–127.

1225 Jefferson, "Opinion on Georgian Land Grants" (May 3, 1790), in *The Works of Thomas Jefferson*, Vol. 6, pp. 467–468.

1226 *Fletcher v. Peck*, 10 U.S. (6 Cranch) 87, at 87.

1227 21 U.S. (8 Wheaton) 543, 1823.

> maintain, as all others have maintained, that discovery gave an exclusive right to extinguish the Indian title of occupancy either by purchase or by conquest, and gave also a right to such a degree of sovereignty as the circumstances of the people would allow them to exercise.[1228]

As one observer tellingly wrote, "The roots of [Marshall's] jurisprudence [as regards this ruling] can be traced to the Bible and medieval interpretations of it to fit expansionist interests of the Roman Catholic Church."[1229] Given that Britain had before possessed title to all lands owned by the natives, Marshall considered that conquest now gave "a title which the courts of the conqueror cannot deny."[1230] Still, this did not entirely neutralize native claims. For instance, Marshall said, the inability of natives to transfer title "may be opposed to natural right, and to the usages of civilized nations, yet if it be indispensable to that system under which the country has been settled, and be adapted to the actual condition of the two people, it may perhaps be supported by reason, and certainly cannot be rejected by courts of justice."[1231]

Lockean arguments that valid titles need to be based on effective use of the land continued to hold sway. Back in 1795, Jefferson wrote that "[w]henever there is in any country, uncultivated lands and unemployed poor, it is clear that the laws of property have been so far extended as to violate natural right. The earth is given as a common stock for man to labour & live on."[1232] Thirty-five years later, Madison would use the same argument whilst discussing Indian land rights in a letter to former Attorney-General William Wirt.[1233] John Quincy

1228 21 U.S. (8 Wheaton) 543, 1823, at 587. See discussed at length in relation to Indian land rights, Blake Watson, "John Marshall and Indian Land Rights: A Historical Rejoinder to the Claim of 'Universal Recognition' of the Doctrine of Discovery," *Seton Hall Law Review*, 36, no. 2, (2006), pp. 481–549.

1229 James Lengel, "The Role of International Law in the Development of Constitutional Jurisprudence in the Supreme Court: The Marshall Court and American Indians," *The American Journal of Legal History* 43, no. 2 (1999), p. 127.

1230 21 U.S. (8 Wheaton) 543, 1823, at 588. Marshall based himself here on letters sent by Henry VII to John Cabot in 1496, which had been modelled on the bulls of Alexander VI to the Spanish monarchs. See discussed in Anthony Pagden, "Law, Colonization, Legitimation, and the European Background," in Michael Grossberg and Christopher Tomlins, *The Cambridge History of Law in America (1580–1815)* (New York: Cambridge University Press, 2008), p. 15.

1231 21 U.S. (8 Wheaton) 543, 1823, at 591.

1232 Jefferson to Madison (October 28, 1795), in *The Works of Thomas Jefferson*, Vol. 8, p. 196.

1233 "The plea, with the best aspect, for dispossessing Indians of the lands on which they have lived, is, that by not incorporating their labour, and associating fixed improvements with the soil, they have not appropriated it to themselves, nor made the destined use of its

Adams, otherwise caught by the nationalist fever, also subscribed to this notion, declaring that "the rights of property result from two sources, occupancy and labor. (...) Possession may be permanently maintained of that which can be cared about with the person."[1234] Thus, where in maritime matters, the United States was a progressive force, in terrestrial matters, it had become a regressive force, climbing down from its original exclusive reliance on purchase in exchange for older doctrines of discovery and conquest coupled with Lockean theories on occupation and settlement.

Still, the example the United States had set as a nation that had freed itself from the clutches of the European powers, and which had managed to carve out a space for itself on the basis of a neutrality doctrine that gained ever deeper roots in the law of nations proved an inspiration for countries south of the Gulf of Mexico. Already back in 1798, a Venezuelan patriot, Francisco de Miranda, had made an offer to Hamilton for the United States to get involved in a plan to liberate South America from the Spanish through a joint naval operation with Britain.[1235] Facing impending conflict with France, president Adams decided at the time against the scheme. After 1815, conditions were very different. The wars of independence in Latin America led numerous American citizens to go south and join the struggle. The government in Washington feared however that such acts could compromise America's neutrality, in particular in light of the struggle over the Floridas. It provided the direct impetus for the Neutrality Acts that the government adopted in 1818.[1236] Nevertheless, various Spanish colonies in Latin America, claiming inspiration from the American War for Independence and based on rights under the law of nations, sought and received recognition as independent states by the Monroe administration in 1822. However, one applicant for such recognition proved to be unsuccessful: Haiti. This very fact showed, in the view of Reinstein, "the extent to which the United States would violate the law of nations to serve the cause

---

capacity for increasing the number and enjoyments of the human race. But this plea, whatever original force be allowed to it, is here repelled by the fact that the Indians are making the very use of that capacity which the plea requires (...)." See Madison to William Wirt (October 1, 1830), in *Letters and Other Writings of James Madison* (Philadelphia: J.B. Lippincott, 1865), Vol. 4, p. 114.

1234 John Quincy Adams, "Lecture on the War with China" (Massachusetts Historical Society), *Niles' National Register* (January 22, 1842), p. 326.

1235 Robert Kagan, *Dangerous Nation*, pp. 122–123.

1236 Whether provocatively or intentionally, the act attributed the status of belligerents to parties in an internal conflict between a sovereign government and rebels. See Nys, *Les États-Unis et le Droit des Gens*, p. 88.

of slavery."[1237] The ultimate -and cruel- irony where Haiti was concerned came in 1823, when Monroe declared that

> [t]he establishment of a Government of people of color in the island [which puts restrictions on employment, citizenship and property rights for whites] evinces distinctly the idea of a separate interest and distrust of other nations. Had that jealousy been confined to the inhabitants of the parent country it would have been less an object of attention; but by extending it to the inhabitants of other countries with whom no difference ever existed the policy assume a character which does not admit of like explanation.[1238]

In other words, a country that itself practiced institutionalized discrimination denied recognition to another country because it plans on introducing similar discriminatory policies. In the end, while France recognized Haiti's independence in 1825, the United States would not do so until 1862.

The events in Latin America brought about a diplomatic exchange between the United States and Great Britain that would eventually lead to the enunciation of the famous Monroe Doctrine—a diplomatic guideline that epitomized American political and international legal notions at the time. The direct occasion that led to its adoption was a proposal by foreign secretary George Canning in the summer of 1823 for Britain and the United States to adopt a declaration that stated the two countries' opposition to any kind of intervention by European powers in the affairs of Latin America. According to Perkins, the proposal of Canning actually amounted to a "limited alliance."[1239] While the exact motives for Canning's proposal have remained unclear, one concern appears to have been that the Holy Alliance was pushing Britain into political isolation.

But sentiment in the United States militated against the notion of alliances with European powers, and was shared across political boundaries. Jefferson for instance wrote that "I have ever deemed it fundamental for the United States never to take part in the quarrels of Europe. Their political interests are entirely distinct from ours. Their mutual jealousies, their balance of power,

---

1237 Robert Reinstein, "Slavery, Executive Power and International Law: The Haitian Revolution and American Constitutionalism" *American Journal of Legal History,* (forthcoming), p. 83.

1238 Monroe, Message to the Senate (February 25, 1823), quoted in Reinstein, "Slavery, Executive Power and International Law: The Haitian Revolution and American Constitutionalism" *American Journal of Legal History,* (forthcoming), p. 89.

1239 Bradford Perkins, "The Monroe Doctrine," in Patrick White (ed.), *The Critical Years: American Foreign Policy 1793–1823* (New York: John Wiley & Sons, 1970), p. 151.

their complicated alliances, their forms and principles of government, are all foreign to us. They are nations of eternal war."[1240] The American Secretary of State, John Quincy Adams, concurred with the former president, saying that: "[f]or the repose of Europe and America, the European and American systems should be kept as separate and distinct from each other as possible."[1241] Canning had hoped that with a joint declaration, he would be able to stave off a new world order organized "on the basis of large, closed continental systems."[1242] But because of Adams' distrust of Canning's motives, he favored issuing a unilateral declaration instead. The Doctrine itself—which was mainly drafted by Secretary Adams—stated that

> The Government of the United States assert[s], as a principle in which the rights and interests of the United States are involved, that the American continents, by the free and independent condition which they have assumed and maintain, are henceforth not to be considered as subjects for future colonization by any European powers (…)

One reason for keeping the two hemispheres separate pertained to differences in their respective constitutional systems: "The political system of the allied powers is essentially different in this respect from that of America. (…) We owe it, therefore, to candor and to the amicable relations existing between the United States and those powers to declare that we should consider any attempt on their part to extend their system to any portion of this hemisphere as dangerous to our peace and safety." Moreover, in further specifying the first point, Monroe added that

> With the existing colonies or dependencies of any European power we have not interfered and shall not interfere. But with the Governments who have declared their independence and maintain it, and whose independence we have, on great consideration and on just principles, acknowledged, we could not view any interposition for the purpose of oppressing them, or controlling in any other manner their destiny, by any

1240 Thomas Jefferson to James Monroe (June 11, 1823), in *The Works of Thomas Jefferson*, Vol. 12, p. 292.

1241 John Quincy Adams to Henry Middleton (July 5, 1820), in *The Writings of John Quincy Adams*, Vol. 7, pp. 50–51.

1242 Wilhelm Grewe, *The Epochs of International Law*, p. 460.

> European power in any other light than as the manifestation of an unfriendly disposition toward the United States.[1243]

Different interpretations have been advanced in explaining the message. The most obvious is that it expressed an isolationist disposition.[1244] In a way, noted historian Dexter Perkins, Monroe's message "made explicit the traditional isolationism of his people, a feeling as old and as more realistic than their pro-republicanism."[1245] But to conclude that this meant that the United States would not reserve the right to involve itself in overseas affairs would be a mistaken reading: "[The] prohibition on the part of the United States against the extension of European influence and power to the New World [did not] necessarily imply (...) that the United States must abstain from all diplomatic activity or all interference in the affairs of other continents."[1246]

The larger implications of the presidential message appear to be much more complex, however, and contain various paradoxes. The first is that while the United States decided against cooperating with Britain against the continental powers, the emphasis on non-colonization appears to be primarily aimed at powers like Spain and Portugal—which wanted to regain control over their overseas possessions—rather than Britain. Implicitly, Monroe and Adams decided to throw in their lot with the British. The Monroe Doctrine was thus, in Mead's words, "the U.S. answer to the strategic dilemma of the first fifty years. (...) It was better to come to an arrangement that would strengthen Britain on the seas than to support the efforts of Continental powers to limit British

---

1243 James Monroe, "President's Message" (December 2, 1823), in *Annals of Congress*, (Senate), 18th Congress, 1st Session, pp. 14, 22–23.

1244 The isolationist sentiment was aptly reflected by Jefferson in a letter to the famous naturalist Alexander von Humboldt: "But in whatever governments they end they will be American governments, no longer to be involved in the never-ceasing broils of Europe. The European nations constitute a separate division of the globe; their localities make them part of a distinct system; they have a set of interests of their own in which it is our business never to engage ourselves. America has a hemisphere to itself. It must have its separate system of interests, which must not be subordinated to those of Europe. The insulated state in which nature has placed the American continent, should so far avail it that no spark of war kindled in the other quarters of the globe should be wafted across the wide oceans which separate us from them." See Thomas Jefferson to Alexander von Humboldt (December 6, 1813), in *The Works of Thomas Jefferson*, Vol. 11, p. 352.

1245 Dexter Perkins, *A History of the Monroe Doctrine* (Boston: Little, Brown and Co., 1955), p. 153.

1246 Perkins, *A History of the Monroe Doctrine,* p. 4. This idea of American intervention in Latin American affairs was of course made more explicit only with the Roosevelt corollary in 1904.

power."[1247] And in practice, it would be Britain that patrolled the waters around South America, not the United States. The consequence was, wrote Alfred Vagts, that "[f]or nearly a century after the Peace of Ghent, [the United States] lived in the umbrella shade of the old mistress of the sea who luckily for [the] ungracious protégé was not also a land power or military power (…)."[1248]

The second paradox is that while Monroe's speech ostensibly addresses non-colonization, in practice it could be read as an expression of domestic imperatives in terms of westward expansion and even beyond. The first priority was, in the words of Sexton, "to bind together the various states, sections and factions of [the] union (…)."[1249] George Herring, focusing on the republic's expansionist ambitions, noted that the Doctrine "reflected America's ambitions in the Pacific Northwest." Moreover, he added, one reason for issuing it without the support of Britain "reflected the nation's keen interest in acquiring Texas and Cuba and its commercial aspirations in Latin America."[1250] Seen in this way, the Monroe Doctrine can be regarded as a balance-of-power device[1251] while at the same time foreshadowing the idea of Manifest Destiny.[1252] Indeed, there were also already voices of concern about what was seen as the inevitable rise of the United States in decades to come. And this was, said a prominent historian of Europe, an important reason for keeping the young nation away from the table in Vienna in 1815, the idea being that Europe needed to be "shielded (…) from extraneous quarrels."[1253]

1247 Walter Russell Mead, *Special Providence* (London: Routledge, 2002), p. 200.

1248 Alfred Vagts, "The United States and the Balance of Power," *The Journal of Politics* 3, no. 4 (November 1941), p. 419.

1249 Jay Sexton, *The Monroe Doctrine: Empire and Nation in Nineteenth-Century America.* (New York: Hill and Wang, 2011), p. 16.

1250 George Herring, *From Colony to Superpower: U.S. Foreign Relations since 1776* (New York: Oxford University Press, 2008), p. 157.

1251 Alfred Vagts and Detlev Vagts "The Balance of Power in International Law: A History of an Idea" *American Journal of International Law* 73, no. 4 (1979), p. 575. The idea that a balance of power could also be a positive means for keeping the peace gained more currency at this time, and was for instance reflected in a letter by Jefferson, expressing hope that "those which are overgrown may not advance beyond safe measures of power, that a salutary balance may ever be maintained among nations and that our peace, commerce, and friendship, may be sought and cultivated by all (…)." Thomas Jefferson to Thomas Leiper (June 12, 1815), in *The Works of Thomas Jefferson*, Vol. 11, p. 477.

1252 Dion noted that this idea existed implicitly in the minds of the Revolutionaries, and was closely connected to notions about the law of nature and fundamental rights. See Leon Dion, "Natural Law and Manifest Destiny in the Era of the American Revolution" *The Canadian Journal of Economics and Political Science* 23, no. 2 (May 1957), p. 239.

1253 Paul Schroeder, *The Transformation of European Politics 1763–1848* (Oxford: Clarendon Press, 1994), p. 574–575.

The third paradox entails the dichotomy between the elements that united the two sides of the Atlantic and those that separated it. To begin with, the post-1815 restoration only helped to sharpen the distinction between republican and monarchical constitutional models. The Monroe Doctrine could therefore easily be read as "a statement of international republican solidarity."[1254] When Austrian Chancellor Klemens von Metternich expressed his concern about the president's message to Russian foreign minister Count Nesselrode, it was precisely over this point, and the moral havoc the United States could wreak should its republican ideas prevail: "These United States of America (...) have suddenly left a sphere too narrow for their ambition, and have astonished Europe by a new act of revolt, more unprovoked, fully as audacious, and no less dangerous (...) in fostering revolutions wherever they show themselves. [Therewith,] they lend new strength to the apostles of sedition, and reanimate the courage of every conspirator."[1255]

At the same time however, despite their republicanism and secularism, Americans also considered themselves to be part of the community of Christian and civilized nations, which shared certain essential values about international conduct. A common concept of international law was certainly among the cornerstones of this community.[1256] This idea was aptly reflected in a pamphlet by Albert Gallatin:

> There is no difficulty in discovering the principles by which the relations between civilized and Christian nations should be regulated and the reciprocal duties which they owe to each other. These principles, these duties, have long since been proclaimed, and the true law of nations is nothing else than the conformity to the sublime precepts of the gospel morality, precepts equally applicable to the relations between man and man and to the intercourse between nation and nation. "Thou shalt love thy neighbor as thyself." "Love your enemies." "As you would that men should do to you, do ye also to them likewise." The sanctity of these commands is acknowledged, without a single exception, by every denomination of Christians, or of men professing to be such.[1257]

1254 Kagan, *Dangerous Nation,* p. 174.

1255 Metternich to Nesselrode (January 19, 1824), quoted in Patrick White, *The Critical Years: American Foreign Policy 1793–1823* (New York: Wilez and Sons, 1970), p. 156.

1256 Wilhelm Grewe, *The Epochs of International Law*, p. 451.

1257 Albert Gallatin, "Peace with Mexico" (1847), in *The Writings of Albert Gallatin*, Vol. 3, pp. 557–558.

As a result, for all the struggles over international law in the United States in the years since independence, Grewe concluded that "the integration of the United States into the international legal community was achieved rapidly and without difficulties—which was only possible because the U.S. was an offshoot of the Christian European family of nations."[1258] At the same time, a realization gradually emerged that the United States had genuinely been able to contribute to the development of the law of nations. James Madison said as much when he wrote in 1823 with reference to the 'free ships, free goods' doctrine that in contrast to the 1790s,

> [t]he U.S. (...) in their Treaties have [now] sufficiently thrown their weight into the opposite scale. And such is the number & character of like weights now in it from other powers, that it must preponderate; unless it be admitted that no authority of that kind, tho' coinciding with the dictates of reason, the feelings of humanity & the interest of the civilized world can make or expound a Law of Nations.[1259]

The confidence that the Doctrine exuded is also illustrated in the fact that it reflected "the emerging American war myth." Concretely, this meant that "[t]he nation would act in self-defense only, and the justice of its cause was clearly implied, even though aggressive national pretensions poked through the mild language of the statement."[1260] Up to 1823, it could be said that this applied much more to territorial than to naval affairs. The Monroe Doctrine could then be regarded as the first major statement in which territorial and naval ambitions were combined, since it concerned the entire Western hemisphere.

A final irony about Monroe's epochal statement is that it took several decades before it was recognized as being epochal. But while it had almost fallen into oblivion at one point in the 19th century, it did constitute, in the words of historian Bradford Perkins, America's "diplomatic declaration of independence."[1261] The statement framed America's future ambitions in realist terms, but in a way, this was only a reflection of its larger ideals. The law of nations was to a large extent still couched in the language of natural law, and

1258 Wilhelm Grewe, *The Epochs of International Law*, p. 296.

1259 Madison to Edward Everett (February 18, 1823), in *The Writings of James Madison*, Vol. 9, p. 121.

1260 Stuart, *War and American Thought from the Revolution to the Monroe Doctrine*, p. 172.

1261 Harry Ammon, *James Monroe: The Quest for National Identity* (New York: McGrawHill, 1971) p. 491, quoted in Perkins, *Cambridge History of American Foreign Relations*, Vol. 1, p. 169.

in that sense, comported well with American ideology as a whole. Even if it is an exaggeration, it could be maintained that the law of nations provided the young nation with a set of principles and rules that not only helped to bring it into existence, but that also enabled its survival into viable nationhood. One British publication held that it had done so deservedly, summarizing its history as follows:

> [It] has survived the tender period of infancy, and outlived the prophecies of its downfall (...) It has been found serviceable both in peace and in war, and may well claim from the nation it has saved (...) the votive benediction of "Esto perpetua."[1262]

1262 Quoted from the *Annual Register* (date unknown), in Perkins, "The Monroe Doctrine," p. 156.

Conclusion

One of the objectives of this book was to demonstrate why and how the law of nations mattered in the history of the early American republic. Traditionally, the historiography of this era has rather neglected this aspect. When such aspects are discussed, say, in the case of impressment or enforcing neutrality rights, this is often done without further reference to legal history or doctrine. This relative neglect is partly due to the fact that international law has simply not been considered a key dimension in explaining the development of the early republic and its foreign relations. A second reason is that many historians are not trained in law, and thus do not have sufficient appreciation for this dimension. Thirdly, the complexity and modes of reasoning that the law brings do not necessarily lend themselves for easy integration into a historical narrative, and thus present a problem for historians, and for legal history as such. This book has been an attempt at redressing this situation.

Understanding the role of international law at the time of the early republic matters because it mattered to the founding generation. Much of their correspondence is filled with references to the law of nations, and the great treatises of Vattel, Grotius and others were directly consulted in cabinet meetings. For this generation, international law was not merely a amalgam of legal abstractions, but suggested rules of statecraft which allowed them to communicate with other nations; to defend American political or commercial interests abroad; and even provided a vehicle for promoting American values beyond its shores.

In these regards, the law of nations was to the Founders much more than a 'weapon of the weak,' which is how various legal scholars and historians have explained the preference the revolutionary generation for couching disputes with foreign powers in the language of international law. First of all, the very notion that the early republic was weak as such is contestable. For sure, as a military power, from its founding until the late 1790s, the republic was indeed a weak country. Yet at the same time, because of its delicate role in the context of the European balance of power, it was able to take on a much more significant role in international affairs than could otherwise be expected.[1263] As a

1263 Another view is that on various occasions during era of the early republic, the United States had simply been lucky given the convulsions that the Europeans found themselves in. See e.g. Bradford Perkins, *The Creation of a Republican Empire* (Vol. 1 of the *Cambridge History of American Foreign Relations,* Cambridge and New York: Cambridge University Press, 1993), pp. 230–231.

 | DOI 10.1163/9789004305687_010

result, the early republic was not forced into abiding by British, French or other doctrines of international law, and had room for developing and promoting its own doctrines, albeit understandably with mixed success. In other words, strength or weakness is not something that is only measured by military power, but can equally be seen as a function of strategic importance as well as perceptions, thus requiring a different approach to thinking about the utility of international law in the early republic.

As a foreign policy instrument, this study agrees with authors such as Douglas Sylvester and Peter and Nicholas Onuf that international law was not only used as a defensive means, but also as a means to assert American political and economic interests. This is very clear for instance with the strategy behind the Model Treaty of 1776 to promote commerce on the basis of the 'free ships, free goods' doctrine, but also with Jefferson's Embargo policy. Economically, the Embargoes were hurtful to American interests, but Jefferson persisted nonetheless to vindicate his interpretation of America's rights. In addition, the law of nations was important in that it helped the Founders to create a new nation that can credibly operate at home and abroad. Reflecting on the law of nations helped expose the shortcomings of the republic under the Articles of Confederation, and led to the adoption of a new constitution in 1787. In that regard, the creation of a federal republic owed much to international legal doctrine.

But apart from using the law of nations as a means to promote its worldly interest, it also attracted the founding generation because in their minds, it constituted a part of the very value system that they wished to propagate, both at home and abroad.[1264] This value system was a combination of many intellectual currents, including Enlightenment liberalism, Protestant ethics, and common law and natural law traditions. This mindset also determined the character of the Revolution itself, which was more informed by the moderate and reform-minded thinking of Montesquieu and Turgot rather than the radical streak represented by Rousseau and materialists such as Diderot and Mably.[1265] The law of nations, with its pedigree in Roman and medieval

---

1264 This is not acknowledged as such in standard surveys of American foreign relations. See e.g. Bradford Perkins, *The Creation of a Republican Empire,* pp. 9–11; or Walter McDougall, "Back to Bedrock: The Eight Traditions of American Statecraft," in Brendon O'Connor (ed.), *American Foreign Policy Traditions* (London: Sage Publications, 2010), Vol. 1, pp. 82–84.

1265 See discussed in Hendrickson, *Peace Pact*, p. 175, who quotes in this context a line from Claude Van Tyne, that "the freest of peoples [were] the first to rebel." See *The Founding of the American Republic: The Causes of the War of Independence*, p. 456. See also the monumental trilogy of Jonathan Israel on the genesis and impact of the Radical Enlightenment.

thinking and customs, very much stood for moderate if not conservative values, and explains why, "[w]hereas the European sympathizers of the French Revolution threw into disrepute 'the sorry comforters' of Grotius, Pufendorf, and Vattel, the American revolutionaries elevated these authorities and wanted to enter the international society the publicists had described."[1266] Bourguignon even noted that because natural law generally "struck a chord" with lawyers in America, "[i]ncorporation of the law of nations (..) must have seemed so obvious to [them] that there was no reason to question its propriety." Critical approaches to the writings of eminent jurists were not considered necessary, nor was it deemed bothersome when they contradicted each other.[1267] This attitude of the Founders towards the great writers on international law was very eloquently captured in a letter written by John Quincy Adams in response to Genêt's contemptuous remarks aimed at Thomas Jefferson:

> When (…) the French Minister "thanks God, that he has forgotten what Grotius, Pufendorf and Vattel have written upon the laws of nations," he ought to be told, that his forgetfulness "is not a thing to thank God on." When he affirms that these writers "were hired jurisprudists, and wrote when they were all enchained," he asserts what is not true. Grotius, the venerable and successful defender of the Christian Faith; the learned and strenuous supporter of the freedom of the sea; the firm and dauntless republican asserter of his country's rights against the encroachments of princely usurpation, was one of the greatest and most illustrious of men, that ever adorned and dignified the human character. Pufendorf was indeed the subject of a monarchical government, but his reputation as a man was such as would have done credit to the most virtuous Commonwealth of ancient or modern times; and his system as a writer pursues the path which Grotius had explored, and is only an improvement upon his principles. Vattel himself declares "that he was born in a country of which *liberty* was the soul, the treasure and the fundamental law. That he would not have written if he could not have followed the light of his conscience. That nothing restrains his pen, and that he was incapable of prostituting it to flattery." To insult the memory and slander the reputation of men like these, of men whose virtues and genius have

1266 Hendrickson, *Peace Pact*, p. 175.

1267 Henry Bourguignon, "Incorporation of the Law of Nations during the American Revolution—The Case of the San Antonio" *American Journal of International Law* 71 (1977), p. 294.

> deserved well of mankind, does as little credit to the head as to the heart of Mr. Genet.[1268]

Before drawing conclusions on the place of the law of nations in the early republic, it is worthwhile to investigate the writings of some of the great early 19th-century American authors in order to get an unadulterated perspective on the legacy of the first fifty-odd years of independence from their point of view. The first treatise to consider is James Kent's *Commentaries on American Law*, "the first comprehensive national survey of the major principles and precedents in American law,"[1269] published in the very year (1826) that both Jefferson and Adams died. Kent was the first law professor at Columbia College—renamed in 1784, having previously been known as King's College—and a judge on the New York Supreme Court. The first part of volume one was devoted to the law of nations.

At the very start of treatise, Kent showed the degree to which he attached great importance to the fact that the United States are considered part of the community of nations that recognizes international law as its basis. Thus, he writes that when the United States became an independent country, "[it] became subject to that system of rules which reason, morality and custom had established among the civilized nations of Europe, as their public law."[1270] Noting that while the law of nations is neither exclusively founded on custom nor on natural law,[1271] he qualified as "dangerous" the view that governments might not be bound by "the obligations of truth, justice and humanity, in relations to other powers."[1272] Further underlining the significance of the natural law of nations, he paraphrased Cicero by saying that "[t]he law of nations, so

---

1268 John Quincy Adams, "Columbus no. III" (December 7, 11 and 14, 1793), in *The Writings of John Quincy Adams*, Vol. 1, pp. 165–166.

1269 Ellen H. Pearson, "Revising Custom, Embracing Choice: Early American Scholars and the Republicanization of the Common Law," in Eliga Gould and Peter Onuf (eds.), *Empire and Nation: The American Revolution in the Atlantic World* (Baltimore/London: The Johns Hopkins University Press, 2005), p. 110.

1270 James Kent, *Commentaries on American Law* (New York: O. Halstead, 1832), Vol. 1, p. 1. In another work, he added that "although [the law of nations] has been transfused into the domestic policy of the several states, yet in a national point of view we are and ought to be, only one people." Kent, *Dissertations, Being the Preliminary Part of a Course of Law Lectures* (New York: George Forman, 1795), pp. 51–52.

1271 As a result of which Janis concluded that Kent had "adopted a middle position (...) called 'mixed' or Grotian, which incorporated both positivist and natural elements." Mark Janis, *America and the Law of Nations 1776–1939* (Oxford: Oxford University Press, 2010), p. 52.

1272 Kent, *Commentaries on American Law*, Vol. 1, pp. 2–3.

far as it is founded on the principles of natural law, is equally binding in every age, and upon all mankind."[1273]

The foundation in natural law was considered very important to Kent, and also helped to single out, in his view, the United States as belonging to a more specific category of nations, namely those that recognize Christianity as a cornerstone of international order:

> [T]he Christian nations of Europe, and their descendants on this side of the Atlantic, by the vast superiority of their attainments in arts, and science, and commerce, as well as in policy and government, and, above all, by the brighter light, the more certain truths, and the more definite sanction which Christianity has communicated to the ethical jurisprudence of the ancients, have established a law of nations peculiar to themselves. They form together a community of nations united by religion, manners, morals, humanity, and science, and united also by the mutual advantages of commercial intercourse, by the habit of forming alliances and treaties with each other, of interchanging ambassadors, and of studying and recognizing the same writers and systems of public law.[1274]

This view is a testimony to the idea that Americans felt that they belonged integrally to the 'European space,' both morally and intellectually. To legal historian Mark Janis, this demonstrated that Kent wished to ensure that America "[is] perceived by other countries as a qualified sovereign partner in the European Christian community of nations."[1275] Kent also noted, perhaps too deferentially, that "[i]n all our foreign negotiations, and domestic discussions of questions of national law, we have paid the most implicit respect to the practice of Europe, and the opinions of her most distinguished civilians."[1276] Being confident about the place that the United States had taken in the community of nations, Kent reaffirmed what had been the country's mission statement in foreign affairs. A pithy summary of Washington's *Farewell Address*, he wrote that "[a] nation that maintains a firm and scrupulously impartial neutrality, and commands the respect of all other nations by

---

1273 Kent, *Commentaries on American Law,* Vol. 1, p. 3.

1274 Kent, *Commentaries on American Law,* Vol. 1, pp. 3–4.

1275 Janis, *The American Tradition of International Law*, p. 37. Elsewhere, Janis wrote that "Kent encouraged Americans to make their country a reliable partner in the extant system." Janis, *America and the Law of Nations 1776–1939* (Oxford: Oxford University Press, 2010), p. 70.

1276 Kent, *Commentaries on American Law,* Vol. 1, p. 19.

its prudence, justice, and good faith, has the best chance to preserve unimpaired the blessings of its commerce, the freedom of its institutions, and the prosperity of its resources."[1277]

At the same time however, Kent's respect for foreign opinion was so great that he did not even attempt to defend the early 'free ships, free goods' doctrine which the United States had pushed for so long. Instead, he conceded that while various treaties involving neutral countries contain just such a stipulation, the general rule that enemy property can be seized outside of territorial waters remained a "clear and established position" under international law.[1278] By the early 19th century, the old rule that enemy goods on neutral ships were liable to seizure was still the prevailing view.[1279] In summary, Kent emphasized the close intellectual bonds on which relations with Europe reposed as well as the country's moral commitment to international law.

In his principal treatise on American law, the *Commentaries on the Constitution of the United States*, Joseph Story also underlined the importance of respect for the law of nations as a passport to admission into the community of nations—that is, the community of European Christian nations. Story argued that the law of nations had been introduced in the United States by way of the common law: "[t]he universal principle (and the practice has conformed to it) has been that the common law is our birthright and inheritance and that our ancestors brought hither with them Upon their emigration all of it, which was applicable to their situation. The whole Structure of our present jurisprudence stands upon the original foundations of the common law."[1280] Having pointed out that the common law "constitut[es] a part of the law of nations," he underlined the principal virtue of the Constitution—to preserve peace at home through "compelling a general obedience (…) and a general respect for the obligations of the law of nations."[1281] In the earlier case of *La Jeune Eugenie* (1821), Story expounded in more detail on his views on the law of nations. Interestingly, in this case, his perspective was much more shaped by natural law considerations. Even more interesting is Story's strong support for newly established principles under international law that are in conformity with "a

1277 Kent, *Commentaries on American Law*, Vol. 1, p. 115.

1278 James Kent, *Dissertations, Being the Preliminary Part of a Course of Law Lectures* (New York: George Forman, 1795), pp. 73–74. See also Kent, *Commentaries on American Law*, Vol. 1, pp. 116–124.

1279 Benjamin Ziegler, *The International Law of John Marshall* (Chapel Hill: The University of North Carolina Press, 1939), p. 242.

1280 Joseph Story, *Commentaries on the Constitution of the United States* (Boston: Hilliard Gray & Co.; Cambridge: Brown, Shattuck & Co., 1833), Vol. 1, p. 140.

1281 Story, *Commentaries on the Constitution of the United States*, Vol. 1, p. 458.

just view of the duties and rights of nations" in the face of customary evidence to the contrary:

> What (...) the law of nations is, does not rest upon mere theory, but may be considered as modified by the practice, or ascertained by the treaties of nations at different periods. It does not follow, therefore, that because a principle cannot be found settled by the consent or practice of nations at one time, it is to be concluded, that at no subsequent period the principle can be considered as incorporated into the public code of nations. Nor is it to be admitted, that no principle belongs to the law of nations, which is not universally recognised, as such, by all civilized communities, or even by those constituting, what may be called, the Christian states of Europe. (...) There are other doctrines, again, which have met the decided hostility of some of the European states, enlightened as well as powerful, such as the right of search, and the rule, that free ships do not make free goods; which, nevertheless, both Great Britain and the United States maintain (...) and scruple not to apply them to the ships of all other nations. And, yet if the general custom of nations in modern times, or even in the present age, recognized an opposite doctrine, it could not, perhaps, be affirmed, that that practice did not constitute a part, or, at least, a modification, of the law of nations.[1282]

In underscoring his belief in principles of the natural law of nations, he concluded:

> I think it may be unequivocally affirmed, that every doctrine, that may be fairly deduced by correct reasoning from the rights and duties of nations, and the nature of moral obligation, may theoretically be said to exist in the law of nations; and unless it be relaxed or waived by the consent of nations, which may be evidenced by their general practice and customs, it may be enforced by a court of justice, whenever it arises in judgment. And I may go farther and say, that no practice whatsoever can obliterate the fundamental distinction between right and wrong, and that every nation is at liberty to apply to another the correct principle, whenever both nations, by their public acts recede from such practice, and admit the injustice or cruelty of it.[1283]

1282 *Report on the Case of the Jeune Eugenie, Determined in the Circuit Court of the United States, for the First Circuit, at Boston, December 1821* (Boston: Wells and Lilly, 1822), pp. 71–73.

1283 Ibid., p. 73.

Few statements better epitomize the American spirit in terms of applying international law in the early 19th century, reflecting a righteousness (whether merited or unmerited) that is in tune with the prevailing legal doctrine in the United States at the time, but also echoes the revolutionary idealism about how the law of nations can help reform international practices.

The last author to consider is Henry Wheaton, whose *Elements of International Law With a Sketch of the History of the Subject* (1836) was the first treatise on international law written in the United States—in fact, in the Anglosphere as a whole. A lawyer and diplomat, Wheaton was very much influenced by the German *Historische Rechtsschule*—which promoted natural law elements—and opposed the legal positivist notions of John Austin. As was the case with Kent and Story, Wheaton also stressed the centrality of Christianity as a cornerstone of civilized international community[1284] when defining international law:

> The law of nations, or international law, as understood among civilized, Christian nations, may be defined as consisting of those rules of conduct which reason deduces, as consonant to justice, from the nature of the society existing among independent nations; with such definitions and modifications as may be established by general consent.[1285]

Indeed, one of the aims of Wheaton was to furnish European international society with "a solid foundation in law"; not to replace the balance of power, but to reinforce and stabilize it.[1286] In this respect, Wheaton professed to be a non-universalist,[1287] believing that "[t]here is (...) no universal, immutable law

---

1284 Janis writes on this aspect that "neither Kent nor Wheaton came to their enthusiasm for international law with any unrealistic expectations that the law of nations was to be for the world as American law was already for the United States. (...) Second, neither Kent nor Wheaton took to morality or to Christendom because they had utopian visions about the efficacy of international law (...)." In a very cautious remark, he concludes that "Kent and Wheaton's affirmation of the 'international law of Christendom' was, very likely, too narrow a view of international law for their century, and, most certainly, for the centuries thereafter." Janis, *America and the Law of Nations 1776–1939*, pp. 70–71. See also discussed in Eliga Gould, *Among the Powers of the Earth: The American Revolution and the Making of a New World Empire*. (Cambridge, MA: Harvard University Press, 2013), p. 7.

1285 Henry Wheaton, *Elements of International Law, With a Sketch of the History of the Subject* (Philadelphia: Carey, Lea and Blanchard, 1836), p. 46.

1286 Nicholas Onuf, "Henry Wheaton and the 'Golden Age of International Law,'" p. 7.

1287 See e.g. discussed in Jesse Reeves, "The First American Treatise on International Law," *American Journal of International Law* 31 (1935), p. 701; Janis, *America and the Law of Nations 1776–1939*, pp. 66–69.

of nations, binding upon the whole human race—which all mankind in all ages and countries, ancient and modern, savage and civilized, Christian and pagan, have recognized in theory and practice, have professed to obey, or have in fact obeyed (...)."[1288] In affirming the fact that "states are independent moral beings (...) only by virtue of rights that confer duties on other, equally independent states,"[1289] Wheaton placed himself in a long tradition going back through Wilson and Wolff, and justified America's policy of neutrality by emphasizing mutual rights and obligations derived from a Christian notion of states as moral entities.

Wheaton thus showed himself to be still firmly wedded to the 18th-century Vattellian tradition of international law whilst also foreshadowing 19th-century currents in legal thinking. Taken together, the works of Kent, Story and Wheaton "may well be taken as an expression of the early American attitude toward international law."[1290] This attachment did not merely derive from the fact that the law of nations was seen as a manifestation of the fundamental norms that inspired the American Revolution, but also because it was seen as the one system of rules that could—and should—ensure a stable and peaceful international order. A good example of this spirit is an 1803 pamphlet by Thomas Pownall, in which he wrote that "until the rights of nations are recognised and established, the law of nations is a betraying mockery, imposed on the minds only of those who are the dupes of it."[1291] The consequences would be far-reaching:

> Unless the essential rights of nations be thus established, the law of nations cannot come into operation; no, not into existence: Unless each nation is recognized as a party participant in the general state of nations; unless the right of its sovereign, equal, independent individuality of political person, be avowed, recognized and admitted; there can be no base even for treaty—no sanction of any pact of alliance or peace: all relations which arise, all actions which pass between nations, can in such case originate only in will, and be put in operation only by force.[1292]

Indeed, part of the reason why the early American statesmen promoted the law of nations was because it was seen as a means that could attenuate the

---

1288 Henry Wheaton, *Elements of International Law*, p. 46.

1289 Nicholas Onuf, "Henry Wheaton and the 'Golden Age of International Law,'" p. 4.

1290 Arthur Nussbaum, *A Concise History of the Law of Nations* (New York: Macmillan Press, 1954), p. 246.

1291 Thomas Pownall, *Memorial Addressed to the Sovereigns of Europe and the Atlantic.* (London: J. Debrett, 1803), pp. 22–23.

1292 Ibid., p. 34.

often negative consequences of pursuing balance-of-power policies that privileged the notion that 'might makes right.' Yes, they recognized that in some ways, the law of nations reflected balance-of-power imperatives. But if the law of nations could be reformed, so statesmen from Franklin to Jefferson thought, it could help to augur in a world in which 'right makes might,' and enable the community of nations to prosper as a result of freedom of commerce. This also explains why throughout the fifty-year period since independence, support for integrating and applying the law of nations in American foreign policy was consistent across party lines, and not marked by the partisan opinions about international law that we witness today. Also interesting to note is that while the reformist zeal that the Founding generation exhibited towards the law of nations was partly inspired by an idea of wresting it from the corrupted hands of European princes so as to reconstitute it on the basis of natural law, ancient common law customs and sometimes religious ideas, there was also a desire to abandon this legacy and to create new foundations, of which the Model Treaty of 1776 is a prime example. Hence, the ambiguity of seeking to create a new society free from the ills that bedevilled old Europe whilst building on the intellectual heritage of the old world was also reflected in the way the Founders approached, interpreted and applied the law of nations.

This ambiguity also resonated in the way in which administrations from Washington to Monroe applied the law of nations. The record of incorporation of international law into constitutional law—was it by dint of natural law, English common law, or through adoption by the states themselves?—remained confused, allowing for different kinds of justifications to be called upon in support of policy positions. This also made it possible for a liberal and progressive type of international law—based on treaties—to prevail in maritime affairs, while policy in regards to territorial acquisition and slavery continued to be inspired by older doctrines. For instance, in the late 18th century, settlers sought to distinguish themselves from their British, French and Spanish predecessors by claiming to only acquire territory through purchase from the natives. Whether this always happened in an honest fashion was already questioned by Alexis de Tocqueville, who wrote years later that "the dispossession of the Indians is accomplished in a regular and, so to say, quite legal manner [that it] is impossible to destroy men with more respect for the laws of humanity."[1293] But in the early 19th century, this idea was gradually abandoned and substituted for older doctrines about conquest—sometimes even with explicit reference to papal bulls. The conquest of East Florida is in this context only the most egregious example, an occasion on which the right to self-defense was

1293 Alexis de Tocqueville, *Democracy in America*, Bk. 1, ch. X.

stretched beyond its limits and the laws of war were flatly disregarded. Some decades later, on the occasion of the war against Mexico in 1848, Albert Gallatin took note of the "inferior standards" of international law that American leaders had applied:

> The United States, though they have the power, have no right to impose terms inconsistent with justice. (…) But in judging the acts of our government, it must be admitted that statesmen think a conformity to those usages which constitute the law of nations not as it should be, but as it is practically, sufficient to justify their conduct. And by that inferior standard those acts and our duties in relation to Mexico will be tested.[1294]

Slavery and the slave trade was the other area in which diverging approaches to the law of nations resulted in the continuing existence of gross iniquities. Given the shared understanding that existed in regards to natural law and the justifications that could be found on the basis of state practice, it was not difficult for lawyers in the early republic to uphold slavery as an institution. Only after the abolition of the slave trade by Britain in 1807 was there some movement in the United States towards ending the slave trade and slavery altogether, although it would still take several decades for the latter to be consigned to the dustbin of history. Perhaps ironically, natural law provided judges Story and Marshall reasons in the *Jeune Eugenie* and *Antelope* cases for condemning the slave trade, even if they had to acknowledge that it had been sanctioned on the basis customary international law for centuries. But foreign policy concerning the slavery issue only became truly confused when slaves in Haiti arose in a quest for independence from France. Wishing to avoid or import a slave revolt, but at the same time wanting to benefit from the lucrative trade with the Caribbean island, the American government did not recognize the island's independence until 1862, thirty-seven years after France itself had done so.

Legal historian Jules Lobel once wrote that "[a]s international relations changed and American military and economic power grew, the status of international law also changed. Increasingly accepted views of absolute sovereignty, nationalism, positivism, and congressional supremacy combined to diminish the force of international law as a limitation on governmental power."[1295] While this is true, this book has tried to demonstrate that the story is more

---

1294 Albert Gallatin, "Peace with Mexico," in *The Writings of Albert Gallatin*, Vol. 3, pp. 558–559.

1295 Jules Lobel, "The Limits of Constitutional Power: Conflicts between Foreign Policy and International Law" *Virginia Law Review* 71, no. 7 (October 1985), p. 1104.

complicated than that. Military and economic power matter, but for the Founding generation, the law of nations was more than just a policy instrument: it was also part of the ideological basis on which the country was founded, and embodied their aspirations for reforming the international order as a whole.

In this respect, the story of the incorporation and application of the law of nations in the first fifty years of the republic provides a capsule history of America's continuous struggle to live up to its own expectations, and of its ambiguous relationship with Europe. The objective of the first European settlers in the new world was not to escape from the old world and leave it to its own devices, but to create a new society that could provide fresh inspiration for moral renewal. The law of nations provided a language with which Americans could communicate these aspirations. It was inevitable that in several respects, Americans would fall short of their own aspirations, and in many cases, they knew it themselves. But, to repeat the point made by Benjamin Franklin, "[w]hy should not this Law of Nations go on improving? Ages have intervened between its several Steps; but as Knowledge of late increases rapidly, why should not those Steps be quickened?"[1296]

1296 Franklin to Benjamin Vaughan (July 10, 1782), in *The Papers of Benjamin Franklin*, Vol. 37, p. 608–610.

Bibliography

Sources

Adams, John. *The Works of John Adams, with Life*. Ed. by Charles F. Adams, 10 Vols. Boston: Little, Brown, 1850–1856.

Adams, John Quincy. "Lecture on the War with China." (Massachusetts Historical Society). *Niles' National Register* (January 22, 1842): pp. 326–330.

________. *Writings of John Quincy Adams*. Ed. by Worthington Chauncey Ford, 7 Vols. New York: The Macmillan Co., 1913.

Adams, Samuel. *The Writings of Samuel Adams*. Ed. by Harry Alonzo Cushing, 4 Vols. New York: G.B. Putnam & Sons, 1906.

Bentham, Jeremy. *An Introduction to the Principles and Morals of Legislation*. [1789] Ed. by J.H. Burns and H.L.A. Hart. London; New York: Methuen, 1996.

Blackstone, William. *Commentaries on the Laws of England*. Oxford : Clarendon Press, 1765–1769. Available at <http://avalon.law.yale.edu/subject_menus/blackstone.asp>.

Burke, Edmund. *Select Works of Edmund Burke*. Ed. by F. Canavan, based on the Payne Edition. Indianapolis: Liberty Fund, 1999.

Burlamaqui, Jean-Jacques. *The Principles of Natural and Politic Law*. [1763] Ed. by Thomas Nugent. Indianapolis: Liberty Fund, 2006.

Bynkershoek, C. van. *Quaestionum Juris Publici Libri Duo*. Classics of International Law. Ed. by James Brown Scott. Oxford: Clarendon Press London (Humphrey Milford), 1930. Available at <http://www.constitution.org/bynk/bynk.htm>.

Chitty, Joseph. *A Practical Treatise on the Law of Nations, Relative to the Legal Effect of War on the Commerce of Belligerents and Neutrals*. Boston: Bradford and Reid, 1812. Available at <http://books.google.com>.

Cicero. *The Offices* [De Officiis]. London: J.M. Dent and Sons, 1953.

Cobbett, William. *Cobbett's Political Register*. London: T.C. Hansard, 1810.

Coke, Sir Edward. *The Selected Writings and Speeches of Sir Edward Coke*. Ed. by S. Sheppard. Indianapolis: Liberty Fund, 2004.

Deane, Silas. *The Deane Papers*. 5 Vols. New York: New-York Historical Society's Publications, 1887–1890.

Duane, William John. *The Law of Nations, Investigated in a Popular Manner, Addressed to the Farmers of the United States*. Philadelphia: William Duane, 1809.

Duponceau, Peter Stephen. *A Dissertation on the Nature and Extent of the Jurisdiction of the Courts of the United States...* Philadelphia: Abraham Small, 1825. Available at <http://books.google.com>.

Franklin, Benjamin. *The Papers of Benjamin Franklin*. Ed. by Ellen Cohn, et al., 37 Vols. Sponsored by the American Philosophical Society and Yale University, 1954–date. Available at <http://franklinpapers.org/franklin>.

Gallatin, Albert. *The Writings of Albert Gallatin*. Ed. by Henry Adams. 3 Vols. Philadelphia: J.B. Lippincott, 1879.

Grotius, Hugo. *The Rights of War and Peace*. Ed. and with an Introduction by Richard Tuck, from the Ed. by Jean Barbeyrac, 3 Vols. Indianapolis: Liberty Fund, 2005. Also available at <http://oll.libertyfund.org>.

Hamilton, Alexander. *The Works of Alexander Hamilton*. Ed. by Henry Cabot Lodge (Federal Edition) in 12 Vols. New York: G.P. Putnam's Sons, 1904.

________. *The Papers of Alexander Hamilton*. Ed. by H. Syrett and J. Cooke. New York: Columbia University Press, 1961–1987.

Hamilton, Alexander, James Madison, and John Jay. *The Federalist Papers* [1787]. Ed. by Isaac Kramnick. Harmondsworth: Penguin Books, 1987.

Hamilton, Alexander. *The Revolutionary Writings of Alexander Hamilton*. Ed. by Richard B. Vernier. Indianapolis: Liberty Fund, 2008. Available at <http://oll.libertyfund.org>.

Heeren, Arnold H.L. *History of the Political System of Europe and Its Colonies*. New York: S. Butler & Son, 1829.

Hobbes, Thomas. *The English Works of Thomas Hobbes of Malmesbury*. Ed. by Sir William Molesworth, 11 Vols. London: Bohn, 1839–1845.

Hoffman, David. *A Course of Legal Study, Respectfully Addressed to the Students of Law in the United States*. Baltimore: Coale and Maxwell, 1817. Available at <http://books.google.com>.

Home, Henry (Lord Kames). *Essays on the Principles of Morality and Natural Religion* [1779]. Indianapolis: Liberty Fund, 2005.

Hume, David. *The Philosophical Works of David Hume*. Edinburgh: Adam Black and William and Charles Teit, 1826. Available at <http://oll.libertyfund.org>.

Iredell, James. *Life and Correspondence of James Iredell*. Ed. by Griffith McRee. New York: D. Appleton and Company, 1858.

Jay, William. *The Life of John Jay: With Selections from His Correspondence and Miscellaneous Papers*, 2 Vols. New York: J. & J. Harper, 1833.

Jay, John. *The Correspondence and Public Papers of John Jay*. Ed. by Henry P. Johnston, 4 Vols. New York: G.P. Putnam's Sons, 1890.

Jefferson, Thomas. *The Works of Thomas Jefferson,* Federal Edition. Collected and ed. by Paul L. Ford, 12 Vols. New York and London: G.P. Putnam's Sons, 1904–1905.

________. *The Writings of Thomas Jefferson*. Ed. by Albert E. Bergh, 19 Vols. Washington, DC: Taylor & Maury, 1907.

________. *The Papers of Thomas Jefferson Digital Edition*. Ed. by Barbara Oberg and Jefferson Looney. Charlottesville: University of Virginia Press, Rotunda, 2008. Available at <http://rotunda.upress.virginia.edu/founders/TSJN.html>.

Jenkinson, Charles (Lord Liverpool). *A Collection of All the Treaties of Peace, Alliance, and Commerce, Between Great-Britain and Other Powers: To which is Prefixed, A Discourse on the Conduct of the Government of Great-Britain in Respect to Neutral Nations.* London: J. Debrett, 1785. Available at <http://books.google.com>.

Kent, James. *Dissertations, being the Preliminary Part of a Course of Law Lectures.* New York: George Forman, 1795. Available at <http://books.google.com>.

________. *Commentaries on American Law* [1826]. New York: O. Halsted, 15th ed., 1985. Available at <www.constitution.org>.

Lecky, Gould F. *An Historical Survey of the Foreign Affairs of Great Britain, with a View to Explain the Causes of the Disasters of the Late and Present Wars.* London: J. Bell, 1808.

Locke, John. *The Works of John Locke in Nine Volumes.* London: Rivington, 12th ed., 1824. Available at <http://oll.libertyfund.org/title/1725>.

Lyman, Theodore. *The Diplomacy of the United States, being an Account of the Foreign Relations of the Country from the First Treaty with France, in 1778, to the Present Time.* Boston, MA: Wells and Lilly, 1828. Available at <http://books.google.com/>.

Mackintosh, James. *Vindiciae Gallicae and Other Writings on the French Revolution.* Ed. by D. Winch. Indianapolis: Liberty Fund, 2006.

Madison, James. *Letters and Other Writings of James Madison.* Published by the order of Congress. Philadelphia: J.B. Lippincott, 1865.

________. *The Writings of James Madison, Comprising His Public Papers and His Private Correspondence, Including His Numerous Letters and Documents Now for the First Time Printed.* Ed. by Gaillard Hunt. New York: G.P. Putnam's Sons, 1900.

________. *The Papers of James Madison.* Ed. by William T. Hutchinson and William M.E. Rachal. Chicago: University of Chicago Press, 1967.

Monroe, James. *The Writings of James Monroe: Including a Collection of His Public and Private Papers and Correspondence.* Ed. by Stanislaus M. Hamilton. New York: G.P. Putnam's Sons, 1898–1903.

Montesquieu, Charles Louis de Secondat, Baron de. *The Complete Works of M. de Montesquieu.* London: T. Evans, 1777. Available at <http://oll.libertyfund.org>.

Morris, Gouverneur. *The Diary and Letters of Gouverneur Morris, Minister of the United States to France; Member of the Constitutional Convention.* Ed. by Anne Cary Morris. New York: Charles Scribner's Sons, 1888.

________. *An Answer to War in Disguise, or, Remarks upon the New Doctrine of England, Concerning Neutral Trade.* New York: Hopkins and Seymour, 1806. Available at <www.archive.org>.

Paine, Thomas. *The Writings of Thomas Paine.* Collected and ed. by Moncure D. Conway. New York: G.P. Putnam's Sons, 1906.

Pownall, Thomas. *A Memorial Most Humbly Addressed to the Sovereigns of Europe on the Present State of Affairs between the Old and the New World.* London: J. Debrett, 1780. Available at <http://www.archive.org/details/memorialmosthumboopown>.

________. *Memorial Addressed to the Sovereigns of Europe and the Atlantic*. London: J. Debrett, 1803. Available at <https://archive.org/details/memorialaddresseoo pownuoft>.

Pufendorf, Samuel von. *De Jure Naturae et Gentium Libri Octo* (*On the Laws of Nature and* Nations [1688]). Classics of International Law. Ed. by James Brown Scott. Oxford: Clarendon Press, 1934.

________. *The Whole Duty of Man according to the Law of Nature* [1673]. Ed. by Jean Barbeyrac. Indianapolis: Liberty Fund, 2003.

Rutherforth, Thomas. *Institutes of Natural Law; being the Substance of a Course of Lectures on Grotius' De iure belli ac pacis.* [1750], Second American Edition. Baltimore, MD: William and Joseph Neal, 1832. Available at <http://books.google.com>.

Stephen, James. *War in Disguise, or the Frauds of the Neutral Flags.* London: J. Hatchard, Piccadilly, 1805. Available at <http://books.google.com>.

Story, Joseph. *Commentaries on the Constitution of the United States.* Boston: Hilliard Gray & Co.; Cambridge: Brown, Shattuck & Co., 1833. Also available at <www .constitution.org>.

Trescot, W.H. *The Diplomatic History of the Administrations of Washington and Adams, 1789–1801.* Boston: Little, Brown and Co, 1857. Also available at <http://books.google .com>.

Tucker, St. George. *View of the Constitution of the United States with Selected Writings.* [1803] Ed. by C. Wilson. Indianapolis: Liberty Fund, 1999 (for page numbers, reference is made to the e-book version at <http://oll.libertyfund.org>).

Vattel, Emer de. *The Law of Nations, or, Principles of the Law of Nature Applied to the Conduct and Affairs of Nations and Sovereigns* [1758]. Ed. and with introduction by Béla Kapossy and Richard Whatmore. Indianapolis: Liberty Fund, 2008.

Ward, Robert. *An Enquiry into the Foundation and History of the Law of Nations in Europe, from the Time of the Greeks and Romans to the Age of Grotius.* Dublin: P. Wogan, P. Byrne, W. Jones and J. Rice, 1795.

________. *A Treatise of the Relative Rights and Duties of Belligerent and Neutral Powers, in Maritime Affairs: In Which the Principles of Armed Neutralities, and the Opinions of Hubner and Schlegel are fully Discussed.* London: Printed for J. Butterworth, by C. Woodfall, 1801.

Washington, George. *The Writings of George Washington.* Ed. by Worthington C. Ford, 13 Vols. New York: G.P. Putnam' Sons, 1889–1892.

________. *Writings of George Washington, 1741–99.* Ed. by John Fitzpatrick. Washington DC: U.S. Government Printing Office, 1931–1944. Available at <http://memory.loc. gov/ammem/gwhtml/gwhome.html>.

Wheaton, Henry. *A Digest on the Law of Maritime Captures and Prizes.* New York: McDermut and D.D. Arden, 1815.

________. "An Anniversary Discourse Delivered before the New York Historical Society" (December 20, 1820). Ms. available at the John Hay Library, Brown University.

________. *Elements of International Law With a Sketch of the History of the Subject.* Philadelphia: Carey, Lea and Blanchard, 1836. Available at <http://books.google.com>.

________. *History of the Law of Nations in Europe and America; from the Earliest Times to the Treaty of Washington*, 1842. New York: Gould and Banks, 1845. Available at <http://books.google.com>.

Wilson, James. *Collected Works of James Wilson.* Ed. by Kermit L. Hall and Mark D. Hall. Indianapolis: Liberty Fund, 2007.

Wolff, Christian von. *Jus gentium methodo scientifica pertractatum* [1749]. The Classics of International Law. Ed. by James Brown Scott. Oxford: Clarendon Press, 1934.

________. *Institutiones Iuris Naturae et Gentium* [1750]. Venezia: Nicolaum Pezzana, 1761. Available at <http://gallica.bnf.fr>.

Documentary Sources

Admiralty Court Reports, or Reports of Cases Argued and Determined in the High Court of Admiralty. Ed. by Christopher Robinson, 6 Vols. Boston: Little, Brown and Co., 1853.

American Diplomatic Code Embracing a Collection of Treaties and Conventions between the United States and Foreign Powers: From 1778 to 1834. Ed. by Jonathan Elliot, 2 Vols., Washington, 1834.

American Political Writing during the Founding Era: 1760–1805, 2 Vols. Ed. by Charles Hyneman and David Lutz. Indianapolis: Liberty Fund, 1983.

American State Papers: Foreign Relations (1789–1838). Library of Congress publication. Available at <http://memory.loc.gov/ammem/amlaw/lwsplink.html#anchor1>.

Annals of Congress, or the Debates and Proceedings in the Congress of the United States (1789–1824). Ed. by Joseph Gales, 42 Vols. Washington: Gales and Seaton, 1834–1856.

Archives des Affaires Étrangères. Correspondance Politique – États-Unis. Vols. 124–135. Paris: Service International de Microfilms, 1994.

Constitution of the United States. Available at <www.constitution.org>.

Convention of 1800 (United States-France) September 30, 1800. Available at Avalon Project <http://www.yale.edu/lawweb/avalon/diplomacy/france/fr1800.htm>.

The Debate on the Constitution: Federalist and Anti-Federalist Speeches, Articles and Letters during the Struggle over Ratification. Ed. by Bernard Bailyn, 2 Vols. New York: Library of America, 1993.

The Debates in the Several State Conventions on the Adoption of the Federal Constitution [1827]. Ed. by Jonathan Elliot, 5 Vols. Published under the sanction of Congress. Available at <http://lcweb2.loc.gov/ammem/amlaw/lwed.html>.

A Digest of International Law as Embodied in Diplomatic Discussions, Treaties and Other International Agreements, International Awards, the Decisions of Municipal Courts, and the Writings of Jurists. Ed. by John B. Moore and Francis Wharton, 8 Vols. Washington, DC: Government Printing Office, 1906.

A Digest of the Decisions of the Supreme Court of the United States: From Its Establishment in 1789, to February Term, 1820. Including the Cases Decided in the Continental Court of Appeals in Prize Causes, during the War of the Revolution. Ed. by Henry Wheaton. New York: R. Donaldson, 1821.

Diplomatic Correspondence of the United States of America, from the Signing of the Definitive Treaty of Peace, 10 Sept. 1783, to the Adoption of the Constitution, March 4, 1789. United States Dept. of State, 7 Vols. Washington DC: Blair & Rives, 1837.

The Institutes of Justinian. Ed. by John B. Moyle. Oxford: Clarendon Press, 1906 Available at <http://books.google.com>.

Instructions to the Envoys Extraordinary and Ministers Plenipotentiary from the United States of America to the French Republic, Their Letters of Credence and Full Powers, and Their Dispatches Received from Them Relative to Their Mission. Philadelphia: W. Ross, 1798. Available at <http://books.google.com>.

Jay Treaty (United States-United Kingdom) Available at Avalon Project <http://www.yale.edu/lawweb/avalon/diplomacy/britain/jaymenu.htm>.

Journals of the Continental Congress, 1774–1789. Ed. from the original records in the Library of Congress. Washington, DC, U.S. Govt. print office, 1904–1937.

Letters of Delegates to Congress, 1774–1789. Ed. by Paul Smith, et al. 25 Vols, Washington, DC: Library of Congress, 1976–2000. Available at <http://memory.loc.gov/ammem/amlaw/lwcite.html#dg>.

Notes on Debates in the Federal Convention of 1787, Reported by James Madison. Available at <http://avalon.law.yale.edu/subject_menus/madispap.asp>.

Official Opinions of the Attorneys General of the United States: Advising the President and Heads of Departments in Relation to their Official Duties. Ed. by Benjamin Hall. 43 Vols. Washington, DC: R. Farnham, 1852.

Records of the Federal Convention of 1787. Ed. by Max Farrand. 3 Vols. New Haven: Yale University Press, 1911. Also available at <http://memory.loc.gov>.

The Revolutionary Diplomatic Correspondence of the United States. Ed. by Francis Wharton. 6 Vols. Washington, DC: U.S. Government Printing Office, 1889. Also available at <http://memory.loc.gov/ammem/amlaw/lwdc.html>.

Report on the Case of the Jeune Eugenie, Determined in the Circuit Court of the United States, for the First Circuit, at Boston, December 1821. Boston: Wells and Lilly, 1822. Available at <http://memory.loc.gov/ammem/sthtml/sthome.html>.

Secret Journals of the Acts and Proceedings of Congress, from the First Meeting Thereof to the Dissolution of the Confederation, by the Adoption of the Constitution of the United States. 4 Vols. Boston: Thomas Wait, 1821.

Selection of Cases and Other Readings on the Law of Nations, Chiefly as it is Interpreted and Applied by British and American Courts. Ed. by Edwin Dickinson, E.W. New York: McGraw-Hill Book Co., 1929.

State Trials of the United States, During the Administrations of Washington and Adams with References, Historical and Professional, and Preliminary Notes on the Politics of the Times. Ed. by Francis Wharton. Philadelphia, Carey & Hart, 1849. Available at <http://books.google.com>.

The Case of Elizabeth Rutgers v. Joshua Waddington, August 7, 1786, Mayor's Court, New York New York: Morrisania, 1866.

Treaty of Alliance (United States-France) February 6, 1778. Available at Avalon Project <http://www.yale.edu/lawweb/avalon/diplomacy/france/fr1788-2.htm>.

Treaty of Amity and Commerce (United States-France) February 6, 1778b. Available at Avalon Project <http://www.yale.edu/lawweb/avalon/diplomacy/france/fr1788-1.htm>.

United States Declaration of Independence. Available at <www.constitution.org>.

The Public Statutes at large of the United States of America. Ed. by Richard Peters. Boston: Little, Brown, 1845. Available at <http://memory.loc.gov/ammem/amlaw/lwsl.html>.

Selected Websites

Avalon Project at Yale Law School: Documents in Law, History and Diplomacy. Available at <http://avalon.law.yale.edu/default.asp>.

The Founders' Constitution. Ed. by P. Kurland and R. Lerner. Available at <http://press-pubs.uchicago.edu/founders/>.

The Internet Archive. Available at <www.archive.org>.

Liberty Library of Constitutional Classics. Available at <http://www.constitution.org/liberlib.htm>.

Rotunda – University of Virginia Press. Available at <http://rotunda.upress.virginia.edu/>.

U.S. Supreme Court Center (Justia.com), Cases and Opinions. Available at <http://supreme.justia.com/index.html>.

Court Cases

United States

Alerta v. Moran. 13 U.S. (9 Cranch) 359, 1815.

The Antelope. 23 U.S. (10 Wheat.) 66, 1825.

Bas v. Tingy. 4 U.S. (4 Dall.), 37, 1800.
Brown v. United States. 12 U.S. (8 Cranch), 110, 1814.
Camp v. Lockwood. 1 U.S. (Dall.) 393, 1788.
Chisholm v. Georgia. 2 U.S. (2 Dall.) 419, 1793.
The Commercen. 14 U.S. (1 Wheat.) 382, 382, 1816.
Findlay v. The William. 9 F. Cas. 57 no. 4790, D. Pa. 1793.
Fitzsimmons v. Newport Insurance Company. 8 U.S. (4 Cranch) 185, 1808.
Fletcher v. Peck 10 U.S. (6 Cranch) 87, 1810.
Foster v. Neilson. 27 U.S. (2 Pet.) 253, 1829.
Glass v. the Sloop Betsey. 3 U.S. (3 Dall.) 6, 1794.
The Hazard. 13 U.S. (Cranch) 205, 1815.
Henfield's Case. 11 F. Cas. 1099, 1108, C.C.D. Pa., 1793.
Hudson v Guestier. 8 U.S. (4 Cranch) 293, 1808.
Johnson v. M'Intosh. 21 U.S. (8. Wheat.) 543, 1823.
La Jeune Eugenie. Crc't Ct., (2 Mason) 409, 1822.
Marbury v. Madison. 5 U.S. (1 Cranch) 137; 2 L. Ed. 60, 1803.
McCullough v. Maryland. 17 U.S. (4 Wheat.) 316; 4 L. Ed. 579, 1819.
Miller v. Hall. 1 U.S. (Dall.), 229, 1788.
Miller v. The Ship Resolution. 2 U.S (2 Dallas) 1, 1781.
Murray v. the Schooner Charming Betsey. 6 U.S. (2 Cranch) 64, 118, 1804.
The Nereide. 13 U.S. (9 Cranch) 388, 1815.
Paquete Habana. 175 U.S., 677, 700, 1900.
Penhallow v. Doane. 3 U.S. (3 Dallas) 54, 1795.
Respublica v. Chapman. 1 U.S. (Dallas) 53, 1781.
Respublica v. De Longchamps. 1 U.S. (Dallas) 111, 1784.
Rose v. Himely. 8 U.S. (4 Cranch), 241, 1808.
Ross v. Rittenhouse. 2 U.S. (Dallas) 111, 1792.
The San Antonio (Debadie v. Russell). 95, Recs. Ct. App., 1783.
The Schooner Exchange v. M'Faddon et.al. 11 U.S. 116 (7 Cranch) 3 L.Ed. 287, 1812.
Talbot v. Janson. 3 U.S. 3 (Dallas) 133, 133, 1795.
Talbot v. Seeman. 5 U.S. 1 (Cranch) 1, 1801.
Thirty Hogsheads of Sugar (Bentzon) v. Boyle. 13 U.S. (9 Cranch), 191, 1815.
Town of Pawlet v. Clark. 13 U.S. (9 Cranch) 292, 1815.
United States v. Guinet, et.al. 2 U.S. 321 (Dallas) 1795.
*United States v. Hudson.*11 U.S. (7 Cranch) 32, 1812.
United States v. Klintock. 18 U.S. (5 Wheat.) 144, 1820.
United States v. Ravara. 2 U.S. 297 (Dallas) 1793.
United States v. Schooner Peggy. 5 U.S. (1 Cranch) 103, 1801.
United States v. Smith. 18 U.S. (5 Wheat.) 153, 1820.

United States v. Worrall. 2 U.S. 384 (F.Cas.) 2 Dall. 384, 1798.
The Venus. 12 U.S. (8 Cranch) 253, 1814.
Ware v. Hylton. 3 U.S. (3 Dallas) 199, 1796.
Williams v. Armroyd. 11 U.S. (7 Cranch) 423, 1813.

United Kingdom

Barbuit's Case. Forr 280; 25 ER 777, 1737.
Calvin's Case. 7 Coke report 1a, 77 ER 377, 1608.
Dr. Bonham's case. 8 Co. Rep. 107a, 114a C.P. 1610.
Heathfield v. Chilton. 4 Burr. 2015, 2016, 1764.
The Immanuel. 2 C. Robinson 186, 1799.
Luke v. Lyde. 2 Burr 882; 97 ER 614, 1759.
The Maria. 1 C. Robinson, 340, 1799.
The Polly. 2 C. Robinson 362, 1800.
Triquet v. Bath. 3 Burr, 1764.
Walsingham Packet. 2 C. Robinson 77, 1799.
Viveash v. Becker. 3 M. and S. 284, 1814.

Books

Adams, Henry. *History of the United States during the Administrations of Thomas Jefferson.* New York: Library of America, 1986a.

________. *History of the United States during the Administrations of James Madison.* New York: Library of America, 1986b.

Adams, Randolph G. *Political Ideas of the American Revolution: Britannic-American Contribution to the Problem of Imperial Organization, 1765–1775.* Durham, NC: Trinity College Press, 1922.

________. *A History of the Foreign Policy of the United States.* New York: The Macmillan Company, 1925.

Adler, David, and Larry George (eds.). *The Constitution and the Conduct of American Foreign Policy.* Lawrence, KS: University Press of Kansas, 1996.

Armitage, David. *The Declaration of Independence, A Global History.* Cambridge, MA: Harvard University Press, 2007.

Bailyn, Bernard. *The Ideological Origins of the American Revolution.* Cambridge, MA: Belknap Press, Harvard University, 1992.

________. *Realism and Idealism in American Diplomacy: The Origins. Homage to Felix Gilbert (1905–1991).* Princeton, NJ: Institute for Advanced Study, 1994.

Bederman, David. *The Classical Foundations of the American Constitution: Prevailing Wisdom.* New York: Cambridge University Press, 2008.

Bemis, Samuel F. *The Diplomacy of the American Revolution: The Foundations of American Diplomacy, 1775–1823*. New York: D. Appleton, 1935.

________. *John Quincy Adams and the Foundations of American Foreign Policy*. New York: A.A. Knopf, 1949.

________. *A Diplomatic History of the United States*. New York: Henry Holt and Co., 1950.

________. (ed.). *The American Secretaries of State and Their Diplomacy* (Vols. 1–4). Totowa (NJ): Cooper Square, 1963–1985.

Benton, Lauren. *A Search for Sovereignty: Law and Geography in European Empires, 1400–1900*. New York: Cambridge University Press, 2010.

Bland, Randall Walton. *The Black Robe and the Bald Eagle: The Supreme Court and the Foreign Policy of the United States 1789–1953*. San Francisco: Austin & Winfield, 1996.

Blumenthal, Henry. *France and the United States, Their Diplomatic Relations 1789–1914*. Chapel Hill, NC: University of North Carolina Press, 1970.

Bowman, Albert H. *The Struggle for Neutrality: Franco-American Diplomacy during the Federalist Era*. Knoxville: University of Tennessee Press, 1974.

Bryce, James. *Studies in History and Jurisprudence,* Vol. II. New York: Oxford University Press, 1901.

Bull, Hedley. *The Anarchical Society: A Study of Order in World Politics*. Houndmills: Palgrave, St. Martin's Press, 2002.

Bull, Hedley, and Martin Wight. *Diplomatic Investigations*. Cambridge, MA: Harvard University Press, 1968.

Burt, Alfred LeRoy. *The United States, Great Britain and British North America from the Revolution to the Establishment of Peace after the War of 1812*. New Haven: Yale University Press, 1940.

Caenegem, Raoul v. *An Historical Introduction to Western Constitutional Law*. Cambridge: Cambridge University Press, 1995.

Castro, William. *The Supreme Court in the Early Republic: The Chief Justiceships of John Jay and Oliver Ellsworth*. Columbia, SC: University of South Carolina Press, 1995.

Combs, Jerald. *The History of American Foreign Policy: To 1920*. Armonk, NY: M.E. Sharpe, 2008.

Corwin, Edward S. *French Policy and the American Alliance of 1778*. New York: Burt Franklin, 1970.

DeConde, Alexandre. *Entangling Alliance: Politics and Diplomacy under George Washington*. Durham, NC: Duke University Press, 1958.

________. *The Quasi-War: The Politics and Diplomacy of the Undeclared War with France, 1797–1801*. New York: Charles Scribner's, 1966.

Dull, Jonathan. *A Diplomatic History of the American Revolution.* New Haven: Yale University Press, 1987.

Dumbauld, Edward. *Thomas Jefferson and the Law.* Norman, OK: Univ. of Oklahoma Press, 1979.

Fenwick, Charles G. *The Neutrality Laws of the United States.* Washington DC: Carnegie Endowment for International Peace, 1913.

Ford, Lisa, and Tim Rowse. *Between Indigenous and Settler Governance.* New York: Routledge Press, 2013.

Gilbert, Felix. *To The Farewell Address: Ideas of Early American Foreign Policy.* Princeton, NJ: Princeton University Press, 1961.

Glennon, Michael. *Constitutional Diplomacy.* Princeton, NJ: Princeton University Press, 1990.

Goebel, Julius. *The Recognition Policy of the United States.* New York: Longman, Green & Co, 1915.

Goebel, Julius Jr.. *History of the Supreme Court of the United States*, Vol. 1. New York: Macmillan, 1971.

Gough, J.W. *Fundamental Law in English Constitutional History.* Oxford: Fred Rothman & Co., 1985.

Gould, Eliga. *Among the Powers of the Earth: The American Revolution and the Making of a New World Empire.* Cambridge, MA: Harvard University Press, 2013.

Gould, Eliga, and Peter Onuf (eds.). *Empire and Nation: The American Revolution in the Atlantic World.* Baltimore/London: The Johns Hopkins University Press, 2005.

Green, L.C., and Olive Dickason. *The Law of Nations and the New World.* Calgary: The University of Alberta Press, 1989.

Greene, Jack P. *Peripheries and Center: Constitutional Development in the Extended Polities of the British Empire and the United States 1607–1788.* New York: W.W. Norton, 1990.

________. *The Constitutional Origins of the American Revolution.* New York: Cambridge University Press, 2011.

Grewe, Wilhelm. *The Epochs of International Law.* Ed. by Michael Byers. Berlin/New York: Walter de Gruyter, 2000.

Griffin, Charles. *The United States and the Disruption of the Spanish Empire 1810–22: A Study of the Relations of the United States with Spain and the Rebel Spanish Colonies.* New York: Octagon Books, 1968.

Grossberg, Michael, and Christopher Tomlins. *The Cambridge History of Law in America (1580–1815).* New York: Cambridge University Press, 2008.

Gulick, Edward V. *Europe's Classical Balance of Power.* New York: Norton & Co., 1968.

Haakonssen, Knud. *Natural Law and Moral Philosophy, from Grotius to the Scottish Enlightenment.* Cambridge: Cambridge University Press, 1996.

Haines, Charles G. *The Revival of Natural Law Concepts.* Cambridge, MA: Harvard University Press, 1930.

Harper, John L. *American Machiavelli: Alexander Hamilton and the Origins of U.S. Foreign Policy.* Cambridge: Cambridge University Press, 2004.

Hartog, Hendrik (ed.). *Law in the American Revolution and the Revolution in the Law.* New York: New York University Press, 1981.

Haskins, George L., and Herbert A. Johnson. *History of the Supreme Court of the United States* (Vol. 2). New York: Macmillan, 1981.

Hendrickson, David. *Peace Pact: The Lost World of the American Founding.* Lawrence, KS: University Press of Kansas, 2003.

________. *Union, Nation or Empire: The American Debate over International Relations, 1789–1941.* Lawrence, KS: University Press of Kansas, 2009.

Henkin, Louis. *Foreign Affairs and the United States Constitution.* Oxford: Clarendon Press, 1996.

Hochstrasser, Tim J. *Natural Law Theories in the Early Enlightenment.* Cambridge: Cambridge University Press, 2000.

Hogan, Michael (ed.). *Paths to Power: The Historiography of American Foreign Relations to 1941.* Cambridge: Cambridge University Press, 2000.

Hogan, Michael, and Thomas G. Paterson. *Explaining the History of American Foreign Relations*, 2nd ed., New York: Cambridge University Press, 2004.

Horsman, Reginald. *The Diplomacy of the New Republic 1776–1815.* New York: Harlan Davidson, 1985.

Horwitz, Morton. *The Transformation of American Law, 1780–1860.* Cambridge, MA: Harvard University Press, 1977.

Hunt, Michael. *Ideology and U.S. Foreign Policy.* New Haven, CT: Yale University Press, 1987.

Hutson, James. *John Adams and the Diplomacy of the American Revolution.* Lexington, KY: University Press of Kentucky, 1980.

Hyde, Charles C. *International Law Chiefly as Interpreted and Applied by the United States.* Boston: Little, Brown & Co., 1922. Also available at <www.archive.org>.

Hyneman, Charles S. *The First American Neutrality: A Study of the American Understanding of Neutral Obligations during the Years 1792 to 1815.* Chicago: University of Illinois Press, 1934.

Janis, Mark. *The American Tradition of International Law: Great Expectations 1789–1914.* Oxford: Clarendon Press, 2004.

________. *America and the Law of Nations 1776–1939.* Oxford: Oxford University Press, 2010.

Jouannet, Emmanuelle. *Emer de Vattel et l'Émergence Doctrinale du Droit International Classique.* Paris: Ed. by A. Pedone, 1998.

Kagan, Robert. *Of Paradise and Power: America and Europe in the New World Order.* New York: A.A. Knopf, 2003.

________. *Dangerous Nation.* New York: A.A. Knopf, 2006.

Kaplan, Lawrence. *Colonies into Nation: American Diplomacy 1763–1801.* New York: The Macmillan Company, 1972.

________. *Entangling Alliances with None: American Foreign Policy in the Age of Jefferson.* Kent, OH: Kent State University Press, 1987.

Keller, Helen. *Rezeption des Völkerrechts: Eine rechtsvergleichende Studie zur Praxis des U.S. Supreme Court, des Gerichtshofes der Europäische Gemeinschaften und des schweizerischen Bundesgerichts in ausgewählten Bereichen.* Heidelberg/New York: Springer Verlag, 2003.

Knalfa, Louis A. *Law and Politics in Jacobean England: The Tracts of Lord Chancellor Ellesmere.* Cambridge: Cambridge University Press, 2008.

Kulsrud, Carl J. *Maritime Neutrality to 1780. A History of the Main Principles Governing Neutrality and Belligerency to 1780.* Boston: Little, Brown, and Company, 1936.

LaCroix, Alison. *The Ideological Origins of American Federalism.* Cambridge, MA: Harvard University Press, 2010.

Lang, Daniel G. *Foreign Policy in the Early Republic.* Baton Rouge: Louisiana State University Press, 1985.

La Pradelle, Albert de. *Maîtres et Doctrines du Droit des Gens.* Paris: Les Éditions Internationales, 1950.

Lewis, James E. *The American Union and the Problem of Neighborhood: The United States and the Collapse of the Spanish Empire, 1783–1829.* Chapel Hill: University of North Carolina Press, 1998.

Lieberman, David. *The Province of Legislation Determined.* Cambridge: Cambridge University Press, 1989.

Lipsky, George A. *John Quincy Adams: His Theory and Ideas.* New York: Thomas Crowell & Co, 1950.

Lutz, Donald. *The Origins of American Constitutionalism.* Baton Rouge: Louisiana State University Press, 1988.

Lycan, George. *Alexander Hamilton and American Foreign Policy.* Oklahoma City: University of Oklahoma Press, 1971.

Macmillan, Ken. *Sovereignty and Possession in the English New World: The Legal Foundations of Empire, 1576–1640.* Cambridge: Cambridge University Press, 2006.

________. *The Atlantic Imperial Constitution: Center and Periphery in the English Atlantic World,* London: Palgrave Macmillan, 2011.

Malone, Dumas. *Jefferson and the Rights of Man.* New York, NY: Little, Brown and Co., 1951.

________. *Jefferson and the Ordeal of Liberty.* New York, NY: Little, Brown and Co., 1962.

Marks, Frederick. *Independence on Trial: Foreign Affairs and the Making of the Constitution.* Baton Rouge: Louisiana State University Press, 1973.

Martin, Francisco F. *The Constitution as Treaty: The International Legal Constructionalist Approach to the U.S. Constitution.* Cambridge: Cambridge University Press, 2007.

May, Henry. *The Enlightenment in America.* Oxford: Oxford University Press, 1978.

McIlwain, Charles H. *The American Revolution, A Constitutional Interpretation.* Ithaca: Cornell University Press, 1958.

McLaughlin, Andrew C. *The Foundations of American Constitutionalism.* New York: New York University Press, 1932.

________. *A Constitutional History of the United States.* New York/London: D. Appleton-Century Co, 1935. Also available at <http://www.constitution.org/cmt/mclaughlin/chus.htm>.

Mead, Walter Russell. *Special Providence: American Foreign Policy and How it Changed the World.* New York: Alfred A. Knopf, 2001.

Miller, Perry. *The Legal Mind in America: From Independence to the Civil War.* Ithaca, New York: Cornell University Press, 1970.

Mowat, Robert B. *The Diplomatic Relations of Great Britain and the United States.* New York: Longmans, Green, 1925.

Mullett, Charles. *Fundamental Law and the American Revolution, 1760–1776.* New York: Columbia University Press, 1933.

Neff, Stephen. *The Rights and Duties of Neutrals: A General History.* Manchester: Manchester University Press, 2000.

Nussbaum, Arthur. *A Concise History of the Law of Nations.* New York: Macmillan Press, 1954.

Nys, Ernest. *Les États-Unis et le Droit des Gens.* Bruxelles: Bureau de la Revue, 1909.

Obering, William. *The Philosophy of Law of James Wilson.* Washington, DC: American Catholic Philosophical Association, 1938.

O'Connor, Brendon (ed.). *American Foreign Policy Traditions.* London: Sage Publications, 2010.

Onuf, Peter (ed.). *Jeffersonian Legacies.* Charlottesville: University of Virginia Press, 1993.

Onuf, Peter, and Nicholas Onuf. *Federal Union, Modern World: The Law of Nations in an Age of Revolutions 1776–1814.* Madison, WI: Madison House, 1993.

Overhoff, Jürgen. *Benjamin Franklin: Erfinder, Freigeist, Staatenlenker.* Stuttgart: Klett-Cotta, 2006.

Palmer, Robert R. *The Age of the Democratic Revolution 1760–1820*, 2 Vols. Princeton, NJ: Princeton University Press, 1959–1964.

Perkins, Bradford. *Prologue to War: England and the United States 1805–1812.* Berkeley and Los Angeles: University of California Press, 1961.

________. *Castlereagh and Adams: England and the United States 1812–23*. Berkeley: Berkeley University Press, 1964.

________. *Cambridge History of American Foreign Relations. Vol. 1: The Creation of a Republican Empire 1776–1865*. Cambridge; New York, NY: Cambridge University Press, 1993.

Perkins, Dexter. *The Monroe Doctrine 1823–26*. Cambridge, MA: Harvard University Press, 1926.

________. *The American Approach to Foreign Policy*. Cambridge, MA: Harvard University Press, 1952.

Picciotto, Cyril. *The Relation of International Law to the Law of England and of the United States of America*. New York: McBride, Nast & Co, 1915.

Pocock, J.G.A. *The Machiavellian Moment: Florentine Political Thought in the Atlantic Republican Tradition*. Princeton: Princeton University Press, 1975.

Potter, Pitman. *Doctrines Américaines de Droit International*. Paris: Centre Européen de la Dotation Carnegie, 1937.

Presser, Stephen. *The Original Misunderstanding: The English, The Americans and the Dialectic of Federalist Jurisprudence*. Durham, NC: Carolina Academic Press, 1991.

Ramsey, Michael D. *The Constitution's Text in Foreign Affairs*. Cambridge, MA: Harvard University Press, 2007.

Redslob, Robert. *L'Histoire des Grands Principes du Droit des Gens depuis l'Antiquité jusqu'à la Veille de la Grande Guerre*. Paris: Rousseau, 1923.

Reid, John Phillip. *Constitutional History of the American Revolution: The Authority to Legislate*. Madison: University of Wisconsin Press, 1986.

________. *Constitutional History of the American Revolution: the Authority of Law*. Madison: University of Wisconsin Press, 2003.

Ruddy, Francis. *International Law in the Enlightenment: The Background of Emmerich de Vattel's Le Droit de Gens*. Dobbs Ferry, NY: Oceana Publications, 1975.

Rudko, Francis H. *John Marshall and International Law: Statesman and Chief Justice*. New York: Greenwood Press, 1991.

Sadosky, Leonard, *Revolutionary Negotiations: Indians, Empires, and Diplomats in the Founding of America*. Charlottesville: University of Virginia Press, 2010.

Scott, Hamish M. *British Foreign Policy in the Age of the American Revolution*. New York: Oxford University Press, 1991.

Sexton, Jay. *The Monroe Doctrine: Empire and Nation in Nineteenth-Century America*. New York: Hill and Wang, 2011.

Shain, Barry Alan (ed.). *The Nature of Rights at the American Founding and Beyond*. Charlottesville: University of Virginia Press, 2007.

Sofaer, Abraham. *War, Foreign Affairs and Constitutional Power: The Origins*. Cambridge, MA: Ballinger Publishing Co., 1976.

Stahr, Walter. *John Jay, Founding Father*. New York: Hambledon and Continuum, 2006.

Stimson, Shannon. *The American Revolution in the Law: Anglo-American Jurisprudence before John Marshall*. Princeton, NJ: Princeton University Press, 1990.

Stoner, James R. Jr. *Common Law and Liberal Theory: Coke, Hobbes and the Origins of American Constitutionalism*. Lawrence, KS: University of Kansas Press, 1992.

Stourzh, Gerald. *Benjamin Franklin and American Foreign Policy*. Chicago: University of Chicago Press, 1954.

———. *Alexander Hamilton and the Idea of Republican Government*. Stanford: Stanford University Press, 1970.

Stuart, Reginald. *The Half-Way Pacifist: Thomas Jefferson's Views of the War*. Toronto: University of Toronto Press, 1978.

———. *War and American Thought from the Revolution to the Monroe Doctrine*. Kent, OH: Kent State University Press, 1982.

———. *United States Expansionism and British North America, 1775–1871*. Chapel Hill: University of North Carolina Press, 1988.

Tatum, Edward H. *The United States and Europe, 1815–1823: A Study in the Background of the Monroe Doctrine*. Berkeley: University of California Press, 1936.

Thomas, Charles M. *American Neutrality in 1793: A Study in Cabinet Government*. New York: Columbia University Press, 1931.

Tomlins, Christopher, and Bruce Mann. *The Many Legalities of Early America*. Chapel Hill: The University of North Carolina Press, 2001.

Tomlins, Christopher, *Freedom Bound: Law, Labor, and Civic Identity in Colonizing English America, 1580–1865*. Cambridge: Cambridge University Press, 2010.

Tuck, Richard. *The Rights of War and Peace: Political Thought and the International Order from Grotius to Kant*. Oxford: Oxford University Press, 2002.

Tucker, Robert, and David Hendrickson. *Empire of Liberty: The Statecraft of Thomas Jefferson*. New York: Oxford University Press, 1992.

Varg, Paul. *Foreign Policies of the Founding Fathers*. Baltimore, MD: Penguin Books, 1972.

Vollenhoven, Cornelis van. *The Three Stages in the Evolution of the Law of Nations*. The Hague: Martinus Nijhoff, 1919.

White, Morton. *The Philosophy of the American Revolution*. New York: Oxford University Press, 1978.

White, Patrick C. (ed.). *The Critical Years: American Foreign Policy 1793–1823*. New York: Wiley and Sons, 1970.

Wight, Martin, and Herbert Butterfield. *Diplomatic Investigations: Essays in the Theory of International Politics*. London: Allen & Unwin, 1966.

Witt, John Fabian. *Lincoln's Code: The Laws of War in American History*. New York: The Free Press, 2012.

Wood, Gordon. *The Creation of the American Republic 1776–1787*. New York: W.W. Norton, 1972.

________. *Empire of Liberty: A History of the Early Republic, 1789–1815*. New York: Oxford University Press, 2009.

Wright, Benjamin. *American Interpretations of Natural Law: A Study in the History of Political Thought.* New York: Russell and Russell, 1962.

Wright, Quincy. *The Enforcement of International Law through Municipal Law in the United States*. Chicago: University of Illinois Studies in the Social Sciences, 1916.

________. *The Control of American Foreign Relations*. New York: The Macmillan Company, 1922.

Yela Utrilla, J.F. *España ante la independencia de los Estados Unidos*. Lérida, 1925.

Yirush, Craig. *Settlers, Liberty, and Empire: The Roots of Early American Political Theory, 1675–1775*. New York: Cambridge University Press, 2011.

Ziegler, Benjamin. *The International Law of John Marshall.* Chapel Hill: University of North Carolina Press, 1939.

Zuckert, Michael P. *The Natural Rights Republic: Studies in the Foundation of the American Political Tradition*. Notre Dame, IN: University of Notre Dame Press, 1999.

Articles

Adair, E.R. "The Law of Nations and the Common Law of England: A Study of 7 Anne Cap. 12." *Cambridge Historical Journal* 2, no. 3 (1928): pp. 290–297.

Alschuler, Albert. "Rediscovering Blackstone." *University of Pennsylvania Law Review* 145, no. 1 (1996): pp. 1–55.

Arcidiacono, Bruno. "Kant et l'avènement de l'état de droit entre les nations: Et non par la guerre, à la manière des sauvages." *Journal of the History of International Law* 8, no. 1 (2006): pp. 39–89.

Armitage, David. "The Declaration of Independence and International Law." *William and Mary Quarterly* 59, no. 1 (2000): pp. 39–64.

Balch, Thomas W. "The United States and the Expansion of the Law between Nations." *University of Pennsylvania Law Review* 64, no. 2 (1915): pp. 113–140.

Bellia, Anthony, and Bradford Clark. "The Federal Common Law of Nations." *Columbia Law Review* 109, no. 1 (January 2009): pp. 1–93.

________. "The Law of Nations as Constitutional Law." *Virginia Law Review* 98, no. 4 (June 2012): pp. 729–838.

Bemis, Samuel F. "The United States and the Abortive Armed Neutrality of 1794." *The American Historical Review* 24, no. 1 (October 1918): pp. 26–47.

________. "Washington's Farewell Address: A Foreign Policy of Independence." *American Historical Review* 39, no. 2 (1934): pp. 250–268.

Bilder, Mary Sarah. "Colonial Constitutionalism and Constitutional Law." *Boston College Law School*, Research Paper 164 (2008).

Bourguignon, Henry. "Incorporation of the Law of Nations during the American Revolution: the Case of the San Antonio." *American Journal of International Law* 71, no. 2 (1977): pp. 270–295.

Bowman, Albert. "Jefferson, Hamilton and American Foreign Policy." *Political Science Quarterly* 71, no. 1 (1956): pp. 18–41.

Brisbin, Richard. "John Marshall and the Nature of Law in the Early Republic." *The Virginia Magazine for History and Biography* 98, no. 1 (1990): pp. 57–80.

Carpenter, William S. "The United States and the League of Neutrals in 1780." *American Journal of International Law* 15, no. 4 (1921): pp. 511–522.

Carson, Hampton. "James Wilson and James Iredell, A Parallel and a Contrast." *American Bar Association Journal* 7, no. 3 (1921): pp. 123–131.

Castro, William. "Foreign Affairs Crises and the Constitution's Case for Controversy Limitation: Notes from the Founding Era." *The American Journal for Legal History* 46, no. 3 (July 2004): 237–270.

Chinard, Gilbert. "Les origines historiques de la doctrine de l'isolement aux États-Unis." *Recueil des Cours* 59 (1937): pp. 225–315.

Corwin, Edward S. "The French Objective in the American Revolution." *American Historical Review* 21 (1915): pp. 33–61.

Corwin, Edward. "The 'Higher Law' Background of American Constitutional Law." *Harvard Law Review* 42, nos. 2 and 3 (1929): pp. 149–185, 365–409.

Davidson, James. "Natural Law and International Law in Edmund Burke." *The Review of Politics* 21 no. 3 (1959): pp. 483–494.

Dickinson, Edwin D. "Changing Concepts and the Doctrine of Incorporation." *American Journal of International Law* 26, no. 2 (1932a): pp. 239–260.

________. "L'interprétation et l'application du droit international dans les pays anglo-américains." *Recueil des Cours* 40 (1932b): pp. 305–395.

________. "The Law of Nations as Part of the National Law of the United States." *University of Pennsylvania Law Review* 101, nos. 1 and 6 (1952–1953): pp. 26–56 and 792–833.

Dion, Leon. "Natural Law and Manifest Destiny in the Era of the American Revolution." *The Canadian Journal of Economics and Political Science* 23, nos. 2 (May 1957): pp. 227–247.

Dumbauld, Edward. "John Marshall and the Law of Nations." *University of Pennsylvania Law Review* 104, no. 1 (1955): pp. 38–56.

________. "Independence under International Law." *American Journal of International Law* 70, no. 3 (1976): pp. 425–431.

Fabel, Robin. "The Laws of War in the 1812 Conflict." *Journal of American Studies* 14, no. 2 (1980): pp. 199–218.

Fenwick, Charles G. "The Authority of Vattel." *American Political Science Review* 7, no. 3 (1913): pp. 395–410.

Fitzsimons, D. "Thomas Paine's New World Order: Idealistic Internationalism in the Ideology of Early American Foreign Relations." *Diplomatic History* 19 (1995): pp. 569–582.

Flaherty, Martin. "History Right? Historical Scholarship, Original Understanding and Treaties as 'Supreme Law of the Land'." *Columbia Law Review* 99, no. 8 (1999): pp. 2095–2153.

Frymer, Paul. "Building an American Empire: Territorial Expansion in the Antebellum Era." *U.C. Irvine Law Review* 1, no. 3 (2011): pp. 913–954.

Ford, Worthington C. "Edmund Randolph on the British Treaty." *American Historical Review* 12, no. 3 (April 1907): pp. 587–599.

Gilbert, Felix. "The 'New Diplomacy' of the Eighteenth Century." *World Politics* 4, no. 1 (1951): pp. 1–38.

Goldsmith, Jack. "Federal Courts, Foreign Affairs, and Federalism." *Virginia Law Review* 83, no. 8 (1997): pp. 1617–1715.

Golove, David, and Daniel Hulsebosch. "A Civilized Nation: The Early American Constitution, The Law of Nations and the Pursuit of International Recognition." Public Law and Legal Theory Research Paper Series, working paper no. 10-58. *New York University School of Law* (2010): pp. 101–228.

Gould, Eliga. "Zones of Law, Zones of Violence: The Legal Geography of the British Atlantic, circa 1772." *William and Mary Quarterly* 60, no. 3 (2003): pp. 471–510.

________. "Entangled Histories, Entangled Worlds: The English-Speaking Atlantic as a Spanish Periphery." *American Historical Review* 112, no. 3 (2007): pp. 764–786.

________. "On the Margins of Europe: The Law of Nations in the Western Atlantic, circa 1755." Paper presented at the conference *The Law of Nations and the Early Modern Atlantic World*, Chicago, February 24, 2009.

Greene, Jack. "The Background of the Articles of Confederation." *Publius* 12, no. 4 (1982): pp. 15–44.

________. "Colonial History and National History: Reflections on a Continuing Problem." *William and Mary Quarterly*, 3rd Series, 64, no. 2 (2007): pp. 235–250.

Grey, Thomas. "Origins of the Unwritten Constitution: Fundamental Law in American Revolutionary Thought." *Stanford Law Review* 30, no. 5 (1978): pp. 843–893.

Haggenmacher, Peter. "Symposium on Parliamentary Participation in the Making and Operation of Treaties: Some Hints on the European Origins of Legislative Participation in the Treaty-Making Function." *Chicago-Kent Law Review* 67, no. 2 (1992): pp. 313–339.

Hamburger, Philip. "Natural Rights, Natural Law and American Constitutions." *The Yale Law Journal* 102, no. 4 (1993): pp. 907–960.

Helfman, Tara. "The Law of Nations in *The Federalist Papers*." *The Journal of Legal History* 23, no. 2 (2002): pp. 107–128.

Hendrik Hartog. *Review, Peripheries and Center: Constitutional Development in the Extended Polities of the British Empire and the United States, 1607–1788* by Jack P. Greene. *William and Mary Quarterly*, 3rd Series, 45, no. 4 (1988): pp. 773–775.

Hendrickson, David. "Independence and Union: Foundations of American Internationalism." *Orbis* 49 (Winter 2004): pp. 37–51.

________. "International Law in Times of Empire: A View from the Eighteenth Century." *Proceedings of the American Society of International Law* 99 (2005): pp. 307–310.

________. "Of Power and Providence." *Policy Review* 135 (March 2006): pp. 1–10.

Henkin, Louis. "International Law as Law in the United States." *Michigan Law Review* 82, no. 2 (1984): pp. 1555–1569.

Hickey, Donald. "America's Response to the Slave Revolt in Haiti 1791–1806." *Journal of the Early Republic* 2, no. 4 (Winter 1982): pp. 361–379.

________. "The Monroe-Pinkney Treaty of 1806: A Reappraisal." *William and Mary Quarterly,* 3rd ser, 4, no. 1 (1987): pp. 65–88.

Higginbotham, Don. "The Early American Way of War: Reconnaissance and Reappraisal." *William and Mary Quarterly* 3rd series, 44, no. 2 (1987): pp. 230–273.

Hulsebosch, Daniel J. "The Ancient Constitution and the Expanding Empire: Sir Edward Coke's British Jurisprudence." *Law and History Review* 21, no. 3 (2003): pp. 439–482. <http://archive.is/HhNKH>.

Horwitz, Morton. "Natural Law and Natural Rights," in Austin Sarat and Thomas Kearns (eds.). *Legal Rights: Historical and Philosophical Perspectives*. Ann Arbor: University of Michigan Press, 1997.

Hostie, Jean. "Contribution de la Cour suprême des Etats-Unis au développement du droit des gens." *Recueil des Cours* 69, no. 3 (1939): pp. 237–348.

Hutson, James H. "Intellectual Foundations of Early American Diplomacy." *Diplomatic History* 1, no. 1 (1977): pp. 1–19.

Hyneman, Charles S. "Neutrality during the European Wars of 1792–1815: America's Understanding of Her Obligations." *American Journal of International Law* 24, no. 2 (1930): pp. 279–309.

Jay, Stewart. "The Status of the Law of Nations in Early American Law." *Vanderbilt Law Review* 42 (1989): pp. 819–842.

Kaminski, John. "Honor and Interest: John Jay's Diplomacy during the Confederation." *New York History* 83, no. 3 (2002): pp. 293–327.

Kaplan, Lawrence. "Jefferson, the Napoleonic Wars and the Balance of Power." *William and Mary Quarterly* 14, no. 2 (1957): pp. 196–217.

________. "Jefferson's Foreign Policy and Napoleon's Idéologues." *William and Mary Quarterly* 3rd. series, 19 (July 1962): pp. 344–359.

Kent, J. Andrew. "Congress's Under-Appreciated Power to Define and Punish Offenses against the Law of Nations." *Texas Law Review* 85 (2006–2007): pp. 843–946.

Koskenniemi, Martti. "The History of International Law Today." *Rechtsgeschichte* 4 (2004): pp. 61–66.

________. "The Advantage of Treaties: International Law in the Enlightenment." *Edinburgh Law Review* 13, no. 1 (2009): pp. 27–67.

Kunz, Josef, L. "Natural-Law Thinking in Modern Science of International Law." *American Journal of International Law* 55, no. 4 (October 1961): pp. 951–958.

LaCroix, Alison, "Drawing and Redrawing the Line: The Pre-revolutionary Origins of Federal Ideas of Sovereignty." *Occasional Papers, University of Chicago* (2008). Available at http://chicagounbound.uchicago.edu/occasional_papers/10/.

Lang, Daniel G. "The Law of Nations and the Balance of Power: The Influence of European Thought on the Founding Fathers." Unpublished PhD dissertation, University of Virginia Library, 1983.

Lang, Daniel G., and Greg Russell. "The Ethics of Power in American Diplomacy: The Statecraft of John Quincy Adams." *The Review of Politics* 52, no. 1 (1990): pp. 3–31.

Langbein, John. "Chancellor Kent and the History of Legal Literature." *Columbia Law Review* 93, no. 3 (1993): pp. 547–594.

Leiner, Frederick. "The *Charming Betsey* and the Marshall Court." *The American Journal of Legal History* 45, no. 1 (January 2001): pp. 1–21.

Lengel, James. "The Role of International Law in the Development of Constitutional Jurisprudence in the Supreme Court: The Marshall Court and American Indians." *The American Journal of Legal History* 43, no. 2 (1999): pp. 117–132.

Lint, Gregg L. "Early American Conceptions of International Law and Their Influence on Foreign Policy 1776–1803." Unpublished PhD dissertation, Michigan State University Library, 1975.

________. "The American Revolution and the Law of Nations 1776–1789." *Diplomatic History* 1, no. 1 (1977): pp. 20–34.

________. "John Adams on the Drafting of the Treaty Plan of 1776" *Diplomatic History* 2, no. 3 (1978): pp. 313–320.

________. "John Adams, Thomas Pownall and the Peace of 1780." Paper presented at conference in Boston and Charlottesville, 21–27 June 2009. Available at <http://www.adamsjefferson.com/papers/Adams_Pownall_Lint.pdf>.

Lobel, Jules. "The Limits of Constitutional Power: Conflicts between Foreign Policy and International Law." *Virginia Law Review* 71, no. 7 (1985): pp. 1071–1180.

Lofgren, Charles. "War-Making under the Constitution: The Original Understanding." *Yale Law Journal* 81, no. 4 (1972): pp. 672–702.

Marks, Frederick. "Power, Pride and Purse: Diplomatic Origins of the Constitution." *Diplomatic History* 11, no. 4 (1987): pp. 303–319.

Matthewson, Tim. "Jefferson and the Nonrecognition of Haiti." *Proceedings of the American Philosophical Society* 140, no. 1 (1996): pp. 22–48.

Morley, Michael. "The Law of Nations and the Offenses Clause of the Constitution: A Defense of Federalism." *Yale Law Journal* 112, no. 1 (October 2002): pp. 109–143.

Onuf, Nicholas, "Henry Wheaton and 'The Golden Age of International Law'." *International Legal Theory*, ASIL Publication, VI, no. 1 (2000).

Onuf, Peter. "To Declare Them a Free and Independant People: Race, Slavery, and National Identity in Jefferson's Thought." *Journal of the Early Republic* 18, no. 1 (Spring 1998a): pp. 1–46.

________. "A Declaration of Independence for Diplomatic Historians." *Diplomatic History* 22, no. 1 (1998b): pp. 71–83.

O'Sullivan, Richard. "Natural Law and Common Law." *Transactions of the Grotius Society* 31 (1945): pp. 117–138.

Overhoff, Jürgen. "Benjamin Franklin, Student of the Holy Roman Empire: His Summer Journey to Germany in 1766 and His Interest in the Empire's Federal Constitution," in Paul Kerry and Matthew Holland (eds.). *Benjamin Franklin's Intellectual World.* Madison: Fairleigh Dickinson University Press, 2012, pp. 77–88.

Pagden, Anthony. "Fellow Citizens and Imperial Subjects: Conquest and Sovereignty in Europe's Overseas Empires." *History and Theory* 44, no. 4 (December 2005): pp. 28–46.

Paust, Jordan. "The President is Bound by International Law." *American Journal of International Law* 81, no. 2 (1987): pp. 377–390.

________. "In Their Own Words: Affirmations of the Founders, Framers and Early Judiciary Concerning the Binding Nature of the Customary Law of Nations." *U.C. Davis Journal of International Law and Policy* 13, no. 2 (Spring 2008): pp. 205–254.

Perkins, Bradford. "Sir William Scott and the Essex." *William and Mary Quarterly* 3, no. 2 (1956): pp. 169–183.

________. "Early American Foreign Relations: Opportunities and Challenges." *Diplomatic History* 22, no. 1 (1998): pp. 115–120.

Peterson, Merrill. "Thomas Jefferson and Commercial Policy 1783–1793." *William and Mary Quarterly* 22, no. 4 (1956): pp. 584–610.

Potter, Pitman. "Relative Authority of International Law and National Law in the United States." *American Journal of International Law* 19, no. 2 (1925): pp. 315–326.

Ramsey, Michael D. "The Law of Nations as a Constitutional Obligation." *International Legal Theory Colloquium*, Georgetown Law School (2005). Available at <http://www.learningace.com/doc/963890/cdd08fca93245bc79b5c795e56a9fa35/ramseypaper>.

Raymond, John, and Barbara Frischholz. "Lawyers Who Established International Law in the United States 1776–1914." *American Journal of International Law* 76, no. 4 (1982): pp. 802–829.

Reeves, Jesse. "The Influence of the Law of Nature upon International Law in the United States." *American Journal of International Law* 3, no. 3 (1909): pp. 547–561.

________. "The First American Treatise on International Law." *American Journal of International Law* 31, no. 4 (1935): pp. 697–702.

Reinstein, Robert. "Executive Power and the Law of Nations in the Washington Administration." *University of Richmond Law Review* 46, no. 2 (2012): pp. 373–456.

________. "Slavery, Executive Power and International Law: The Haitian Revolution and American Constitutionalism." *American Journal of Legal History* (2013, forthcoming).

Rosen, Stephen P. "Alexander Hamilton and the Domestic Uses of International Law." *Diplomatic History* 5, no. 3 (1981): pp. 183–202.

Rowe, G.S., and Alexander W. Knott. "The Longchamps Affair (1784–1786), the Law of Nations, and the Shaping of Early American Foreign Policy." *Diplomatic History* 10, no. 3 (1986): pp. 199–220.

Ruddy, Francis S. "The Acceptance of Vattel," in Alexandrowicz, C.H. (ed.). *Grotian Society Papers*, (1972), pp. 177–196.

Ruskola, Teemu. "Canton is Not Boston: The Invention of American Imperial Sovereignty." *American Quarterly* 57, no. 3 (2005): pp. 859–884.

Sears, Louis M. "Jefferson and the Law of Nations." *American Political Science Review* 13, no. 3 (1919): pp. 379–399.

Sheridan, Eugene R. "The Recall of Edmond Charles Genet: A Study in Transatlantic Politics and Diplomacy." *Diplomatic History* 18, no. 4 (1994): pp. 463–488.

Sherry, Suzanna. "The Founders' Unwritten Constitution." *The University of Chicago Law Review* 54, no. 4 (Fall 1987): pp. 1127–1177.

________. "The Intellectual Origins of the Constitution: A Lawyers' Guide to Contemporary Historical Scholarship." *Constitutional Commentary* 5 (1988): pp. 323–347.

Smith, Charles A. "Credible Commitments and the Early American Supreme Court." *Law and Society Review* 42, no. 1 (2008): pp. 75–110.

Sofaer, Abraham D. "The Presidency, War and Foreign Affairs: Practice under the Framers." *Law and Contemporary Problems* 40, no. 2 (1976): pp. 12–38.

Sprout, Harold. "Theories as to the Applicability of International Law in the Federal Courts of the United States." *American Journal of International Law* 26, no. 2 (1932): 280–295.

Stanlis, Peter. "Edmund Burke and the Law of Nations." *American Journal of International Law* 47, no. 3 (1953): pp. 397–413.

Starke, J.G. "The Influence of Grotius upon the Development of International Law in the Eighteenth Century." in Alexandrowicz, C.H. (ed.). *Grotian Society Papers* (1972), pp. 162–176.

Stinson, J. Whitla. "The Common Law and the Law of Nations under the Federal Constitution." *California Law Review* 9, no. 6 (1921): pp. 470–483.

Sylvester, Douglas. "International Law as Sword or Shield? Early American Foreign Policy and the Law of Nations." *NYU Journal of International Law and Politics* 32, no. 1 (1999): pp. 1–87.

Vagts, Alfred. "The United States and the Balance of Power." *Journal of Politics* 3, no. 4 (1941): pp. 401–449.

Vagts, Alfred, and Detlev Vagts. "The Balance of Power in International Law: A History of an Idea." *American Journal of International Law* 73, no. 4 (1979): pp. 555–580.

Washburn, Albert. "The American View of Neutrality." *Virginia Law Review* 2, no. 3 (1914): pp. 165–177.

Watson, Blake, "John Marshall and Indian Land Rights: A Historical Rejoinder to the Claim of 'Universal Recognition' of the Doctrine of Discovery." *Seton Hall Law Review* 36, no. 2, (2006) pp. 481–549.

Westengard, Jens. "American Influences upon International Law." *Journal of Comparative Legal and International Law* 18 (New Ser.) no. 1 (1918): pp. 2–14.

White, Edward G. "The Marshall Court and International Law: The Piracy Cases." *American Journal of International Law* 83, no. 4 (1989): pp. 727–735.

Wilson, George G. "International Law and the Constitution." *Boston University Law Review* 13, nos. 2 and 3 (1933): pp. 234–260, 462–499.

________. "The United States and International Law." *Proceedings of the American Society of International Law* 30 (1936): pp. 14–25.

Wiltse, Charles. "Thomas Jefferson on the Law of Nations." *American Journal of International Law* 29, no. 1 (1935): pp. 66–81.

Witt, John Fabian. "The Power of War and Peace," chapter from *Lincoln's Code: The Laws of War in American History*. Presented at NYU legal history colloquium (February 17, 2010). Available at <http://www.law.nyu.edu/ecm_dlv2/groups/public/@nyu_law_website__academics__colloquia__legal_history/documents/documents/ecm_pro_064378.pdf> (retrieved on March 26, 2010).

Wright, Quincy. "International Law and Ideologies." *American Journal of International Law* 48, no. 4 (1954): pp. 616–626.

Zink, James. "The Language of Liberty and Law: James Wilson on America's Written Constitution." *American Political Science Review* 103, no. 3 (2009): pp. 442–455.

Zoller, Elisabeth. "Aspects internationaux du droit constitutionnel: contribution à la théorie de la fédération d'Etats." *Recueil des Cours* 294 (2002): pp. 39–166.

Index